Regionalism and Globalization i

Regionalism and Globalization in East Asia

Politics, Security and Economic Development

Second Edition
2014

Mark Beeson

First edition 2007
Second edition 2014

Published by
PALGRAVE MACMILLAN

Palgrave Macmillan in the UK is an imprint of Macmillan Publishers Limited, registered in England, company number 785998, of Houndmills, Basingstoke, Hampshire RG21 6XS.

Palgrave Macmillan in the US is a division of St Martin's Press LLC, 175 Fifth Avenue, New York, NY 10010.

Palgrave Macmillan is the global academic imprint of the above companies and has companies and representatives throughout the world.

Palgrave® and Macmillan® are registered trademarks in the United States, the United Kingdom, Europe and other countries

ISBN 978-1-137-33236-3 hardback
ISBN 978-1-137-33235-6 paperback

This book is printed on paper suitable for recycling and made from fully managed and sustained forest sources. Logging, pulping and manufacturing processes are expected to conform to the environmental regulations of the country of origin.

A catalogue record for this book is available from the British Library.

A catalog record for this book is available from the Library of Congress.

Typeset by Cambrian Typesetters, Camberley, Surrey, England, UK

Printed in China

Contents

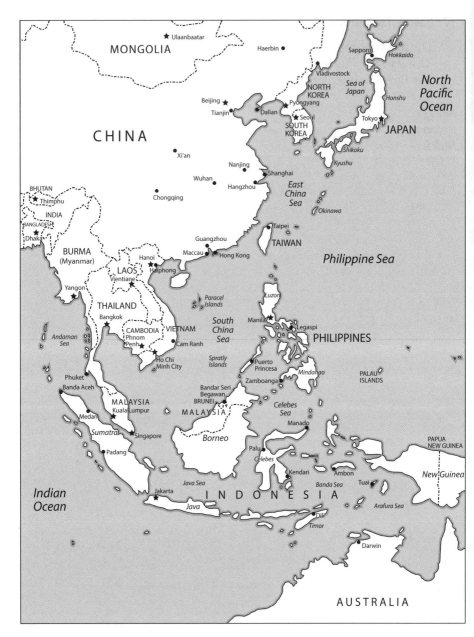

Map of East Asia

Preface

This is an extensively revised and updated version of a book that was originally published in 2007. In addition to bringing the text up to date in a rapidly changing region, there are several completely new chapters which reflect the evolution of East Asia, notably on the impact of the crises in the global economy and on the region and on the continuing rise of China. The final chapters have also been extensively revised and rewritten to take these and other changes into account. In addition, some material has been reorganized to make chapters more reader-friendly and of a more uniform length.

I am indebted to a number of people for helping to bring this new version about. The enthusiasm of my publisher, Steven Kennedy, for the project has – as ever – proved difficult to resist. I would also like to thank Doug Watkin and Shaomin Xu for their valuable research assistance, and my new colleagues at Murdoch University for allowing me the time so soon after my appointment to complete the current volume.

MARK BEESON

List of Abbreviations

AFC	Asian financial crisis
AFTA	ASEAN Free Trade Area
AMF	Asian Monetary Fund
APEC	Asia-Pacific Economic Cooperation
APT	ASEAN+3
ARF	ASEAN Regional Forum
ASA	Association of Southeast Asia
ASEAN	Association of Southeast Asian Nations
ASEAN+3	Association of Southeast Asian Nations plus China, Japan and South Korea
ASEM	Asia–Europe Meeting
CBMs	confidence-building measures
CCP	Chinese Communist Party
CMI	Chiang Mai Initiative
DPP	Democratic Progressive Party
DPRK	Democratic People's Republic of Korea
EAC	East Asian Community
EAEC	East Asian Economic Caucus
EAS	East Asia Summit
EASG	East Asia Study Group
EAVG	East Asia Vision Group
EPZs	export processing zones
EU	European Union
FAOFAD	Food and Agricultural Organization: Fisheries and Aquaculture Department
FAOUN	Food and Agriculture Organization of the United Nations
FDI	foreign direct investment
FILP	Fiscal Investment and Loan Program
GAFF	General Agreement on Tariffs and Trade
GFC	global financial crisis
GIC	Government of Singapore Investment Corporation
IFIs	international financial institutions
IMF	International Monetary Fund
IPCC	Intergovernmental Panel on Climate Change
JSDF	Japan Self-Defence Forces
JSP	Japan Socialist Party
KMT	Kuomintang
LDP	Liberal Democratic Party

MCA	Malayan Chinese Association
MIC	Malayan Indian Congress
MITT	Ministry of International Trade and Industry
MNC	multinational corporation
MoF	Ministry of Finance
NAFTA	North American Free Trade Agreement
NATO	North Atlantic Treaty Organization
NEP	New Economic Policy
NGO	non-governmental organization
NICs	newly industrialized countries
NIEs	newly industrializing economies
ODA	official development assistance
OECD	Organisation for Economic Co-operation and Development
PAFTAD	Pacific Trade and Development Conference
PAP	People's Action Party
PBEC	Pacific Basin Economic Council
PECC	Pacific Economic Cooperation Council
PLA	Peoples' Liberation Army
PNG	Papua New Guinea
PRC	People's Republic of China
ROK	Republic of Korea
SARS	severe acute respiratory syndrome
SEZs	Special Economic Zones
SOEs	state-owned enterprises
SPDC	State Peace and Development Council
TPP	Trans-Pacific Partnership
UMNO	United Malays National Organization
UNCTAD	United Nations Conference of Trade and Development
UNEP	United Nations Environment Program
TRT	Thai Rak Thai party
VCP	Vietnamese Communist Party
WTO	World Trade Organization
ZOPFAN	Zone of Peace, Freedom and Neutrality

Introduction

This book provides an introduction to, and an analysis of, 'East Asia' – a region that will exert a profound influence on the course of global history in the twenty-first century. Whether it has the capacity to overcome growing tensions and work as a collective actor is less clear, however. In the seven years since the first edition of this book appeared, a number of things have changed in East Asia that have raised important questions about its collective future – not the least of which is whether the region will actually be organized on a collective basis. The rise of China has continued to gather pace and it encapsulates much that is positive (and potentially negative) about the remarkable transformations that continue to shape and distinguish the region. But even if the territorial disputes that are currently attracting so much attention prove intractable, this may only make the region more rather than less important. For the reality is that it is not only East Asia's remarkable, historically unprecedented economic success that has made it a focus of world attention; its potential to spark a major conflict has also grown rather than diminished over the last few years. There are, in short, many reasons to take the countries of East Asia very seriously.

The story of East Asia's emergence as one of the most important regions in the world is long and complex. But one of the major overarching arguments I develop in what follows is that we cannot understand why the region is becoming such a prominent global force unless we consider economic, political and security issues simultaneously, in the specific historical circumstances that shaped them. Unlike many other books on East Asia, therefore, this volume provides an analysis of regional development that is grounded in the region's long, highly distinctive and often bloody history, simply because it is not possible to make sense of the region's development without it; nor is it possible without this analysis to understand the significance of the territorial disputes that are currently threatening to tear the region apart. Many of the most striking characteristics of East Asia – the preoccupation with sovereignty and security, the close ties between business and government, and the frequently fractious nature of its internal relations – have their origins in the region's unique formative experiences; they help to explain the course of national and regional development to this day. In short, history matters.

Armed with a sense of East Asia's distinctive history, we are in a better position to make sense of the contemporary era. For all the talk of 'globalization', one of the most striking things about East Asia and the countries that compose it is its internal heterogeneity and distinctiveness from other regions. Indeed, if there is one observation that is always made about East Asia it is about its diversity. Whether this is measured in terms of living standards, political systems or religious beliefs, there is much that distinguishes one East Asian country from another. Yet, despite all this diversity and uncertainty, there has also been increasing interest in attempting to give political and institutional expression to a distinct East Asian region – or there has until recently, at least. Now the course of regional development is looking less assured. But if a more self-consciously realized, increasingly coherent regional development process does continue, it will be one of the most important regional and *global* political developments since the Second World War. For, despite the East Asian crisis that erupted so unexpectedly in 1997, and despite the moribund performance of the Japanese economy throughout the 1990s, East Asia remains a crucial, increasingly important part of the global economy – a reality that the continuing 'rise of China' has only reinforced. The intention of this book is to unpack the component parts and dynamics that are either encouraging or inhibiting this process. To develop a sense of how these complex processes might unfold, therefore, I explore East Asia's interconnected political, economic and strategic processes in the overarching geopolitical context of which they are an increasingly influential part.

That the countries constituting the geographical region of East Asia will be influential is no longer in doubt, despite the financial crisis that gripped the region in the late 1990s. Overall, the East Asian states have more than regained the ground they lost, but the region's significance has been further enhanced by the remarkable, seemingly unstoppable, rise of China. China's astounding growth has already had a profound effect on the global economy, but it is also forcing a major reconfiguring of international relations both within East Asia itself, and between East Asia and the rest of the world. Deciding whether China's rise presents more of a threat or an opportunity is the key question with which all its neighbours must deal. Until recently, China's rise seemed unambiguously positive; now, in the wake of China's growing assertiveness, the picture is less clear.

The relationship between Japan and China will be the key to the region's future development, or at least to the possible development of a self-consciously organized and coherent region along the lines of the European Union. Given the European Union's current problems, it is unlikely that many in Asia will want to replicate it too closely, but if an East Asian variety of regionalism is to amount to anything more than a series of reports and mission statements, it will need to find a way of accommodating an increasingly powerful China and an economically colossal, but politically marginal, Japan. This may be even more difficult than it may seem at first glance: not only does Japan's single most important relationship lie outside the 'East Asian region' with the USA, but its relations with China are poisoned by an often violent, invariably acrimonious history that threatens to derail permanently the chances of developing an inclusive regional grouping. For this reason, Chapters 2 and 3 of this volume provide an overview of the region's history, without which it is impossible to understand the obstacles to regional development, or the bilateral relations within it.

Before undertaking this historical grounding, however, I provide an introduction to some of the debates that surround the growing interest in regional developments and the relationship of such developments to processes of 'globalization'. In Chapter 1, I spell out what is meant by a region, and why regions have become increasingly important even in an era in which globalization is the apparently dominant metaphor, if not material reality. This apparent paradox helps to explain, and actually drives, regionally based processes: simply put, regional co-operation potentially offers members advantages that equip them to respond more effectively to 'global' pressures. Indeed, when we unpack the discourse of globalization a little more carefully, it becomes apparent that it has a very strong regional accent. Interest in regional development is consequently growing, and not just among academics. Policy-makers, too, are increasingly alive to the potential competitive advantages and sheer political clout that regional collaboration offers – especially when their peers in other parts of the world are undertaking similar initiatives. In this context, regionalism is an idea whose time appears unambiguously to have come.

And yet the history of 'East Asia' also serves to remind us that there is nothing new under the sun. While it may not have been described as such – especially when there were no other regions to contend with – East Asia has always had an important regional quality. For some three or four thousand years, China has been at the centre of a regionally based order that it dominated and was remarkably orderly for long periods of time. In Chapter 2, I explain that, for all the differences in the development of individual East Asian 'nations', Chinese hegemony gave an underlying continuity to much of East Asia's commercial and political relations. Indeed, it could be argued that the common experiences of more recent European colonization and integration into a world order dominated by the superpowers has reinforced rather than undermined common regional experiences. This claim is contentious, but the idea that regional coherence is fundamentally alien to East Asia is not as obvious as some would have us believe. Chapter 3 puts the very different Southeast Asian part of the overall region in its distinctive historical place, something that helps us to understand the subsequent course of political and economic development there.

Security issues, or more straightforwardly, war and violence, have had a profound impact on the course of development in East Asia. This is true of much of the world, of course, but there are issues and events that distinguish East Asia and make universal assumptions and generalizations of questionable value. As Chapter 4 explains, some quite distinctive ways of conceptualizing security issues have emerged in East Asia, and the region's unique history has left an enduring legacy that has given a particular shape to its evolution. The friction between Japan and China, for example, cannot be understood without the relationship being placed in its specific historical and strategic context. But security, and the thinking that informs it, also spills over into political and even economic issues. Consequently, it is one of the central claims and themes of this book that understanding East Asia at either the level of the individual nation, or as a potential regional actor, involves looking not only at conventional political and economic factors, but also at the overall geopolitical context in which they have emerged. The implications for regional security are spelled out in Chapter 5, paying particular attention to the ongoing territorial disputes that are undermining the prospects for regional co-operation and even peace itself.

Chapter 6 looks at the importance of nationalism and domestic politics. While I stress repeatedly in this chapter and the ones that follow that political and economic processes are deeply integrated and ultimately inseparable in East Asia, it is useful to highlight some of the formal distinctions between regimes that are democracies, such as Japan; versions of democracies, such as Malaysia; and non-democracies, such as China. This is important not just at the national level, but also because it has implications for possible regional collaboration. Plainly, states that are radically different in terms of their internal structures, social embeddedness and basic operational styles are likely to find it much more difficult to co-operate regionally than, say, the democracies of Western Europe. As a consequence, the possibility of developing a collective identity is also more remote.

One of the most distinctive aspects of East Asian development, if not a regional invention, has been the 'developmental state', which is the focus of Chapter 7. Though some would argue that it is no longer effective or relevant, it remains one of the most distinctive features of East Asia's remarkable economic expansion, and its legacy endures in much of the region. Indeed, some would argue – and let me say at the outset that I am one of them – that under certain conditions effective state capacity and intervention in economic processes may still be an important part of stimulating the economic development process, especially for countries attempting this process relatively late in the day. But whatever the merits of this argument, the fact remains that the developmental state has had a dramatic impact on the region, and the distinctive relationships between government and business that it encouraged have not disappeared.

Chapter 8 considers the most important inheritor of the developmental state tradition, even if it is realized in ways that mark it out from Japan and the rest of the region. The rise of China is affecting the development of the rest of the region profoundly in both economic and strategic terms and so it merits an entirely new and separate discussion. While there is no simple 'China model' that other countries can copy, China is exerting an increasingly powerful influence over its neighbours and the region's fate will be determined to a large extent by what China's leaders do with their growing power – for better or worse.

Chapters 9 and 10 consider different aspects of the region's political economy. First, I explain how the region is increasingly integrated into the wider global economy, a process in which the legacy of the developmental state becomes especially significant. It is clear that different states have responded to the complex array of challenges and opportunities associated with globalization in different ways. Much has depended on the sorts of strategies individual states have pursued, and the capacity of various governments to implement them. Much has depended, too, on the timing of the integration process, the scale and structure of the economy involved, and their potential attractiveness to international investors. As Chapter 10 makes clear, though, there are potential pitfalls and dangers associated with the economic dimension of globalization, and these have resulted in a series of crises, which have not been confined to Asia. The impact of such crises on the region and its overall enthusiasm for collective action are detailed.

The question of whether East Asia has the capacity to develop coherent, regionally based political institutions is the subject matter of Chapter 11. Here the evidence is rather mixed. On the one hand, East Asia already has a history of institutional development, but it is patchy and generally disappointing in terms of its outcomes. On the other hand, the fact that *any* institutional development and collaboration has occurred in a region with all of East Asia's apparent problems and differences is no small achievement in itself. The final chapter considers some of the challenges that any regional institution or the individual states of East Asia will have to confront in the future. Much will depend on the region's overall ability to keep the developmental process going in the (generally) highly successful way it has for decades. Nowhere is more important in this regard than China. Without continuing rapid development, the legitimacy of the ruling elite in China may be fatally undermined and the country plunged into political chaos.

Unfortunately, and despite the formidable economic development that has already occurred, the success of this project may hinge on more than simply technocratic competence or continuing foreign investment. The most formidable, and perhaps insurmountable, hurdle to endless economic growth may be the natural environment and its capacity to sustain massive economic and demographic expansion. The final chapter considers East Asia's environmental constraints and its capacity for addressing them. The region's ability to address this challenge will have ramifications that extend far beyond East Asia. It may have become rather clichéd to say so, but the world's centre of economic gravity really has tilted decisively toward the region. For better or worse we have little option but to try to understand the factors that are likely to determine its future trajectory.

Chapter 1

Conceptualizing East Asia: From the Local to the Global

Identifying 'East Asia' is more difficult than it might seem at first glance. One of the problems inherent in describing any region is deciding where to draw the boundaries: who's in and who's out? Which countries can be considered 'authentic', unambiguous members of a region, and which should be excluded? On what basis should inclusion or exclusion occur? Are there differences in the way political and economic regionalism occur? Even more problematically, is it possible that regionally based 'security communities' might even overturn some of the most widely held expectations about regional security and the possibilities for co-operation rather than conflict in East Asia as a consequence? This chapter begins the process of answering these questions by providing some conceptual tools for thinking about regions. It also suggests why it makes sense to consider East Asia as potentially constituting a region in the same way we think of Western Europe or Latin America.

The main purpose of this chapter is to consider the nature of regions generally, and of the East Asian region in particular. In so doing I shall highlight one of the central themes and questions that animates this entire book: what, if anything, is different about East Asia? Are such differences diminishing in the face of seemingly irresistible global forces, or are they sufficiently robust and institutionalized to remain distinctive and different from much of the rest of the world? There are no simple answers to these questions, and much depends on the country and the specific issue area we consider. As we shall see in this chapter and those that follow, however, despite the existence of powerful forces actively encouraging change and reform within the East Asian region, there remains much that is very different from comparative 'Western' experiences.[1]

East Asia contains some of the world's most important and distinctive political economies. There are signs that East Asia's undoubted economic and strategic weight is gradually being institutionalized in new regionally-based organizations that have the potential to alter the global distribution of power and influence. This is occurring as part of a complex adjustment on the part of states to increasingly global pressures and influences, some of the most powerful of which emerge from domestic actors as they try to shape national policy outcomes to their advantage (Baccini and Dur 2011). What is especially distinctive about this process is that it has a pronounced regional dimension. States have discovered the potential utility and benefits of co-operation with their more immediate neighbours. This chapter provides an overview of some of the key forces that are driving and mediating these processes, and a framework for capturing the dynamic nature of regional interactions, development and the construction of regions themselves. The key point to emphasize at the outset is that there is nothing 'natural' or inevitable about the course of regional development; it reflects specific national and regional histories, contingent constellations of power and interest, and the wider global environment of which they are a part.

Consequently, the first part of this chapter reviews some of the more illuminating ways that regional processes have been considered. While there are some general principles involved in regionally-based phenomena, this chapter and the ones that follow also make it clear that we need to place each regional experience in a specific historical context to capture the particular political, economic and strategic circumstances that gave it a distinctive shape. The process of identifying what is specifically East Asian about the area that is of primary concern in this book begins in the second part of this chapter. I introduce the main countries of the region and suggest why it makes more sense to think of them as being part of 'East Asia', rather than, say, the Asia-Pacific or any of the other possible ways of describing the countries of the area under consideration. The final part of the chapter considers regional processes in the context of the all-encompassing globalization phenomenon. In particular, I consider how states everywhere are attempting to mediate between various levels of activity, and how we can understand their varying capacities to do so. The overall intention here is to provide a conceptual framework within which both the individual states of the region and their emerging collaborative activities can be understood.

Recognizing regions

One of the most widely noted features of the contemporary international system is the persistence and importance of regionally-based modes of co-operation and organization. The European Union (EU) is by far the most important exemplar of regional integration and co-operation, and its development is often seen as a benchmark against which other regions are measured (Börzel and Risse 2012). The prominence of the EU experience in these debates also reinforces the inherent Eurocentrism of our understanding of regional and historical development more generally (Hobson 2012). While East Asia is nothing like as coherent or established as the EU, especially as far as political co-operation is concerned, nevertheless there are substantial grounds for considering it as a discrete region in much the same way as we think of Western Europe. It is important to emphasize that the prominence of regions anywhere is somewhat surprising: we live in an era that is routinely characterized as 'global', so the persistence of regional variation, let alone the self-conscious pursuit and active creation of regional organizations and identity, is not what some of the most enthusiastic observers of globalization might have led us to expect.

Historically, interactions with immediate neighbours have always been important and largely as a consequence of simple geography. For much of human history, what Geoffrey Blainey (1982) has famously described as the 'tyranny of distance' has meant that things could hardly have been otherwise: the sheer difficulty of interacting over long distances placed fundamental constraints on the nature of possible relationships. But the advent of more reliable forms of communication and transport has led some observers to claim that we now inhabit a deeply integrated world in which global, rather than national or regional, processes will predominate, sweeping aside earlier forms of political and economic order (Ohmae 1990). And yet not only are states proving to be highly resilient and important forms of political organization in places such as East Asia, but they are increasingly exploring ways of co-operating on a regional rather than a global basis. How are we to explain this apparent paradox?

Interest in regions at both a policy-making and a theoretical level gained momentum in the period following the Second World War, though it is not an exclusively post-war phenomenon (Mansfield and Milner 1999). Chapter 2 illustrates how both Japan and (especially) China have attempted to assert an influence over the region for considerable periods. But it was the development of the EU in the post-war period that really galvanized scholarly interest in regionalism. It also caused policymakers in other parts of the world to try to emulate what until recently had been its unambiguous success. Consequently, the formation of the EU in particular cannot be understood in isolation from the particular geopolitical circumstances and regional order that emerged in the aftermath of the Second World War. Not only was there an understandable desire to ensure that the western European powers did not engage in the sort of internecine struggles that had devastated Europe, but the emerging Cold War confrontation with the Soviet Union also meant that the United States was intent on ensuring that western Europe would be a successful capitalist bulwark against Soviet expansion (Beeson 2005).

Strategic considerations and dynamics have also been equally important factors in shaping regional co-operation in East Asia. But they have also been crucial obstacles to regional integration: the East Asian region was divided by the ideological and strategic cleavages of the Cold War period, effectively precluding the possibility of regional co-operation that included all of the states of Northeast and Southeast Asia (Cumings 1997). Consequently, the 'first wave' of theorizing about the emergence of coherent regions in the post-war period focused predominantly on the EU experience and was strikingly 'functionalist' in tone. The leading theorists of this time were people such as Ernst Haas (1964) and David Mitrany (1965), who saw European development as an essentially technocratic exercise, in which policy-makers co-operated to create new regionally-based institutions for mutual gain. There are some well-known problems with this sort of functionalist analysis, which have seen it lose influence as a way of explaining regional dynamics.[2] Functionalist explanations have always been preoccupied with explaining how regional processes work and the benefits that flow from their capacity to generate 'spillovers', but they were less good at explaining the creation of regional orders in the first place (Hurrell 1995).

Nevertheless, the neofunctionalist analysis drew attention to something of a problem for conventional International Relations (IR) theory: if the world really was composed of discrete nation-states locked in a never-ending struggle for survival in an anarchical world order, then the sort of regionally based co-operative relations that the EU embodied was difficult to explain. Until recently, the EU clearly generated mutual benefits and seemingly changed the underlying logic and practice of international relations in western Europe as it institutionalized co-operative relations and made the prospect of conflict between the European powers increasingly remote (Wallace 1995). Even now, some observers argue that the EU continues to exert a powerful influence over organizations such as the Association of Southeast Asian Nations (ASEAN) (Jetschke and Murray 2012). The sorts of tangible economic and political benefits the EU was seen as embodying in its heyday – benefits that are sharply at odds with the expectations of conventional IR theory – encouraged renewed interest in regional processes.

Louise Fawcett (1995) suggests that a number of key factors have underpinned the emergence of the 'new regionalism'. While a renewed practical and theoretical interest in regionalism was evident in the 1980s, the end of the Cold War provided a crucial impetus for regional processes. As noted briefly above, and as we shall see in more detail in subsequent chapters, it was simply not possible for a broadly-based form of East Asian co-operation to take hold while the region was divided along ideological lines. The ending of the Cold War has also encouraged the decentralization of the international system, which Fawcett considers a second critical factor encouraging regional processes. Economic and even security relations are assuming a greater regional character as organizations such as the North Atlantic Treaty Organization (NATO) expand, and as institutions for regional economic co-operation such as the North American Free Trade Area (NAFTA) attempt to co-ordinate co-operative efforts at a regional level.

The early success of the EU in particular provided a further spur to regional collaboration, Fawcett argues, as countries became concerned about the implications that flowed from 'fortress Europe' for their own economic welfare. In addition to NAFTA, we have seen the emergence of organizations such as Mercosur in Latin America, and the Asia-Pacific Economic Cooperation (APEC) forum, which includes parts of Latin America, Australasia and East Asia. For some areas of the world, regional co-operation offered a way of warding-off the possible negative impacts of global processes and providing a degree of insulation for regional polities and economies. This is an argument that still has some relevance for contemporary East Asia: regional processes seem to offer a way of responding to the ubiquitous challenges thrown up by globalization (Oman 1994). To understand more clearly how global–regional interaction occurs, it is helpful to consider how regional processes have come to be understood in the most recent wave of theorization.

Theories of regional co-operation and integration

One of the most widely employed distinctions made in the theoretical literature is between regionalism and regionalization (Breslin and Higgott 2000). Regionalism implies a degree of intentionality as states and other actors engage in an essentially political process of collaboration. Regionalization, by contrast, is a less self-conscious and coherent process, primarily driven by the private sector. This is an especially important consideration in the context of East Asia because – in sharp contrast to the European experience – regional integration has thus far been driven primarily by the uncoordinated impact of corporate restructuring and investment in the region. However, there is no reason to suppose that there is only one possible pattern of regional development, or that the EU represents the successful end point of such processes (de Lombaerde *et al.* 2010; Söderbaum 2012). Such claims look even less plausible in the light of the EU's recent problems. Nevertheless, it is possible to identify a number of features of regional processes that give some indication of their importance, and which help to distinguish politically driven forms of regionalism from the underlying forms of regionalization associated with private-sector activities and international economic restructuring.

Regional awareness and identity, Andrew Hurrell (1995) argues, are two of the potentially most important features of regional processes. If regions are to amount to anything more than fairly arbitrary geographical demarcations, then they necessarily have a discursive and ideational component which gives some sense of what it means to belong to the region, and the factors distinguish members from non-members. Formal institutional development at the regional level is a powerful marker of this process. Consequently, identity issues are important, because 'all regions are socially constructed and hence politically contested' (Hurrell 1995: 334). Equally important, as Benedict Anderson (1983) famously pointed out, the creation of 'imagined communities' is challenging enough within national political spaces, especially for newly independent countries such as those of Southeast Asia, let alone at a regional level, where a putative sense of identity may be far more tenuous and undermined by long-running local tensions.

This sort of regional identity or common outlook on key issues is an important determinant of the success of regional projects generally, and of what Hurrell describes as 'regional cohesion'. There are, Hurrell (1995: 337) suggests, two aspects of regional cohesion: first, when the region plays a defining role in relations between regional states and the rest of the world; and second, when the region forms the basis for policy co-ordination within the region itself. While the EU has not always proved capable of playing the sort of coherent and significant role that its strategic, political and especially economic weight might suggest it could, it has clearly been greater than the sum of its parts (Ash 2004; Menon 2008). This was plainly one of the motives behind the original development of ASEAN, though it has actively avoided the sort of sovereignty pooling and institutional integration that has been the hallmark of the EU (Beeson 2009a; Narine 2002).

However, the sort of *de jure* regionalism, or formally organized co-operation, which is so characteristic of the EU, has proved more elusive elsewhere. East Asia has thus far been associated primarily with *de facto* regionalism, which is one way of thinking about the potential for regional co-operation that flows from what Hettne and Söderbaum (2002: 41) describe as the 'real region'. Of course, this begs the question of what the basis of the 'real region' might be. As we shall see when we consider the respective fates of some of the more important organizations such as APEC, 'ASEAN+3' (APT) and the increasingly prominent East Asian Summit (EAS), there are very different ideas about where the boundaries of regions should be drawn and what purpose such groupings should pursue. But before examining these initiatives in any detail, it is useful to look more closely at the countries that potentially constitute the region – however it is defined.

East Asia: unity in diversity?

One of the most frequently noted features of East Asia, and one of the principal reasons why the prospects for EU-style regional co-operation generates such scepticism, is the sheer diversity of the countries of the region. Table 1.1 gives an indication of how heterogenous East Asia is: not only does the region contain every major religion and form of government, it is also distinguished by massive disparities in wealth distribution. Even if we put to one side the troubled history of the region for a moment, and concentrate solely on contemporary indicators of GDP and per capita income, it is plain that there are very significant differences in the underlying economic circumstances of the region's members. Compounding the differences in economic weight are the very different demographics of the region, ranging from China's gigantic population to the micro-states of Singapore and Brunei. Even within these figures there are major differences in the circumstances confronting countries in the region: for example, the contrast between Japan with its rapidly ageing population and somewhere like Indonesia, which continues to experience rapid population growth.

Despite all this diversity, it is helpful to make a broad distinction between the countries of Northeast and Southeast Asia. As we shall see in more detail in subsequent chapters, Northeast Asia includes two major powers – China and Japan – which have exerted a long-term influence on both Northeast Asia in particular and East Asia more generally. In China's case, this influence, primarily indirect and cultural, has stretched back over thousands of years. More recently, Japan's highly successful industrialization process not only demonstrated that Asian powers were capable of becoming major economic and strategic forces in international affairs, but it also initiated a process of more generalized economic development in Northeast Asia, as Taiwan and Korea followed in its wake (Kohli 2004). In Southeast Asia, in contrast, industrialization and economic modernization occurred significantly later and were delayed partly as a consequence of European colonization – a fate that the countries of Northeast Asia largely escaped. This also explains differences in the extent and depth of the industrialization process in Southeast Asia (Yoshihara 1988). In Chapter 7 I explain how the superior 'state capacity' of Northeast Asian countries such as Japan enabled them to promote and direct the course of industrialization more effectively. While a number of Southeast Asian countries such as Singapore, and to a lesser extent Malaysia and Thailand, have also displayed an ability to guide

Table 1.1 Population, politics, wealth and religion

Country	Area (000s sq. m)	Population (million)	GDP (US$)	GDP per capita (US$)	Government	Main religion
Burma (Myanmar)	678	55	83	1,323	Transitional (nominally civilian parliamentary democracy)	Buddhism
Brunei Darussalam	6	0.409	21	49,536	Constitutional sultanate	Islam
Cambodia	181	15	34	2,239	Democracy under constitutional monarchy	Buddhism
China	9,597	1,343	11,300	8,386	Communist	Atheism (official), Daoism
Hong Kong, China	1	7	351	49,417	SAR	Multiple
Indonesia	1,905	249	1,125	4,666	Democracy	Islam
Japan	378	127	4,444	34,748	Democracy under constitutional monarchy	Shintoism/Buddhism
Korea, South	100	49	1,554	31,220	Democracy	Christianity, Buddhism
Korea, North	121	25	40	1,800	Communist one-man dictatorship	Suppressed
Lao PDR	237	7	17	2,768	Communist	Buddhism
Malaysia	330	29	464	16,240	Quasi-democracy under constitutional monarchy	Islam
Philippines	300	104	391	4,080	Democracy	Christianity
Singapore	0.697	5	315	59,710	Quasi-democracy	Buddhism
Taiwan	36	23	876	37,715	Democracy	Buddhism/Daoism
Thailand	513	67	602	9,398	Democracy under constitutional monarchy	Buddhism
Vietnam	331	92	300	3,359	Communist	Buddhism
United States	9,827	314	15,075	48,328	Democracy	Christianity

Sources: 2012 data from CIA *World Factbook* and IMF *World Economic Outlook.*

and facilitate economic development, there is still a distinct difference in both the timing of the industrialization process and the sheer scale of the much larger economies of Northeast Asia, which makes the basic differentiation between Northeast and Southeast Asia meaningful. The recent 'rise of China', examined in more detail in Chapter 8, looks set to cement this historical divergence and reinforce the economic, political and strategic dominance of the north.

Consequently, East Asia appears to lack the kinds of commonalities that have distinguished the EU in particular, which were frequently thought to account for the relative success of the European project. And yet we need to treat the conventional wisdom with a degree of caution. The extent of European homogeneity is frequently overstated, and the degree of identification with, and enthusiasm for, the European project is not necessarily universal, especially in the aftermath of the recent crisis (Erlanger 2011; Overbeek 2012). But even if we accept that historical circumstances have played a crucial role in preparing the ground, at least, for the sort of sovereignty-pooling and political co-operation that distinguished the EU in its heyday, this merely begs the question of whether East Asia has similar preconditions. Richard Stubbs (2002) has argued that the rapid emergence of ASEAN+3 owes much to common historical experiences – particularly Japan's economic and military impact on the region – common cultural traits, the impact of the Cold War, and the distinctive nature of East Asia's business and political relations. All of these factors will be explored in more detail in subsequent chapters, but the point to emphasize at this stage is that there are at least some potential grounds for possible co-operation and identification even in a region with a troubled past and a problematic present.

This possibility is particularly clear in the case of ASEAN, which, for all its shortcomings, remains the most enduring multilateral institution of its kind in the developing world. More importantly, perhaps, it has arguably changed the nature of inter-state relations between Southeast Asia's highly disparate states in ways that are surprising and suggestive of possibilities for the larger East Asian regional project. As I argue in more detail in subsequent chapters, ASEAN owes much of its importance and success to a unique set of geopolitical circumstances which provided both the impetus for inter-state co-operation between the ASEAN states, and which help to account for the organization's surprisingly high profile as a consequence. While the sceptics are right to point to ASEAN's limited record of achievement, the sheer existence of ASEAN has had some impact in socializing its members into patterns of behaviour that are unlikely to have come about otherwise (Ba 2009; Jetschke 2012). The question is whether such bonds of solidarity can withstand shifts in the overall geopolitical context, which we shall explore in Chapter 11.

The extent to which a common sense of purpose and identity may be developing is an especially important consideration when we remember that the idea of Southeast Asia as a distinct region is something of a historical accident. During the Second World War, when the British fought the Japanese in Burma and elsewhere, they began to refer to 'Southeast Asia' to describe the countries of what we not now think of as the ASEAN grouping (Emmerson 1984). The emergence of 'Southeast Asia' highlights a more general point about the contingent nature of regional definition on the one hand, and the process by which regions are defined, on the other. Edward Said (1985) has highlighted how particular discourses effectively create the idea of an 'other' that constitutes and reinforces identity – even ones with negative connotations. As far as contemporary East Asia is concerned, the significance of this insight is that it highlights what might be described as the self-reflexive element of regionalism and its inevitable connection to larger global processes: the *idea* of 'Asia' was necessarily an outgrowth of the interaction between an increasingly self-conscious European continent and the land mass to its east (Hobson 2007). As Korhonen (1997: 349) points out, this interaction had its greatest impact with the outward expansion of the European powers in the nineteenth century, a process that culminated in the displacement of a Sinocentric regional order by European perceptions of geographical space and political practices. Thus regional definitions are somewhat arbitrary, mutually-constitutive, politically-contested, and reflect a particular distribution of power and influence in the international system (Rozman 2012). This is why the self-conscious pursuit and creation of regional institutions is such a defining part of regional orders.

Theories of regional definition

The possibility that regional definition reflects something other than simple geography can be seen in the attempts to use the idea of the 'Pacific Age' or, more recently, the 'Asia-Pacific' as ways of self-consciously constructing an idea of regional identity that might be used to encourage particular economic or political outcomes. The idea of a Pacific Age has waxed and waned, and is a measure of American enthusiasm about engagement with Asia (Cumings 2009; Korhonen 1996), about which I shall say more in the next chapter. The more recent invocation of the 'Asia-Pacific' region was intended to promote a vision of mutually-beneficial co-operation and economic prosperity that glossed over many underlying tensions and contradictions (Beeson 2006a), not the least of which was that much of East Asia was not capitalist. Even those countries that were aligned ideologically with the United States were not necessarily enamoured of the sort of liberal, market-oriented capitalism that it promoted (Woodside 1993). The all-encompassing Asia-Pacific idea has proved unable to sustain the hopes of its advocates, especially as a consequence of the Asian financial crisis of the late 1990s. This is partly why there has been renewed interest in the more narrowly defined East Asian region.

However, even if the notion of an East Asian region has more potential resonance among Asian policy-makers than the Asia-Pacific idea, there are still a number of major obstacles to be overcome if East Asia is to achieve what Björn Hettne (1999) describes as 'regionness'. Hettne suggests that a number of qualities are needed for a region to be an effective actor and meaningful entity. In addition to basic geographical barriers and ecological characteristics, regions should contain a social system that transcends the local and effectively constitutes a regional security community. While some observers consider that such a community already exists in the Southeast Asian part of the region (Acharya 2001), the creation of an authentic security community at an East Asian level continues to present a formidable challenge, especially as a result of China's increasingly assertive behaviour. As we shall see, there are some well-known internal obstacles to the development of close security ties in the region, which are compounded by the continuing importance of the USA and its bilateral ties with a number of key East Asian powers such as Japan. As a result, there are potentially insurmountable structural constraints to this aspect of regionness (Emmers and Tan 2011).

At the level of organized co-operation in the fields of cultural, political, economic and military affairs – the third of Hettne's measures of regionness – there are at least some hopeful signs. The basis for institutionalized security co-operation in the form of the ASEAN Regional Forum (ARF) exists but, as Chapter 5 illustrates, there are some formidable continuing impediments to effective regional security co-operation. More positively, concerted efforts have been made to encourage deeper economic integration. While it is important not to overstate this, or to exaggerate the role that governments – as opposed to the private sector – have played in this, sufficient progress has been made to at least give a veneer of regionness to political and economic integration. At the level of 'culture' the picture is less clear, as I explain in Chapter 6. Certainly, there are a number of commonalities, particularly Confucianism and a predilection for authoritarian government, but the attempted cultivation of 'Asian values' across much of the region during the mid-1990s was brought to a shuddering halt by the Asian economic crisis.[3]

Consequently, the picture regarding common values – Hettne's fourth criterion of regionness – is consequently mixed and evolving. On the one hand there are some common views about forms of political and economic organization, as well as sensitivities about Western intrusion.

On the other hand, however, these views are being diluted by global processes and the expansion of civil society. And yet, despite long-established traditions of democratic rule in places such as Japan and the remarkable process of democratization that has occurred in Indonesia, much of the region remains undemocratic, and civil society remains under-developed, as I explain in Chapter 6. Thus there is even less potential for the rise of the sort of *transnational* civil society that Hettne takes to be a measure of substantive regional integration and consolidation (see Beeson 2001). Nevertheless, Hettne's final suggested measure of regionness is the capacity of the region to act as a subject with a distinct identity, legitimacy and structure of decision-making. Here the signs had been quite promising, until recently at least. At the best of times, however, there are limits to the development of co-operative decision-making processes in Asia – a legacy of the jealously guarded nature of national sovereignty across much of the region and the reluctance to pool sovereignty in a similar way to the EU.

Despite that, by the measures of Hettne's criteria of regionness, East Asia looks to be nowhere near as developed as the EU, it still makes more sense to consider the countries of East Asia as being members of a putative political and economic grouping, rather than simply as individual countries that happen to inhabit the same part of the planet. Even in the seemingly least promising area of regional interaction – security co-operation – it is important to remember that threats travel most directly over short distances, and neighbours have little choice other than to attempt to accommodate each other if they wish to avoid conflict (Buzan and Waever 2003). Interpreting the rise of China is, as we shall see, critical in this context: whether China's intentions are peaceful, co-operative or aggressive will prove to be the central determinant of intra- and inter-regional relations during the twenty-first century. While it is clearly impossible to predict how China's rapid rise to prominence will influence its strategic thinking and behaviour in the longer term, what we can say is that it will happen in a profoundly reconfigured geopolitical environment and regional order: the end of the Cold War means that regional co-operation within and across East Asia is no longer foreclosed by the divisions of the Cold War. As a consequence, some observers consider that the new post-Cold War environment may actually encourage a reversion to the kind of Sinocentric regional order that prevailed for hundreds, if not thousands, of years before European engagement (Kang 2003a). The question is whether this underlying order and potential can be translated into an institutionalized regional framework.

Interest in East Asian regionalism was given added momentum as a consequence of the East Asian crisis, as I explain in more detail in Chapter 10. A key motivating factor here was the possibility that regionally based institutions might have the potential to provide collective regional responses to external challenges. The crisis highlighted the region's vulnerability to external economic and political forces, and many in the region wanted to develop indigenous mechanisms to manage future crises and make East Asia more autonomous (Grimes 2009; Pempel 2005a). It remains to be seen how successful such initiatives will be, but the desire to act in this manner and resist some of the unwanted impacts of 'globalization' highlights a theoretical and practical issue that will recur throughout this book: are the countries of East Asia inevitably 'converging' on Western styles of economic organization and political representation, or are the differences that distinguish the region sufficiently embedded and institutionalized that they will continue to diverge from the idealized free-market, liberal democratic model? To put it even more starkly, is there something about the nature of socially and institutionally embedded political economies that gives regional, as opposed to global, dynamics a particular immediacy and power? The rest of this introductory chapter explores these questions and highlights some of the theoretical and practical issues that may help to answer them.

Regional divergence or global convergence?

One of the most fundamental problems in thinking about international relations of any sort revolves around which 'level of analysis' to employ. The regional level that is the principal focus of attention in this book has only come to prominence relatively recently. Traditional IR theory tends to focus on the state and its place among a system of other states, with less attention being given to either regional forces or the array of new actors that are subsumed under the rubric of globalization. To help clarify what is an extremely complex set of interactions and processes, it is useful to add to the discussion of regional processes by unpacking the broadly conceived global and national categories, to understand better how they influence each other, and how they may ultimately shape the development of East Asia as a distinct entity.

The global level

One of the problems with making sense of the idea of globalization is that the associated literature has become so vast, and draws on such a diverse range of perspectives. Sociologists, geographers, political scientists and economists have all employed the term to highlight different aspects of transnational processes.[4] Given the many different uses to which the term has been put, there are grounds for questioning whether it retains much theoretical or descriptive utility. Despite the rather indiscriminate way the term is often used, I suggest that it serves a double purpose: first, if globalization is carefully defined, it serves as useful shorthand for a range of transnational processes that have become more prominent since the early 1960s and which are characteristic of the contemporary era. Second, globalization serves as a convenient counterpoint to regionalization, and allows us to make better sense of the way these levels interact.

As with regional processes, globalization has distinctive economic and political aspects. While these features are often treated separately, they are inextricably intertwined. There is a good deal of debate about when globalization might have begun (Frank and Gills 1993), and how extensive it might actually be (Hirst and Thompson 1996). However, there is little doubt that the institutional order created under the auspices of American hegemony, which we now think of as the Bretton Woods regime, was absolutely pivotal in creating the sort of 'open', liberal economic order that encouraged economic integration across state borders (Eichengreen and Kenen 1994; Latham 1997). Not only did the Bretton Woods institutions – the International Monetary Fund (IMF), the World Bank, and the General Agreement on Tariffs and Trade (GATT)[5] – encourage the development of international money markets, massive growth in trade and foreign investment, and the restructuring of corporate activities across national borders, but they were also instrumental in promoting a particular normatively-based policy agenda which came to be associated with neoliberalism (Brenner *et al.* 2010; Wilson 2009; Zurn *et al.* 2012).

Historically, much of East Asia has proved to be remarkably unenthusiastic about the neoliberal model and the agenda of liberalization, deregulation and minimal government with which it is associated (Beeson and Islam 2005). This has caused a good deal of friction between the USA and a number of East Asian countries in recent decades, and highlights the inescapably political and contested nature of globalization. Having said that, however, there is an underlying process of economic restructuring that interacts with political and regulatory initiatives, and helps to explain the particular shape of the international order (Ruigrok and van Tulder 1995; Tickell and Peck 2003). The next chapter illustrates how such processes have unfolded over the longer term, and how entire regions such as East Asia have been drawn into an expanding web of capitalist production structures that have profoundly affected existing patterns of social relations across much of the world. In assessing the extent of global influences and the degree of change that has occurred as a consequence, much depends on the time frame employed (Tilly 1984). As Chapter 2 demonstrates, there has been a fundamental transformation in the political structures and social relations of East Asia as a direct consequence of its interaction with 'the West' and its associated economic and political practices.

In debates about convergence and divergence, therefore, this process of long-run change may prove to be the most significant: the fact that formerly feudal or socialist countries adopt *any* form of capitalism is ultimately the critical point, not whether they are interventionist or laissez-faire in their public policy (see Strange 1997). However, the principal focus of this book is on the recent past, and here the evidence about the impact of globalization – especially in the narrowly defined economic sphere – is more ambiguous. Despite the consolidation and increasingly sophisticated organization of multinational corporations being one of the most important developments of the post-war period (Dicken 2011),[6] its impact has been uneven and contradictory for a number of reasons. First, there is no such thing as a typical multinational corporation (MNC). Different industrial sectors present different organizational challenges, and company strategies differ as a consequence (Abbott and Snidal 2009; Dunning 1988). Moreover, it is possible to disaggregate the entire production process and locate different aspects of the 'commodity chain' in different countries depending on their value and the locational advantages of specific areas. Consequently, the underlying logic of production is vastly different in the textile, automotive or resource industries, not to mention some of the increasingly sophisticated service sector industries that are an increasingly large part of the global economy (Gerrefi *et al.* 2005). The implication of this, of course, is that some regions of the world will be integrated into the global economy differently because they offer particular attractions for potentially mobile MNCs (Henderson *et al.* 2002).

And yet, a striking, counter-intuitive characteristic of MNCs is that they continue to display a surprising degree of national identity. For all the talk about the supposedly footloose nature of international business, the irresistible competitive pressures associated with globalization, and the need for firms to adopt 'international best practice', the reality is that corporate organizations across the world continue to display distinctive local features that distinguish one part of the global economy from another (Doremus *et al.* 1999; Sturgeon 2007). The major economies of Northeast Asia, Japan, Korea and China continue to display noteworthy local characteristics, making any notion of rapid convergence unlikely. The implications of these differences are drawn out more fully in Chapter 9. The point to emphasize here is that the attractiveness of different countries as potential investment locations is not solely a function of their 'natural' endowments, such as cheap labour or natural resources, but will also be influenced by specific national regulatory environments and policies. Crucially, the experience of the EU and recent policy initiatives in the East Asia suggest that such attractions may be aggregated at a regional level (Baldwin 2011).

In such circumstances, when there is no longer a necessary correlation between national economic and political identities, and where the effectiveness of government appears to be undermined by forces associated with globalization, it is understandable that governments should look to regional co-operation as one way of reclaiming authority and competence (Hameiri and Jayasuriya 2011). Until recently, the EU had served as an important benchmark for regional initiatives and an exemplar of what co-operation could achieve. Indeed, some argued its very existence changed the nature of and expectations about international relations (Manners 2002). Such claims may look rather inflated in light of recent events, but it is still legitimate to ask whether East Asia could achieve something similar – always supposing regional elites actually wanted to, of course. Before attempting to answer that question, we need to look more closely at the ability of states themselves to develop and enact policies that might produce EU-style outcomes. In other words, we need to consider the nation-state level of analysis before we can assess the possibilities for regional co-operation.

The nation-state in a global context

A focus on the national or individual state level is especially important in the context of East Asia. The state has been at the centre of the highly successful developmental project that has attracted much interest in the region. Indeed, the East Asian experience has been a major reason for 'bringing the state back in' to the study of comparative political and economic development (see Skocpol 1985; Weiss and Hobson 1995; see also Bremmer 2010). The historical role of the state is one of the common qualities that serves to distinguish the region, and which potentially offers, if not some form of common identity, then at least some basis for a common approach to public policy that might ultimately be transposed to the regional level. Consequently, it is helpful to have some conceptual tools with which to make sense of the role of the state generally, and of its particular place in East Asian development in particular.

In the context of potential regional collaboration, there are major differences between the EU and East Asia – especially in the quantity and quality of their respective institutional infrastructures – which raise questions about the ability of East Asia to replicate the European experience. Such differential capacities are significant because one of the most widely noted political aspects of the globalization process has been the emergence of what some observers have described as global civil society (Dryzek 2012). Yet it is clear that there are significant, historically-determined differences in the extent of domestic civil society in Europe and Asia, the nature of the social formations within which states are embedded, and constraints on the sorts of political outcomes that are possible as a consequence. The relatively limited experience of democratic rule, the influence of authoritarianism, and the continuing importance of the state as the central arbiter of political outcomes, means that the influence of civil society at either the domestic or the international level is relatively limited in East Asia (Gerrard 2013). This has significant implications for the development of a sense of regional identity and the depth of regionness as a consequence.

Prominent strands of the globalization literature have suggested that we are witnessing a profound reconfiguration of political organization, which is fundamentally undermining the autonomy of the state (Ohmae 1996; Strange 1996). In this reading, the ability of the state to act independently is undermined both as a consequence of global economic processes it is increasingly unable to control, and because of a transfer of power and regulatory responsibility to a new array of actors on the global stage (Boli and Thomas 1999; Mathews 1997). If this analysis is correct, it would have especially important ramifications for the role, and even the legitimacy, of East Asian states that have been at the centre of national development projects. Certainly, there is little doubt that states generally have voluntarily ceded authority to the private sector in many key areas of economic regulatory activity (Braithwaite and Drahos 2000). It is also clear that national governments are subject to the judgement of non-state authorities such as ratings agencies in a way that they have not been previously, thus as a consequence potentially constraining their policy-autonomy (Sinclair 2005). But it is far less certain that states have lost their ability to act effectively, either individually or collectively.

Analytically, there have been a number of important contributions to our understanding of why some states have been effective and others have not. One way of conceptualizing this variable degree of effectiveness is as 'state capacity', which essentially means a government's ability to formulate and implement policy successfully (Back and Hadenius 2008; Bell and Hindmoor 2009). There are a number of critical factors influencing this apparently simple requirement. Peter Evans (1995) famously argued that unless states – or more specifically, bureaucratic elites acting in the 'national interest' – enjoyed a measure of 'embedded autonomy', there was a danger that they would either be ineffective, or would simply act in the interests of whichever powerful domestic interest managed to capture them. The trick, then, according to Evans, was to be sufficiently embedded in society so that the plans and policies of government could be implemented successfully, but not so close to powerful vested interests that they lost their independence or became corrupted as a consequence. This is an especially relevant consideration in the case of East Asia as there is a major debate about just how independent and non-corrupt state elites across the region actually are.

Other writers have also drawn attention to the importance of state–society relations, suggesting that states must have the ability to reach down into the society within which they are embedded to extract the resources necessary to underpin development (Mann 1993). Joel Migdal (1988, 1994) has provided an especially useful series of analyses of state development and strength in the 'Third World',[7] which have particular relevance for an East Asian region that contains both 'strong' and 'weak' states, and as a consequence, different levels of economic development. State strength is essentially a synonym for state capacity, but what is distinctive about Migdal's analysis is the link he makes between a lack of state capacity and the specific challenges of state-building and economic development in the Third World. Too often, analysis of political organization and economic management are focused on the developed world – circumstances that have only limited relevance to East Asia as a whole. If what Migdal calls 'social control' is unrealized, and if political authority is contested and considered illegitimate, he suggests that the chances for the development of effective state capacity or strength are remote. It is increasingly widely recognized that, without social stability and functioning institutions, the prospects for development remain weak (Fukuyama 2004). What is significant about Migdal's analysis in this context is that he highlights the dynamic nature of state–society interaction and its mutually constitutive effect:

> As the state organization comes into contact with various social groups, it clashes with and accommodates to different moral orders. These engagements, which occur at numerous junctures, change the social bases and the aims of the state. The state is not a fixed ideological entity. Rather it embodies an ongoing dynamic, a changing set of goals, as it engages other social groups ... The formulation of policy is as much a product of this dynamic as it is a simple outcome of the goals of top state leaders or a straightforward legislative process. (Migdal 1994: 12)

What is distinctive and different about such processes in the contemporary era, of course, is that they occur within an increasingly influential and constraining international context. While the state may be a more dynamic, politically-contested space than many conventional analyses suggest, and while domestic competition may continue to be a central determinant of national policy, such contests occur in a wider global environment. Understanding the relationship between individual states, their national policy-making capacities, and regional or global processes is therefore, vital.

It is clear that states remain crucial parts of the contemporary international system. Without the regulatory and legal frameworks that states provide, the complex patterns of social interaction associated with capitalism simply could not survive (Bell and Hindmoor 2009; Heilbroner 1985). There is nothing natural or inevitable about the existence of market-mediated social relationships and modes of economic organization, as Karl Polanyi's (1957) influential analysis of British economic and social development reminds us: even in supposedly laissez-faire Britain, capitalist social relations were not the spontaneous response of individuals to the hidden hand of the market, but had to be imposed coercively through state auspices. Similarly, one of the most fundamental changes in East Asia – a transformation that is still under way today – has been the incorporation of the region into an increasingly pervasive and global capitalist economy; and it has completely overturned pre-existing patterns of social relations, economic organization and political authority in the process. Indeed, it is important to remember that the Westphalian state[8] that is such a central and taken-for-granted part of the international system, and which is generally charged with managing the adjustment process, was itself actually introduced to East Asia as part of the expansion of European political and economic power – a process that is described in more detail in the next chapter.

At this stage, it is useful to make a distinction between the state as part of a system of states and the state responding to global processes on the basis of more particularistic national strategies. In the contemporary global era, there is a functional requirement for the provision of various collective goods that transcend national borders. International exchange rate systems, for example, are critical parts of the international political economy that only states can ultimately underwrite, but which they can only provide by acting collaboratively (Cerny 1995). In other words, at one level the state remains fundamental, but only as a co-operative part of a system of states. It is the recognition by individual states in East Asia that mutual gains are not only possible through collaboration, but may actually be impossible to realize without it, that has spurred recent interest in regional co-operation. We might expect, therefore, that the response of individual states to ubiquitous global pressures might become increasingly similar – even if such responses have a regional dimension. Some of the most sophisticated analyses of global processes have, indeed, suggested that states are locked in a process of 'regulatory arbitrage' that leaves them very little room for manoeuvre (Cerny 1996). And yet, when we look at the responses of individual states to the challenges of globalization, we see continuing differences in terms of both capacity and in the strategies they have chosen self-consciously in response to seemingly universal pressures (Berger and Dore 1996; Hall and Soskice 2001).

There are two particularly useful general explanations of this apparent paradox, in which individual states seem to be assailed by competing centres of power and authority, and yet are still able to initiate policy. On the one hand, states – or some states, at least[9] – seem to have the ability to adapt to changing circumstances and adjust policy accordingly. Linda Weiss, for example, argues that globalization actually *requires* states to act proactively if economic development is to occur, and that states retain an 'enabling' capacity which allows them to develop new forms of economic management predicated on co-operation, co-ordination and social partnership (Weiss 2003: 308). Clearly, not all states will have this sort of capacity, but even where the ideology of neoliberalism has made state 'intervention' unfashionable and controversial, the empirical record suggests that a more directive and 'hands-on' approach to economic management is still feasible (Beeson and Pham 2012).

The other way of explaining the persistence of state effectiveness involves considering the internal architecture of states themselves, and their relationship with nationally demarcated societies and even the regions of which they are a part (Hameiri and Jayasuriya 2011). The fundamental dilemma confronting states today is the disjuncture between political and economic space: as a consequence of globalization, economic activity and political authority are no longer coterminous. What Ruggie (1993) calls the 'unbundling' of territoriality, in which the old relationship between nationally demarcated political authority and economic space has broken down, to be replaced by a more complex, fluid set of relationships that transcend national borders. Such changes have transformed both the environment within which states operate, and to varying degrees, the state itself. The contemporary state occupies a 'crossroads position' in a complex network of actors, institutions and processes (Cerny 2005), as it attempts to mediate between 'domestic' and 'external' forces. In such circumstances some of IR's most fundamental ideas about the nature of states and their capacities come under challenge, as does the capacity of individual states to respond to such challenges.

The tension between the old, state-centric conception of territorialization, and the new processes of de-territorialization that emerge as a consequence of economic globalization have been well highlighted by economic geographers (Agnew 1994; Brenner 1999). But if it has become clear that economic activity increasingly occurs in a space 'beyond' national borders, it is also apparent that political structures are being reconfigured as a consequence too. As Reinicke (1998: 66) points out, globalization challenges the state's 'operational sovereignty', and forces it to develop new ways of adjusting to an array of global *and* local or national pressures that emerge as a consequence of the long-term restructuring of the international political economy. Kanishka Jayasuriya (2001) has explained how global pressures are encouraging a reconfiguration of the internal structures of the state, as various agencies and institutions – central banks are the quintessential example – assume greater independence and authority. Significantly, formerly national organizations are developing closer relationships with their counterparts elsewhere, creating a form of 'regulatory regionalism' in the process, Jayasuriya (2009) argues. While this process has gone furthest in the EU, it is also apparent that policy networks and institutionalized relationships that cross national borders and integrate formerly discrete polities on a regional basis are also a central part of the processes of sovereignty-pooling that is such a distinctive part of the Western European experience (Wallace 1999).

Given the series of economic and political crises that have gripped the EU since the start of the 'global financial crisis' (GFC) in 2008, the EU might look like more of a model to avoid than to emulate (Beeson and Stone 2012). I consider the impact of the GFC and the earlier 'Asian financial crisis' (AFC) in more detail in Chapter 10. The point to note here is that we should be careful not to assume that Europe's past is Asia's future, or that there is only one response to globalization or one road to regional integration. Nevertheless, the EU experience illustrates some potentially universal issues that East Asians may have to confront if regionalism is to take hold there.

Conclusion

Despite the well-known heterogeneity that characterizes the countries of East Asia, there are a number of reasons for thinking that, when taken together, they constitute a distinct region. The story of East Asia's recent attempts to institutionalize and deepen intra-regional co-operation is told in detail in Chapter 11. This chapter has provided ways of making sense of that empirical evidence. One of the most important points to emerge from the theoretical literature is that regional processes have interconnected economic and political aspects that emerge in particular geopolitical circumstances. The effectiveness of regional initiatives is largely dependent on how deeply political and economic processes are linked and co-ordinated, and how deeply co-operative mechanisms are institutionalized. The EU has gone furthest in this process, and until recently provided something of a benchmark. It remains to be seen whether East Asians now have either the desire or – equally importantly – the capacity to replicate European-style institutional structures.

It is possible, of course, that East Asian forms of regional integration will take a different form from those of the EU. Indeed, we should expect that this will be the case, given the very different geopolitical circumstances that prevail in East Asia, the different ways and times at which they were incorporated into emerging global processes, and the specific patterns of political and economic organization that have emerged as a consequence. The 'thickness' of Europe's institutional infrastructure, especially at the non-state level, means that some forms of transnational co-ordination and co-operation are simply more feasible in Europe than they are in East Asia (Beeson 2001). As subsequent chapters suggest that, despite East Asia's association with authoritarianism, significant movement towards greater democratization is occurring across the region, and the extent and influence of civil society is expanding at both the domestic and – to a more limited extent – the transnational level. But there are plainly limits to this process, and the desire or ability to replicate the EU experience, especially given the EU's recent troubles and the growing tensions caused by territorial disputes in East Asia, make it more likely that regionalism in East Asia will follow its own distinctive trajectory.

The East Asian experience consequently has important comparative significance for much of the non-Western European world. States everywhere find themselves subjected to an array of new pressures. Not only is their ability to develop and implement policy autonomously compromised, but expectations about what states ought to deliver for their citizens have generally grown – despite the neoliberal preoccupation with minimal government and reduced government spending. While it is clear that states are far from powerless, and that proactive responses to the challenge of globalization not only exist but also help to determine the way in which different parts of the world are integrated into the global economy, one of the most striking paradoxes of this process is that states may need to sacrifice – or at least redefine – their sovereignty to do it. This has been the EU's solution: collective regional action has generally proved to be an effective way of responding to global pressures and increasing the influence of Europe as a whole. To begin the process of assessing East Asia's particular national and regional dynamics, we need to place them in their specific historical context.

Chapter 2

Northeast Asia and the Weight of History

All states and societies are products of their particular historical circumstances. Even where countries or regions have been profoundly influenced by external forces, such forces are mediated by local institutions, actors and contingent factors that give a distinctive character to seemingly ubiquitous influences. The impact of contingent factors can be seen in the different responses to the impact of European imperialism in Latin America and East Asia, for example. Equally important and revealing, such forces can be seen in the very different impacts that apparently similar influences had on countries within various regions. Japan and China not only responded very differently to the challenge of European economic and political expansion, but their subsequent historical development has been distinctive as a consequence. If we want to understand the contemporary economic, political and strategic positions of the various countries of East Asia, and why there are important differences between both the developmental experiences of individual countries, as well as between Northeast and Southeast Asia, then we need to place recent developments in their historical context.

In this chapter I outline the key historical patterns and developments that underpin contemporary East Asian intra- and inter-regional relations. Given the extent of the region's history this is no easy task and the result is necessarily a broad-brush sketch. China alone has been a distinct civilization for more than 3,000 years. While it is not possible to do justice even to China's history and its influence over what we now think of as East Asia in the course of one chapter, it is vital to have a sense of the legacy of Chinese hegemony and its place at the centre of a relatively stable East Asian order. Indeed, some observers think that the older, China-centric world order may be re-emerging and providing the basis for a more narrowly defined East Asian regionalism (Kang 2003a). Even if such analyses prove to be wide of the mark, the tensions between countries such as Japan and China, which may actually frustrate greater regional integration, cannot be understood without placing their bilateral relations in the context of some of the grimmer episodes of recent history. Likewise, the disparity in developmental outcomes that distinguishes Northeast and Southeast Asia cannot be explained unless we recognize the impact of colonial rule on countries such as Indonesia, Malaysia and the Philippines (Sidel 2008).

The central argument of this chapter is not just that history matters, but that it continues to shape contemporary relations within the region, and between the region and the rest of the world. The impact of the growing contact with Europe is perhaps the most obvious and dramatic illustration of this possibility. China's position at the centre of an East Asian order was overturned by this process, inaugurating a 'century of shame' from which it is only just recovering. Similarly, Japan's post-war subordination to, and reliance on, the United States, and the impact this has had on its place in the world, cannot be understood without an appreciation of the historical context that has shaped Japan's recent foreign policies. The strategic implications of these developments will be taken up in subsequent chapters. The point to emphasize here is that historical factors have been crucial determinants of the course of economic, political and strategic developments within the region and help to account for the comparatively late development of regional processes in East Asia.

The first part of the chapter looks at the relative decline of China and the internal and external factors that have brought it about. Following this, I look at Japan's very different response to the challenge of European expansion – a story that has important comparative lessons and continuing contemporary relevance. While the sometimes violent relationship between China and Japan has been the most important bilateral interaction in the East Asian region, an historically informed analysis also makes it clear just how influential outside forces have been – especially the hegemonic powers of the day. This observation is particularly apposite for the countries in Southeast Asia that are examined in the next chapter. While it is not possible to do justice to the complex and distinct histories of the countries of the region in a couple of chapters, I shall identify some of the key historical influences that continue to shape the intra- and inter-regional relations of East Asia to this day.

The decline of Chinese hegemony

Lucian Pye (1990: 58) famously observed that China was 'a civilization pretending to be a nation'. While this may not be as true as it once was, it captures something important about the unique historical position of China in the world, and especially its regional history. Though there is some doubt about just how far back Chinese civilization stretches, it can be traced to the Three Dynasties of Ancient China – the Xia, Shang and

Zhou – which existed in the 2,000 years before the birth of Christ. Many of the imperial and cultural institutions that came to be associated with dynastic rule in China were established in this period. Confucius (551–479 BC), for example, lived during the Zhou dynasty, developing a social and moral code that continues to exert an influence to this day, and which largely preceded the Ancient Greeks and the dawn of Western civilization. Despite developing the world's first great civilization, sophisticated social and cosmological perspectives, to say nothing of a series of remarkable technological innovations that would ultimately provide an important impetus to Western development (Hobson 2004), Chinese history is punctuated by often convulsive dynastic transformations and the threat of foreign conquest.

While the principal focus of this chapter is on recent Asian history and the impact on East Asia of 'globalization' in the form of European economic and political expansion,[1] it is important to acknowledge briefly the legacy of this earlier period. During the Han dynasty (206 BC–AD 220), for example, not only was there an internal consolidation and expansion of Chinese rule and the establishment of 'imperial Confucianism' (Fairbank 1994), which incorporated the idea of the 'Mandate of Heaven' and cosmological harmony,[2] but such ideas were also spreading to other parts of the region. Korea began to adopt Chinese writing and administrative practices by the fourth century AD, and Japan followed suit during the fifth and sixth centuries. Though this period marked the beginning of China's cultural hegemony over its neighbours, its own position was not assured. For all the disdain the Chinese have displayed for 'barbarians', it is no small irony that their history has been powerfully shaped by them.

The invasion of China in the late thirteenth century by the Mongols under Kublai Khan was the most traumatic example of external intervention. The major lasting impact on China of the Mongol interlude was to pave the way for the introverted Ming dynasty (1368–1644), which withdrew behind the Great Wall and isolated itself economically by closing land and sea connections with the West (Huang 1997). In the context of world historical change it is difficult to overstate the significance of this period in helping to determine the relative fates of Europe and China. By 1400, Chinese shipbuilding and nautical expertise, as well as expanding commercial links had made China a major economic force in East Asia.[3] Existing trade patterns with the countries of what we now think of as Southeast Asia were consolidated. And yet concerns about renewed Mongol power, and the in-principle objections of Confucian-trained scholar-officials[4] to commercial activities helped to encourage a further turning inward and isolationism. Though there is some dispute about how complete this process was, the contrast with what was happening in

Europe is striking and it is worth making a few comparative observations as they help to explain both the remarkable expansionary dynamism of Europe and the inevitability of its collision with East Asia. They also help explain the region's ill-preparedness when confronted with the European challenge.

However, it is also important to recognize that, in its heyday, China's influence and its relationship with other 'states' of the region was profound and formalized in the 'tribute system'. While the political structures of pre-modern Asia were a good deal looser, less precisely delimited geographically, and more personalized than their Westphalian equivalents in Europe (Wolters 1999), China presided over a regional hierarchy that recognized its own dominance in the tribute missions dispatched by the likes of Japan, Korea, Vietnam, Thailand, Burma and Cambodia. As far back as the Tang dynasty (AD 618–907), China's neighbours acknowledged its status as the leading power in the region by sending diplomatic delegations to pay homage. At one level this was ritualistic performance which had a limited impact on the subordinate powers that acknowledged China's superior status. But while the tribute system may have been largely symbolic, it has been argued that it provided an important stabilizing influence in a region with no formal mechanisms to manage intra-regional relations. David Kang (2010: 10) suggests that 'far more than a thin veneer of meaningless social lubricants, the tribute system and its ideas and institutions formed the basis of relations between states'. At the very least, therefore, there are historical precedents for Chinese domination of the region.

Seen against this backdrop, China's ultimate inability to respond to the challenge posed by European expansionism is all the more remarkable when we consider that China, as Frank (1998) has argued persuasively, was at the *centre* rather than the periphery of world trade until at least the end of the eighteenth century. In Frank's view, China's isolationism is overstated and reflects in part the bias of the Eurocentric interpretation of world history that has occurred in parallel with European military and economic domination. According to Frank, it was only the discovery and exploitation of the Americas that really gave the previously backward Europeans an entrée to the emerging world economy. While this thesis is still controversial, it is clear that the massive flows of wealth – especially in the form of gold and silver – from both South America and Africa provided a crucial stimulus to European development and helped to establish Europe as a *capitalist* society (Blaut 1993).

While the transformation of European social relations that saw the overturning of feudalism and the emergence of new forms of market-mediated societies was a complex process that spanned hundreds of years (see Wood 2002), it is important to highlight the contrast with China's much more rigid social order. Whereas much of Europe was experiencing profound upheaval in its domestic social relations, institutions of governance, political ideas and economic dynamics, China was comparatively more institutionally inert (Jones 1981). China's effective, but highly conservative structures of governance are widely considered to have been an obstacle to the sort of flexibility and adaptability that characterized the often convulsive social change that swept through Europe from the fifteenth to the nineteenth centuries. China, by contrast, was paralysed by the 'ethnocentric complacency of Confucian officials and the imperviousness of Chinese culture to outside stimuli' (Hsü 1983: 106). For millennia, Chinese elites considered they had had nothing to learn from the barbarians outside their empire. This, combined with an overburdened and cumbersome imperial decision-making process, meant that by the time the Europeans had become increasingly forceful in their attempts to break into Asia, China's leadership under the final Qing dynasty (1644–1911) was 'stultified below and worn out at the top' (Fairbank *et al.* 1965: 103).

While market mechanisms existed within the Chinese empire, economic development remained stunted in comparison to Europe. Despite China's early lead in technological development and the spur this provided to the West (Hobson 2004), it was Europe's technological development that really accelerated its development and paved the way for its subsequent economic and military dominance (Pomeranz 2000). Crucially, China's failure to make the transition to capitalism was as much ideational as it was institutional. As Wong (1997: 147) points out, 'Chinese rulers had no reason to imagine, let alone promote, the mercantilist policies invented by European rulers'. In other words, the competitive economic and interstate dynamic that had underpinned both the rise of European economic *and* military power in a mutually reinforcing virtuous circle (Tilly 1990) was absent in China; China's comparative stability engendered complacency and a disdain of the sort of systematic, break-neck, interconnected economic development that was the hallmark of Western Europe's increasingly region-wide developmental process. By contrast, East Asia would have to wait for the rise of industrialized Japan to work a similar miracle.

The end of empire

While the collapse of the Qing dynasty marked the end of the imperial system, it is worth remembering that for its first 150 years of existence the Manchu-led empire[5] experienced the greatest territorial expansion since the time of Mongol domination. Why was the subsequent collapse so rapid and inexorable? At one level, this was clearly a consequence of what David Abernathy calls European imperialism's 'triple assault' on domestic institutions of governance, on established patterns of economic organization, and on indigenous ideas and values that gave meaning to life. The combined effects and superior organizational capacities of European states' soldier-administrators, merchants and missionaries had a generally overwhelming impact on colonized countries. The net effect, Abernathy (2000: 9) argues, was the European powers' 'capacity to undermine the power and legitimacy of other expanding political systems'. While there is still a good deal of debate about the underlying dynamics of imperialism,[6] there is less doubt about its impact: not only did the imperial era establish the preconditions for the most recent phase of globalization and the almost complete adoption of capitalism as a system of economic organization across the world, but it also led to the universal expansion of the inter-state system and the dominance of the nation-state as a consequence (Watson 1992).

And yet, even if we accept that the Europeans had developed more effective institutions with which to co-ordinate economic and military activities, and a technological edge with which to underwrite them, we should not jump to the conclusion either that Europe's domination of China was complete, or that it came about solely as a consequence of European, rather than Chinese, attributes. China was simply too big and too difficult to conquer, and the impact of European ideas and commercial practices outside of key elites is easy to overstate – especially in the Chinese hinterland. Moreover, not only did Chinese culture exert an important influence on Europe,[7] but a good deal of the feebleness of China's response to the European challenge was a consequence of internal degeneration, rather than simple European superiority. In short, 'foreign aggression was made possible only by the weakening of dynastic leadership and efficiency' (Fairbank *et al.* 1965: 81). The inflexible and overloaded nature of the imperial administrative system noted above, combined with increased corruption, a stagnant economy and the relentless population pressures that have haunted all administrations in China, meant that the internal dynastic cycle was as much to blame for China's weakness as was Europe's comparative strength. With a more competent, vigorous and responsive leadership in the nineteenth century, regional, not to say world, history might have looked very different.

As it was, Europe's economic expansion and the demands that accompanied it were implacable. The Opium War (1839–42) was emblematic of the new economic and strategic relationship between China, Europe and Britain in particular. The opium trade was dominated by private merchants and the British East India Company, and it was these that encouraged the British government to underwrite their commercial interests with naval fire-power when the Chinese authorities threatened their freedom of economic action. The Treaty of Nanjing, which ended the Opium War, forced China to accept a massive increase in opium imports and cede control over a series of Chinese ports – guaranteeing foreign traders commercial access to the mainland. Why were the British so enthusiastic about peddling addictive drugs to China's masses in violation of the wishes of the Chinese government? Because the opium trade offered a way of solving a perennial British trade deficit with China. Europe consumed Chinese silk, spices and especially tea, but exported very little in return. Britain and Europe were able to pay their bills with bullion plundered from the 'New World' and derived from the slave trade, but the systematic cultivation of a market for opium produced in another of Britain's colonies – India – promised to solve the trade problem. The overall impact on China is summarized pithily by Pomeranz and Topik (1999: 103):

> The Chinese not only lost their battle to exclude dope and their war with the British navy; they lost their tariff autonomy, a large indemnity, the right to subject foreign residents to Chinese law, and the land that would soon be Hong Kong. The worst was yet to come: its military weakness exposed, China entered a calamitous century of foreign aggression, domestic disorder, and civil war. Skyrocketing opium use – to perhaps 40 million addicts by 1900 – played no small role in this.

Clearly the opium wars were not the single cause of China's decline, but it certainly highlighted the fundamental military and political weakness of the Chinese state and imperial system relative to the European intruders. It also highlighted how important China's economy was to the rest of the world even at this early stage of globalization, and how far other countries were prepared to go to try to ensure that economic relations were conducted on a favourable basis. In this regard, there are, as we shall see in Chapter 5, interesting parallels with China's recent accession to the World Trade Organization: while China's entry is voluntary rather than coerced by gun-boat diplomacy, the two episodes shed a revealing light on the different nature of British and American hegemony. I comment further on the latter in Chapter 8. What is important to note here is the general historical potential for even the most powerful countries to come under the sway of extra-regional powers.

Nothing highlighted the potential imbalance of influence and authority better than the 'standard of civilization' by which the European powers judged China and other states as potential members of the interstate system. As Gerrit Gong (1984: 7) points out, the standard of civilization idea might have provided a justification and legitimacy for the global expansion of the Western powers, but 'it represented an insult, a humiliation, and a fundamental threat to the proud and culturally independent non-European countries'. In this context, the existence of the Treaty ports and European extraterritoriality came to be seen as a badge of inferiority and subordination. This is why the reforms undertaken in the final days of the imperial system were so significant, argues Zhang:

> The Imperial reforms in the first decade of the century instituted fundamental changes in nearly every sphere of Chinese life. The changes in the Chinese values system and traditional institutions brought about by the reforms called into being a New China, similar to the rest of the world in terms of its political attitudes and values and in its legal institutions. Whether intentionally or not, this was not just a transformation of empire, but also a civilization. (Zhang 1991: 10)

Ironically, of course, the belated attempts at 'self-strengthening'[8] and modernization that had been resisted by the Confucian elites accelerated the Empire's demise, rather than rescuing it. Education about Western ways was not confined to technical matters, but introduced new political doctrines that further undermined the ideological legitimacy of the old order. In little more than a hundred years, the foundations of a dynastic order that had lasted for millennia had been fatally eroded. From being at the centre of regional order that dominated its neighbours and accepted their tribute as a mark of its due status,[9] China found itself reduced to being a subordinate power on the brink of catastrophic internal collapse.

Internal struggle

The last years of the Qing dynasty were marked by increased unrest and declining authority. The Boxer Rising (1898–1901) was one of the most important expressions of growing discontent. It highlighted widespread popular unhappiness about the impact of Christian missionaries and China's loss of face as a consequence of European and Japanese intervention in the country. China was losing control of its territory to the British, Germans, French, Russians and – most gallingly, perhaps – the Japanese. In Godement's (1997: 26) colourful phrase, 'the country was being carved up like a watermelon'. While this is something of an overstatement, it does capture the sense of powerlessness and consequent humiliation that gripped many Chinese in the face of their country's apparent dismemberment, infiltration and subordination. In such circumstances the stage was set for a major internal struggle about China's future.

Ironically, the final decade of Qing rule, 1901–11, was marked by significant attempts at social and institutional reform, but they proved too late to save it. Once the reform process was under way it proved impossible to control; the heady mixture of social transformation and ideological contestation was too much for an imperial system that was legitimated by its stability and autonomy. Not only was the need for modernization widely accepted by the beginning of the twentieth century, but the modernizing impulse was synonymous with nationalism. Even more remarkably, the revolution when it did finally come was 'largely made in Japan' (Fairbank *et al.* 1965: 631). Japan's remarkable – and highly successful – modernization process, and the nationalism that had been such a prominent part of it, made it a role model for other would-be modernizers across Asia. Sun Yat-sen (1866–1925), one of the key figures in the revolutionary movement in China and a future nationalist leader, spent time in Japan absorbing new ideas and establishing a support base among Chinese students studying there. The Japanese were happy to support Sun and encourage his republicanism.

The actual revolution of 1911 was 'singularly unviolent' (Fairbank *et al.* 1965: 640). The old order had been thoroughly undermined and discredited by the nationalists and modernizers, and the hollowed-out shell required surprisingly little to make it shatter. It is important to remember that the Qing dynasty had initially been established by the Manchu minority; the nationalist movement offered the majority Han Chinese a chance to re-establish their dominance, as much as did the prospect of establishing democracy and institutional reform (Fung 1995: 182). Resolving questions of national identity that had been long-standing sources of tension and resentment provided a powerful underlying dynamic for the nationalist movement above and beyond the general promise of reviving China and enabling it to stand up to external challenges.[10] This was an entirely predictable consequence of China's integration into the international states system, which had the effect of making China a nation-state rather than an imperial civilization, and making nationalism a key part of the new order. Nationalism remains a potent force in Chinese politics to this day (Gries 2004).

However, the initial post-revolutionary compromise, which saw Sun Yat-sen sacrifice his leadership ambitions in favour of a military strongman, Yuan Shikai, for the sake of national unity and stability, proved unsustainable. Indeed, the country collapsed into a prolonged period of warlordism and internecine conflict in which the centralized authority of the state essentially broke down. In some ways this is unsurprising: given the longevity of the imperial system it might be expected that developing new institutions and patterns of authority would prove difficult. What is more surprising, perhaps, is the degree of intellectual dispute that accompanied the new order. On the one hand, the May Fourth Movement[11] epitomized the desire of many modernizers to reject the traditional, Confucian order and adopt a more independent posture toward the West. On the other hand, however, the West's influence was clearly manifest in the ideological struggles that erupted between the nationalists and the communists – divisions that would eventually culminate in civil war. At the outset of this contest, however, there was a noteworthy degree of co-operation between differing factions. Initially, the Kuomingtang (KMT), which was led by Sun and was the main manifestation of the nationalist impulse, co-operated with the Chinese Communist Party (CCP), which drew its inspiration from Marxism–Leninism and the successful Russian Revolution.

Following Sun Yat-sen's death in 1925, the KMT assumed power under Chiang Kai-shek (1887–1975), who exploited nationalist sentiment to establish a modernizing government in Nanjing. Significantly, both the nationalists under Chiang and the communists under Mao Zedong (1893–1976) were able to exploit hostility towards Japan and its aggressive takeover of Manchuria to bolster their own positions. Chalmers Johnson (1962) has demonstrated how the CCP was able to mobilize the peasantry – traditionally a conservative and unpromising source of revolutionary potential – as a direct consequence of the war with Japan that broke out in 1937 and lasted until the end of the Second World War. Indeed, Johnson's analysis suggests that Chinese communism was primarily a form of nationalism and a response to Japanese aggression. The great achievement of the CCP was to establish a power base in the countryside – an area neglected by the more urban-oriented KMT. One of the critical failures of the KMT government was its inability to penetrate the countryside and exercise the sort of infrastructural power that is one of the hallmarks of effective state capacity. Chiang's dominance of the regime meant that while government became more centralized, the KMT became less influential and the administrative infrastructure of the Nanjing government failed to develop adequately. It relied on coercion to maintain its authority, and as a consequence resources were directed towards the military. Perhaps most important, though, Chiang's failure to institute reform and win over the countryside allowed his communist rivals to survive and regroup despite his best efforts to crush them (Eastman 1986).

The great mass of China's population has always lived on the land, so the peasants have occupied an especially important place in Chinese history. Even now, 40 per cent of China's population live and work in the agricultural sector,[12] despite the major internal migration and structural transformation of the economy that has occurred over recent decades. In the first half of the twentieth century, however, the peasantry represented an even greater section of the population, and one that had been destabilized by the collapse of imperial rule and the rise of warlordism. Part of Mao's genius, and part of what marked him out as a potential leader of the CCP, was his flair for theory and his attempt to replace the patron–client relations that predominated in the countryside with the ideology of class struggle. During the Long March of 1934–36, in which the CCP traversed much of western China while being pursued by Chiang's nationalist forces, the Party leadership was consolidated under Mao. It also allowed the CCP to shake off the influence of Moscow and establish a distinctive doctrine and the Sinification of Marxism – a split that would have long-term implications for future international relations within the region and beyond.

Japan's invasion of Manchuria in 1937 and the war it sparked exposed the potential weaknesses of the Nationalist government. Despite the collaboration between the CCP and Chiang's nationalist government to fight the Japanese invaders it was a marriage of convenience that could not last. Significantly, it was the United States – already revealed as the key external power in the East Asian region – that attempted to unify the Chinese forces. Roosevelt's suggestion that the command of all Chinese forces should be united under American General Stilwell proved too much for Chiang, however, as it revived the spectre of foreign domination that the nationalists had taken such pains to overcome. Yet it should also be emphasized that American assistance for China eventually occurred only as a consequence of the wider Second World War and a calculation of the USA's own strategic interests. Before that, and despite the violation of Chinese sovereignty and Japan's brutal occupation, the USA remained isolationist and uninvolved. Indeed, it is particularly significant – and understandable, perhaps – that in the aftermath of the Second World War, and despite the emerging outline of the ideologically divisive Cold War, the Americans should have shown little enthusiasm for intervening in the resolution of China's internal struggles (see Iriye 1967).

As we now know, of course, this policy would allow the communists to triumph in their struggle with the nationalists, and contribute to the 'loss' of China to the Soviet sphere of influence. We also now know that the idea that there was a homogenous anti-capitalist bloc was an overly simplistic reading of the complexities of relations among the communist powers. The consequences that flowed from such ideologically blinkered assumptions are taken up in more detail in the next chapter. What is of most significance at this stage is the historical legacy of this period: China became a communist country in 1949 and the nationalists were driven off the mainland to Taiwan,[13] thus setting the stage for the major strategic confrontation between the capitalist and communist powers that would distinguish global politics for the next 40 years or so.

There are a number of points about China's pre-war experience emerging from this brief overview of Chinese history that merit emphasis. First, the demise of the dynastic system that constituted China's civilization and identity for millennia was always going to be traumatic and difficult to accommodate, and arguably the process is still under way. Second, the 'century of shame' that the break-up of the old order and the intervention of external powers inaugurated also had a profound impact on both China's internal and external relations that can be seen to this day (Wang 2012). Nationalism remains a potent force in China and one that the authorities struggle to control. Third, China's recent history has been – and continues to be – powerfully shaped by external influences. Fourth, state strength or capacity is a powerful determinant of how effectively countries will be able to manage and accommodate both external *and* internal forces. In China's case it took decades for the old order to die and a new one to be born under communist auspices. The question now is whether those structures are any longer able to cope with the new pressures and challenges that globalization generates. Paradoxically, much the same is true of Japan – China's pivotally important neighbour – which, despite a much more successful initial response to the challenge posed by the West, is also facing profound adjustment problems as its tries to reconfigure its historically embedded institutions. To see why, we need to look more closely at Japan's history, too.

The rise of Japan

The comparative historical experiences of Japan and China in response to European contact and expansion could hardly be more different. True, for a time, Japan also attempted to turn inwards when confronted by the West's potentially destabilizing beliefs and practices. But when Japanese elites did decide to learn from, rather than to ignore, the West, they set in train a process that would see Japan become the second-largest economy in the world and – for a short time – a formidable military power. Japan's very different response to incipient global processes is not just important in the context of intra- and inter-regional relations, it is also a powerful historical reminder that there is nothing inevitable about the impact of external forces or the way individual states will respond to similar challenges. Indeed, the Japanese experience has provided a major challenge to those theoretical perspectives that either assumed that Asia was in some way incapable of developing because of inappropriate cultural values, or because the structurally entrenched dominance of the West made significant development in the 'periphery' of the global economy all but impossible. As we shall see in Chapter 7, so significant has been the experience of Japan and its acolytes, in fact, that it has generated an influential school of thought which argues that there are actually advantages in 'late' development (Gerschenkron 1966). Such possibilities were not immediately apparent in Japan's early history, however.

In 1603, Ieyasu, founder of the Tokugawa house, established the Tokugawa shogunate and national dominance after a series of civil wars during the fifteenth and sixteenth centuries. Like China, Japan had an imperial system, and the shogun or principal military leader was notionally the emperor's deputy. In reality, however, power resided with the shogun and his central administration, or *bakufu*. Power outside the capital Edo (now Tokyo) was held by various feudal lords or *daimyō*, who enjoyed greater or lesser degrees of independence from the centre depending on personal connections with the shogun. The *daimyō* positions were primarily hereditary and dependent on the distribution of land by the Tokugawa. Beneath the *daimyō*, society was broadly divided between the samurai, a small but expanding merchant class, and the mass of the people who lived on the land. The samurai had originally been a warrior class dependent on specific lords for their support, but as Japan changed and became more peaceful, many samurai became civil officials – achieving social mobility and creating a skilled cadre of skilled administrators in the process. This would prove invaluable when the modernization process began in earnest in Japan (Beasley 1993).

Before this happened, however, Japan had been deliberately cut off from the rest of the world. For around 200 years from the early 1600s to 1854, Japan had either rejected or attempted rigorously to control contact with the outside world. Japan's leaders were uncomfortable about the destabilizing impact of ideas that Portuguese traders and missionaries brought during the sixteenth century. Isolationist policy was feasible because, unlike China, Japan was of little interest to the Europeans, who regarded Japan as a poor and inaccessible country. And yet the picture of backwardness and isolation is misleading: not only were literacy rates in Japan comparable with Europe's by the nineteenth century, but the emerging domestic capitalist class was a cause and consequence of the economic development that had already occurred during the Tokugawa period. Crucially, and in sharp contrast to China, there was no inherent disdain of commerce in Japan, something that encouraged urban merchants and even rich peasants to invest in longer-term economic activities. Consequently, by the nineteenth century, 'the Japanese probably had the most advanced and thoroughly monetised economy in Asia and were well prepared for further economic development' (Fairbank *et al.* 1965: 191).

There are a number of other factors that help to explain why Japan was better placed to respond to Western demands to open its economy.

First, the speed with which integration with the West occurred was far greater than it was in China. Rather than responding gradually to a growing threat that they initially failed to take seriously, as imperial China did, the superiority of Western arms, technology and even governmental structures was rapidly evident to Japan's ruling elites (Moore 1973: 251). Indeed, there was a greater diversity and pragmatism in Japanese thought, evidenced by the tradition of 'Dutch learning', in which Dutch traders had become an important source of knowledge and eventually a synonym for all Western scientific knowledge. Neither did Japanese elites suffer from the sort of civilizational hubris that left China fatally ill-prepared to respond to the West. Japan's leaders recognized the vulnerable nature of their small country and determined to learn from the West in order to overcome their weaknesses. In this context they were aided by the realization that the old feudal structures were outmoded and increasingly irrelevant. The samurai, for example, had been transformed by peace and were irked by a lack of social mobility, and were in many cases psychologically prepared for the transition from feudal retainer to 'salary man' (Fairbank *et al.* 1965: 192). But despite such propitious preconditions being in place, before this internal transformation could begin, Japan still required a decisive prod from outside.

The opening of Japan and the Meiji Restoration

The arrival of US Commodore Matthew Perry in what is now known as Tokyo Bay in 1853 is rightly seen as a defining moment in modern world history. Not only was Japan drawn irrevocably into the international system, but it also heralded the arrival of the United States as a major power in the Asia-Pacific region – one that would continue to exert a direct influence over the course of national and regional developments in East Asia. It also marked the beginning of what has come to be the largest economic, and one of the most strategically important bilateral relationships in the world. From this point in East Asia's history, the centre of power and influence began to shift from Europe to North America. Understanding East Asia now also meant understanding American foreign policy.

Perry's arrival highlighted some uncomfortable realities with which the Japanese would have to come to terms. First, American technology was plainly far ahead of Japan's, something the presence of Perry's new steam-driven ships made painfully apparent. Second, the USA was already part of an emerging global economy and willing to use its superior technological and military capacities to pursue its commercial interests. In this context, Japan was a potentially crucial source of coal for the steamships that conducted the rapidly growing trade between the USA and China. But underlying these commercial imperatives was an expansionist foreign policy and a sense of 'manifest destiny' which, if not imperial in the British sense, certainly helps to explain the sense of moral rectitude and God-given duty that has often accompanied America's foreign affairs (Smith 1994). As Iriye points out, from the outset, America's relations with East Asia have been underpinned by something akin to missionary zeal:

> Few were so naïve as to believe that America was the embodiment of perfection and that all its ideas and institutions could be transplanted abroad. But all were convinced that American society was a step nearer to perfection than other societies, and that if these latter sought to reform themselves there was much that Americans could do to help … the nations of Asia seemed to be waiting for precisely such help. Americans could teach the Chinese and the Japanese rudiments of technology and modern science; they could introduce Western ideas and customs; they could assist the Asian governments as they struggled to survive in a turbulent world; above all, Americans could bring Asians to a new and higher level of spirituality. (Iriye 1967: 18)

Consequently, interaction with Japan in particular and East Asia more generally has always been marked by fundamentally different – frequently incompatible – differences of opinion about the ways that political, economic, social and even religious life should be organized, and much mutual misunderstanding as a result. In the context of Japan–America relations, there has been an unrelenting clash of value systems and basic forms of institutional organization as a result of the different ways their societies have been organized (LaFeber 1997).

This is an important and enduring consideration, especially given that the Meiji Restoration, which occurred not long after the USA forced Japan to open up, involved a transformation of some of Japan's most fundamental institutions. While the actual events of 1868 constituted 'little more than a shift of power within the old ruling class' (Jansen 1989: 308), the Meiji Restoration signalled the end of the feudal era in Japan and the consolidation of centralized power under a modern monarch. It was not an easy process, however. The Commercial Treaty of 1858, negotiated by Townsend Harris, marked the definitive opening of the Japanese economy, but this bland-sounding document triggered a crisis within Japan's ruling elite. The leadership of Ii Naosuke, who took responsibility for the opening of Japan, was cut short by his assassination, revealing the inability of the *bakufu* to cope with foreign encroachment. Loyalists looked to the emperor as an alternative around whom to rally, under the banner of 'revere the emperor, expel the barbarians'

(W. Cohen, 2000). A complex struggle developed between rival *daimyō*, which culminated in an alliance against, and the eventual defeat of, the shogun. The young Emperor was reinstalled as a symbol of national unity, while the real power lay with a rising generation of young samurai who had usurped the old *bakufu*.

The point to emphasize here is that, unlike in China, the social revolution that foreign contact was instrumental in triggering did not lead to the complete dismemberment of the old institutional order. On the contrary, the emperor became a key element of continuity, albeit a largely symbolic and ceremonial one. What is of even greater long-term significance is that the young generation of reformers that came to hold real power in Japan instituted a series of reforms that would have far-reaching implications, changes that would provide the basis for Japan's highly successful accommodation to external challenge. While the development of new political institutions to replace those of the Tokugawa era would take a generation and not be finalized until 1889 with the promulgation of a constitution (Beasley 1989), this did not stop the more broadly based modernization process, nor the overarching desire to build up Japan's national strength relative to the imperialist powers.

It is a measure of how completely the Japanese were able to redefine key elements of their domestic institutions and foreign policy practice that they adapted to the European 'standard of civilization', and the specific notions of statehood and international behaviour that implied, far more successfully than had China (Gong 1984). Whether the prize was worth the effort is, of course, a moot point, but it is nevertheless an important indicator of the transformation Japan had undertaken – and one that Japanese elites pursued self-consciously as a marker of their new status in the international system. Before this could be achieved, however, a series of reforms – generally drawing on European models[14] – had been undertaken in the Japanese military, legal system and bureaucratic structures. One of the most important reforms in this context was the abolition of the domains of the *daimyō*, which allowed the further centralization of power and co-ordination of the reform process. Six key ministries, headed by an oligarchy of court nobles or feudal lords, came to dominate an authoritarian decision-making process in the first decade of Meiji rule. Of the other reforms that were put in place, perhaps the most important was the desire to import and copy Western technology – especially in armaments and communications. This would eventually underpin Japan's dramatic rise as a regional and military power.

The reorganization of the military, initially along French lines, and the establishment of a conscript army involving compulsory national service, were major steps in this process. Subsequently, a military police was established as well as staff colleges for the army (1884) and navy (1888).

The highlighting of military reforms is deliberate because they came to assume such long-term significance. As early as 1873, some were agitating for war with Korea – partly as a way of defusing the domestic tensions that the rapid reform process was generating.[15] Eventually, Japan contented itself with a punitive expedition against Chinese-controlled Taiwan. This development was, in some ways, an entirely predictable part of the modernization of Japan as a distinct nation-state, and the concomitant desire to define it boundaries. The slogan 'rich country, strong army' had encapsulated many of the Meiji regime's ideas about the interconnectedness between military and economic strength (Samuels 1994). The status of Taiwan was uncertain, and Japan's forceful assertion of its position was in keeping with its overall desire to emulate European-style imperial practice and a measure of the effectiveness of the new Meiji regime (Iriye 1989). There was one other major consequence of Japan's imperial phase that needs to be emphasized. Both Taiwan's and Korea's deep ties with Japan were established in a process that Bruce Cumings argues laid the foundations for the more generalized industrialization process across Northeast Asia: both colonies experienced an early form of the 'administrative guidance' of a sort that became such a crucial part of Japan's post-war renaissance. As a consequence, Cumings (1984: 11) argues, 'a highly articulated, disciplined, penetrating colonial bureaucracy substituted both for the traditional regimes and for indigenous groups and classes that under "normal" conditions would have accompanied development'.

Japanese imperialism would not only have long-term implications for the development of Taiwan but it also highlighted the changing balance of power between China and Japan. Relations with Korea assumed a similarly important symbolic quality: on the one hand, Japan was keen to ensure that Korea acknowledged its new status, while on the other, the evolving regional order simultaneously highlighted China's relative decline and the end of Korea's tributary relationship with it. As a consequence of Japanese expansionism and nascent imperialism, it established colonial enclaves or dominance over parts of China, Korea and Taiwan between 1880 and 1895, in the process becoming the first country to force Korea – the 'hermit kingdom' – to open itself to foreign engagement. Whatever we may think of these achievements in retrospect, it is important to recognize that they were very much in keeping with the practices of the 'great powers' of the day. They were also a clear indicator of how successful and rapid the reform process in Japan had been: not only were the characteristics of a modern state in place by the 1880s, but Japan already had a capacity to redefine the region of which it was an increasingly influential part. Significantly, in a pattern that was to be repeated more peacefully elsewhere in later years, Japan's control of

Korea was consolidated by the establishment of deep economic ties – links which helped to drive Japan's own process of domestic industrialization (Iriye 1989).

Tensions between China and Japan over Korea culminated in the Sino-Japanese War (1894–95) and Japan's decisive naval victory over China, which eventually led to the latter's complete withdrawal from Korea. Japan's dominance over China was highlighted by its subsequent annexation of Korea in 1910, and later occupation of Manchuria. This highlighted China's diminished status and capacity, and created a long-running source of bilateral tension in the process. The subsequent Treaty of Shimonoseki (1895) confirmed China's humiliation and its failure to modernize as successfully as Japan had done. It also gave the Japanese Taiwan and the Liaodong peninsula. Russia insisted that the Liaodong peninsula be handed back to the Chinese, as it had its own imperial ambitions in China. But given that Japanese elites were by now steeped in the logic of empire and supported by an increasingly nationalistic population, it was entirely predictable that one of the principal longer-term consequences of this period was to set the scene for future conflict and the outbreak of the Russo-Japanese War (1904–05).

Japanese imperialism and militarism

Japan's growing imperial ambitions coincided with its modernization and militarization, and confirmed its status as a major power at the beginning of the twentieth century. The signing of the Anglo-Japanese alliance in 1902 was one indication of Japan's new status, but its inter-imperialistic war against Russia – and the unprecedented defeat of a major European power it subsequently yielded – highlighted just how far Japan had developed. Again, it is important to emphasize that the violent resolution of Japan's imperial conflict with Russia over their rival claims to Manchuria enjoyed widespread popular support in Japan: patriotism, militarism and imperialism were producing precisely the same sort of heady cocktail in Japan as they had in Britain and Germany; and they would ultimately produce equally tragic results. It is worth noting that – at this stage, at least – questions of national prestige and relative international standing would seem to have had as much, if not more, to do with Japanese expansionism as any strictly material explanations of the sort that have distinguished influential Marxist analyses (see Hoogvelt 2001: 21–8). In Japan's case, the defeat of Russia and the destruction of its fleet fuelled the national appetite for further expansion. By 1910, Japan had completed the annexation of Korea, converting it into a fully fledged colony – instituting governmental and organizational reforms that would have far-reaching consequences for both the subsequent economic development in South Korea, and for contemporary Japan–Korea bilateral relations.

Though Japan had begun a process of modernization at the beginning of the twentieth century that was transforming its economic infrastructure and governmental institutions, it was still a predominantly agricultural country. True, the Japanese government was trying assiduously to develop its shipbuilding and steel-making capacities, and establish a national rail network, but the picture of a far-sighted and competent state single-handedly driving forward Japan's industrialization process needs to be treated with some caution. As Tessa Morris-Suzuki's careful analysis has demonstrated:

> Technological change in Meiji Japan was not confined to state-owned enterprises, nor to the handful of embryonic *zaibatsu* who possessed close links to government. Instead, the really significant feature of Meiji innovation is that it was quite widely spread through many companies and craft workshops in many parts of the country. (Morris-Suzuki 1994: 85)

The debate about the importance and competence of the state and its role in Japan's development will be taken up in more detail in Chapter 7, as it remains one of the most important issues not just for Japan, but for debates about the role of the state more generally in East Asia. What we can say about this earlier period is that the 'second phase of modernization' in Japan was accompanied by an average level of government investment in the economy of more than 40 per cent per year during the period 1887–1940 (Fairbank *et al.* 1965: 493–4). The targeting of this scarce capital towards specific business groups established a pattern that would become a distinctive feature of Japan's post-war development; it also helped to establish the handful of major *zaibatsu* or industrial conglomerates that would come eventually to dominate the economic landscape.

All this investment underpinned an accelerating transformation of the Japanese economy, and its rapid integration into the wider world system. As in Britain's early industrialization, and as China has recently demonstrated, the development of a major textile industry was a key step in the journey to industrial development. In Japan's case, textiles constituted 50 per cent of its industrial output in 1891, and an even bigger slice of exports (Fairbank *et al.* 1965: 499). But as Japanese exports of manufactured goods took off, so did the need to import raw materials – a dilemma that has been at the centre of Japanese public policy since the modernization process began, and which helps to explain all that is distinctive, and occasionally tragic, about Japanese foreign and economic policies. But even before Japan's foreign and domestic policies led it inexorably into further military conflict, the ambivalent nature of greater integration into the international system had become apparent during the Great Depression, which resulted in a crippling blow to international economic activity across the world.

Japan was not affected as badly as most by this crisis, however – not in terms of its immediate economic prospects, at least. Not only were Japanese goods still cheap and comparatively attractive, even in greatly reduced international markets, but military adventurism in Manchuria in 1931 gave further buoyancy to the Japanese economy. This is an even more surprising development than it might seem, given the benefit of hindsight and present knowledge about the outcome of Japanese militarism. Between 1918 and 1931, the prospects for political reform, internationalism and peaceful coexistence had looked surprisingly bright in Japan. During the 'liberal 1920s' the growth of Japan's cities, the expansion of a domestic bourgeoisie, improving levels of education and a greater knowledge of Western ideas, all created pressure for political reform (Beasley 1993). Party politics had become established in Japan by the end of the First World War, and men over the age of 25 were given the vote in 1925. At the same time, however, authoritarian controls were introduced to control political dissent, especially on the left. The tensions between the move towards liberal democracy and authoritarian militarism were resolved in favour of the latter, following a series of political assassinations.

These tensions culminated in a major insurrection and political crisis in 1936, which had the effect of tilting the country further towards authoritarianism, intimidating the political class, and increasing the relative power of the military. The army presented itself as a force for national unity in the face of destabilizing political contestation and extremism. The insulation of military matters – including the authority to decide questions of war and peace – reflected and consolidated the shift of power to the military and the service chiefs. A descent into warfare was the all-too-predictable consequence of these domestic convulsions. Equally predictably, perhaps, given the long-running regional tensions, it was a war with China. We have already seen the impact of the war that broke out in 1937 on China itself, but it is also important to recognize how important China was to Japan, and what a watershed the colonization of Manchuria was in this context. Japan had established a puppet government in 'Manchuku', as the Japanese called it, in 1932, after engineering their own military intervention. The subsequent exploitation and occupation of Manchuria provided both a model of military-style colonialism and a way of also cultivating support for the army at home:

in concrete ways, aggression abroad brought about the militarisation of politics at home. The bubble of enthusiasm for the Manchurian occupation restructured the balance of bureaucratic power in favour of the army, which in turn ensured the perpetuation of the new policy of military expansionism. (Young 1998: 129)

The war with China generally, and the occupation of Manchuria in particular, are significant, therefore, not just because of the long-lasting impact they had on Sino-Japanese relations, but because they served as a model for what Young (1998: 240) describes as the 'advance guard of Japanese industrial capitalism'.[16] The potential significance of this development became clearer as the Second World War unfolded.

The latter war and its aftermath are considered in greater detail in the next chapter, but at this stage it is important to make a couple of preliminary points. First, there was a certain inevitability about the looming clash between the USA, which had rapidly become the premier power in the Pacific, and Japan, which was increasingly reliant on imports of raw materials to fuel both its industrialization and its militarization. As early as 1936, Japanese military strategists were looking towards Southeast Asia to provide critical raw materials. By 1940, the conflict in Europe was seen as providing a suitable distraction for Japan to expand into the region – aggressively if necessary. Although Japanese strategists wanted to avoid a clash with the USA, the inexorable logic of Japan's distinctive military-industrial complex drove them on.

Predictably enough, the USA was becoming increasingly concerned about Japanese militarism and expansionism, not least as a consequence of Japan signing the Tripartite Pact with fascist Germany and Italy in 1940. The increasingly painful sanctions the USA imposed on Japan in an effort to rein in its expansionary ambitions during 1940 and 1941, were seen by the Japanese military as an explicit and fundamental threat to Japan's autonomy and economic security – and thus providing the trigger for conflict. From the perspective of Japan's dominant military elites, its dependence on Southeast Asia for crucial supplies of natural resources such as oil and rubber left it with few options if it wanted to maintain economic independence and military autonomy (Willmott 1982). The tragic consequences and ultimate result of Japan's misreading of both American strength and willingness to fight are well known. Before concluding the discussion of Japan's historical legacies, though, it is important to say something about Japan's Southeast Asian empire, for no matter how short-lived it might have been, it had a profound impact on the region and continues to influence the conduct of Japan's relations with the Southeast Asian sub-region to this day.

How not to do regionalism

One of the most important consequences of the war as far as Japan was concerned – and by extension, much of the rest of the putative region, as well – was its impact on Japan's sense of itself as a nation and as a member of an international order. Even before the outbreak of the Second World War, Japanese elites were preoccupied with Japan's place in an emerging regional order, and many were actively promoting a vision of 'pan-Asianism'. For all its demonstrated capacity to learn from, and even become part of, a Western-dominated international economic and political order, by the outbreak of the Second World War the idea that Japan could and should be the leader of a regional order that incorporated the whole of East Asia – including China – was becoming firmly established. Indeed, Japanese regional leadership was seen in some quarters as a way of ridding the region as a whole of a pernicious European and American presence. Seen in this light, Japan's subsequent occupation of Southeast Asia takes on a different aspect:

> The Japanese never disguised the fact that their primary interest lay in obtaining the rich resources of the colonial region. The difference this time was that in trying to achieve this goal, they were engaged in an expulsion of Westerners from Asia ... The rhetoric of pan-Asianism provided a ready-made rationale for such action. At the same time, however, this rhetoric required something more substantial than defeating American and European forces. The Japanese had to develop a vision of the new Asia that they were purportedly constructing. (Iriye 1981: 64)

In reality, the vision was never coherently developed or realized. The Greater East Asia Co-Prosperity Sphere was intended to be a mechanism for unifying East Asia under Japanese leadership, with the Japanese economy acting as its principal engine of growth. From its inception, however, the proposed structure was plagued by bureaucratic infighting in Japan and outright hostility in some of its critical constituent parts – especially the Philippines and Malaya. As Beasley (1993: 206) points out, in North East Asia the Japanese were able to use a common Confucian heritage to try to win over converts to the East Asian idea. In the Southeast part of the region, however, there was no such common cultural glue to overcome resentment of Japanese dominance. The idea of 'co-prosperity' that supposedly lay at the heart of Japan's pan-Asian vision was never realized either: the demands of Japan's war-time economy meant it was unable to replace Western markets or supplies of consumer goods, despite the relentless exploitation of Southeast Asia's raw materials. Predictably enough, living standards across Southeast

Asia declined as a consequence of its economic isolation, lack of investment and economic dependence on Japan. Moreover, from a Japanese strategic perspective, the – often brutal and widely resented – occupation of China and Southeast Asia tied down troops that might otherwise have been occupied in fighting the enemy.

Strategically and economically, then, the Greater East Asia Co-Prosperity Sphere was ill-conceived and unsuccessful. Misguided as it was, though, it is important for a number of reasons that merit spelling out. At one level, it represents the first attempt to think explicitly of 'East Asia' as a distinct region in its own right. While the underlying rationale and motives might have been dubious and self-serving, it did have the effect of drawing attention to putative notions of 'Asianness' in opposition to a 'Western' other.[17] At another level, and despite the appalling impact that Japanese occupation had on much of Southeast Asia and its people, it had the effect of demolishing the idea of European superiority and the invincibility of the white races. As we shall see, prior to Japan's violent intrusion into the region, the European powers had generally enjoyed an untroubled ability to exploit ruthlessly their colonial possessions. After the Second World War and the crushing defeats the Japanese – crucially, an *Asian* power – inflicted on Britain in particular, the days of European colonization were definitively over. Only the timing of their withdrawal remained to be decided.

Before we consider that process and the circumstances that preceded this process in Southeast Asia, it is important to spell out the long-term consequences of this period for Japan. As we shall see in Chapter 5, one of the most important impacts of the Second World War generally has been Japan's military and – to a lesser extent – political subordination to the USA. In a regional context, not only were future relations between Japan, Southeast Asia, and especially China, poisoned as a consequence, but any prospect of Japan's overt regional leadership being resurrected was rendered inherently problematic. As far as much of the region was concerned, Japan's image was tarnished almost irrevocably. Governments across the region, especially in China, have ruthlessly exploited Japan's awkwardness and guilt about its wartime activities to extract maximum diplomatic and material advantage.

Conclusion

Even the most powerful countries of the region were profoundly affected by the impact of European imperialism – even if they were not colonized directly, as were Japan or Thailand, as we shall see in the next chapter. The key consequence of this period as far as the region was concerned was that it precipitated an abrupt shift in the relative fortunes of China and Japan – a position that has only recently been overturned. China had been at the centre of regional affairs – even if not strictly 'East Asian' regional ones – for hundreds, if not thousands, of years. Its toppling from this accustomed pinnacle was the cause of internal upheaval and national shame. The humiliation was all the greater given that Japan, its smaller, hitherto subordinate neighbour, was not only instrumental in bringing about its downfall, but prospered directly as a consequence. Despite the recent shift in the standing of China and Japan, earlier humiliations continue to rankle and make the resolution of contemporary problems all the more difficult.

And yet both Japan and China demonstrate that positive and effective responses to external challenges are possible, even if, as we shall see, it has been after a number of false starts in China's case. Indeed, China's much later economic take-off demonstrates that even the most traumatic and unpropitious historical circumstances can be overcome, given effective leadership and policies. Without them, however, long-term development outcomes are likely to be much less impressive. This has generally been the experience of the smaller, more recently independent states of Southeast Asia to which we now turn.

Chapter 3

Southeast Asia's Dependent Development

As we saw in Chapter 1, considering 'Southeast Asia' as a distinct region is a relatively recent development (Emmerson 1984). The fact that it was an external power – the British – that began this practice is emblematic of a wider set of relationships, and the way in which Southeast Asia has been drawn into contemporary international political and economic structures. The manner of this integration will be taken up below and in other chapters, but it is noteworthy that Southeast Asia as a whole has never really shaken off this somewhat dependent, even subordinate position. While there is currently a good deal of excitement about the possibility of Indonesia becoming the next 'BRIC' (Brazil, Russia, India and China) economy, if it manages to do so, it will be the exception that proves the rule: hitherto, Indonesia and Southeast Asia more generally have had little influence and standing in the world's most important forums. Even acting collectively, the influence of the Association of Southeast Asian Nations (ASEAN) has been relatively modest and might actually be undermined by the prominence of Indonesia and the possible unravelling of Southeast Asian solidarity (Ruland 2009).

Despite the widely noted heterogeneity of the Southeast Asian region, for our purposes it makes sense to consider the countries of the region collectively as there are sufficient commonalities in their respective historical experiences to make some degree of generalization about this sub-region possible. One of the most important distinctions to make within the Southeast Asian region itself is in the fundamental difference between mainland and maritime Southeast Asia. This has resulted in major differences between the development of such states as Vietnam, Laos, Cambodia, Burma and Thailand, which would ultimately emerge on the edge of the East Asian landmass, and those such as Indonesia, Malaysia, the Philippines, Singapore and Brunei, which were maritime states. Predictably enough, the first important centres of power in Southeast Asia developed on the mainland, in Funan, from around AD 100–600, mainly in what is now Cambodia, and in Champa, from about AD 200–1700, in what is now Vietnam. Yet even within the broad division between mainland and maritime centres, there is a further distinction to be made between the permanent settlements that grew up around rice production in key river systems like the Mekong, and the more thinly populated regions outside this area. Anthony Reid (2000: 4) describes this as the 'fundamental dualism of hill and valley, upstream and downstream, interior and coast'. The legacy of these early divisions can still be found in the hill tribes of countries such as Vietnam. Such basic geographical features of Southeast Asia help to explain the fundamental challenges of governance that have confronted political elites historically across much of the region. This is particularly true of maritime states such as the Philippines and Indonesia. Modern Indonesian governments, for example, have had to try to impose centralized order on a sprawling archipelago that encompasses thousands of small islands in addition to the main – very different – population centres of Java, Sumatra, Bali, Sulawesi and Kalimantan, as well as the currently troublesome region of West Papua.

Indonesia may be something of an extreme example, but it highlights another surprisingly common experience among the diversity of populations: Southeast Asia has been influenced profoundly by contact with the outside world, and not just during the period of European colonization, which is the principal focus of attention here. Evidence of the influence of other cultures on Southeast Asia can be seen from the extensive impact of Hinduism and Buddhism, though the historical record of the region's early development is sketchy and imperfect. It is clear, however, that as early as the seventh century AD, major new centres of power and economic activity were emerging in maritime Southeast Asia, as the development of the important trading empire of Srivijaya in Sumatra demonstrates (see SarDesai 1997). What is of the most significance for our purposes is that, from about the fifteenth century, access to Southeast Asia became easier as a consequence of improvements in maritime transport and technology. There had certainly been contact with Indian, Chinese and Arab traders before this period, but from 1500–1800 there was an intensification of trade relations. There was also one other enduring and important consequence of the period before European domination of Southeast Asia's trade routes that we must note: the introduction and steady spread of Islam, something that was marked by the conversion of the strategically important Malay trading port of Melaka in the fifteenth century (Watson Andaya 1999).[1]

The effect of this period was to incorporate the region into an existing political and economic order, a process that had profound implications for the societies of what we now think of as Southeast Asia. But before considering this process in detail, it is important to consider how life was organized before the encroachment of both European capitalism and the inter-state system that emerged alongside it, which has come to define exclusively *national* political space in the process. While Southeast Asians have generally taken up the ideas of nationalism, sovereignty and all the other trappings of the inter-state system with great enthusiasm, there was nothing inevitable about this. On the contrary, the dominant patterns of relationships that existed before European imperialism transformed the region suggest that things could have developed differently.

Perhaps the most fundamental and far-reaching aspect of the transformative process that European contact encouraged initially was the development of colonial relations and, subsequently, independent nation-states where none had existed before. Prior to European colonization, the demarcation of political space, which we in the West take to be such a familiar part of national and international life, was unknown in Southeast Asia. While the increasingly fine-grained delineation of time and space, and the more instrumental and objective nature of authority, have been hallmarks of modernity in the West (Harvey 1988), in Southeast Asia, by contrast, the extent of rule and the nature of authority were by turns imprecise and personal. As Nicholas Tarling (1998: 47) puts it, 'what concerned a ruler was the people not the place'. In other words, not only were the boundaries of the pre-European kingdoms of Southeast Asia generally highly uncertain, but power and authority were also closely bound up with the personal qualities of the ruler. To quote Tarling again:

> The concept of a frontier was uncommon, if not unknown, in Southeast Asia. The idea that the ambit of a state was geographically fixed was rarely accepted. What counted in Southeast Asia, sparse in population, was allegiance. Whom, rather than what, did the state comprise? States might indeed advance or retreat, grow or decline, but in terms of adherents and followers, [were] a network of familial and supra-familial relationships. (Tarling 1998: 47)

The idea that political – and by implication, economic – life in Southeast Asia might be dependent primarily on personalized relationships is in some ways not unlike the situation that prevailed in China before its abrupt incorporation into the wider international system. What distinguishes Southeast Asia, though, is the importance and prevalence of patron–client ties.[2] In what Lucian Pye (1985) has described as 'the Asian view of power', consensus, paternalism and deference are the distinguishing features of a system based on personal authority. In the West, by contrast, the expectation is that authority will come to be invested in particular institutions or the specific office an individual holds. It was precisely this sort of underlying differentiation that led thinkers as diverse as Max Weber and Karl Marx to believe that capitalism could not flourish in Asia in the absence of the sort of state structures, legal systems, individual attitudes and formal rationality[3] that had developed in the West (Sayer 1991).

We now know, of course, how wrong such assumptions were. Asia has generated some of the most successful capitalist countries ever seen – at least when judged in terms of rising per capita incomes and gross domestic product (GDP). We also know, as we shall see in more detail in subsequent chapters, that within the overarching framework of capitalist production structures, great variations are possible in the way that political and economic processes are organized, *and* in the interaction between them. While we should be careful about making sweeping generalizations based on civilizational distinctions of the sort that Pye, Marx and Weber claimed, it is clear that local differences in social structures and norms help to account for the way that various parts of East Asia responded to external economic pressures and the spread of global capitalism. It is also clear that vestiges of these earlier patterns continue to distinguish different forms of capitalist organization in the region to this day.

But it is not just our understanding of capitalist development that is modified when refracted through an Asian prism: the early development of Southeast Asia also reminds us that even the practice of international relations system itself – which many IR scholars take to be timeless, unchanging and a universal phenomenon – can look very different across time and space. Because of the highly personalized nature of rule, and the great imprecision of geographical boundaries in early Southeast Asia, Wolters (1999: 29) has argued that we should think of the distribution of power in the region as being characterized by a series of overlapping *mandalas* or 'circles of kings', rather than the types of clearly demarcated national boundaries that were becoming such a prominent part of Western Europe and its subsequent colonies. Wolters argues that this pattern of personalized relationships helped to define relationships within and between loosely configured kingdoms across much of Southeast Asia before European colonization.

Amitav Acharya (2000: 24) has drawn on Wolters' *mandala* metaphor to claim that 'one could at least imagine a *regional pattern* of inter-state relations in classical Southeast Asia based on essentially similar political forms'. While this may seem a slender reed upon which to build too great a conceptual structure, it does highlight one important fact, nevertheless: when the Europeans (like the Indians, Chinese, Arabs and even Japanese that went before them) eventually did arrive and impose themselves on the region, they were not writing the subsequent history of their colonial rule on a blank page. Previously established patterns of indigenous rule, relationships and authority would be transformed rather than completely erased as a consequence of Europe's entry into the region.

The coming of the Europeans

One of the most noteworthy features of Southeast Asia before 1750 was the remarkably low levels of population density, especially compared with Northeast Asia. Even as late as 1800, 80 per cent of the region was still covered by dense jungle, and the 20–30 million people of Southeast Asia were concentrated in a few scattered trading states and the agricultural centres that emerged around the mainland's major river systems and in Java. Two of the most important changes in the region since the early 1800s have been the dramatic increase in population and the startling physical transformation of the natural environment – phenomena that are clearly not unrelated. One of the most important forces underpinning these interconnected processes was the incorporation of the region into global economic structures.

Though the Chinese played a major role in pioneering trade with Southeast Asia, their retreat into isolationism in the fifteenth century left the way open for others to take their place. Indeed, from as early as the fifteenth century the lure of the 'spice islands' proved irresistible for Portuguese traders, and the Dutch East India Company (VOC) established a monopoly over Southeast Asia's spice trade as early as the 1620s (Reid 1999: 116–21). Of course, trade was not the only thing the Europeans were interested in or brought with them. The Portuguese also brought Christianity. It is worth noting in light of more recent events that Christianity clashed with the Islamic traditions imported by Arab traders, with Islam providing an important rallying point for those hostile to European intrusion and the disruption of hitherto Muslim-dominated trade routes (McCloud 1995: 115). The Dutch were less confrontational than the Portuguese and thus were able to profit from the enmity the latter had generated, and establish themselves in the region following their capture of Melaka in 1641. Indeed, the European powers had quite different imperial styles and impacts (Parry 1971: ch. 5). In what we now think of as Indonesia in particular, the Dutch, and more specifically, the VOC, established effective control over the archipelago, but we need to be careful not to overstate the immediate impact of this on traditional Indonesia society. As Robert Elson points out:

> A deliberately self-limiting exercise, mercantile capitalism eschewed interference with indigenous polities except to make necessary arrangements for the delivery of desired trade goods; apart from

strategically placed forts and 'factories', it avoided territorial conquest and the overheads which administration and defence of such territories involved unless these were deemed necessary to protect its more important commercial interests. While sometimes it imposed itself upon the indigenous setting through its activities as tribute gatherer and trade director ... mostly it meshed its activities into the practices and routines already well established in Southeast Asia. (Elson 1999: 132)

This is a surprisingly modern-sounding approach to economic control and exploitation, and one with contemporary parallels. Though the style of rule developed by the Dutch was not as directly intrusive as we might think when seen retrospectively, the cumulative, long-term impact of integration into the general European-dominated economic and political system was profound, and 'seriously diminished the sense that the region enjoyed any substantial and inherent shared identity or characteristics or destiny' (Elson 2004: 17). Other observers go even further, and argue that Britain's belated intervention into Southeast Asia, for example, 'introduced social, economic, and political changes that left the fabric of indigenous society threadbare' (McCloud 1995: 119). When we look at the impact of British colonialism, it is clear that a number of Southeast Asian nations developed their particular social structures and economic profiles – with all the problems that have subsequently flowed from them – as a direct consequence of their position in Britain's imperial economy.

The most obvious manifestation of Britain's colonial presence was the series of trading colonies it established in Penang (1786), Melaka (1824) and Singapore (1819). These developments reflected more than the simple commercial imperatives that might be expected to flow from one country, or even company, pursuing its interests, however. The colonization and carving up of Southeast Asia reflected intense intra-imperial competition among the Europeans themselves as they jockeyed for control and influence. Under such circumstances, it becomes easier to see why the Japanese felt that this was the natural order of things and emblematic of great power status. For Southeast Asia, it meant that societies and economies were reshaped as a consequence of much larger, extra-regional forces and contests. Even where local actors proved decisive, invariably it was as a consequence of wider struggles. The complex rivalries, occasional conflicts and shifting alliances between the Dutch, British and French in Europe had their counterparts in the colonies.[4] Britain's rise and the relative decline of the Dutch allowed the British to expand its imperial possessions steadily – frequently at the expanse of the Dutch. But whichever European power was in the ascendancy, relations in the colonies were always complicated and overlaid by European imperatives and the capacity of their colonial officials.

The quintessential 'man on the spot', Stamford Raffles, was in fact the Lieutenant-Governor of Java before he helped to establish Singapore as a key part of Britain's expanding trade empire in the region. Raffles was unhappy at the concessions the British government had made to the Dutch in return for their support against the French in Europe's continuing struggle for supremacy. Not only did the establishment of the Straits Settlements – as Singapore, Penang and Melaka were known – reveal the amount of autonomy colonial representatives frequently had in the far-flung outposts of empire, but it consolidated Britain's economic position and secured the vital trade route to China. And yet there was often a good deal of ambivalence on the part of British governments about the wisdom of accumulating additional colonial responsibilities. Despite the existence of extensive tin mines in Malaya, for example, the British government was initially reluctant to intervene in the Malay states. However, the growing importance of tin for industrializing Europe, improvements in communication and a concomitant rapid expansion in the tin trade meant that British merchants lobbied their government to establish more secure conditions and minimize foreign competition. In another revealing example of what could be described alternatively as initiative, arrogance or chutzpah, Britain's governor-designate for the Straits Settlements proceeded to engineer, with the more-or-less willing compliance of the traditional Malay chiefs, a de facto extension of the British empire across the Malay peninsula (Tarling 1966).

It is also typical of the imperial mindset of the time that the British considered that, far from exploiting native peoples and their natural wealth, they were actually introducing them to the benefits of civilization and imposing an order the peoples were incapable of realizing for themselves (SarDesai 1997: 107). However, the reality was rather different. Assets such as the tin mines and the new, rapidly expanding rubber industry were not only developed ruthlessly, but they were also worked by 'coolie' labour imported from China. This pattern of importing labour from China was repeated across much of Southeast Asia, where the seemingly endless supply of cheap labour from the mainland was also put to work in the rapidly expanding, completely alien, plantations that sprang up in the sugar, rubber, palm oil and tobacco industries of the Philippines, Cambodia, Vietnam and Sumatra (Elson 1999). In Malaysia, Chinese labour was also supplemented with large numbers of Indians and Tamils. It is not simply that the working conditions confronting these immigrants were generally appalling and almost comically at odds with the purported civilizing mission of British empire that this period is noteworthy. For Malaysia in particular, the long-term legacy of British colonization was the profound impact it had on the ethnic and social make-up of the country, and the structural distortion this wrought on the resulting Malaysian economy. It is a legacy that has shaped public policy and hampered indigenous development ever since.

British imperial preferences also had a similarly dramatic and ultimately even more tragic impact on Burma. Burma's principal significance as far as the British were concerned was political: the British wanted to keep the French out and establish hegemonic influence as they had in India (SarDesai 1997). The fact that Burma also offered a potential trade link with China was an important strategic bonus. The seriousness of British intent can be gauged from the fact that there were no fewer than three Anglo-Burmese wars as the British attempted to impose their authority. During the third of these, the gratuitous British humiliation of the Burmese royal family sowed the seeds of the enduring enmity of the Burmese, and caused a major guerrilla war. But poor as Britain's colonial record frequently was, it was possibly not as inept or imbued with as much hauteur as that of the French. Nor would it prove as painful and traumatic to dislodge.

While the French had had a presence in Vietnam since the seventeenth century, it did not consolidate imperial power there until the latter part of the nineteenth century. Proselytizing Catholic missionaries had been at the forefront of early French intrusions into Vietnam, but the French wanted to replicate Britain's success in opening China to foreign commerce. The persecution of French missionaries proved to be a convenient justification for a more extensive intervention, culminating in the signing of a treaty with the Vietnamese Emperor Tu Duc in 1862. This gave the French control of 'Cochin China', or the southern provinces around Saigon.[5] The French were also granted the right to navigate the Mekong delta as part of the settlement, something that facilitated their further expansion into Cambodia. Internecine warfare between the Siamese (Thai), the Vietnamese and the Cambodians had left the latter in a vulnerable state and actively seeking the support of external allies – something that helped the French to consolidate their presence in the region.[6] By 1884, France had established control over the whole of Vietnam. This triumph would prove short-lived, however, and usher in a period of turbulent colonial government that would ultimately culminate in France's expulsion from the region. Paradoxically, France's 'superior' state capacity and the heavy-handed use of military repression would undermine traditional village life and organization in Vietnam, instituting unpopular administrative reforms that would fan peasant unrest and eventual rebellion (Trocki 1999: 103). Though it would prove to be the most traumatic and drawn-out, France's experience was not uncommon as Southeast Asia became swept up in series of revolutionary, nationalist and independence movements in the first half of the twentieth century.

Nationalism, revolution and insurrection

The circumstances in which some of the most important countries of the region achieved independence are considered in more detail in subsequent chapters. At this stage, it is important to outline the circumstances behind the independence movements and the way that relations between what might be described as the 'centre' and the 'periphery' developed before the Second World War.[7] While it is difficult to disentangle all the factors that encouraged the steady, unstoppable progress toward independence in the new, post-war Asian order, it is possible to identify a number of pivotal influences that were prominent in the period between the First and Second World Wars.

One of these, of course, was the First World War itself. There were a number of major consequences of this period for East Asia as whole, and for the Southeast Asian sub-region in particular that merit emphasis. In the north, China was able to escape the most intense European predations and Japan to confirm its status as a great power (Edwardes 1961). In Southeast Asia, the First World War helped to undermine the idea of a united, superior European civilization, revealing the potential vulnerability of the European empires, and fuelling an upsurge of anti-colonial organization and thinking in the process (Christie 1996: 11). Likewise, the potential perils of economic integration into the expanding international system – a recurring theme of Asia's relationship with the economies of the West – were also illustrated vividly during the Great Depression. Southeast Asia's increased exposure to capitalist vicissitudes increased social instability and political unrest across the region. More immediately, the Europeans themselves provided Southeast Asians with a new nationalist conceptual framework and vocabulary around which to mobilize in opposition to colonial power.

Nationalism was not an entirely novel force in East Asian political life – the Vietnamese and Burmese had employed 'nationalist' sentiment in opposition to Chinese rule at various times, for example. But it is the steady introduction of the distinctively modern and European form of nationalism that is the really distinctive feature of this period. As we shall see in more detail in Chapter 6, nationalism has been a crucial force in the evolution and consolidation of, first, the European nation-state (Smith 1998), and subsequently the very idea of a national polity where none existed previously in Southeast Asia. Ironically, it was the introduction of Western forms of education, and in particular political ideas, that really paved the way for the emergence of a nationalist discourse across the region. Not only were European notions of liberty, equality and justice imported from Britain and France, but so too was the even more incendiary doctrine of revolutionary Marxism.

Marxist ideas would prove to be especially influential in Indochina, but their eventual ascendancy was not a foregone conclusion. The commercialization of rice production and the integration of Vietnam into the global economy exacerbated the impact of France's colonial administration as noted above, creating potentially incendiary conditions (Wolf 1969). Yet the peasantry were a conservative rather than a revolutionary force, and generally preoccupied with maintaining rather than overturning the status quo. Unsurprisingly, given the peasantry's social circumstances and lack of education, there was little ideological content to the mass rebellions that developed. As Godement (1997: 38) observes, 'In Asia, nationalism and communism both came into being not in a blaze of fire, but with a spark which needed intellectual momentum and organisational power to fan the flames.' It was the capacity of middle-class intellectuals such as Ho Chi Minh – who absorbed these new ideas while in Paris – who provided the revolutionary leadership and doctrine that was able to interpret and take advantage of the combustible aftermath of, first, French colonialism, and then the world war. In the same way that the Chinese communists had gathered strength during the Second World War, Vietnam's revolutionary leaders established themselves in the hinterland before launching an independence movement that would eventual expel the French.

In light of recent events and the attention given to Islamic movements in Southeast Asia, it is also important to note that Marxism was not the only doctrine available to those disenchanted with colonial rule. On the contrary, Islam's role as a force for political mobilization against perceived oppressors is far from unprecedented. Low (1991: 26) argues that, in Indonesia during the first decades of the twentieth century, it was Muslim movements such as *Sarekat Islam* (Islamic Union) that were more powerful vehicles for political mobilization than strictly nationalist organizations, which did not develop until later (see Elson 2005). It is also clear that, as with Ho in Vietnam, Indonesia's eventual independence leader, Sukarno, was educated by the Dutch and as a consequence absorbed the political ideas of the West. But Sukarno's particular genius lay in his ability to blend the secular, modernizing impulse he derived from Europe with customary Javanese notions about the nature of power and leadership. As in Vietnam, traditional Javanese village life was overturned by the penetration of Western political and especially economic practices, once again preparing the way for an independence movement – in Indonesia's case, one given extra momentum by the impact of Japan's war-time colonization. We shall look more closely in Chapter 6 at the role nationalism has played since Indonesia's independence. At present, though, it is necessary to say a little about two countries that have as yet played little part in this narrative: Thailand and the Philippines.

Both of these countries are distinctive – even among all the heterogeneity that is Southeast Asia. Thailand, was the only country in Southeast Asia to avoid direct colonization by an external power; and the Philippines is unique in that it was the latter-day champion of anti-colonialism – the United States – that exercised colonial authority most recently, and continues to cast a long shadow over contemporary developments in the country. Despite the fact that Thailand escaped direct colonization, from the nineteenth century onwards the European powers exercised 'considerable indirect control' (Vandergeest 1993: 139). The Thai monarch was compelled to sign a series of treaties with European and US governments that limited autonomous control of trade and taxation. As in Japan, the perception of weakness and vulnerability encouraged Thai elites to undertake far-reaching reforms, including an expansion of the bureaucracy. Significantly, the ethnic Chinese that had arrived in earlier waves of migration to Southeast Asia, and had established themselves as an increasingly powerful force within Thai society, played a growing a part in this process. These domestic reforms culminated in the end of the absolute monarchy and the moral and intellectual order that had previously prevailed. The cultivation of a national language, the extension of universal education, and the development of a national rail system were key elements of the deliberate process of nation-building that Thai elites undertook. Perhaps the most enduring legacy of this period was the emergence of the military as the most powerful force in Thailand. As Chai-Anan Samudavanija put it: 'During the first three decades after the overthrow of the absolute monarchy in 1932, the military was the most powerful political actor, dominating every facet of Thailand's political life and keeping in place a dictatorial regime that ruled almost unchallenged for most of that period' (1993: 271).

As with Thailand, the high colonial period had long-lasting effects on the Philippines that are still working themselves out. It is important to note that in the case of the Philippines, the history of anti-colonial resistance is longer than anywhere else in Southeast Asia. As early as the eighteenth century, there was a series of revolts against the rule of the Spanish colonists. As the Philippine economy was drawn inexorably into the wider international system during the nineteenth century, the basis of domestic production and class relations changed. As in other parts of the region, the country was exposed to new ideas and values. In part, this was a consequence of the revolutionary changes that were gripping Spain itself, but the ending of the short-lived Spanish republic led to political repression rather than liberalism in the Philippines. And yet the demand for greater political rights had established a foothold in the Philippines: the demand for greater political freedom championed by indigenous leader Jose Rizal and the nascent sense of national consciousness it engendered would prove difficult to suppress – despite Rizal's death. But the events that transformed the status of the Philippines decisively were occurring on the other side of the world as a consequence of the Spanish-American War that broke out in 1898.

When the Americans inherited remnants of the Spanish empire as a consequence of their victory, they were uncertain quite what to do with it. This was an especially acute dilemma as the Filipinos themselves had launched a revolution designed to overthrow Spanish rule before the Americans arrived, and which the US government found itself having to suppress when it assumed control. The subsequent war – or insurrection, as the Americans preferred to term it – between the USA and the local population was surprisingly drawn-out and costly (Boot 2002). The eventual result of America's first imperial venture was a 'structure of accommodation, or collaboration' (Thomson *et al.* 1981: 117), in which the US government cultivated indigenous elites to deal with the local people and run the Filipino economy,[8] while the Americans guaranteed order and imposed overall leadership. This arrangement proved agreeable to all parties as it was predicated on the idea that the Philippines' eventual independence was guaranteed – though this became a less important issue as time went on. However, the Americans' dependence on a small group of local intermediaries helped to create an enduring social structure that has been at the heart of many subsequent political and economic difficulties:

> America's reliance upon collaboration and suasion to maintain its insular empire made the collaborators a privileged group. Positioning themselves between the two real loci of power and authority in the islands, the American government and the mass of the Filipino people, they became indispensable mediators. Since the only credible collaborators – the only people with the authority, outlook, and education necessary to deliver the allegiance of the people – were members of the established elite, the imperialism of suasion thus became the bulwark of class interest ... While protecting and institutionalising the power of the Filipino elite, the Americans allowed themselves to be used as an external device for deflecting criticism of their regime. (Thomson *et al.* 1981: 119)

The pattern of relations established between the USA and the Philippines has not entirely disappeared even after independence; the USA remains a critically important partner of contemporary Philippines governments as a consequence. The nature of the relationship also highlights a more general feature of American power and influence: the preference for arms-length, rather than direct control. This issue is explored more extensively in the next chapter, but it is important to highlight just how jarring America's role as an imperial power was for many in the USA, which then, as now, saw itself as a beacon for freedom, democracy and independence (Smith 1994). The contradictory nature of American policy was further highlighted by the fact that the USA locked the Philippines into a highly restrictive set of trade agreements during the first three decades of the twentieth century, effectively cementing its dependence on the United States. Moreover, the predominantly agricultural exports that went to the USA failed to benefit the mass of the population and served to entrench the power of the large-scale rural landholders (SarDesai 1997).

The case of the Philippines highlights in a dramatic and rather depressing fashion a historical legacy and policy failing that has afflicted all the states of Southeast Asia to a greater or lesser degree. The failure to institute effective land reform continues to set the Southeast Asian states apart from their northern counterparts, and helps to account for the southerners' much less impressive developmental outcomes. As a consequence, in the Philippines in particular, anachronistic class structures inhibit indigenous development as a parasitic land-owning class inhibits vital reform. As Joe Studwell (2013: 26) points out, in much of southeast Asia:

> post-colonial governments toyed with land reform but never followed through to fundamentally restructure their rural economies. And the United States failed to apply the external political pressure that it used to such positive effect in northeast Asia. This lack of domestic and international political conviction over the importance of household farming in development was the first step towards relative economic underperformance of the southeast Asian region. No country bears this out more painfully than the Philippines.

The Philippines is something of an anomalous outlier in many ways, even by Southeast Asia's less demanding benchmark. Part of the explanation for the country's underperformance can be traced back to this colonial period. Spain's initial colonization did little to integrate the Philippines' economy into the developing international trading system. There was consequently little development of indigenous bureaucratic capacities to manage increased commercial activities, as happened in Thailand, and even in Indonesia (Crouch 1985). This comparative handicap was compounded by subsequent American colonization. The Americans had little sympathy with, or interest in, the development of indigenous government, land reform, or the types of extensive state structures that would become synonymous with much of the region. Consequently, the main impact of American colonialism, as Paul Hutchcroft (1998) argued, was to consolidate the position of an indigenous oligarchy that was able opportunistically to enrich itself and use the state as a vehicle to maintain its own position, rather than as a means of nationally-based economic development.

Conclusion

Given the importance of the colonial period in enabling and possibly foreclosing subsequent paths of development for all the countries of the region, it is worth highlighting a few general comparative points. With the exception of Thailand – which was also not immune to imperial pressures – all the colonial powers needed to establish working relations with indigenous collaborators if they were to maintain control and exploit the economic resources of the colony. But the style of rule and the manner of exploitation varied as a consequence of both the nature of the colonizer and the colonized. As Trocki (1999: 83) points out, the Dutch empire in the East Indies and that of the Spanish in the Philippines were 'pre-modern creations', established as early as the sixteenth and seventeenth centuries. The attenuated nature of colonial control meant they were more reliant on co-opting local elites into their administrative enterprises. But the consequences of colonial power could be quite different: the declining status of Java's administrative class stands in stark contrast to the experience of the Philippines, where colonial rule strengthened the position of the *mestizo* classes.[9]

When the ruling power was Britain, with its multiple colonies, noteworthy differences of administration and state formation could emerge even within one empire. In Malaya, the British worked with the existing Malay rulers to prop up at least the façade of traditional rule. Throughout the Straits Settlements, the actual implementation of British rule relied heavily on the Straits Chinese, who had established themselves as an increasingly important bureaucratic and economic force. In Burma, by contrast, 'the British were prepared to risk dramatic change' (Tarling 2001: 173). The fact that this change was frequently ill-conceived, and the country difficult to pacify, should not obscure the larger point about colonial differentiation. The distinction is captured in the notion of direct and indirect rule (see Trocki 1999: 90–7). The former refers to the attempts to impose 'rational' governmental practices on indigenous peoples, who were invariably conceived of as inferior and incapable of achieving effective self-rule. The British in Burma and the French in Indochina came closest to this model. Indirect rule, by contrast, described the sort of collaborative relationships that existed between the

British in the Straits Settlements, and the Dutch in some parts of Indonesia. The Americans in the Philippines attempted the first and entrenched the latter.

In short, the consequences and style of colonial rule in Southeast Asia are highly uneven and contradictory. Nicholas Tarling (2001: 199) suggests that 'the overall impression of the imperial regimes must be one of fragility and lack of penetration. Indeed, greater penetration was likely to increase fragility'. And yet, if we need to be careful about over-emphasizing the immediate consequences of colonial rule, we need to be equally alert about the possibility of understating the long-term impact of the colonial period. However resilient some indigenous beliefs and patterns of social relations might have been, the reality is that the countries of Southeast Asia are now part of a larger international system that has affected unambiguously domestic political and economic development. At the very minimum, the countries of Southeast Asia are now part of a globe-girdling system of states and a ubiquitous capitalist system. One of the most important and enduring consequences of this transformation has been the consolidation of the domestic state in Southeast Asia, something that has generally been accompanied by a growth in the size, penetration, competence, centralization and range of functions of national governments as a consequence (Elson 1999). The development and relative strength of this sort of state capacity has been at the heart of the entire region's subsequent development, albeit with important variations, as we shall see in Chapter 7.

When seen in the long sweep of history that forms such an important backdrop to contemporary international relations and comparative developmental outcomes, exogenous forces seem to have played a greater role in shaping contemporary Southeast Asia than they have in Northeast Asia. True, China was eventually transformed by the impact of European expansion – or at least China's structures of domestic governance were. But even in China there has been an enduring sense of civilizational identity and coherence that is not always evident in the more recently minted states of Southeast Asia. Having said that, we also need to recognize that within those comparatively recently established independent states of Southeast Asia, their political structures and the course of political development reflects internal contests and struggles for power. In part, Southeast Asia's political formations reflect a universal process triggered by the transformative impact of capitalist development. However, the precise forms the resultant patterns of social development and class structures actually took reflected the relative strength of indigenous forces and their ability to take advantage of structural change at the national and international level (Sidel 2008).

Such background considerations are not only important when trying to explain the relative success or otherwise of political and economic development, but they are also crucial parts of our understanding of Southeast Asian attitudes toward security. The preoccupation with internal stability and the aversion to outside 'interference' in domestic affairs may not be uniquely Southeast Asian attributes, but they are unusually prominent and distinctive parts of the Southeast Asian inheritance. The next chapter explains how some of these concerns feed into the evolution of the entire East Asian region's security agenda.

Chapter 4

The Evolving Security Agenda

There are a number of ways of thinking about 'security'. Traditionally this has tended to mean focusing of the capacity for, and responses to, collectively organized violence – usually at the hands of the state. Much of the literature dealing with security still tends to have a state-centric focus. While this is an entirely understandable and justified approach, given the state's historical importance as a source of, or a defender against, violence and conflict, it is not the only security concern facing states these days. On the contrary, and despite the preoccupation with *state* security in much of East Asia, there are new security challenges confronting states everywhere. Whether it is international terrorism, the deterioration of the natural environment, or even the uncertainties triggered by economic downturns, human beings are subject to a range of threats and dangers that go well beyond the conventional security agenda that typified the security concerns of policy-makers and academic specialists in former times (see Newman 2013).

Having said that, one of the most important features of the historical development of security concerns in the region was the prominent role played by the military in the course of national development, especially in Southeast Asia. As we shall see in this chapter and the next, however, the military also remains an important actor in the People's Republic of China, and this is contributing to both the style and content of China's increasingly assertive foreign policy at the time of writing. China is also a reminder of the growing nexus between issues such as the environment and economic development – problems that threaten the very existence of the current order in the longer term – as well as the unresolved historically based territorial disputes that continue to dog the region. But whether it is the individual or the state, 'new' or traditional security concerns, without some sense of the distinctive concerns and contingent factors that have influenced thinking about security in East Asia we cannot hope to understand the region's overall development.

'Security governance'

There are a number of different levels at which we can begin to conceive of and think about security issues. At the broadest level it is possible to distinguish between security issues that are primarily 'national' and those that are more 'international' or outward-facing. In some ways, this is something of an artificial distinction, because the intersection between the international and the national is far less clear than it has been in the past, but this is not to say that it is meaningless. For all the attention that has rightly been paid to the erosion of a clear separation between 'inside' and 'outside' (Walker 1993), especially in the economic realm (Cerny 2013), there are still some activities that remain dominated by states, and where the state is reluctant to cede authority. Indeed, one of the biggest influences on state behaviour in Southeast Asia has been, as we shall see, a desire to protect state sovereignty and autonomy. While this goal may be manifest primarily at the national level, it has also played out in the Southeast Asian region's transnational politics, most obviously in the formation and operation of the ASEAN.

One way of capturing the multidimensional nature of security issues is to see them as part of a more generalized form of governance. 'Security governance' in this regard, James Sperling (2010: 1) argues, 'represents a bundle of policies which may individually or jointly exacerbate or mitigate the problem of collective action'. Significantly, the notion of security governance captures a wider array of concerns than a traditional focus on military capability and hardware. In contrast, 'a comprehensive approach to security governance must also include threats posed to systemic or milieu goals of states, the legitimacy or authority of state structures, or national social cohesiveness and integrity' (Sperling 2010: 5). While the security governance approach has been applied mainly to a European context, it also has great potential significance for the East Asian region (Beeson forthcoming). Indeed, it is possible to argue that some of the basic ideas associated with security governance have actually been pioneered in the region, albeit under a different rubric. To see how, we need to examine the historical experience of the country that has arguably done more to develop a distinctive regional approach to security than any other: Japan.

Japan and 'comprehensive' security

Given the persistence of Japan's very distinctive security relationship with the USA, it is worth spelling out in more detail just how it has worked and what its implications have been. Japan's approach to security and foreign policy in the post-war period was shaped by its own recent, traumatic past, and by the emerging logic of the Cold War and American grand strategy. There were revealing tensions in the American camp over policy towards occupied Japan, with some, like Occupation

Commander General Douglas MacArthur, wanting to concentrate on dismantling Japan's *zaibatsu* business groups, while others, like the architect of the US containment policies, George F. Kennan, being preoccupied with stabilizing Japan and reviving the economy. Indeed, it is important to note that some informed observers argue that 'the purpose of the alliance was not only to defend *but also to restrain Japan*' (Pyle 2007: 349, emphasis added). Suffice to say at this stage that the concentration on economic revival that emerged from this period established a larger pattern that would come to define Japanese policy over the next several decades.

The key figure in developing Japan's distinctive policies after the Second World War was Shigeru Yoshida, Japan's first post-war prime minister and the architect of the 'Yoshida doctrine'. It was Yoshida who proposed stationing American troops permanently on Japanese soil as he wanted to 'ease Japan back into the world community without incurring the costs of rearmament or alienating the United States' (Schaller 1997: 27). In the context of the unfolding Cold War, an expansionist Soviet Union, a shaky Korean peninsula, a hostile China, and an East Asian region that had fresh memories of Japanese brutality and occupation, it was a shrewd move. It also gelled with a basic antipathy towards militarism on the part of a Japanese population that remained traumatized by the war and the nuclear devastation it brought to Japan itself (Katzenstein 1996). In such circumstances, the American imposition of the 'peace constitution' of 1947, including the celebrated Article 9, in which the Japanese renounced the sovereign right to use force to resolve international disputes, was less remarkable than it might seem initially. As Christopher Hughes (2005: 21) points out, the most enduring impact of the war had been the development of a 'strong strain of anti-militaristic sentiment amongst Japan's policymaking elites and general citizenry, and a genuine ambivalence about the centrality and efficacy of military power in ensuring security'.

The essence of the bilateral relationship that developed between Japan and the United States in the aftermath of the Second World War was one in which Japan relied on the USA to underwrite its security while maintaining a low diplomatic profile and concentrating on the job of reconstructing the Japanese economy. While contingent circumstances might have provided the preconditions for a fundamental shift in Japanese policy goals, 'the fundamental orientation toward economic growth and political passivity was also the product of a carefully constructed and brilliantly implemented foreign policy' (Pyle 1988: 452). In other words, Japanese foreign policy in the post-war period may have been in part 'reactive' and affected by bureaucratic rivalries within the policy-making establishment, as Calder (1988a) has argued, but it also reflected a careful and highly original calculation of what Japan's 'national interests' actually were and the best means of pursuing them.

In short, nothing about Japan's post-war foreign and domestic policy suggests that it has been driven by essentialist, immutable, culturally derived factors, or by the ineluctable, universal structural logic of the international system. On the contrary, Japan's foreign policy-making has evolved over time and reflected shifting balances of domestic forces and foreign pressures, in much the same way as it does anywhere. What the Japanese experience does remind us of, though, is that national policies are products of unique geopolitical circumstances and histories, and it is these factors that give national policies their distinctive qualities and delimit the range of possibilities open to policy-makers. In addition to the constraints placed on Japan by the war and American occupation, Japan's post-war leaders were keen to ensure the economic security of a country that lacked the basic resources to fuel its rapidly expanding reconstruction and industrialization. The disastrous consequences of Japan's aggressive wartime expansion into Northeast and Southeast Asia had demonstrated the dangers and futility of the military option as a way of securing Japan's economic future. The consequence of the long-term redefinition of Japanese security and the best means to achieve it was the formalization of the doctrine of 'comprehensive security' that emerged in 1980 under Prime Minster Ohira Masayoshi.

Japan's vulnerability to major economic and political changes in the international system was highlighted by the twin 'oil shocks' of the 1970s. Adding to Japan's sense of insecurity was the pronouncement of the so-called 'Nixon doctrine' in 1969. Richard Nixon, chastened by America's ruinously expensive and strategically futile involvement in the Vietnam War, warned America's Asian allies that the US was no longer prepared to commit troops to Asia, and that they must assume greater responsibility for their own defence (Kimball 2006). This led to an emphasis on 'self-help' in Japan, and a gradual rethinking of the role of the Japan Self-Defence Forces (JSDF).[1] While this may seem conventional enough, the other noteworthy aspect of Japan's new security thinking was the development of 'resource diplomacy', in which the Japanese government employed an elaborate array of official development assistance (ODA) packages, and helped Japanese corporations to secure access to vital resource supplies overseas (Arase 1995; Hatch and Yamamura 1996). Such policies have been given renewed life and importance as part of the rivalry with China (Yoshimatsu and Trinidad 2010). The long-term significance of these strategies will become more apparent when we look at the expansion of Japanese business into East Asia, as well as the impact on China as it has sought to replicate elements of Japanese policy (Wilson 2013).

Overall, Japan's notion of security is far more comprehensive than either the notion of security generally proffered in IR theory, or in the security practices of Western counterparts.[2] Comprehensive security goes beyond conventional military security to include political, economic and sociocultural factors. As Alagappa (1998: 624) put it, 'underlying the notion of comprehensive security is the belief that survival and prosperity are better served by all-round strength than by reliance on military power alone'. This basic insight not only allows us to make sense of the specific content of Japan's multidimensional, integrated developmental strategies that emphasized the control of strategically important technological processes (Heginbotham and Samuels 1998), but it also helps to explain the attractiveness and emulation of such policies in other parts of East Asia.

While some observers have flatly denied the idea that there is any such thing as an 'Asian' approach to security (Segal 1995), it is clear that there are concerns in East Asia that go beyond a narrow preoccupation with military matters (Harris and Mack 1997). Plainly, they are products of the region's specific historical circumstances. While it is difficult to generalize about such a disparate group of countries, it is evident that 'for most states, the core component of comprehensive security is still political survival' (Alagappa 1998: 625). This may be a concern of all states everywhere, as conventional IR theory might suggest, but this observation has particular significance in an East Asian context because of the region's unique history. As we have already seen, East Asia was affected profoundly by imperialism, an episode that revealed the region's vulnerability to Europe's superior military technology, and galvanized Japan in particular into a rush to modernization. But the decolonization and independence processes have been equally influential in shaping the more broadly conceived notions of security that have come to distinguish the region.

Southeast Asian security dynamics

The more explicitly political aspects of the post-war decolonization process are considered in Chapter 6, but at this point it is important to sketch briefly how the military has developed in the region, as this has had major implications for both the types of political regimes and even the nature of the development processes that have emerged as a consequence. In much of Southeast Asia it is possible to make a general observation about the legacy of the colonial period on the region's militaries:

> rather than imbuing the armed forces with military professionalism which required absolute obedience to the civil authority, colonial rule

left behind armed forces more often oriented towards maintaining internal order than to external defense, and therefore implicitly attuned to domestic politics. (May *et al.* 1998: 1)

Consequently, the military has often assumed a uniquely powerful role, sometimes as a force for liberation from colonial oppression, sometimes as a vital tool of nation-building and development, but almost always as one of the most powerful institutions in the country (Beeson and Bellamy 2008).

Indonesia is the most complete exemplar of these interconnected possibilities and the highly distinctive role that the military has played in the nation's political and economic life as a consequence. Not only did Indonesia's army have its origins in the revolutionary struggle against the Dutch colonialists, but it also played a crucial role in unifying 'Indonesia' from the highly disparate elements that had made up the Dutch East Indies. The pivotal nature of the ABRI's[3] role in Indonesia's development was captured in the notion of *dwifungsi* or dual function, which describes its military and non-military ideological, political, economic and socio-cultural roles. In terms of effective state capacity, the ABRI has been one of the most important expressions of political as well as more directly coercive power. The Indonesian army is also deeply involved in economic activities (Beeson 2008). To some extent it had little choice: by some estimates, 60–65 per cent of the military's operating expenses come from 'off-budget sources' rather than the central government (Cochrane 2002). This has not only encouraged the development of close ties between political, economic and military elites in Indonesia, but has also encouraged the growth of corruption, illegal activities and cronyism. While the extent and institutionalized nature of some of these problems may be uniquely Indonesian, the final point that country highlights is more general: the military in Indonesia, like its counterparts across Southeast Asia, has been almost entirely preoccupied with *internal* threats to the survival of the state and, with the notable exceptions of South Korea and Taiwan, quite resistant to civilian-inspired reform (Croissant and Kuehn 2009; Croissant and Wurster 2013).

The preoccupation with internal security helps to explain the remarkably infrequent clashes and inter-state conflicts, despite widespread concern about the numerous supposed flashpoints and threats to Southeast Asian security and stability (Tan 2000). It is not simply because this sort of behaviour is sharply at odds with what much Western theorizing and policy practice might lead us to expect that makes the Southeast Asian experience interesting; it also represents very different ways of accommodating specific historical circumstances and geopolitical pressures. Variations on the Indonesian theme can be multiplied throughout Southeast Asia. In Thailand, for example, the military was at the centre of national politics from the time it overthrew the monarchy in 1932, until the actions of a newly assertive civil society in 1992 appeared to have significantly curtailed its influence. That the military should have assumed such an important position in the political life of the country for so long is explained by the fact that Thailand's modern military has from its inception been 'explicitly political', and was 'modernised to protect the regime from domestic enemies and enforce its policies, and was not intended for external defence' (Ockey 2001: 191).

The growth of civil society in Thailand and elsewhere in the region has potentially major implications for both the military and regional development more generally. The potential tensions between military and civil society are also evident in other parts of the region – especially those with a history of authoritarian rule. While the Philippines currently has one of the most vibrant civil societies in Southeast Asia, it has not always been the case, nor is it clear that the military's role in politics has ended permanently. Again, it is important to emphasize how important the historical legacy of the colonial period and the subsequent geopolitical context has been in shaping both the form of the military itself and its relationship to other social and political institutions. Not only was the military preoccupied with internal threats – in this case communist insurgency – but it became a direct extension of the authoritarian rule of Ferdinand Marcos following his imposition of martial law. Significantly, under the guise of enhancing national security, the military became a deeply institutionalized part of the Philippines economy and politics, as well as gaining control over the legal system and media (Hedman 2001). As in Indonesia, power and patronage became increasingly concentrated in the hands of an authoritarian leader. Loyalty was to Marcos rather than the state, thus cementing the ties between political and military power. All this was tolerated, if not encouraged, by the USA in the context of the Cold War and the perceived need for 'strong' allies (Cha 2010).

Though the concern with domestic threats to national security is one of the defining characteristics of the Southeast Asian region, the precise role the military plays in achieving this varies. In Malaysia and Singapore, for example, despite the persistence of non-democratic political practices and rather repressive forms of rule, the militaries are generally professional and not directly involved in maintaining domestic order.[4] At the other end of the spectrum is Burma, where a military dictatorship has until very recently dominated every aspect of national affairs. The release from house arrest of Burma's principal champion of democratic reform, Aung San Suu Kyi, is clearly an encouraging sign that has generated much excitement. It is important to remember that, historically, the military has controlled Burma's principal export industry and cash crop, and supplies something like 70 per cent of the world's opium and heroin as a result (Neher 2001: 161). There are, therefore, serious grounds for doubting how much of a transformation the current reform agenda – surprising and welcome though it may be – can actually bring about in civil–military relations given the military's hitherto dominant and highly institutionalized position (Huang 2013).

An objection might be made that while these sorts of national-level contingent factors are of interest in countries with little strategic weight or international significance, they matter less when it comes to the universal and timeless concerns of the 'great powers'. And yet we have already seen that Japan, which clearly has the potential to become a major power if it so chooses, has – until recently at least – preferred to renounce aggressive militarism. Japan serves as a powerful reminder that nationally-embedded values and ideas about the appropriate role of the military can help to determine the role of the military in particular and the nature of foreign policy more generally. Recent history suggests there may be limits to this process, and that Japan may indeed be becoming a 'normal' country. But before we consider this possibility in any detail, it is important to say something about China's military – China being a country that everyone agrees is a 'rising power', and which some believe to be on an inevitable collision course with the current hegemon (Carpenter 2006).

Security and the PRC

If there is agreement about China's increased significance in regional and global affairs, there is less consensus about what this might mean, or what informs China's security perspective. The humiliation inflicted on a weak China by the European powers in particular, sparked a transformation of the country's key institutions, and had a profound influence on the People's Republic of China's (PRC's) leadership's views about China's place in the international system. From the outset of PRC rule, much of China's interlinked foreign and security policies have been driven by the essentially nationalist desire to regain the country's place among the great powers (Deng 2008). While this might seem a conventional enough aspiration, and one that is perfectly in keeping with much standard IR analysis, the fact that China is notionally a communist country may also make its policies and goals different. Indeed, history seen through the lens of Marxism–Leninism *ought* to look rather different from when seen by Thucydides or Hans Morgenthau. Thus, one of the enduring questions about China's place in the international order is whether it is, or may become, a 'normal' country, or whether its unique historical legacy

– especially 'the century of shame', its more recent revolutionary origins and the seemingly non-negotiable status of Taiwan – mean that it is inevitably a non-status quo power.[5]

Despite the fact that the Chinese case has sparked a good deal of interest in the impact of different, nationally based 'strategic cultures' (see Booth and Trood 1999), the most exhaustive study of China's strategic culture, and one of the principal triggers for much of the ensuing debate, came to a slightly paradoxical conclusion: while individual strategic cultures do make a difference and influence the views of policy-makers, in China's case such views are 'long-term, deeply rooted, persistent and consistent' (Johnston 1995: 258). In other words, broadly similar views about security can be found in China both before and after the revolutionary period in which the PRC came to power, and – equally important historically – they are not significantly different from the views of other major powers, Johnston claims:

> Chinese strategic culture – with its stress on the overall efficacy of force for achieving state security, and on careful, capabilities-based assessments of opportunities for applying force – arguably predisposes those socialised into it to make strategic decisions roughly along realpolitik expected utility lines. (Johnston 1995: 260)

This may help to explain why realist theoretical perspectives initially became so popular among Chinese international relations (IR) specialists (Shambaugh 1994: 44). Of late, however, it is significant that liberal and even constructivist perspectives have come to exert a greater influence over IR scholars in China (Qin 2009), a development that helps to account for the emphasis placed on China's 'peaceful rise' and the benefits of interdependence (Shih 2005). This is not an entirely unprecedented or inconceivable development: it is clear that the PRC leadership has operated in an environment where non-material factors have been important. China's communist leadership found itself confronted by a formidable opponent in an international and regional order divided primarily along *ideological* lines. Mao in particular saw American hegemony in ideological terms, reflecting a Marxist-inspired reading of history, which was cognisant of the inherent contradictions that supposedly drive imperial powers. While the end result may have been the same – potential conflict between major powers – the possibility that it might have been the consequence of the ineluctable workings of long-run historical-materialist forces made the prospects for the diplomatic resolution of difference infinitely more problematic. The fact that the PRC leadership actively aspired to become a leading force in and role model for the Third World compounded the ideological divide (Van Ness 1970).

It would be remarkable if there were not any major differences in the way that Chinese policy-makers and strategists view the world – especially when compared with the United States's view. Since its inception, the USA has been blessed by a uniquely favourable set of strategic circumstances, with weak and/or friendly neighbours to its north and south, and oceans into which to project power to its east and west. To this benign picture can be added resource wealth and self-sufficiency, to say nothing of a remarkably productive combination of relative social stability and underlying dynamics. China, by contrast, has not only been torn apart by foreign intervention and domestic upheaval within living memory, but it is bordered by poor, unstable, frequently hostile countries that challenge its foreign policy capabilities (Beeson and Li 2014). How China is coping with some of these problems will be taken up in more detail later. At this stage, it is sufficient simply to note the hugely different geopolitical circumstances that have confronted the two principal protagonists in the unfolding strategic drama in East Asia.

Comparative grand strategies

Before considering how USA–China relations are evolving, and how this is affecting the wider East Asian region, it should be noted that not only are the views of China's strategic thinkers different from those of the USA, but they are much closer to the notion of 'comprehensive' security developed by Japan. As in Japan, Chinese conceptions of security incorporate both an economic component and a recognition of the importance of technological development (Shambaugh 1994). Wu (2001) argues that there has been a major shift in the thinking of Chinese strategists since the early 1990s, in which there has been a notable shift from a preoccupation with national survival, to one in which there is a greater emphasis on national economic development. Crucially, this process is seen increasingly as being dependent on integration with the wider, capitalist world economy. China's growing participation in, and even enthusiasm for, multilateral institutions is one of the most important manifestations of this change in thinking and practice (Kuik 2008; Sohn 2008). This would, indeed, seem to confirm China's integration and socialization into the global international order established under American hegemony in the aftermath of the Second World War. But for some observers, however, this may be an interim phase. For example, Chan *et al.* (2012: 39) argue that:

> as soon as China feels confident enough in its status as a great power, it may no longer feel totally obliged to comply with the established norms and rules of Western-dominated international institutions ... At

issue is whether or not China can harness enough soft power to modify the existing norms in its favour, convincing others to follow the Chinese way of thinking.

We shall examine the possible implications of such arguments in more detail in Chapter 8. The point to note at this stage is that China's foreign-policy thinking generally and its 'grand strategy' in particular has been an evolving work-in-progress that has been reactive and responsive to changing circumstances. China's policy may still be overwhelmingly realist in orientation and driven by the pursuit of what its policy-makers take to be the 'national interest', but as Zhang Feng points out, this has been a process of 'learning by doing', the principal consequence of which has been that 'today's China is unclear about its international purpose and unable to clarify what it stands for' (Zhang 2012: 340). China's security policy, therefore, is subject to some of the same competing influences and pressures as the rest of its foreign-policy-making processes. While the construction of foreign policy in China remains frustratingly opaque – for reasons that are explained in more detail in Chapter 8 – the Peoples' Liberation Army (PLA) continues to enjoy an institutionalized presence in the most senior ranks of Chinese governing elites and this clearly influences to conduct of policy, especially in security-related areas.

In many ways this is unsurprising, of course. As in parts of Southeast Asia, the military in China played a pivotal role in the civil war and defeat of the nationalists. The difficult geopolitical and developmental challenges the PRC leadership has confronted subsequently have also meant that conventional military security has been an important part of state policy. And yet it is also true to say that 'the most fundamental change in the dynamics of foreign policy decision-making has been the shift of emphasis since 1978 on the part of the central leadership from the nation's physical security to its economic development' (Lu 2001: 57). In other words, there has been a long-term recalibration of foreign policy priorities, which had seen – until fairly recently, at least – the formal standing of the PLA diminish as other priorities and parts of the state became more important. However, recent events have provided a reminder that the PLA is far from inconsequential.

It is important to remember that, as elsewhere in parts of Asia, 'the PLA's primarily mission has always started at home – to keep the Party in power' (McGregor 2010: 105). The close relations between the governing political elite (about which I say more in Chapter 6) were dramatically revealed in the spectacular, politically embarrassing downfall of the former Communist Party chief of Chongqing, Bo Xilai. Whatever offences Bo may actually have committed, he was a high-profile champion of a rather old-fashioned form of Maoism that had a substantial number of sympathizers, not least among the conservative ranks of the military. Indeed, it was Bo's links to the PLA, and even rumours of a possible coup, that may ultimately have been responsible for his political demise (Page and Wei 2012). Two other points are worth making about the PLA's continuing role behind the scenes: first, prominent military commentators are assuming a much higher profile in debates about the country's foreign and security policies. As we shall see, this helps to explain the growing assertiveness, even aggression, of recent Chinese policy. Second, the PLA still appears to exercise an influence over the selection of its ostensibly civilian superiors. Xi Jinping's ascension to power was apparently facilitated by his cultivation of ties with influential military figures (Lam 2012).

All of this is a long way from the usual focus of attention as far as China's military is concerned, which is overwhelmingly concerned with China's military capability and capacity to project power. China's uncompromising behaviour in its territorial disputes in Northeast and Southeast Asia would seem to vindicate such attention. Indeed, there is a long-standing, very influential strand of realist strategic analysis which argues that war between a rising, militarily modernizing China and a declining United Sates is highly likely, if not inevitable (Friedberg 2011; Mearsheimer 2001). And yet until quite recently one of the most remarkable features of China's overall policy agenda was the comparatively modest scale of its military spending (Nathan and Ross 1997). Even now it is important to recognize that Chinese military spending remains a fraction of America's, and that the USA enjoys a significant lead over China in terms of its military technology and – let us not forget – the battle-hardened quality of its military personnel too. China's last military conflict was a border with its neighbour Vietnam, in which China's forces were revealed to be no match for the Vietnamese. Nevertheless, the conventional policy wisdom in the USA is that:

> The People's Republic of China is pursuing a long-term, comprehensive military modernization program designed to improve the capacity of China's armed forces to fight and win 'local wars under conditions of informatization', or high-intensity, information-centric regional military operations of short duration. (Office of the Secretary of Defence 2005: iv)

The strategic basis and consequences of such claims are considered in more detail in the next chapter. What merits emphasis at this stage is that China's experience is another reminder that the particular preoccupations that galvanize specific national elites invariably have local roots. True, the wider geopolitical context provides a critical, overarching conditioning environment within which strategic calculations are made, but the latter have always been deeply overlaid by contingent factors and domestic sensibilities. The second striking thing to note is that such contingencies can have a regional component: not only did East Asian countries suffer similar historical challenges and traumas, but some of their responses show a degree of commonality. The prevalence of a comprehensive approach to security – even where the detail or ideology that informs it may vary as a consequence of distinct national experiences – is a surprisingly common feature of East Asia's approach to security and as a consequence has influenced the way that the region's nascent security architecture has developed. As we shall see in more detail in Chapter 8, such considerations also continue to influence the conduct of economic policy. Indeed, economic security might well be considered in the same context as a number of other 'new' non-military forms of security that have potentially powerful national consequences.

Conclusion

Most analyses of security in East Asia focus on relative military capacities. This is clearly a crucial determinant of the significance of individual states. Despite having an enormous army, North Korea would plainly not have the same strategic significance if it did not have nuclear weapons. Similarly, the fact that China's economic development allows it to purchase new weapons systems is not unimportant; but we also need to remember that its still lags far behind the USA in terms of defence spending and technological sophistication (Crane *et al*. 2005). Indeed, Beijing's strategic planners are painfully conscious of their strategic inferiority and vulnerability relative to the still far superior power of the United States, even under an Obama administration that is less enthusiastic about open-ended foreign entanglements (Homolar 2012). Under such circumstances it is remarkable, perhaps, that up to now China has not made military modernization an even greater priority.

The principal focus in the chapter has been national security policies and perspectives, and while there are some basic considerations that inform the strategic calculations of states everywhere – the most important of which is the preservation of the state itself – the way states go about this and the way they prioritize security issues varies as a consequence of distinct, historically contingent circumstances. Indeed, the very definition of 'security' continues to display noteworthy national and even regional variation. This latter point is potentially especially significant: despite all the well-known variation in the circumstances that influence strategic thinking in the countries of East Asia, there is a widely held belief that the achievement of security is more 'comprehensive' process than it is generally seen to be in the West. Though such distinctive, regional orientations to security questions are no guarantee that East Asia's security relations will either be orderly or revert to some sort of pre-existing order centred on China, it does suggest that even in the contentious, seemingly non-negotiable security arena there may be some common ground. But whatever potential there may be for co-operation within the region, it will depend on the wider context within which the region is embedded – a subject that forms the basis of the next chapter.

Chapter 5

Regional Security[1]

Having looked primarily at the national basis of security issues in East Asia thus far, it is now time to turn to a more conventional examination of East Asia's intra- and inter-regional relations. There are, however, some limitations in the state-centric approach that dominates conventional analyses that need to be acknowledged at the outset. Most significantly, many of the most influential interpretations of state behaviour entirely neglect the sort of domestic level analysis presented in the preceding chapter. Indeed, some of the most prominent analyses of international security suggest that the actions of states are the entirely predictable consequences of the structure of the inter-state system itself (Waltz 1979). And yet not only have these sorts of predictions about the inevitable nature of state behaviour in the post-Cold War period not materialized (Waltz 1993), but the very structure of the international system itself has also undergone a profound metamorphosis. The predicted return to a 'normal', multipolar system has not happened, even if it is beginning to look slightly more possible (Schweller 2011). We may not be living in quite the sort of unipolar system that distinguished the administration of George W. Bush at the height of its powers (Daadler and James Lindsay 2003), but nor are we in an era of unambiguous multipolarity either.

One of the most important issues that is central to both the security dynamics that are the principal focus of attention in this chapter, and to the evolution of the United States' relationship to the regional economy, is whether the USA itself is undergoing a long-term process of economic decline. Though the USA is not a direct part of the region, it has exerted a profound influence on its development and will inevitably continue to do so, even if some of the claims about its relative decline prove to be well founded (Layne 2012; Pape 2009). It is not simply that the USA has effectively shaped the global international order and the norms and practices it reflects that is crucial here, but that there may be a real 'peer competitor' with which the USA must contend. While some aspects of the 'rise of China' may be overstated, there is no doubt that it represents a challenge of a different order from that presented by Japan, for example, which may have been a powerful economic force, but which was subordinate to the USA in the security sphere (Samuels 2007). China, in contrast, presents a very different sort of challenge.

The regional strategic context

Before we consider the prospects for what has been described as 'hegemonic transition' and its possible implications for security in the region, it is important to note that even before China emerged as a potentially destabilizing, threatening force in the region, some analysts thought that the region was famously 'ripe for rivalry' (Friedberg 1993/94). Europe's past was thought to provide a model for Asia's future, but in the sense of nineteenth-century-style regional, multipolar competition, not the increased levels of transnational co-operation and institutionalization that characterized the twentieth century. While Friedberg is right to highlight the increased salience of the region as a focus of security concern, inter-state conflict has of late been the rare exception in East Asia, not the rule. Despite the ongoing territorial disputes in the region and the unpredictable behaviour of North Korea, it is entirely possible that the situation may remain the same.[2]

It is worth noting at the outset that many of the most influential analyses of Asian security are produced in the USA and this undoubtedly influences their content despite their claims to objectivity (Smith 2002). This matters because the basic premise found in so much North American scholarship in particular – that America's strategic presence is the necessary glue that stabilizes an otherwise combustible region – may not be as self-evident as many observers seem to think. It is noteworthy that co-operative approaches to security issues have progressed the furthest in Southeast Asia, where the United States is least engaged, and remained relatively underdeveloped in Northeast Asia, where the USA is heavily involved in directly managing intra-regional relations (Alagappa 2003: 594). It is also worth remembering that 'maintaining stability' has also involved the USA fighting major wars over Korea and Vietnam.

Thus the USA has played a major, occasionally highly interventionist role in the history of East Asia since the early 1960s. While it is important to acknowledge that the countries of East Asia have also been influenced powerfully by the region's distinctive historical experiences and the challenge of integration into an international strategic, political and economic order dominated by the West, the United States' role has been decisive at times. Two further implications of this general situation merit emphasis: on the one hand, the countries of East Asia have developed an – understandable – preoccupation with shoring-up national sovereignty, security and the integrity of the state. On the other hand, the region has been fundamentally divided. The principal example of these divisions was the ideological splits of the Cold War, which occasionally became 'hot', but which were invariably reinforced by older enmities and suspicions. It is, of course, in the interests of hegemonic power that things should remain this way. As Michael Mastanduno points out,

> since the United States does not want to encourage a balancing coalition against its dominant position, it is not clear that it has a strategic interest in the full resolution of differences between, say, Japan and China or Russian and China. Some level of tension among these states reinforces their individual need for special relationships with the United States. (Mastanduno 2002: 200)

Some observers go further and argue that the 'hub and spokes' strategy the USA has employed in East Asia is both in America's interest and necessary for regional stability (Joffe 1995). Others emphasize that, even if the USA was itself the principal beneficiary of its policies, its role as an 'off-shore balancer' was critical to maintain stability in an otherwise unstable and conflict-prone region (Art 2003). What we can say is that the series of bilateral security relationships that the USA established in the region with countries such as Japan, Thailand and the Philippines as well as Australia in the wider Asia-Pacific were key components in a USA-dominated regional security order. It was, of course, very much a product of and a response to the exigencies of the Cold War. Whatever one thinks of the rationale for such alliances, at the height of the Cold War they divided the region and made region-wide economic and political co-operation impossible (Beeson 2005). The USA's alliance relationships were necessarily asymmetrical and, as Victor Cha (2010: 158) points out, 'designed to exert maximum control over the smaller ally's actions'.

Thus, despite not being directly part of the East Asian region, the USA played a crucial role in the overall 'regional security complex' that determined strategic outcomes in the region (Buzan and Waever 2003). The reality now, however, according to former US National Security Adviser Zbigniew Brzezinski (2012: 101), is that 'the United States must realize that stability in Asia can no longer be imposed by a non-Asian power, least of all by the direct application of US military power'. One of the reasons that the likes of Brzezinski – formerly an advocate of a much more interventionist grand strategy on the part of the USA – have revised their opinions about the strategic balance in East Asia is because it has begun to shift in quite dramatic ways. At the centre of this rethinking has been China's remarkable rise. While the economic consequences of the rise of China may be largely benign, many observers think that, at the very least, this could presage a destabilizing struggle for supremacy in the wider Asia-Pacific region (Friedberg 2011; Mearsheimer 2006).

Hegemonic transition?

In one of the most influential realist analyses of the nature of power in the international system, Robert Gilpin (1981: 48) argued that it is 'the differential rate of change between the international distribution of power and the other components of the system that produces a disjuncture or disequilibrium'. Such disjunctures – especially changes in the relative economic standing of different states – undermine the balance of power, introduce instability and tension, and encourage rising states to try to transform the international system to reflect their interests. In this reading, conflict is inevitable as declining powers will seek to resist a process that inevitably diminishes their relative position. It is this underlying claim about the inevitable, materially-driven nature of competition and potential conflict that is at the heart of so-called 'hegemonic transition theory' (Chan 2008; Organski 1968). Given that in Britain we have arguably only experienced one fully fledged hegemonic transition, when Britain was (peacefully) replaced by an (initially reluctant) United States, this might seem to be a rather limited framework when trying to assess East Asia's strategic prospects. However, it is not necessary to accept the deterministic prophecies of the likes of Gilpin or the most prominent current realist Mearshiemer (2001) to recognize that its claims and ideas need to be taken seriously – if only because so many policy-makers in the USA and China are also avowed realists.

For traditional, state-centric analyses of hegemonic power and transition, military might is a pivotal measure of influence and a determinant of dominance (Lemke 2002). In this context, it is important to emphasize that despite the concerns of many realist scholars about the rise of China and the supposed likelihood, if not inevitability, of conflict, American military ascendancy remains largely in place. As has frequently been pointed out (Ferguson 2004), the USA spends more on military hardware than the next 15–20 powers combined. Moreover, despite concerns about the vulnerability of American aircraft carriers to Chinese missile capability (Bradsher 2012), the USA has an unrivalled ability to project power, as well as a major and expanding lead in the technical sophistication of its weapons systems – something many observers take to be an unambiguous and enduring expression of America's continuing dominance (Brooks and Wohlforth 2002). And yet, it is not obvious that this military strength is as decisive as it once was, or that the ability of other countries such as China to challenge American dominance should be judged exclusively, or even primarily, by their ability to counter conventional military might. On the contrary, it is possible that the nature of contemporary international relations, in which the declining incidence and utility of traditional inter-state conflict is such a noteworthy part

(Gartzke 2007; Pinker 2012), may be opening a political space within which to challenge American primacy with comparative impunity – especially where this is reinforced with other, increasingly relevant and usable forms of structural power.

The key question, of course, is which nation might provide alternative leadership in the region. The obvious candidate is China. This raises a number of important, if controversial, questions. First, given the USA's (frequently violent) involvement in East Asia, would the region perhaps actually be *more* stable in the absence of the USA? Second, are the ways in which we think about security and stability too focused on the conventional military aspects of the question? There is a certain irony to this, given that one of the most enduring elements of American hegemony – and one of the principal sources of its legitimacy and the stability of the overall system – was not military at all, but a consequence of the sort of 'soft power' that is such a crucial feature of its political dominance (Nye 2004). Many realist analyses fail to make this connection to the multi-faceted nature of hegemony, which is a striking omission because it is arguably in this context – and not in the narrowly conceived military arena – that China has most ground to make up.

Intriguingly, though, a historically informed analysis that focuses on what Braudel famously described as the *longue durée* reminds us that the possibility of Chinese hegemony and a stable regional order is far from unprecedented or unimaginable. As we saw in Chapter 2, for hundreds, if not thousands, of years, China was the centre of a generally stable and remarkably durable 'international' order, in which the other nations of what we now think of as East Asia accepted its dominant position and frequently benefited from it. At a time when it seems inevitable that China will again become the dominant economic power of the region and a major strategic force, it is not unreasonable to ask whether an older, more enduring regional order might also be re-emerging. It is precisely this possibility that informs David Kang's (2003a: 57) contention that 'a rich and strong China could again cement regional stability'. Not only does Kang reject the assumption that an American withdrawal from the region would necessarily generate instability, but he suggests that Japan would have little to gain from initiating the sort of great power competition that many Western analysts consider inevitable.

While it is clear that Japan's post-war behaviour has been far from 'normal', and not what much Western IR theory might lead us to expect, it is not clear that it can reorient itself as easily as Kang implies. On the one hand, from a strategic perspective, Japan is 'overly dependent on the US, to the position where it cannot extricate itself from the alliance' (C. Hughes, 2005: 144). While much of the legitimating rhetoric for these initiatives revolves around either the war on terror or – in the case of the Ballistic Missile Defense System – 'rogue states' such as North Korea, the real driver of the Japan–USA alliance is the rise of China. In this regard, China's own recent behaviour and the increasing tensions over unresolved territorial claims have not only undermined stability in the region, but they have also raised long-term questions about China's capacity to provide regional leadership (Beeson 2013a).

Managing territorial politics

At the centre of recent tensions between China and Japan, as well as China and Southeast Asia, are unresolved territorial disputes in the South China Sea over what the Japanese call the Senkaku Islands and the Chinese call the Diaoyu Islands. In both the Northeast Asian and Southeast Asian cases, the islands in question are unprepossessing, or barely existent in the case of the Spratly and Paracel Islands, but none the less they are potentially valuable possessions.

By some estimates, oil reserves in the South China Sea, for example, may amount to over 200 billion barrels, second only to Saudi Arabia if this proves to be true (Fabi and Mogato 2012). Since becoming an oil importer as recently as the mid-1990s, questions of energy security have begun to assume an increasingly prominent place in China's foreign policy priorities and calculations (Leung 2011). Fuelling China's continuing growth is crucial to development, social stability and the legitimacy of the 'communist' elites that still govern China (Zhu 2011). The South China Sea could play a crucial role in maintaining the political status quo in China, which helps to explain both China's confrontational stance and its interest in developing the capacity to protect the vital sea lanes through which resources must travel (Collins and Erikson 2011). This helps to explain the non-negotiable nature and extent of China's claims, however implausible they may seem (see ICG 2012).

Important as such material considerations might be, the dispute with Japan also highlights the remarkable continuing importance of the history of the East Asian region. At one level, this may 'only' be a dispute over unresolved borders, such as might occur wherever legal precedent is unclear or contested. What makes the disagreement between China and Japan so much harder to resolve, however, is the historical baggage both bring to the table. As we saw in Chapter 2, China suffered terribly at the hands of Japan during the twentieth century. Many Chinese believe that the Japanese government has never fully acknowledged the nature of its wartime role. The rapid growth in China's barely-controlled social media sites and the legions of frequently nationalistic 'netizens' who populate them makes any perceived weakness in pursuing national interests extremely dangerous for the Chinese government (Parello-Plesner and Anti 2013). But it is also important to recognize that nationalism is on the rise in Japan too (Hayashi 2012). The newly installed (at the time of writing) government of Shinzo Abe is similarly constrained by his government's commitment to defend 'Japanese interests'. In short, unresolved historical grievances as much as contemporary conflicts are threatening to lock both sides into dangerous, non-negotiable positions.

Some informed observers think that, for all their importance to China, there is still room for the negotiated settlement of its territorial claims (Fravel 2011: 296). One potential obstacle in this context, and a key test of the region's ability to manage its own intra-regional relations, is China's reluctance to multilateralize its territorial disputes. Despite the existence of the ASEAN Regional Forum (ARF), an organization that ought to be uniquely well placed to play a mediating role (as I explain below) China prefers to exercise its greater power and leverage through bilateral channels on this particular issue (Raine 2011). While China has demonstrated a willingness to play an active role in regional, and even global, institutions, this has not been at the expense of national sovereignty, which remains paramount in Chinese strategic thinking (Rozman 2010; Shambaugh 2013). In this respect, at least, for all the unhappiness China's behaviour may cause among Southeast Asian political elites, the country's preference for sovereignty-enhancing regional institutions is entirely in keeping with ASEAN's own fundamental principles. The question is whether such an approach can provide the basis for a leadership role for China at the regional level, let alone on the global stage.

Can the ARF manage regional security?

The most important attempt to institutionalize security co-operation in the region thus far has been the development of the ASEAN Regional Forum (ARF) (see Yuzawa 2012). The ASEAN grouping that was instrumental in bringing this about is considered in more detail in Chapter 11, along with what is potentially its most important offshoot so far: ASEAN+3. However, it is important to make a couple of preliminary observations about ASEAN as they help in understanding the potential significance of the wider geopolitical context in shaping security relations in the region. While ASEAN was notionally intended to 'accelerate ... economic growth, social progress and cultural development' (ASEAN 1967), it was very much a product of the Cold War and the geopolitical imperatives it generated. Shared concerns about the rise of China and the spread of communism, combined with anxieties about the USA's long-term commitment to the region, provided the impetus for regional co-operation (Emmers 2003). Nearly 30 years later, the ending of the Cold War and the redefinition of the overarching international security situation provided a similar stimulus for the formal establishment in 1994 of the ARF.

It is significant that from its inception the ARF was designed to engage, and if possible to manage relations with, the major regional powers. Its membership consequently includes all the key countries with the capacity to shape security outcomes in the region.[3] Equally significantly, the ASEAN governments conceived of the ARF as 'ASEAN writ large' (Leifer 1996: 25). In other words, the sorts of operational practices, norms and behaviours that were part of the ASEAN grouping's modus operandi would also form the basis of those of the ARF. As we shall see in Chapter 11, this mode of operation has some clear weaknesses, and the ARF has also suffered from similar problems. But given that there was a perceived need to make sure that all the participants – especially China – felt 'comfortable' with the format, it was perhaps inevitable that membership of the ARF would have limited implications and obligations. But as critics have been quick to point out, consensus, voluntarism and inclusiveness – the hallmarks of the 'ASEAN way' – have their limitations (Jones and Smith 2007).

The major criticisms of the ARF in particular, and ASEAN's security initiatives more generally, centre on their apparent ineffectiveness, or on the necessity of there being a congruence of interest with the major powers. ASEAN initiatives such as the 1971 Zone of Peace, Freedom and Neutrality (ZOPFAN), for example, are frequently seen as being contradictory and unrealizable, intended to limit extra-regional intervention, while simultaneously recognizing and even encouraging the involvement of the major powers in the economic and security affairs of the region (Collins 2003: 161). Likewise, the resolution of the 'Cambodian problem',[4] which is frequently cited as ASEAN's finest hour and the pre-eminent exemplar of its diplomatic effectiveness, is seen by others as being wholly dependent on a coincidence of interests between the United States and China, thus allowing the ASEAN grouping to play a prominent role (Smith and Jones 1997). Both the USA and China wanted to see Vietnam withdraw from Cambodia following its invasion to remove the murderous Pol Pot regime. It was this confluence of interests, rather than the effectiveness of ASEAN diplomacy in influencing either its neighbours or the major powers, that was decisive, critics claim.

However, it is the potentially crippling ineffectiveness of ASEAN-style approaches to conflict management that has drawn some of the sharpest criticism. Smith and Jones (1997: 147) claim that ASEAN 'is not really a conflict avoidance organization. It is rather an *issue* avoidance organization'. In other words, ASEAN is primarily a mechanism for sidelining problems that regional leaders consider politically too difficult or sensitive. Equally problematical, there is a potentially irreconcilable difference of approach between the ARF's East Asian and 'Western' members that mirrors the sorts of divisions that have hamstrung APEC and made the concept of an 'Asia-Pacific' grouping inherently disputable. With the noteworthy exception of Japan, ASEAN members and China prefer general, non-binding discussions about security issues, whereas countries such as Australia and the USA want to develop specific confidence-building measures (CBMs) capable of rapid implementation. Such differences have undermined the potential effectiveness of the organization and its ability to provide the sort of 'preventative diplomacy' that the region desperately seems to need (Emmers and Tan 2011).

The capacity of the ARF actually to make a difference and address the region's increasingly pressing security challenges is important for both theoretical and practical reasons. After all, the institutionalization of security relations could have important effects and actually reconfigure, or at least ameliorate, inter-state tensions. Some observers think that ideas are important and the construction of particular security orders is not simply a manifestation of brute material preponderance. Amitav Acharya (2004), for example, has suggested that ideas about security are not simply mediated by local actors and 'grafted' on to local circumstances, but may in fact come to shape the behaviour of major, extra-regional powers. Acharya suggests that the Americans' acceptance of ASEAN's and the ARF's norm of 'co-operative security' – which was based on a non-legalistic inclusiveness and rejection of deterrence-based security systems – is indicative of the way in which the less powerful Southeast Asian states were able to influence the behaviour of the hegemon. Given the low priority the USA has given to both ASEAN in particular and to multilateral institutions more generally, especially in the Bush era, it remains to be seen how binding these norms will be, especially at moments of crisis.

The great hope at the heart of ARF initiative was that China could not only be engaged, but that it might also be socialized into 'good' behaviour. While we should remember that, as we saw earlier, there are multiple, frequently competing interests at work in the construction of China's foreign policy, and that this is necessarily an elite-level process, there is evidence that 'China' is being socialized in precisely the way ASEAN desired. Johnston (2008: xiv) argues that 'there is considerable, if subtle, evidence of the socialization of Chinese diplomats, strategists, and analysts in certain counter-realpolitik norms and practices as a result of participation in these institutions'.

There seems to be an increasingly sophisticated recognition on the part of Chinese elites that multilateral institutions offer a way of consolidating their position, pursuing their interests, and reassuring a nervous neighbourhood about their long-term intentions (Beeson and Li 2012; Shambaugh 2013). Indeed, China's elites appeared to have undergone a profound shift in their thinking about regional and international relations, changes that extend beyond security issues and reflect some of the central assumptions about the nature of interdependence (Yahuda 1997).

The limits to socialization?

There are, however, some apparently non-negotiable issues that threaten to cloud this potentially bright picture and undermine the idea of China's 'peaceful rise' that has been cultivated so carefully by China's ruling elites (Buzan 2010; Zheng 2005). In addition to the territorial disputes that are attracting so much attention, the PRC continues to regard Taiwan as a 'renegade province', an internal matter, and sees its eventual reunification with the mainland as a core, non-negotiable goal of foreign policy. The principal reason for its routine citing as one of the key East Asian flashpoints is because 'China will not commit itself to rule out the use of force … and has the right to resort to any necessary means' (PRC 2000: 18). Though it has been argued plausibly that China is happy with the face-saving status quo and unlikely to act pre-emptively against an American-backed Taiwan (Swaine 2004), the unambiguous nature of the PRC's language, and the significance of the Taiwan issue in China itself, is grist to the mill for those in the USA who advocate the 'containment' of, rather than 'engagement' with, China.

Clearly, conflict over Taiwan cannot be ruled out. Miscalculation, misunderstanding, accident or – more likely, perhaps – ungovernable nationalism on the mainland (Gries 2004; Miles 2000–01), could all overturn 'rational' calculations of advantage and plunge the region into a potentially catastrophic conflict, with entirely unforeseeable consequences. The reality thus far, however, has been that China has shown an increasingly nuanced capacity to calculate its national interests and the best ways of pursuing them. In the continuing debate about the potentially pacifying impact of liberal interdependence, in the case of Taiwan, at least, there does seem to be increasingly persuasive evidence that economic links and market imperatives are bringing about a significant change in the bilateral relationship (Chan 2009). Indeed, noted China watcher Robert Ross suggests that the extensive nature of the economic interdependence between Taiwan and the mainland, and the scale of Taiwanese investment in the PRC mean that 'Taiwan's business community has become what Hirschman called a "commercial fifth column"'

(Ross 2006: 386). Other observers are far less sanguine and argue that nothing less than full control of Taiwan will satisfy the leaders of the PRC because of it geopolitical importance. Robert Kaplan, for example, argues that the return of Taiwan is central to the ambition of escaping from the confines of geography and allowing China to project its growing naval power outwards (Kaplan 2012: 217).

One important test of China's ability to play the sort of 'responsible stakeholder' role that Robert Zoelick (2005) famously asked for, will be its ability or even willingness to play a constructive role on the Korean peninsula. Of all the world's potential flashpoints, Korea has always looked potentially the most combustible and unpredictable – a reputation the recent brinkmanship of North Korea's young leader Kim Jong-un has only reinforced. China's record and motivations towards North Korea are mixed and demonstrate both the advances it has made, but also the difficulties it has experienced in becoming an effective international actor. On the one hand, China has been a key player in, and driver of, the 'Six Party Talks' that were intended to at least create the conditions for dialogue between parties, if not actually achieve a long-term resolution of the underlying problems (see Haggard and Noland 2009).[5] On the other hand, China continues to support an increasingly erratic, unpredictable and morally indefensible regime. Plainly, China is concerned about the prospect of a disorderly collapse of its neighbour that might trigger an outpouring of refugees, not to mention the creation of a formidable new power on its doorstep in the form of a unified Korea. And yet even prominent domestic commentators are beginning to break ranks and call for China finally to abandon North Korea because its strategic rationale is outdated and damaging (Deng 2013).

A number of features of the Korean situation merit emphasis. First, the sort of American unilateralism and willingness to use military strength that was so characteristic of the Bush era have made it far less likely that the Democratic People's Republic of Korea (DPRK) will want to give up its nuclear capability. This is not to defend or justify DPRK policy or the regime itself, simply to point out the non-productive nature of American policy, and the reality that the North has pursued the development of nuclear weapons as a way of ensuring its own survival (Pritchard 2007). Given the potential importance of distinct national experiences and strategic cultures noted in the previous chapter, the DPRK's traumatic recent history and its reliance on the aggressive use of military force has tended to reinforce its pursuit of strategic autarky. A second point to consider, therefore, is whether the complex clash of identities and goals that shapes both the behaviour of the North and the response of the USA (Bleiker 2005; Kang 2009) is likely to be influenced by the application of force alone. This question assumes even greater importance in the light of the much discussed recent recalibration of American strategic policy.

The pivot to Asia

While this book is concerned primarily with East Asia, one of the most prominent features of the region's development – especially in the period since the Second World War – has been the influence of American power. The impact of 'American hegemony' was on display most visibly during the Cold War, when the idea of 'East Asia' was restricted to a geographical signifier. But American power continues to influence the region's evolution, especially in the strategic sphere. Nothing better captures the continuing significance of the USA's geopolitical concerns and influence than the so-called 'pivot to Asia' that President Obama (2011) announced during a visit to Australia – arguably the USA's most dependable ally in the wider Asia-Pacific region.

The decision to 'pivot' back to Asia marks an important moment in American foreign-policy-making. In some ways, of course, the USA has never 'left' the region: American troops have remained in South Korea and Japan, and its navy has access to places such as Singapore and, of course, Australia. What is arguably most significant about the recent statements by President Obama and Hillary Clinton (2011) is that they felt compelled to make them in the first place. The perception was that, not only was China a newly assertive potential peer competitor in the Asia-Pacific, but the USA had been neglecting the region while being preoccupied with seemingly interminable conflicts in the Middle East. For the Obama administration, the obvious economic importance of East Asia, which is explored in later chapters, was being reinforced by a renewed strategic salience. American policy-makers were keen to ensure that had a say in shaping the increasingly important region's future. As Hillary Clinton (2011) put it:

> At a time when the region is building a more mature security and economic architecture to promote stability and prosperity, U.S. commitment there is essential. It will help build that architecture and pay dividends for continued American leadership well into this century, just as our post-World War II commitment to building a comprehensive and lasting transatlantic network of institutions and relationships has paid off many times over – and continues to do so. The time has come for the United States to make similar investments as a Pacific power.

A number of points are worth highlighting here. First, American policy-makers clearly still believe that, not only is the USA not in decline, but they still have the capacity to determine the course of political, economic and strategic development in the broadly conceived region of which East Asia is a part, as they did in Europe. Second, America's overt leadership is a necessary part of this process. As we shall see when we look more closely at the evolution of regional institutions in East Asia, there was a moment when it seemed that the USA would be frozen out of some of the more important emerging forums. Now, however, the picture looks rather different. As a result largely of China's rather inept diplomacy and bullying approach to regional territorial disputes, many of the region's smaller powers are looking to shore up or develop closer ties with the USA. Strikingly, it is not just the 'usual suspects' such as Japan, Australia and the Philippines that are moving ever closer to the USA. On the contrary, so unnerved have many of the region's states been by China's behaviour that even Vietnam, with which the USA fought a long and bloody war less than 40 years ago, is exploring the possibility of developing closer strategic ties with the United States (Whitlock 2012).

While Obama is an avowed multilateralist, the 'pivot' to Asia looks to many like an expression of traditional great power politics in which the focus is primarily on conventional strategic balancing and 'containing' China's influence, if not its rise (Ross 2012). This is certainly the way American policy has been viewed in China (Swaine 2012). There are a number of questions to ask in the context of a discussion of regional security. First, what impact is such a strategy likely to have, even if it is successful? Indeed, how would the success of such a strategy be measured, even if we accept at face value that the intention is to stabilize the region rather an attempt to contain China?

For all the attention given to grand strategic objectives in the USA (and China too, for that matter), it is worth considering whether policy goals of the 'great powers' are either feasible or appropriate. Such a question might seem easy to answer in the case of China's rather implausible territorial claims and the heavy-handed, counter-productive manner in which it has gone about pursuing them. But we might also ask the same sorts of questions of the USA: does the region really need the sort of geostrategic maneuvering that seems more reminiscent of the Cold War rather than the beginning of the twenty-first century? It is important to remember that for all the country's remarkable recent economic development, many of China's people are comparatively impoverished and their lives remain relatively insecure; and much the same could be said about many of China's neighbours. To conclude our discussion, therefore, it is worth considering some of the 'new' security issues that are arguably a more appropriate and pressing part of any putative regional security agenda.

The emergence of 'new' security issues

Whether we should consider the 'new' security agenda as a regional or a domestic issue is a moot point: all have an international aspect, but all also have profound domestic consequences, highlighting the inherently arbitrary and imprecise nature of the domestic–international interface. Nevertheless, what we can say is that for all the attention that is given to high-profile issues such as Taiwan, North Korea and the South China Sea, the reality is that the most likely long-term threats to East Asian security come not from the possibility of traditional interstate conflict, but from a new array of transnational issues that transcend national borders and may be beyond the control of individual states. At one level this has triggered an overdue debate about the very nature of 'security' in the broadly conceived Asia-Pacific area, and a welcome refocusing on human rather than state security as a result (see Burke and McDonald 2007; Newman 2010). At another level, however, the focus on the new security agenda serves as a powerful reminder of just how challenging and multifarious the new security issues are likely to be, and raises serious questions about the capacity of states in the region to manage them.

Alan Dupont (2001) has provided one of the most extensive surveys of the new security challenges and their possible impact on East Asia. Most fundamentally, the region's relentless population expansion and urbanization drives a series of interconnected environmental problems: soil erosion, deforestation, declining air quality, increasing water scarcity and the manifold consequences of rapid urbanization, to say nothing of a looming energy crisis that threatens to put a fundamental constraint on the region's prospects for continuing rapid economic development (Dent 2012; Elliott 2012; Jasparro and Taylor 2008; Roberts and Kanaley 2006). Even more problematical, some observers think it is inevitable that conflict over diminishing resources will be the trigger for future wars (Klare 2008).

Energy and environmental issues will be addressed in more detail in Chapter 12, as they have the capacity to derail the entire development-oriented East Asian project. At this stage, it is worth noting briefly other problems highlighted by Dupont, caused by unregulated population movements, people-smuggling and environmental refugees, as well as transnational crime, drug trafficking and the impact of AIDS and other possible pandemics. This is a formidable and intimidating list of problems that inspires little optimism about their easy resolution, especially in parts of Southeast Asia, where less effective structures of governance have been the historical norm (Haque 2007). Challenging though such problems may be, however, they highlight an enduring reality that conventional analyses of security relations generally neglect: 'transnational threats are primarily non-military in nature and constitute a broader set of security considerations relating to survival, resource allocation and the health of the planet. They are therefore unlikely to be resolved by military force or ameliorated by traditional security approaches' (Dupont 2001: 32). Many of the traditional analyses of East Asian security that remain preoccupied with the relative strength of rival militaries – an approach that continues to inform policy at the highest levels – generally fail to acknowledge the importance of either the underlying trends that Dupont and others have identified or the redundancy of military options. The key security threat posed to states such as Cambodia or Burma, for example, is not invasion by a foreign power – for what possible incentive could there be to do so? – but the disintegration and collapse in authority in what are already fragile states.

At its most dramatic this can lead to a process that Mary Kaldor (2001: 5) has described as 'more or less the reversal of the processes through which modern states evolved'. This internal fragmentation of the state and concomitant inability to govern is most pronounced in sub-Saharan Africa, a region dotted with 'failed' states, ineffective governance and consequently appalling economic development outcomes (Duffield 2002; Newman 2009). Ironically, parts of Africa cannot persuade foreign governments to become involved with their countries under any circumstances; and the fear of invasion is the least of their problems. While Southeast Asia is not in a similar position, and while it is rightly known for its highly impressive development outcomes, there are other threats that have the potential to place additional pressure on regional governments, and which may undermine both their legitimacy and their capacity to govern effectively.

One of the key challenges for the governments of Southeast Asia in particular comes from their association with the spread of terrorism across the region. The perceived need to combat terrorism was given particular prominence as a consequence of the American-led 'war on terror' that began as a consequence of the attacks of 11 September 2001 ('9/11'). Unfortunately, there was nothing new about the existence of insurrectionary movements in Southeast Asia. There have been long-running struggles with an assortment of independence movements, rebellions and separatists in the Philippines, Southern Thailand and Aceh (Chalk 2001). What distinguished the war on terror was the focus on Islamic terrorism, and the assumption that 'the West' was threatened by an implacable enemy bent on establishing a Muslim caliphate across Southeast Asia. Such fears already look overblown despite the continuing threat post by rebel groups and terrorists, in Thailand and the Philippines in particular. The effectiveness of the response in Indonesia has been especially striking (Emmers 2009).

But Indonesia also serves as a powerful reminder that the security challenges facing regional states are complex and unconventional. While Indonesia has little to fear from conventional military threats and has apparently even managed to get to grips with the threat of domestic terrorism, it is debateable whether these are the primary challenges about which policy-makers should be concerned. For a country with serious environmental problems, and a still rapidly expanding population with rising expectations, the principal challenge will be meeting the aspirations of its people in a sustainable manner. Much the same could be said for other major regional actors such as the Philippines, Vietnam or China, for that matter. Security discourse may still be externally focused, but some of its most tangible impacts are unrelentingly domestic.

Conclusion

At the very least, the growing strategic tensions within the region mean that the possibilities for effective security governance in East Asia look more problematic. Indeed, the construction of an East Asian 'security community', or a 'transnational region comprised of sovereign states whose people maintain dependable expectations of peaceful change' (Adler and Barnett 1998: 30), looks a fairly remote prospect at this stage. Even some of the most persuasive advocates of this possibility concede that such a community is 'nascent' at best (Acharya 2001: 208). Similarly, Buzan and Waever (2003: 177) argue that despite the increased importance of China at the heart of East Asia's intra-regional relations, unless and until China becomes democratic the development of a regional security community is simply not feasible. Such conclusions only serve to reinforce one of the underlying themes of this chapter: that national differences remain crucially important determinants of both domestic security arrangements and external relations. The distinct histories and patterns of social relations that distinguish East Asian nations will continue to delimit the range of possible relations within and between the countries of the region. To see whether such distinctive histories will indeed prove to be insurmountable barriers to greater regional co-operation, we need to look more closely at the political development of the countries of the region and at the prospects for change.

Chapter 6

Nationalism and Domestic Politics

East Asia has attracted most attention over recent decades because of its remarkable, and historically unprecedented, economic development. But before we explore how so many East Asian countries escaped from poverty quite as quickly as they did, we need to consider the political context within which this development occurred. It is one of the animating ideas of this entire volume that politics and economics are intimately linked. Economic governance implies the existence of an institutionalized political order in which arm's-length relationships can develop. The precise nature of such social relationships is generally determined by political contestation, even if their outcome is far from inevitable. There is no reason to suppose that East Asia (or anywhere else, for that matter), will inevitably reproduce the earlier European experience, despite the obvious advantages that many of the latter's institutional innovations conferred on the West (Morris 2010; North and Thomas 1973). On the contrary, the recent sub-optimal performance of most 'Western' economies and the resilience of their Asian counterparts has raised questions about precisely which part of the world might have the best institutions for economic development and 'good governance', leading some to suggest that a synthesis may be both possible and desirable (Berggruen and Gardels 2013).

Such debates and questions hover in the background to much of the discussion in this and subsequent chapters. But to begin to answer them, we need to look more closely at the actual practice of politics in the East Asian region. Although forces associated with globalization are undermining the simple domestic–international dyad, most politics remain local and often fiercely nationalistic. East Asia's historical association with very different forms of political rule, ones often characterized by authoritarianism and political repression, the protection of sovereignty, and the abuse of human rights, reinforce this point, and make claims about possible political convergence on a liberal democratic 'Western' model of more than academic interest (see most famously Fukuyama 1992; also Huntington 1991). Indeed, if the claims about the course of political development were accurate, then the very existence of East Asia's traditional political order and that of the political elites who have benefited from it would be in question. Given that political elites the world over are generally resistant to change that disadvantages them or threatens their power, we might expect such apparently ineluctable historical forces to be resisted vigorously. That is precisely what has happened in much of the region. And yet it is also clear that democratic forces are also making progress. Once again, there is no single 'East Asian model' or experience. There are, however, some important continuities and commonalities that distinguish the region, which could conceivably serve as the basis for a common approach to regional integration. At the very least, East Asia's national political structures and traditions will delimit the range of possible regional outcomes effectively and thus merit detailed consideration (Brownlee 2007; Hicken and Kuhonta 2011).

While it is not possible to provide a single, all-encompassing explanation for East Asia's political heterogeneity, or even elaborate a consistent set of variables that accounts for specific national circumstances, it is possible to identify a number of key issues and forces that are common across the region. In this context, the legacy of history and the impact of the distinct set of geopolitical and strategic circumstances detailed in earlier chapters have exerted a powerful influence across East Asia. More recently, individual countries are attempting to accommodate the challenges of 'globalization' and the array of external pressures that are encouraging – and some times compelling – changes in the internal regulatory architectures of individual states and the sociopolitical milieus within which they are embedded (Jayasuriya 2001). Economic development and integration are reconfiguring domestic class structures and political relationships in unpredictable ways that defy easy generalization, but reflect the particular history of each country and the manner in which it has responded to, and articulated with, the wider international system (Beeson 2012). As we shall see in this chapter and those that follow, the success of this adaptation depends in large part on the 'strength'[1] of the state and the kinds of capacities discussed in Chapter 1. There is a variety of ways of responding to the interconnected challenges of internal transformation and external pressure.

The primary concern of this chapter is with the internal political changes and accommodations found in East Asian polities. Consequently, it surveys the different political structures found in the region, which run the gamut from genuine democracy to military dictatorship, with various forms of authoritarianism and 'semi-democracy' in between. It also explains the specific circumstances that have made authoritarian rule such a common part of East Asia's collective history, and why nationalism continues to exert such a powerful appeal despite the emergence of apparently universal pressures for change and emancipation. Political repression has left a powerful legacy, and as a result civil society in much of East Asia remains underdeveloped (Majid 2010). Even where civil society has developed in countries such as the Philippines, this is no guarantee of either good governance or immunity from military takeovers (Beeson and Bellamy 2008). Even global forces are filtered through domestic institutions and may not have the impact we might expect.

This chapter is the first part of a longer discussion of the political economy of the region. While political and economic forces are deeply interconnected and cannot be understood in isolation from each other (Underhill 2001), for the sake of convenience I shall examine initially some of the more formal expressions of political activity across the region, before showing in the next chapter how this has affected national patterns of governance and economic development. Consequently, after examining theoretical claims about the nature of democratization, globalization and their potential impact on authoritarianism, I explain the particular circumstances that have led to the wide variety of political outcomes across the region. I do this initially by considering Japan and the countries of Northeast Asia, followed by Southeast Asia. China is discussed separately and more fully in Chapter 8, because of its growing importance as a regional actor and potential role model.

East Asia's democratic moment?

Before looking at specific East Asian experiences, it is worth putting these general developments into their historical and theoretical context. It should be emphasized at the outset that much of 'our' thinking about the prospects for East Asia, and the type of political and economic trajectory it *ought* to follow, is a consequence of the bias of Eurocentrism (Hamilton 1994; Hobson 2007). Because the West has come to dominate much of the rest of the world through imperialism – be it the older economic variety or the more recent cultural version – it becomes easy to believe that this is the 'natural' order of things and that no other outcomes were (or are) possible. This was certainly implicit in the writings of the so-called 'modernization' theorists who were so influential during the Cold War period (Latham 2000). And yet, it is plain that there is a good deal of resistance to the some of the most pervasive and insidious expressions of globalization (Barber 2001). More pertinently for the purposes of this chapter, there are real doubts about how durable the current 'wave' of democratic expansion is actually likely to be (Diamond 2008a). Moreover, it is not at all clear that there is only one way of responding to global forces politically or in policy terms (Heilmann and Schulte-Kulkmann 2011). The questions we need to consider in this chapter are whether the very diverse political regimes that are found across the region are likely to persist in the face of global pressures, and whether they might provide fundamental obstacles to more regionally based relationships if they do.

The temptation to view the East Asian experience through Western lenses may be strong, but it needs to be resisted. It is important to remember that 'the rise of the West', and the distinctive political practices, belief systems and economic relationships it generated were products of a very specific set of historical circumstances (Hall 1986; Spruyt 1994; Tilly 1990). The transformation of social relations that the development of capitalism began in Western Europe was not replicated in what was then a more stable China or other parts of Asia until much later (Sidel 2008). This is important to keep in mind, because the transformation in European social structures associated with the rise of a domestic capitalist classes, and in the kinds of concomitant changes in the distribution of political power that the rising classes demanded, simply did not happen in the same way in Asia. In terms of political development this was a double blow: not only did much of Asia not experience the kinds of improvements in living standards and technological development that occurred in much of the West, but they did not receive the same impetus for political emancipation and democratization either. This is crucial, because the development of more 'progressive', economically dynamic class structures appears to be one of the prerequisites for any move towards more democratic political practices (Rueschemeyer *et al.* 1992).

One of the crucial factors that came to distinguish parts of Europe, which stands in sharp contrast to the East Asian experience, is what Held (1995: 69) calls the 'reciprocity of power'. The growing dependence of national governments on co-operative subject populations brought about a long-term change in state–society relations, change that was consolidated by the growing legitimacy of emerging nation-states, ultimately entrenched in systems of representative democracy, and codified in new regulatory architectures. In Western Europe's case, the accommodation between economic and social forces has proved to be remarkably durable, adaptive and capable of encompassing significant variations on the overall theme of capitalist democracy (Boyer and Hollingsworth 1997; Jessop 2003). The ubiquity of the capitalist-democratic form in Western Europe has evidently also made the development of regional co-operation much easier. This resilience, and the historical tendency for the capitalist state to supplant all rivals, is undoubtedly a major reason why observers such as Fukuyama have claimed that there is a certain inevitability about the technically superior form of Western political organization sweeping all before it. Yet not only is the ascendancy of the state not as assured as was once thought, but the associated triumph of democracy – at least, a democracy worthy of the name[2] – is even more uncertain.

Again, it is important to emphasize how unexpected and counter-intuitive all this is. The state has rightly come to be seen as the dominant political institution of the modern period, and its association with economic development has underpinned expectations about the course of political reform. However, while economic development may make the transition to democratic patterns of government more likely, in that it has the capacity to encourage the growth of new class forces that may undermine non-democratic or authoritarian forms of rule and demand greater emancipation (Huntington 1991: 72), this does not guarantee political reform. On the contrary, not only are some forms of non-democratic, authoritarian rule actually associated positively with economic development (Bertrand 1998; Leftwich 2000), but there is no necessary link between democracy and development either (Przeworski *et al.* 2000: 271). Moreover, it has been argued that the emergent middle classes of East Asia, which might be expected to demand greater political rights, may be prepared to trade them off for more economic development and security (Jones 1998). What we can say is that forms of corporatism, characterized by state bureaucratic domination, monopolistic political representation, ideologically exclusive executive authorities, and anti-liberal, authoritarian or mercantilist states (Schmitter 1979: 22), have been surprisingly prominent across much of East Asia.

These are issues that need to be explored by looking at the very different accommodations that have been arrived at in East Asia. Before doing so, however, it is possible to make a few generalizations that will help to make sense of the ensuing discussion. First, though the path to democracy may still be more uncertain and varied than some of the Fukuyama-esque analyses might have us believe, there does seem to be strong evidence to suggest that if the transition is made, 'democracy is almost certain to survive in countries with per capita incomes above [US]\$4,000' (Przeworski *et al.* 2000: 273). This matters because many of the countries of the region – including large parts of China – have either achieved such income levels, or have them in sight. Consequently, the prospects for democratic consolidation, all other things being equal, look good if the initial hurdle of transition can be negotiated safely (Diamond 2008b; Lind 2011). The second point to emphasize is that, while stable growth and democratic consolidation may have the potential to become a virtuous circle, its realization 'depends on the development of political institutions that can effectively mediate policy debates and coordinate relations among contending social and economic interests' (Haggard and Kaufman 1995: 335). However, one potential obstacle must be negotiated in this process: the enduring importance of nationalism.

That nationalism is such a powerful force in East Asia, and has the capacity to influence the course of development there should not surprise us. After all, nationalism was a central part of the earlier European experience and an essential part of the nation-state coupling in particular and the dominance of Europe more generally (Hobsbawm 1987). Indeed, nationalism has been considered to be one of the essential qualities of European-style modernity and a prerequisite for the development of industrial economies and societies (Gellner 1983). While the importance of nationalism and the purposes to which it has been put vary across the region, for some countries – Indonesia is perhaps the most important exemplar – it potentially offered the glue with which to bind together the disparate and arbitrary remnants of the Dutch empire. As Anderson (1983: 12) observed: 'It is the magic of nationalism to turn chance into destiny.' Put more prosaically in the language of social science, nationalism provided what Giddens (1985: 219) called the 'cultural sensibility of sovereignty'. In other words, if the emergent independent states of Southeast Asia – and the liberated, reconstituted states of Northeast Asia for that matter – were to amount to more than lines on a map and notional claims to jurisdictional authority, then their leaders needed the support of the populations they claimed to represent and the populations needed to recognize themselves as part of the same collectivity.

When seen in this light, it becomes easier to understand why so many of East Asia's political elites have been preoccupied with developing national myths, protecting sovereignty and generally resisting external intrusion: the nation-state was often a fragile entity, but one that, if realized successfully, held out the prospect of more effective governance and control within politically demarcated boundaries – however arbitrary, contested and contingent their origins might be (Tilly 1990). The great paradox for East Asia is that, at the very moment when it might be expected that nationalism would come into its own, the entire nationalist project is being undermined by global processes that are eroding 'national' borders and bringing the authority and competence of national governments into question (Cerny 1999). Moreover, in many parts of the world there is a growing tension between the national identities established in the original nation-building period, and the sorts of local and even transnational identities that have become more prominent or reconstituted by processes associated with globalization (Ariely 2012). At a moment when – in much of the trail-blazing West, at least – individual identities are becoming much more contingent, reflexive and detached from national boundaries, there are important questions to be asked about the future of nationalism and even its possible mutation into 'supra-nationalism' (see Smith 1998) These are questions that are central to the future of East Asia and its constituent parts. Before considering them, however, it is necessary to look back at the evolution of the various political regimes in the region.

Japan and Northeast Asia

This section examines the political development of Japan, the two Koreas and Taiwan. Most attention is given to Japan, partly because it is one of East Asia's unambiguous major powers, but also because it has played such a central role in shaping the overall region's post-war development. Japan is especially important as an exemplar of a highly successful Asian state and a capitalist one at that: whatever problems Japan might have experienced recently in attempting to adjust to competing regional and global pressures, the fact remains that it pioneered a very distinctive way of accelerating the developmental process. The nature of Japan's early successes and its more recent problems is in part a reflection of its political system and the competence of its political class.

The riddle of Japan

Even by East Asia's remarkably diverse standards, Japan is something of an anomaly. On the one hand, it is the region's most enduring democracy and frequently cited as proof that 'Western' forms of democratic rule can be transplanted successfully to other parts of the world. Even though the formal mechanisms of democracy have been established in Japan, it is a fairly unusual variant. Not only has Japanese democracy been associated with a form of what Johnson (1987) called 'soft authoritarianism', but it has also been dominated by the Liberal Democratic Party (LDP) in the period since the Second World War. Those analysts enamoured of culturalist explanations of what Pye (1985: ch. 6) called the 'riddle of Japan' attribute its distinctive political development to factors such as the influence of Confucianism, and 'traditional' social values based on merit, respect, filial piety and so on. There are, however, some rather more tangible, specific and mundane explanations for Japan's distinctive patterns of political life, reasons that have as much to do with war and peace, and the familiar staples of interest-driven politics, as they do with anything distinctly 'Asian'.

A number of specific events helped to give a particular shape to Japan's post-war politics. Most decisive, of course, was that Japan not only lost a major war, but lost it to the United States (Johnson 1999). That Japan might have lost enthusiasm for militarism and been amenable to a new national paradigm was understandable, given that over 2 million Japanese were killed during the Second World War and their country was devastated economically (Katzenstein 1996). What was equally important, though, was America's vision of itself as an instrument of political emancipation (Smith 1994) – something that allowed America's forces to adopt a paternalistic role once Japan had been occupied peacefully

(Dower 1986: 305). That such attitudes were often racist and ill-informed did not make them any less effective. Significantly, the demilitarization and democratization of Japan were seen by the Americans as being deeply intertwined, with the latter guaranteeing the former. Equally significantly, in the early phases of this process, political change was 'fundamentally progressive' (Dower 1995: 166): even the Communist Party was legalized, and trade unions were allowed to organize freely.

And yet this pattern of political mobilization, openness and expanding civil society – which is what we might expect a genuine democracy to look like – could not survive in the bleak atmosphere of the Cold War and the geopolitical constraints it imposed. While the Americans had only limited success in modifying Japan's bureaucratic and corporate structures, they were far more effective in crushing Japan's post-war labour militancy. The significance of this process should not be underestimated for the eventual triumph of Japan's distinctive, highly co-operative managerial style of labour relations is anything but a 'natural' expression of underlying social harmony (Gordon 1993). Likewise, the eventual course of Japanese politics and its crystallization into its distinctive one-party dominance owes much to the overarching imperatives of this period.

At a formal level, the most significant changes in post-war Japan revolved around the imposition of the so-called 'peace constitution', and the shift of sovereign power from the emperor to Japan's parliament, the Diet. The intention was to create a Westminster-style political structure in which executive power would reside with the prime minister and Cabinet. The other goals of the reforms were to broaden participation in the political process by allowing women to vote and curbing the power of big business and rural landlords. There were also rather ineffectual attempts at bureaucratic reorganization and decentralization, but as far as the formal trappings of democratic rule were concerned, Japan experienced a major post-war makeover (see Stockwin 1999).

At the same time as these changes to the formal structure of the political system were being enacted, major developments were occurring within Japan's political parties. In the first decade after the war, Japan experienced a number of short-lived coalition governments between socialists and conservatives. Predictably enough, these coalitions proved to be unstable. In 1955, in one of the defining moments of Japan's post-war political history, the various conservative parties came together to form the LDP. It has hardly been out of office ever since. The key to the LDP's dominance has been its ability to attract support from big business, the agricultural sector and Japan's expanding urban middle class on the one hand, and skilfully to manage and accommodate internal disagreements, on the other. The other factor that consolidated the position of the LDP was American support for the party over its Soviet-oriented socialist opponent, the Japan Socialist Party (JSP). Again, the Cold War context proved pivotal.

An important aspect of the LDP's long-running domination of Japanese politics has been its ability to accommodate internal differences. This is primarily because internal divisions are non-ideological, but revolve around power struggles between different factions within the LDP itself (Eccleston 1995). The absence of internal ideological competition mirrored a wider social consensus that emerged during the 1960s: the primary objective of the government and the people more generally, for that matter, was an unrelenting focus on economic growth. This allowed key bureaucratic agencies to take responsibility for planning Japan's economic renaissance, as we shall see in the next chapter. It also consolidated a basic division of labour among Japan's elites and further encouraged the growth of factional politics within what was effectively a form of one-party rule. This helps to explain some other novel features of Japanese politics.

One of the most striking aspects of Japan's post-war political system is not just the very prominent role assumed by unelected officials within the bureaucracy, but also the comparatively uninfluential role of the political class that is notionally in charge. For most of the post-war period, Japan's political class simply has not played anything like the same sort of active, policy-making and implementing role that similar groups have elsewhere. There are signs. however, that after many false starts this relationship is changing, and the key institutional actors such as the prime minister may be acquiring the sort of power enjoyed by their counterparts in the West. However, this is a relatively recent development, and for most of Japan's post-war history things were very different. In the so-called 'iron triangle', a mutually rewarding division of labour and responsibility was maintained between the bureaucracy, professional politicians and business elites (van Wolferen 1989).

If one individual epitomizes much that is unique about Japan's post-war politics, it is Kakuei Tanaka, who, despite being dogged by corruption scandals throughout his career, and being forced to resign the prime-ministership in 1974 after being accused (and ultimately convicted) of taking bribes from the American Lockheed Corporation, still exerted a powerful influence over the LDP as a 'shadow shogun'. He was able to do this by making his own faction the largest in the LDP and ensuring that it 'became impossible for anyone to become prime minister without the support of the Tanaka faction' (Curtis 1999: 82). Tanaka was the quintessential kingmaker to whom any prime minister was beholden, and who could insist on control of key cabinet posts in proportion with the strength of his faction. Tanaka was able to influence the selection of perspective LDP candidates, something that ensured their loyalty was to him personally, rather than to the LDP as a whole (Schlesinger 1999). The cost of competing in Japan's complex electoral system meant that such ties were often reinforced through the direct distribution of resources. The consequence of this, of course, was to entrench the role and importance of so-called 'money politics'.[3]

The great paradox the Japanese case reveals is that corrupt politicians are not necessarily obstacles to development, but neither is it clear whether more competent ones will be able to institute needed reforms. The rapid and continual change in Japan's political leadership and the damaged reputation of the bureaucracy have combined to undermine public confidence in governments of all persuasions. The recent rejection of the Democratic Party of Japan and the re-election of the LDP led by a recycled leader (Shinzo Abe) with a record of failure are indications of the parlous state of Japanese politics. More worryingly for Japan's neighbours, perhaps, is the stridently nationalistic platform upon which Abe returned to power (Soble 2013). Such notionally domestic changes assume greater significance when we consider some of the challenges facing Japan's Northeast Asian neighbours, and in Korea's case, a similarly untested but nationalistic leader (Piling 2012).

Korea and Taiwan

The first point to make about both Korea and Taiwan is that, like Japan, the political histories of both countries directly reflect the wider geopolitical context of which they are a part. Both countries are divided, either internally in Korea's case, or from the larger entity of which it was originally a part, in Taiwan's. The consequences for their respective political development and structures have been profound and cannot be understood without reference to this wider historical legacy. As we saw in earlier chapters, both countries owe their existence – in their current forms, at least – to struggles that occurred more than half a century ago. The division of Korea in particular reflects an initial post-war superpower compromise consolidated by the Korean War. The most enduring consequences of this period have been both the tragic, anachronistic division of Korea itself, and the creation of the world's last Stalinist outpost. North Korea – the Democratic People's Republic of Korea (DPRK) – is, indeed, so bizarre, sui generis and destabilizing that it is as well to deal with it first.

The DPRK's principal significance – other than being a unique comparative case study for social scientists – is strategic. Because the

DPRK has nuclear weapons, because its very existence poses a continuing threat to the South, and because it has the capacity to plunge the region into a major conflict with unforeseeable but inevitably catastrophic consequences, we need to take it seriously and try to understand it. The defining characteristic of the DPRK is that it has become a family dynasty, perpetuating a style of charismatic, strong-man leadership that has recently been disappearing from much of East Asia. The current leader, Kim Jong-un, is an unimpressive and untested figure, like his father before him – both inheriting the leadership on his father's death. The insular, opaque nature of the regime means that it is difficult to know quite how the DPRK operates, but what we can say is that the Kim dynasty dominates every aspect of life in the North, centralizing power in a form of what Bruce Cumings (1997: 399) describes as 'conservative corporatism', and establishing a personality cult the like of which has rarely been seen (Suh 1988).

Initially, Kim Jong-un's grandfather, Kim Il-sung (in power 1948–1994), was a creature of the Soviets. It is indicative of his views that Khrushchev's de-Stalinization of the Soviet Union prompted a split with the DPRK's former sponsors and a closer alignment with China. Kim Il-sung developed the ideology of *chuch'e* or self-reliance, which continues to exert an influence to this day, with disastrous consequences for the North's economy. While Kim Il-sung consolidated his control through the apparatus of the workers' party, it is, as Chung (1986: 35) points out, 'more a personalised system than a communist state'. His ideology drew on older, romanticized, traditions to create a regime in which power radiated outwards in concentric circles (Cumings 2004: 124). Thus far, the dynasty that Kim Il-sung established has proved to be remarkably durable, and yet this may prove to be an illusory and brittle strength might may be shattered very rapidly, with potentially dramatic consequences for its neighbours (Cha 2012).

No country feels this uncertainty and insecurity more acutely than its neighbour to the south – the Republic of Korea (ROK). Sandwiched between Japan and China, Korea has found itself subject to continual long-term pressures from its more powerful neighbours. When combined with the later traumas of civil war, the seemingly never-ending Cold War, foreign occupation, and the social upheaval caused by rapid industrialization, it is perhaps unsurprising that the history of South Korea, along with North Korea, has been marked by fairly extreme politics of one sort or another. The fact that for much of the South's post-war history this should have taken the form of repressive authoritarian rule is also not surprising. After all, the ROK was attempting to achieve stability and development in unpromising conditions, by building on the foundation of Japanese authoritarianism and military rule established during the colonial period (Kohli 2004). Not only did this mean 'salvation' for those who had collaborated with the Japanese, but it also marked a systematic attempt to 'depoliticise civil society, and to destroy the social foundations on which a unified nation-state could be established' (Choi 1995: 18).

That the first leader of the new Republic of Korea – Syngman Rhee – was an authoritarian who also used Japan's coercive apparatus to maintain control, was consequently an entirely predictable artefact of the emerging Cold War. The Americans wanted to establish strong, anti-communist leaders across the Third World (Gaddis 1982), and Rhee's election was in keeping with this goal. Indeed, in some ways the Korean War, for all its trauma, was instrumental in shoring up Rhee's position as it effectively eliminated leftist opposition in the South, while anti-communism provide the ideological basis for the First Republic established in the war's aftermath. The state became the key to stabilizing the regime and driving development, but it was a state that was established in very different circumstances and much more rapidly than had been the case in Europe, or even Japan. Thus, from the outset, the ROK was a product of American hegemony and was defined in opposition to the 'communist' regime in the North (Woo 1991).

In a significant harbinger of future social struggles, however, Rhee's downfall in 1960 came about as a consequence of student unrest and mounting opposition to his regime in a nascent civil society. Given that the overwhelming majority of the South's population was still involved in agriculture, this development is all the more remarkable. But the limited extent of the ROK's civil society at this time makes it less surprising that the initial foray into democratic rule proved short-lived, and a military coup installed a new authoritarian leader, Park Chung-hee (whose daughter, Park Geun-hye, is the current president). The distinctive features that came to characterize South Korea throughout the 1960s and 1970s – authoritarianism, political repression, and state-led developmentalism – were laid down at this time. Crucially, land reform was undertaken that effectively broke up the old class structures and allowed new economic and eventually political structures to emerge. By the mid-1970s, the bulk of the population had moved off the land into the cities, and become part of the emerging export-oriented industrial economy. In short, the class structure of the ROK rapidly evolved, creating the basis for a general expansion of civil society and the often violent labour struggles that became such a high-profile part of its subsequent development.

Evidence of this potential was seen following Park Chung-hee's assassination in 1979 and the subsequent imposition of martial law, when labour unrest became even more widespread and intense. Significantly, opposition to the government of Chun Doo-hwan (leader from 1979–88), which was installed by another military coup, included students, workers, religious groups, and the expanding 'middle class' of urban professionals. This coalition of forces engineered a major social uprising in 1987, which eventually brought down the Chun government. The capacity of the next government, of Roh Tae-woo, to deal with the underlying social unrest was made more complex by the emergence of a reunification movement in 1988, but somewhat easier by the 'demobilization' of the democracy movement itself. The middle-class pro-democracy forces believed they had achieved their principal goal and transformed the formal political structures of South Korea. However, despite the fact that the ROK adopted all the trappings of democracy, and the military appeared to have relinquished its interventionist role in Korean politics, many considered that the post-1987 changes were 'only cosmetic' (Chin 2003: 204).

Nevertheless, there have been a number of elections in the intervening period and a peaceful transfer of power from one democratically elected civilian president to another. The transfer of power between competing elites in the 1990s is a substantial indicator of the durability of democratic forms in the ROK. Paradoxically, however, although most observers agree that the formal trappings of democratic rule appear to be firmly established and that alternatives are increasingly unthinkable, there is some doubt about the degree to which individual Koreans have internalized the norms that go with democratic processes (Shin *et al.* 2003). Historically, there has been a much higher tolerance of 'corruption' in the ROK, and an expectation that politicians will use their office to enrich themselves personally (Morriss 1997). Legitimacy in this context is much more about performance than probity (Gilley 2009).

South Korea's political development provides a useful counterpoint to Taiwan's: in South Korea, organized labour – despite its militancy and high profile – has been excluded from what Buchanan and Nicholls (2003) consider its corporatist governance structures. In Taiwan, by contrast, organized labour has been closely aligned with the state and is as a consequence much less of an independent political force. That labour would effectively be nullified as an independent political force, and that other forms of civil society might be subdued is not surprising, given Taiwan's recent history. It needs to be remembered that the modern Taiwan was established by the defeated Kuomintang (KMT), Nationalist forces under Chiang Kai-shek. The manner in which the 1.5 million new arrivals established their hegemony over the 7 million-strong indigenous population established a pattern of rule that was to endure for decades: the KMT supplanted Japanese officials, brutally subdued local opposition to KMT rule and created a socially insulated corporatist-style state apparatus that was unrepresentative but enjoyed significant capacity. Significantly, the new regime was able to initiate major land reform that removed a potentially obstructive landlord class. When combined with the incorporation of labour, as noted above, the 'authoritarian corporatist'[4] governments of the KMT were able to dominate the policy-making process and institute the sorts of economic initiatives discussed in more detail in the next chapter.

For all the remarkable success of Taiwan's economic development, though, many indigenous Taiwanese regarded mainlander rule as 'a foreign imposition akin to colonial domination' (Alagappa 2001: 12). For the first four decades of KMT rule, it was possible to neutralize the pursuit of democratic reform because of the overall geopolitical context: the threat of invasion by the mainland gave the nationalist leadership a convenient rationale for authoritarian rule and the privileging of national security. However, when the larger international climate began to change in the 1980s political reform became more feasible, if not inescapable. Decades of rapid regional expansion, the increased stability it seemed to generate, and a more generalized international movement towards democratization, all helped to create the preconditions for change. Even for Taiwan's authoritarian leadership, democratic reform was potentially attractive as it gave an increasingly internationally isolated Taiwan a way of positioning itself as a beacon of regional democracy in contrast to the autocratic mainland (Lu 1991). The birth of the Democratic Progressive Party (DPP) in 1986 was a tangible manifestation of the democratizing impulse.

However, it was not until the opposition actually won an election and there was a handover of power by the entrenched KMT elite that public confidence in the substance as well as the form of democracy became stronger. When long-time KMT president Lee Teng-hui's nominated successor, Lien Chan, was defeated by DPP challenger Chen Shui-bian in 2000, it represented something of an 'electoral earthquake' that consolidated democratic rule and gelled with the wider international climate (Diamond 2001). The KMT's defeat can be attributed to what Diamond calls its 'moral and political exhaustion': after so long in office, the growth of corruption and factionalism had become an electoral liability. However, the DPP's authority was subsequently undermined by a corruption scandal revolving around Chen that culminated in his imprisonment and the eventual return to power of the KMT under the leadership of Ma Ying-jeou. Two points are worth emphasizing here: first, for all its tribulations, democracy has endured in Taiwan; and, second, the KMT's advocacy of closer ties with the mainland has not been an electoral disaster, despite the sensitivity many feel about maintaining independence from the PRC (Kastner 2009).

Paradoxically, therefore, Taiwan is both important and marginal when thinking about the impact of domestic political conditions on regional development. On the one hand, Taiwan is generally conspicuously absent from major regional and global forums such as the United Nations and – in a regional context – the emergent ASEAN+3 process. Deference to the increasingly powerful mainland has meant that the ranks of Taiwan's allies, especially those that are willing to express support for Taiwanese independence, have become remarkably thin. Even the USA, the avowed champion of democracy and free speech, has traditionally maintained a position of 'strategic ambiguity' regarding its intentions toward Taiwan and its status as an independent entity (see Tow 2001: 108). All sides prefer to maintain the polite fiction that Taiwan remains an 'internal' problem for the PRC that will be resolved at some point in the future. On the other hand, however, Taiwan's increased penchant for democracy and freedom of speech threatens to puncture this politically convenient, if somewhat farcical, arrangement by pursuing independence. In that case, Taiwan has the capacity not to simply make regional co-operation and confidence-building more difficult, but, as some analysts think, it may destabilize the entire international system (Kaplan 2012).

Consequently, while it is difficult to see how the more independently minded Taiwanese will achieve their goal of independence, Taiwan's position highlights an issue with wider ramifications: regional and extra-regional powers will continue to turn a blind eye to authoritarian regimes, human rights abuses and inter-state bullying, even if this means snubbing a genuinely democratic regime to do so. The relationship between external and internal pressure for political reform is a function of the overarching geopolitical context, something that also helps to explain the durability of authoritarianism and the distinctive patterns of political order in Southeast Asia.

Southeast Asia and the making of nations

Southeast Asia is synonymous with heterogeneity and this makes generalization difficult, if not foolhardy. And yet it is possible to identify historical patterns and commonalities which, if they do not entirely explain the course of subsequent political development, at least give us a sense of the parameters in which it occurred. The overwhelming common historical reality that – with the exception of Thailand – distinguished Southeast Asia, was that it consisted of newly independent states confronted by the dual challenges of national political consolidation and economic development. In such circumstances, when the very boundaries of nascent states were not always certain, and where the capacities of the emergent independent governments remained underdeveloped, it is hardly surprising that newly empowered elites across the region would turn to nationalism as the glue with which to bind frequently disparate communities together (Stockwell 1999; Tarling 1998).

The Second World War provided a decisive break with the colonial era. Not only were the Europeans encouraged to leave the region by increasingly effective independence movements in Indonesia, Burma and Vietnam, but they did so also at the urging of the USA. The geopolitical imperatives of the gathering Cold War meant that, from a US perspective, it was essential to cultivate pro-capitalist allies in Southeast Asia, lest they fall like so many dominoes to communist expansion (see Rotter 1987). While such assumptions reveal a remarkably unsophisticated grasp of both the diversity of regimes within Southeast Asia and the long-standing intra-regional rivalries that prevailed there, it did have one noteworthy effect: the USA was prepared to tolerate, and even to encourage, the development of 'strong-man' leaders if they were anti-communist. Even the somewhat erratic, independently minded Indonesian independence leader Sukarno was initially wooed by the USA as a potential bastion against communist expansion (McMahon 1999: 85).

Not surprisingly, therefore, the military has played an important historical role in a number of Southeast Asian countries, especially Indonesia, Burma, the Philippines, Thailand and, of course, Vietnam – a country that has spent much of its modern history fighting one external power or another. What is more surprising, perhaps, is that there has been a shift away from modes of governance dominated by strong-man leaders and/or the military, to ones in which some form of democratic rule appears to be consolidating. But while there are some general trends emerging, there are also significant continuing differences in the nature of political regimes across the region. It is worth spelling out briefly what these are in the most important and illuminating countries.

The democracies

That Indonesia and the Philippines should be considered to be Southeast Asia's most genuine democratic regimes is remarkable and rather surprising. Given their often traumatic histories, internal divisions, limited state capacities and prominent positions in the 'war on terror', the omens were not good. Indeed, Thailand's recent history and the continuing danger of military intervention serves as a salutary reminder that the process of democratic consolidation is fragile, unpredictable and without guarantees (Beeson 2008; Connors 2009).

Indonesia's newfound democratic status is especially noteworthy, given its history since independence. Both of the country's most important post-independence leaders – Sukarno and Suharto – put their own distinctive mark on Indonesian politics. Sukarno instituted 'guided democracy' in 1959 in response to domestic unrest. He also banned elections, suspended the constitution and consolidated his own pre-eminence in the process. The ostensible motivation for this was to achieve national stability, but in a familiar regional pattern, and the trampling of political liberty was justified with reference to Indonesian 'cultural values' (Vatikiotis 1996). It was a pattern of rule that was to become entrenched and be given unique expression by his successor, Suharto. The precise details of Sukarno's downfall in 1965 remain uncertain (see Cribb 1990), but it is clear that his increasingly erratic behaviour, his closeness to China and his support of Indonesia's domestic communist party, the PKI, made him a liability in the eyes of many. In contrast, Suharto's vehement anti-communism and antipathy towards China made him highly acceptable to the United States and its strategic and economic interests (Tanter 1990).

Suharto's 'New Order' established a form of authoritarian corporatism that became a more widespread part of East Asia's political landscape during the Cold War. The specific challenges of political consolidation and economic development in Indonesia were crystallized in the ideology of 'Pancasila'. The five principles of Pancasila were initially propounded by Sukarno,[5] but under Suharto they were turned into 'the basic credo to which all Indonesians had to adhere' (Liddle 1999: 40). While the People's Consultative Assembly had formal responsibility for electing the President,[6] and while the People's Representative Council has notional responsibility for authorizing the budget and legislation, under Suharto there was only the form and not the substance of popular control. Pancasila provided a theoretical justification for the rejection of Western-style political pluralism by appealing to an 'integralist or organicist stream of thought' (Elson 2001: 240). In other words, in a pattern that would distinguish much of Southeast Asia, Suharto justified political repression in the name of supposedly traditional Indonesian cultural values and practices. When reinforced by a military that the ex-soldier Suharto kept under close control, and a political party that dominated stage-managed electoral processes,[7] the New Order achieved a remarkable degree of ideological and social control in what was a new and developing country.

The other key qualities that distinguished the Suharto regime were his ability to 'personalize' control of the military (Elson 2001: 244), and to place himself – and eventually the rest of his family – at the centre of a dense network of political–business relationships. These relationships were central to the web of patronage-based connections that consolidated Suharto's power (Robison and Hadiz 2004: 43). The multifaceted domination of Indonesia by the New Order regime not only militated against the development of an independent civil society, but it also meant that the authority and legitimacy of the regime was fatally undermined by the East Asian economic crisis and its aftermath. Moreover, the collapse of the regime was sudden, unanticipated and left little in the way of effective alternative structures of governance and co-ordination. Two further points merit emphasis: first, the regime collapsed despite, and not because of, an effective, organized opposition (Elson 2001: 293). Second, in the absence of such an internal opposition, external, global forces in the shape of international controllers of mobile capital and the newly assertive international financial institutions (IFIs) created an irresistible economic and political momentum for change. The actual implementation of reform post-Suharto was nothing like as meaningful or wide-ranging as many outsiders had hoped, however (Walter 2008).

The ever more integrated international economy of which Indonesia is necessarily a part, and in which the IFIs continue to exert such influence, forms the increasingly influential environment within which Suharto's successors must operate (see Beeson 2006b). When added to the rising popular expectations that have accompanied the transition to democracy, it becomes easier to understand why governance has proved so difficult in Indonesia, and why there was initially a rapid turnover of leaders in the new democratic environment.[8] The sad irony is that, despite establishing successfully the mechanisms of democratic rule, they have not made the sprawling, ethnically diverse and economically underdeveloped archipelago any easier to govern. On the contrary, some of the neoliberal initiatives urged by external agencies, such as decentralization, for example, have actually exacerbated problems of central control and fuelled corruption in the provinces (Hadiz 2004a). Indeed, for all the accolades President Susilo Bambang Yudhoyono has been accorded for his influence in consolidating democracy and pursuing domestic threats to security, efforts to improve governance generally and reduce corruption in particular have been disappointing (Bellman and Barta 2012).

In this regard, the Philippines gets an even more mixed scorecard, despite being one country in Southeast Asia that ought to be democratic and in possession of a robust, independent civil society. After all, the Philippines was colonized by not just the most powerful country in the world, but also its most ardent champion of democracy. And yet the tragic paradox of the Philippines is that, while it may be democratic at present, its independent history has been punctuated by military coups and authoritarian rule. Indeed, the Philippines can lay claim to having had one of the most spectacularly corrupt, repressive and incompetent regimes in the whole of Asia. Adding a further layer of irony to this doleful picture is the fact that the American colonists must shoulder much of the blame. As Hutchcroft (1998: 26) pointed out in his definitive study of the Philippines' underwhelming development record, 'the legacy of US colonialism was considerable oligarchy building, but very little in the way of state building'. Put differently, the Americans' antipathy to the sort of 'strong' states that abounded elsewhere in the region meant that they paid little attention to establishing an effective state apparatus with which to oversee the developmental project following independence.

The Philippines' woeful economic performance is considered in more detail in the next chapter, but it is important to note that the enfeebled state the USA left behind was 'so lacking in autonomy from dominant economic interests that even the most basic regulation of capital is continuously frustrated' (Hutchcroft 1998: 15). The pivotal moment in independent Philippines history that entrenched and institutionalized this state of affairs was the declaration of martial law by Ferdinand Marcos in 1972. Prior to this, the Philippines was 'one of the last strongholds of civilian control over the military in the Third World' (Hernandez 1986: 262). It is all the more remarkable, then, that the reversion to a repressive, military-backed authoritarianism that occurred under Marcos should have happened in a former American colony. The reason the USA took an indulgent view of the Marcos dictatorship was the same as it was elsewhere: better a pro-capitalist dictator than even the most progressive, possibly even pro-American left-wing leader.[9] Whatever the overarching strategic rationale for this policy, the net effect was clear in the steady erosion of the Philippines' domestic political institutions, a centralization of power around the presidency, and an increasing reliance on coercion to maintain order (Doronila 1985).

And yet the coercive apparatus that underpinned the patterns of corruption, cronyism and patronage that were central to Marcos's rule, ultimately proved to be just as brittle in the Philippines as it had in Indonesia. At one level, the outbreak of 'people power' that swept Marcos from office in 1986 was a remarkable expression of popular discontent and capacity for social mobilization. At another level, however, the installation of Corazon Aquino as the new president was not a decisive break with the past. On the contrary, Aquino was 'a member of one of the wealthiest and most powerful dynasties within the Filipino oligarchy' (Anderson 1988: 3). The diverse coalition of forces that rallied behind Aquino following the murder of her husband, Benigno, in 1983 began to unravel when she became president. Given the nature of the problems she faced – dealing with internal insurrection movements, attempting to implement land reform, keeping the military on-side and under control, to say nothing of finally kick-starting development in the Philippines – it is perhaps not surprising that the high hopes that accompanied her accession to power remained largely unfulfilled.

The so-called GRINGOs (government regulated and initiated NGOs) that are one of the principal manifestations of the Philippines' distinctive civil society are not simply oxymoronic, they are often preoccupied with maintaining control of decentralized resources and pork-barrelling (Gonzalez 2001: 279), rather than in promoting more widely based, 'progressive' social causes. Indeed, even the work of international aid agencies has reinforced the existent status quo as a consequence of their ideological stances and commitment to non-confrontation (Rodan and Hughes 2012). The only post-Marcos administration that is widely considered to have made some progress in both igniting domestic economic activity and in confronting some of the powerful vested economic interests that have made economic reform and development so problematic, was led by Fidel Ramos during the mid-1990s. Yet even Ramos was not able to reform key elements of the economy such as the banking sector (Hutchcroft 1999), nor was his administration free of accusations of electoral malpractice of a sort that has led William Case (2002) to describe the Philippines' political system as a 'stable but low quality democracy'. The networks of patronage and privilege that characterized the subsequent administrations of Estrada and Arroyo only reinforced this record of underperformance and maladministration (Hutchison 2006). For some observers, the lesson to be drawn from both the Philippines' and Indonesian experiences is that:

> In both, corruption and the privilege of elites remains relatively unassailable, and weaker or more marginal populations cannot often depend on government to make progress against important social and economic needs. In part, this disappointment has to do with the ability of both governments, in different ways, to develop a style of rule that combines democratic and authoritarian elements in an effort to thwart oppositional challenges and narrow the range of social concerns to which it must actually respond. (Boudreau 2009: 234)

Thailand too has a long history of military rule and periodic coups in which rival elites established their relative pre-eminence, but it is currently democratic. In 1992, it seemed that Thailand's own version of people power had ensured that there had been an irrevocable transformation in the nature of domestic politics. And yet, while the military may not be the threat to civilian political authorities that they once were, the nature of the political process itself is still far short of the democratic ideal. 'Money politics', or less euphemistically, the outright bribing of large numbers of the electorate, continues to be prominent part of the elections that have taken place since the 1990s. When combined with political violence and intimidation, especially in rural areas, and a history of domination by a 'bureaucratic polity' (Riggs 1966), it is not surprising that Maisrikrod and McCargo (1997: 132) conclude that 'power remains the preserve of the few. The mass of the population continues to be excluded from a significant say in the way the country is governed'.

Corruption has been a fundamental part of the political and bureaucratic processes for decades in Thailand, but has become especially prominent and pervasive since the 1980s (Phongpaichit and Piriyarangsan 1994). The quintessential example of the way centres of political, bureaucratic and economic power can coalesce to underpin a particular government can be seen in the case of former prime minster Thaksin Shinawatra (McCargo 2005). The organization with which Shinawatra has sought to guide his developmentalist agenda, the Thai Rak Thai (TRT) party, was hardly a vehicle for political emancipation. On the contrary, as Pasuk and Baker (2004: 228) have pointed out, Shinawatra's control of the media, use of money and appeals to nationalism were designed to 'delegitimize all non-formal politics and close down political space'. Nevertheless, he enjoyed popular support, but was ultimately removed in yet another military coup in 2006. The net effect of the Shinawatra period has been to entrench divisions within Thai society that have their basis in very broad divisions between the urban middle class and the rural poor, and between forces linked to the monarchy and those associated with the Shinawatra era (Hewison 2010). The fact that Thaksin Shinawatra's sister, Yingluck Shinawatara, is currently the prime minister – albeit at the head of the new Pheu Thai Party – has done little to resolve definitively the underlying, deep-seated political divisions that may well come to a head once again when the ageing king dies.

If the potential for a return to authoritarian politics remains a significant risk in Thailand, the prospects for genuine democratic reform may be even more fragile for those countries that have never actually achieved real democracy in the first place.

Semi-, non- and putative democracies

Whether we call them 'semi' or 'pseudo' democracies, Singapore and Malaysia share common historical legacies that help to explain their distinctive political accommodations (Slater 2010). The fact that both were former colonies of Britain and briefly part of the Federation of Malaysia gives them some significant commonalities, but the nature of their subsequent political, and in particular their economic trajectories, since Singapore left the Federation in 1965 also suggests some important differences. Perhaps the single most significant political reality that helps to explain Singaporean development has been the dominance of the People's Action Party (PAP) generally and the pivotal role played by Lee

Kuan Yew in particular. Lee was prime minister from 1959 to 1990, and has established something of a family dynasty as his son, Lee Hsien Loong, is the present incumbent. Though the PAP's dominance under the Lees and interim premier, Goh Chok Tong, has been so complete it seems difficult to imagine any other possibility, at the outset its hegemony was not so assured.

The PAP was originally an uneasy alliance between British-educated middle-class nationalists such as Lee, and indigenous Chinese labour and student movements. Lee Kuan Yew's great achievement, if that is the way to describe it, was to not only oversee the transformation of Singapore's economy, but also the island's political system. Following the break with Malaysia, the PAP began to develop a corporatist regime that conferred a good deal of autonomy on the state itself, while simultaneously co-opting potential sources of political opposition such as organized labour (Brown 1995). The net effect of a process that was perfected over the ensuing decades was, as Garry Rodan (1996a: 95) describes it, a reconfiguring of 'the expanding realm of the state through the extension and refinement of the mechanisms of political co-optation, not the evolution of a more expansive civil society'. The PAP has skilfully nullified or deflected potential sources of political opposition by incorporating business, civil society and labour leaders into corporatist networks. Similarly, effective political opposition has been marginalized through initiatives such as the Societies Act (1967), which makes political mobilization outside of government-approved boundaries all but impossible.

More recently, the PAP has maintained its tight grip on the population in general and possible sources of political opposition through a number of innovative strategies. On the one hand, supporters of the PAP are rewarded with government largesse through the upgrading of public housing estates. On the other hand, the Singaporean government has made increasing use of a compliant judiciary to bankrupt political opponents and to intimidate the local and international media (see Rodan 2006). Indeed, it is important to make a general comparative point about the legal system in countries such as Singapore with more authoritarian traditions: while the liberal tradition sees legalism as a restraint on the excessive powers of the state, 'in East Asia, it is employed as a managerial and technocratic device for the effective organization of the market and the state' (Jayasuriya 1996: 377). While this may not be quite as accurate a description of the entire region as it once was, and East Asia's legal distinctiveness may be 'fading' (Dowdle 2012: 235), the main point to make about the Singaporean experience in particular is that there is no easy, straightforward or inevitable relationship between rising living standards and the achievement of genuinely democratic government: populations may be compliant and willing to trade off political freedoms for economic growth, and states may prove themselves to be adept at developing new modes of social and political control (Rodan 2009).

It might be thought that the fate of a small island economy with a population of less than four million is not of great historical consequence or comparative significance. Yet Singapore has assumed a surprisingly important place in debates about economic development in the region, and an even more prominent place in discussions of the possible significance of cultural values in that process. When the Southeast Asian economies were expanding rapidly in the 1990s, Singapore became synonymous with so-called 'Asian values'. According to Lee Kuan Yew (in Zakaria 1994: 114), one of the most prominent figures in this discourse, Singapore's remarkable economic development was attributable to 'thrift, hard work, filial piety and loyalty in the extended family, and, most of all, the respect for scholarship and learning'. These basic assumptions came to be elaborated and associated with what was variously described as Asian values, an 'Asian way' or 'Asian ethic'.

Supporters of Asian values adopted a position of unabashed cultural relativism in making a two-pronged claim that, first, there was no 'objective' position from which to judge the relative worth of different cultural and social systems; and second, because different societies have different histories and thus different values, and there are no universal forms or values that apply equally across all cultures at all times. The implication of this point was stated unambiguously by Mahathir: not only could democracy look and operate differently in different societies as a consequence, but 'not all forms of democracy are productive. There is good and productive democracy as well as bad and destructive democracy. Democratic freedom must go hand-in hand with democratic responsibility' (Mahathir 1997: 9).

It is no coincidence that Malaysia also played a major part in the Asian values debate, and has a political system that is generally characterized as authoritarian. Malaysia is also a country in which the contemporary political trajectory has been influenced powerfully by its colonial history. British imperialism not only skewed Malaysia's subsequent economic development, but it also determined the distinctive ethnic mix that has been such a central feature of its concomitant political policies. Because the British solved their labour shortages by importing workers from other parts of Asia, little more than half of Malaysia's population are indigenous Malays or *bumiputera*, with the rest being made up of Chinese (26 per cent), Indians (8 per cent) and other indigenes. The distribution of these ethnic groups is uneven, however, and some areas are dominated by particular groups, such as the Chinese in Penang and 'other indigenes' in Sarawak. Not only are Malaysia's ethnically based communities not evenly distributed spatially, neither are their relative incomes. The more commercially minded Chinese rapidly came to dominate economic activities in Malaysia – as they have in other parts of the region (Studwell 2007). This economic ascendancy generated great resentment among the majority Malays, and despite generally rising living standards post-independence, ethnic tensions culminated in major riots in 1969. This social upheaval led to the abandonment of gradualist development polices and the inauguration of the New Economic Policy (NEP) that was designed explicitly to discriminate positively in favour of the hitherto economically marginalized Malaysian majority (see Khoo 1995).

One of the immediate consequences of the 1969 riots was that the Malaysian political system 'turned in a markedly authoritarian direction' (Crouch 1996: 26). The government claimed it needed more coercive powers to maintain social stability and to ensure the economic development that, it was hoped, would bring about generalized improvements. One of the principal mechanisms with which the Malay majority ensured its political hegemony was through the United Malays National Organization (UMNO), the dominant component of the Barisan Nasional (BN) alliance governments that have enjoyed unbroken power. The BN allowed UMNO to bring other ethnic communities into the alliance, through the Malayan Chinese Association (MCA) and the Malayan Indian Congress (MIC). The fact that UMNO dominated the alliance, the key levers of political power, and thus the control of economic resources, meant that as far as the Malay community was concerned 'much of its appeal lay in its patronage-dispensing function' (Crouch 1996: 37). This gave an implacable economic logic to UMNO's political activities as its power was determined and dependent on not just successful economic development, but also control of the economic resources it generated.

The underlying logic of the NEP had been developed by the dominant political figure of post-independence politics in Malaysia: Mahathir bin Mohamad. In *The Malay Dilemma*, Mahathir (1998 [1970]) spelled out why he thought the indigenous population merited preferential treatment. But Mahathir did not become prime minister until 1981, and arguably did not cement his position unambiguously until 1987, when he finally saw off internal rivals for the leadership of UMNO and thus also the country (Case 2002). What made Mahathir so dominant, however, was his ability to personalize his power, and the authoritarian nature of the regime he led through what Dan Slater (2003: 82) describes as 'packing, rigging, and circumventing'. Mahathir strengthened potentially authoritarian institutions and undermined more democratic ones, systematically 'packing' key bodies like the judiciary with compliant allies. The potential importance of this strategy became clear when Mahathir was able to use the legal system to destroy his former deputy and leadership rival Anwar Ibrahim, a strategy that has also been employed – albeit less successfully – by the current prime minister, Najib Tun Razak. The 'rigging' Slater describes refers to Mahathir's ability to manipulate UMNO's rules and procedures that determine leadership positions to his advantage. 'Circumventing' refers to the way resources are directed towards loyal allies in 'packed' institutions, making potential centres of opposition more difficult to develop. As with Singapore, Malaysia has a similarly cowed media that offered little criticism of these developments (Rodan 2005).

By winding back civil liberties, manipulating UMNO elections (where the 'real' competition for political power occurs), and changing the procedures governing general elections, Mahathir was able to retain the trappings of democracy without running the risk of a regime change (Case 2002). As a result, Mahathir developed a dominant, authoritarian position within Malaysian politics. And yet it was never entirely hegemonic and there were always potential sources of opposition and tensions within the regime (Hilley 2001). Indeed, the Anwar affair revealed major divisions within UMNO itself (Khoo 2003), and Anwar's re-emergence as a significant political force is indicative of the declining domination of UMNO in Malaysian politics. It is also indicative of the possibility of widespread disenchantment with the old regime and real pressure from civil society for meaningful reform and change (Case 2010). As in Singapore, however, the ruling elite is not without options or a capacity to respond, co-opt or coerce – much depends on the relative strength, organization and leadership of civil society groups (Giersdorf and Croissant 2011).

Malaysia's authoritarian past and potential notwithstanding, it can at least lay claim to being some sort of democracy. The rest of the region's diverse polities are generally even further from the democratic ideal, though the recent dramatic political change in Burma/Myanmar is an important reminder that situations can alter in unexpected ways. Whether Burma's apparent move towards democratic reform proves to be genuine and sustainable is unclear at this point, but whatever happens it raises important questions about the influence of regional organizations such as ASEAN, which are taken up in Chapter 11. More impervious to change is the micro-state of Brunei, which, while run by a sultan rather than a military junta, shows little sign of similar political development. The key to the ruling family's domination is oil and gas wealth, which allows them effectively to buy the support of the general population. Similarly, Southeast Asia's newest potential member – East Timor – is so small and new that its significance at this stage is primarily as a focus of intra- and inter-regional concern and manoeuvring, rather than as a major actor in its own right (Hughes 2009).

The main point to make about the political development of the former French colonies in Indochina is that they are marked not just by imperialism, but also by the colossal impact of the Vietnam War. Unbelievably enough, tiny Laos lost 50 per cent of its population during the 20-year civil war that ended in 1975 with the declaration of the communist-led Lao People's Democratic Republic (Fry and Faming 2001: 147). Any country faced with that sort of demographic collapse might struggle to cope, let alone one with very limited state capacity.

Cambodia has been similarly ravaged by internal conflict, most notoriously at the hands of the tyrannical Pol Pot, who managed to murder perhaps a sixth of the population during fewer than four years in power in the late 1970s. Though elections now occur, they are marred by violence and intimidation, and have seen power consolidate around strong-man leader Hun Sen (Hughes 2009).

Vietnam is by far the most important of this group of countries, its population size (over 80 million) and economic potential making it a potentially major force in Southeast Asian and perhaps eventually East Asian politics; it is integrating rapidly into the international capitalist economy, but its political system remains dominated by the Vietnamese Communist Party (VCP). In many ways, Vietnam faces similar sorts of problems to its giant neighbour China, in that it must make the transition from a rather ideologically rigid, authoritarian form of communist rule, to a political structure that can accommodate the demands of global economic integration (see Beresford 2008; Gainsborough 2011). I detail this transition in more detail in the next chapter.

Conclusion

A number of points emerge from the preceding discussion that are worth keeping in mind when thinking about economic development and the potential for regional and even inter-regional co-operation. First, East Asia is a diverse place and this is nowhere more apparent than when thinking about its remarkable political diversity. This in itself reminds us that history and path dependency matter. and there is nothing inevitable about the course of political development. Second, and contra the expectations of many commentators in the West, liberal democracy is not the inevitable endpoint of human history. On the contrary – and Burma's welcome reforms notwithstanding – the experience of a number of Southeast Asian regimes suggests that they are indeed 'hybrid regimes', though 'not as imperfect versions of liberal democracies but as possible political regimes in their own right, with their own internal dynamics and qualitatively distinct institutional forms' (Jayasuriya and Rodan 2009:

773). Such a conclusion is in keeping with what Levitsky and Way (2010: 5) describe as 'competitive authoritarianism', in which

> formal democratic institutions exist and are widely viewed as the primary means of gaining power, but in which incumbents' abuse of the state places them at a significant advantage vis-à-vis their opponents. Such regimes are competitive in that opposition parties use democratic institutions to contest seriously for power, but they are not democratic because the playing field is heavily skewed in favor of incumbents. Competition is thus real but unfair.

In this regard we also need to recognize that globalization may provide some of the necessary but not all of the sufficient conditions for political reform. In other words, though external pressures and influences may be consequential at particular times, they may not in themselves be determinative. The relationship between the domestic and the international is dialectical but not necessarily decisive. As Milner and Mukherjee (2009: 177) put it, 'democracy may help foster economic globalization but globalization does not promote democracy'. A final point to consider is whether, at a time when the reputation of both Western capitalism and more particularly the effectiveness of the American political system is subject to extensive critique (Mann and Ornstein 2012), the possible geopolitical erosion of 'Anglo-American primacy' is actually reducing the attractiveness of democratic reform (Narizny 2012). This is an especially important consideration when we consider the potential political trajectory and attractiveness of China. But before we do that, we need to consider the broadly conceived role that political processes have played in the rise of the East Asian economies.

Chapter 7

East Asia's Developmental States[1]

One of the most distinctive and original features of East Asia's political and economic history since the Second World War has been the emergence of what has been described as the 'developmental state'. In the aftermath of the Asian financial crisis (discussed in Chapter 10), many observers thought we had heard the last of the developmental state, which seemed anachronistic and associated with cronyism and corruption. A number of recent developments suggest that it may be premature to write it off, however (Stubbs 2009, 2012). First, the reputation and influence of Anglo-American capitalism has been diminished substantially as a consequence of economic crises in North America and Europe (Posner 2010; Wu 2010). Second, the fact that China has adopted what can only be seen as a very successful model of development that is much closer to the developmental state pattern than it is to the now discredited neoliberal alternative has renewed interest in the interventionist model, as we shall see in Chapter 8. Because the East Asian experience has potentially important lessons for other parts of the world where development is still sorely needed (Fukuyama 2004; Sachs 2005), and because its imprint is still clearly evident across East Asia, it is important to examine it more closely.

At its simplest, the developmental state has become a generic term to describe governments which try to 'intervene' actively in economic processes and direct the course of development, rather than relying on market forces. The ability of states to influence the course of development and business activity depends in large part on state 'strength' and capacity, and the ability to establish effective relations with economic actors. While the developmental state is associated predominantly with East Asia because of being identified with the so-called East Asian miracle (World Bank 1993), it is important to note that some scholars have claimed that the developmental state pre-dates the East Asian experience and has been around for a long time in one form or other (Bagchi 2000), and that successful economic development *everywhere* has required major state assistance (Chang 2002).

Of late, however, one country in particular has been considered as the pioneer of both rapid economic growth and industrialization in East Asia, and of the developmental state itself. Japan has come to epitomize all that was most successful and remarkable about economic take-off in a region that was once associated with inescapable backwardness. For this reason, Japan's experience will be given extensive consideration. A noteworthy aspect of the discussion of Japan – and the rest of East Asia, for that matter – is that precisely the same structures, practices and values that were once thought to be part of the 'secret' of Japan's success and the cause of the 'East Asian miracle' are now considered as the cause of its economic problems. One of the primary tasks of this chapter is to try to make sense of recent debates about the rise and apparent fall of the developmental state (Beeson 2004b), and identify what went right, and wrong, in Japan's case, and in some of the countries that followed its lead. One possibility to keep in mind is that Japan's developmental experience in the high growth era[2] and the strategies that underpinned it may still have much to teach us, despite any problems it has recently experienced. It is important to remember that at the outset both Japan's rapid industrialization and that of the other 'newly industrializing economies' (NIEs) following in its wake was remarkable, unparalleled and unexpected. While the region's developmental states were clearly not solely responsible for this process – the fortuitous historical circumstances described in earlier chapters combined with the activities of local and international capital plainly helped (Vu 2010) – the state's role is sufficiently distinctive and the outcomes generally so successful that they merit detailed analysis.

Despite important variations in the way that developmentalism has been approached, and significant differences in state capacity, most of the states of the region have attempted to pursue some form of state-led development of a sort that seems vital for successful development (Commission on Growth and Development 2008; Rodrik 1997). Consequently, it is important to understand how and why this happened, not only because it is at odds with much of the prevailing Western wisdom, but also because it provides an important element of commonality in the political and economic practices of the East Asian region as a whole.

The Japanese exemplar

Before considering how Japan's post-war recovery was engineered, it is worth spelling out what makes the developmental state conceptually distinctive and why it is so contentious as a consequence. Nearly everything about the developmental state is sharply at odds with the conventional economic wisdom that prevails in the Anglo-American nations and in the policy prescriptions of the IFIs. Consequently, the developmental state has been both a direct intellectual and ideological challenge to the dominant economic orthodoxy associated with the Washington consensus or neoliberalism, and a practical challenge because of the rapid rise of highly competitive East Asian economies.

Thinking about the developmental state

Neoclassical economics, which still provides much of the intellectual foundation for the dominant economic orthodoxy that has come to be associated with neoliberalism, emerged at the end of the nineteenth century and continues to exercise a powerful influence over contemporary economic thinking. At the heart of neoclassical economics is a belief in the efficacy of markets, which are considered to be the most efficient means of allocating economic resources. There is an assumption that individuals are best able to make 'rational choices' about their own interests, and that these will intersect with the decisions of producers to ensure the most efficient distribution and production of goods and services. The key point about this highly simplified sketch of conventional economic thinking is that economic well-being is seen as being dependent, not on the state or the collective actions of human beings, but on individual decision-making in response to spontaneously occurring market forces. On the contrary, in this highly abstract, historical reading of the nature of economic activity, states were seen as a potentially major *obstacle* to the efficient production and allocation of economic resources (Stilwell 2002).

This remarkably benign view of market processes, in which the 'laws' of supply and demand enable informed consumers to make individual consumption choices, to which there are rapid responses by competitive, entrepreneurial producers leading to a state of 'equilibrium' and harmony, is noticeably at odds with historical reality. Capitalism been punctuated repeatedly by profoundly disruptive periods of massive economic *dis*equilibrium (Kindleberger 1996), and the very adoption of capitalist social relations was frequently resisted and traumatic, not just in East Asia, but also in its European heartland (Polanyi 1957). Moreover, the neoclassical vision of frictionless markets, well-informed consumers, and competitive producers pays little heed to the constraining impact of the initial distribution of power, privilege and property rights in society (Gourevitch 2005; Rothkopf 2012). More fundamentally, the neoclassical model has little to say about the lack of competition in, and the strategic significance of, key industrial sectors – a possibility that is central to understanding East Asia's different approach to industrial development (Chang 2000).

Despite its well-known pretensions to 'scientific' status and methodology, economics remains an imprecise social science, subject to all the difficulties this implies. Put differently, understandings of economic processes are contingent and socially determined; they are consequently also value-laden and reflective of a specific set of social circumstances – even if it is one in which international factors play an increasingly influential part. The socially constructed understanding of economic 'reality' will both reflect and *help to construct* the very economic processes and forms that policy-makers and theoreticians seek to comprehend and manage. The major methodological failing of the dominant neoclassical model, therefore, is not just that it generally remains uninterested in its own ontological and epistemological status, but that its universalizing, ahistorical abstractions are incapable of dealing with the wide varieties of economic forms that continue to distinguish 'global' capitalism (Hodgson 1996). This failing not only helps to shed light on why the Japanese model has proved so difficult to explain by many Western economists, but also why mainstream Western economists were both unable to predict *and* were complicit in causing the recent global financial crisis that affected the USA so badly (Colander 2011; Tett 2009).

Economic thought in Japan, by contrast, is a good deal more heterodox and pragmatically oriented (Morris-Suzuki 1989), and consequently not driven by a particular economic philosophy. The relatively obscure German political-economist Friedrich List has been a far greater influence than Adam Smith on Japanese policy-makers, and the Japanese view of themselves and the potential role of the state is profoundly different as a consequence.[3] Rather than relying on what Smith described as the invisible hand of the market to determine the production and distribution of goods and services, List's ideas reinforced and legitimated a proclivity for industrial targeting in Japan that began in the late Tokugawa period and which was reinforced from the Meiji period onwards (Beasley 1993: 103). Such policies were especially important as a direct consequence of the fact that Japan was a comparatively 'late'-developing country. Because Britain, Western Europe and the United States had already industrialized successfully, there was a proven developmental template that Japanese planners could draw on and use to accelerate the course of economic development. The key insight of Alexander Gerschenkron (1966) was that late-developing states could make use of existing technology and developmental techniques to compress the rate at which the industrialization process took place.

There are a couple of other major assumptions which inform the state-led approach to economic development that are widely recognized in the literature, and which provide the rationale for the 'interventionist' approach. First, and most fundamentally, perhaps, it is clear that some industries and productive processes are inherently more valuable, wealth-generating and consequently 'strategic' than others. This is the basis of the claim that 'manufacturing matters' (Cohen and Zysman 1987): manufacturing provides higher productivity gains, and greater technological 'spillovers' in the form of skill development and economic linkages across the economy in a way that other sectors such as agriculture and resource extraction simply cannot. While the nature of economic activity has become considerably more complex and disaggregated of late, this basic insight still has a good deal of validity – especially when considering the initial development of the industrialization process.

There is a further salient point that flows from this basic claim, however, that has both policy and ideological implications: the assumption that some forms of economic activity are intrinsically more valuable would – or possibly should – suggest that governments have an interest in seeing them occur within their national jurisdictions. The key question then becomes whether such activities occur 'naturally' as a consequence of market forces, or can actively be encouraged through government incentives or policies. Japan plainly chose the latter course, which was a direct refutation of the conventional economic wisdom.

Japan's elite bureaucrats have long recognized the impact on national power and security implications that flowed from the possession of an indigenous manufacturing capacity (Heginbotham and Samuels 1998). Without industrialization and borrowing from the West, Japan would not have risen to the front rank of the imperial powers before the Second World War. But it was equally apparent to Japan's post-war technocrats that the wealthy countries of the world were also complex, industrialized nations having a number of key economic sectors with self-sustaining domestic linkages. Once in place, such technologically rich industrial processes had the capacity to 'lock-in' increasing returns and rising living standards in a virtuous circle (Arthur 1989). A failure to industrialize and adopt productivity-enhancing technology threatened an equally path-dependent vicious circle of declining returns and living standards.

A major reason why some countries are highly successful in encouraging technological innovation and industrial development is that they provide a supportive institutional order (Boyer and Hollingsworth 1997; Rodrik 2000). Consequently, Japan's economic bureaucrats set out, quite self-consciously and intentionally, to *create* a comparative advantage in industrial production in defiance of Western economic 'laws' and orthodoxy. While Japan's pre-war industrialization meant its policy elites were not starting from a blank slate, the extent of war-time damage to the Japanese economy meant that the scale of the reconstruction and development was enormous and the results equally staggering. It was Japan's ability to 'custom design policy instruments to fit the differing priorities, needs, and circumstances of individual industries' that was central to the 'industry policies' its bureaucrats implemented (Okimoto 1989: 9).

Historically, the idea of a powerful, interventionist state playing a pivotal role has enjoyed a good deal of legitimacy in Japan, even if things are rather different now. From the latter part of the nineteenth century, Japan's political elites were preoccupied with drawing on the American and European industrialization experiences to plan a similar process of economic development in Japan. As a result, many of the techniques and strategies that would become synonymous with 'Japan Inc.' and the development state following the Second World War, were already well developed in the first half of the twentieth century (Terry 2002). In other words, a particular view of the appropriate role of the state in economic development was in place even before the Americans arrived at the end of the Second World War. Nevertheless, when the USA occupied Japan in the aftermath of the war it had a profound impact on Japan's political system and values, but not on its traditions of interventionism and the position and structure of the bureaucracy. As Chalmers Johnson (1982) points out in his seminal work on Japan's capitalist developmental state, while the Americans wanted to reform both the bureaucracy and the *zaibatsu* system, they were constrained by geopolitical imperatives, and by the sheer difficulty of penetrating the bureaucracy itself. As a result, not only did the *zaibatsu* return to prominence in the post-war period (albeit re-badged as the *keiretsu* networks), but key agencies such as the Ministry of International Trade and Industry (MITI) and the Ministry of Finance (MoF) were in position to guide the process of industrial regeneration.

Development in practice

Therefore the American occupation had only a limited impact on the bureaucratic and corporate structures that had been consolidated before the Second World War. Consequently, established relationships between the bureaucracy and business played a prominent role in shaping the direction of Japan's subsequent, unprecedented, economic renaissance. At the centre of Japan's post-war reconstruction efforts was what Johnson (1982) described as the 'plan rational', known more commonly now as the developmental state. The key word here is 'plan', for that is precisely what Japan's political elites did: rather than waiting for the market to determine the most 'efficient' allocation of available economic resources, Japanese policy-makers made a judgement about precisely which industries and economic sectors they considered to be strategically the most important, and set about encouraging their long-term development. Some of these judgements had been made before the war, when the demands of militarism and the perceived need for industrial self-sufficiency meant that a number of key industries such as ship-building were targeted for development. The logic of targeted economic development through the use of specific industry policies was taken up again after the war, when key bureaucratic agencies were given responsibility for directing the development process.

In Japan's case, the possibility that the state would play a dominant role in not just economic planning, but in society more generally, was made more likely by its specific historical circumstances. On the one hand, the Japanese had already become accustomed to the highly successful role played by its reformist elite in the nineteenth and early twentieth centuries. On the other hand, the overwhelming need to reconstruct the economy in the wake of war-time devastation gave a further impetus to the state-led reconstruction project and a broad social consensus about its legitimacy. While there have been industrial failures that serve as salutary reminders about the fallibility of Japan's economic planning elite after the initial 'catching-up' phase had been accomplished (Callon 1995), nevertheless, in the immediate aftermath of the war, the Japanese pioneered particular relationships and policy tools that allowed its bureaucratic elites to guide the course of largely successful economic development.

Some of the most significant early initiatives taken in the 1950s involved limiting the import of finished manufactured goods, but encouraging the inward transfer of new technologies. Significantly, Japanese planners also borrowed selectively from Western management practices, leading to the development of Japan's life-time employment system and the more systematic usage of labour force skills – initiatives that were long thought to give Japan a distinct competitive advantage over its Western rivals (Johnson 1982: 216). Perhaps even more important than the distinctive labour relations and corporate practices that evolved in post-war Japan were the sorts of relationships that developed between the state and business. Both of the latter two terms need unpacking because, in reality, 'the state' was primarily agencies such as MITI, the MoF and the Bank of Japan, and 'business' was the handful of mega-corporations that came to dominate Japan's post-war economic landscape. There is some contention about where the balance of power in these relationships lay, with some emphasizing the power and autonomy of agencies such as MITI (Okimoto 1989: 112–13) – in precisely the way that Peter Evans suggested defined 'embedded autonomy'; see Chapter 1, and others who stress the 'reciprocal' nature of business–government relations (Samuels 1987: 2–8). However we describe it, though, there are a number of institutionalized elements of the relationship that made it productive and facilitated the development process.

The distinctive nature of Japanese politics helps to account for the bureaucracy's extraordinary power and authority: the political class was preoccupied with politicking and raising money, and happy to leave the management of the economy to the technocrats. The dangers of this process would eventually become all too apparent, but initially this arrangement worked well and opened up a regulatory space that the bureaucrats were happy to occupy. But this does not explain the willingness of Japan's capitalist class to go along with the initiatives that emerged from the likes of MITI. The state's dominance was partly a consequence of Japan's 'late developer' status and the catalytic role the technocratic elite had played even before the war. But MITI and the other elements of the bureaucracy were able to exercise what came to be known as 'administrative guidance' – that is, 'informal regulatory power or indirect control' (George Mulgan 2005: 23) – in the war's aftermath because they had the policy tools and regulatory authority that gave them both political and economic influence.

In the early phases of Japan's post-war recovery, MITI's control over access to foreign currency and the overall tariff regime was crucially important, and gave the bureaucracy powerful leverage over companies wanting to operate overseas or to receive government protection. Likewise, MITI's endorsement of a company or industry made it far easier for it to obtain relatively scarce capital through low-interest-rate loans (Krauss 1992: 50). This was an especially important consideration given that, unlike most Western economies, Japan's system is much more dependent on bank finance rather than equity markets for raising capital (Zysman 1983). One of the key innovations that facilitated bureaucratic control and industrial development was the remarkably bland-sounding Fiscal Investment and Loan Program (FILP), which utilized the substantial funds deposited in the Postal Savings System to channel cheap capital to targeted industries. The FILP and its policies were ultimately controlled by the MoF and intended to both encourage Japan's already substantial savings rate and to reinforce the overall direction of developmentalism (Tabb 1995: ch. 4).

Reinforcing this economic leverage were a series of more direct, personal relationships that allowed Japanese policymakers to implement their plans and encourage the growth of targeted industries; initially petro-chemicals, steel and ship-building, and subsequently the electronics and automotive sectors. What is common to all, of course, is that they are industries essential to the development of a sophisticated industrial economy with complex, mutually reinforcing linkages across various sectors. In Japan's celebrated (or reviled) system of *amakudari*, senior civil servants joined the boards of private sector companies upon their (generally early) retirement. This system was in part compensation for the nugatory legitimate rewards given to bureaucrats, but more important, a potentially crucial conduit for the transmission of advice from the state, and the provision of feedback from business (Schaede 1995). Once again, this is in line with the idealized concept of embeddedness that Evans considered to be a part of effective state capacity.

However, these arrangements are not without their potential dangers and pitfalls. While close connections between business and government can be important mechanisms for the transmission of information, they can also become mutually rewarding 'circles of compensation' or reciprocal networks designed to further the material goals of participants (Calder 1988b). This potential is especially likely to be realized when such networks become increasingly self-serving and endure beyond their original purpose (Beeson 2003b). It is precisely this possibility that has given rise to some of the – frequently highly generalized and imprecise – claims about 'crony capitalism'. Despite such accusations being often little more than caricatures and part of a broader attempt to destroy the credibility of the developmental state more generally, there were, nevertheless, major problems with and inherent dangers in the state-led approach to development, and Japan illustrates many of them.

Japan in crisis

Japan's economic problems have both domestic *and* international origins. In Japan, and in most of the other East Asian developmental states, changes in the *international* political economy have either undermined the country's economy or highlighted weaknesses in it. In Japan's case, it did both. On the one hand, there were major systemic weaknesses that developed within an increasingly dualistic domestic economy. However, these vulnerabilities and potential flaws might not have been exposed quite so dramatically, or become such liabilities, had it not been for the operation of the wider international order generally, and the actions of American foreign-policy-makers in particular. The key development in this regard was the so-called Plaza Accord of 1985 in which Japanese policy-makers – under intense pressure from their American counterparts[4] – agreed to allow the yen to appreciate in the belief that this would solve the 'problem' of America's ballooning trade deficit with Japan (Murphy 1997).

Given that history is currently repeating itself, as the Americans try to talk the new trade villain – China – into revaluing its currency, it is worth spelling out some of the implications of this process. At the very least, it is a timely reminder that the most powerful country in the world has the capacity to compel compliance with its policy preferences, whatever their consequences might be. Nevertheless, the Japanese felt compelled to go along with the policies of the Reagan administration if they wanted to ensure continued access to America's vital domestic market. Between 1985 and 1988, in a process the Japanese called *endaka*, the value of the yen increased by 56 per cent in trade-weighted terms, and by 93 per cent against the US dollar (Brenner 2002: 106).

This sort of dramatic currency appreciation would have been a problem for any economy, but it was especially acute for Japan because of the nature of its domestic economy and the logic of its developmental model. Paradoxically, some of Japan's seemingly greatest strengths – high savings rates and a phenomenally successful export-led developmental strategy – eventually became liabilities as the economy matured. 'Excessive' domestic savings led to 'under-consumption' and an ever greater reliance on exports to underpin the overall national growth strategy (Katz 1998). This highlighted another strength that seemed to have become a weakness: 'dedicated capital'. At the peak of the developmental state's powers, it had been able to redirect Japan's high levels of domestic savings towards targeted companies through a process of 'financial repression'. Financial repression occurs when governments keep interest rates 'artificially' low, or lower than market-clearing rates. This provides one way of supplying targeted industries or borrowers with cheap capital, gives policy-makers leverage over private industry, and helps to account for the high investment and growth rates in much of East Asia.[5] But the steady liberalization of the financial sector and the growth of domestic savings meant that firms no longer needed to rely on the government, or even local financial institutions, to access capital. Consequently, the effectiveness of a major policy tool of government from Japan's high-growth era was permanently undermined.

If the net effect of changes in the financial sector had simply been a diminution in the effectiveness of governmental industry policy and economic leverage, all might have been well. Unfortunately, however, the MoF made what is widely regarded as a major policy mistake in not raising interest rates and controlling credit growth as the currency appreciated. They may have done so for the best of reasons – understandable concern about the impact on the economy of the rising yen and the all-important export sector – but the net effect of this was to inflate the 'bubble economy' of the late 1980s and early 1990s. The consequences of this period of 'free money', when the combination of low interest rates and banks desperately searching for new customers made credit all too easily available, are well-known: a (temporary) stratospheric rise in the equity and real estate markets, a dramatic increase in the number of non-performing loans held by Japanese banks, and an outpouring of Japanese capital overseas (Wood 1992).

The implications of this latter development were not all bad, and were crucial in driving the regionalization process in East Asia. In Japan, however, the impact of the bubble economy was not only profound in economic terms, but also politically damaging. As T.J. Pempel (1998: 148) makes clear, as the bubble started to deflate, 'government policies were no longer a cohesive strategy directed at national improvement, but rather an eclectic mixture of ad hoc efforts to plug holes in competing dikes'. Public officials, who had formerly been held in high public esteem, began to be seen as increasingly incompetent and even corrupt (Hartcher 1997: 42–8). From experiencing a state of national self-confidence bordering on hubris during the boom years, a mood of introspection and doubt took hold as the difficulties involved in resolving Japan's economic problems became clearer, and confidence in the competence and honesty of public officials declined.

The ineffectiveness and compromised nature of public policy exacerbated underlying problems in the Japanese economy that had been disguised, but largely created by the high growth, developmental state era. Richard Katz argues that at the centre of Japan's domestic difficulties was an industrial policy that had 'degenerated into little more than political pork barrelling and logrolling', designed to prop up uncompetitive industries (Katz 1998: 31–2). Again, what had been a source of strength and central to Japan's unambiguous developmental success, gradually degenerated into self-serving networks bound together by mutual obligation and patronage, at least in the uncompetitive domestic sector. Two aspects of this process were especially damaging: first, public policy reflected and helped to entrench the 'dual economy', in which uncompetitive domestic industries were protected by government, actually encouraging a shift of workers from more efficient, export-oriented industries. Indeed, many of Japan's most competitive and successful companies moved off shore during the 1990s, exacerbating the lack of domestic competitiveness and increasing the need for greater government support (Katz 1998: ch. 3).

This latter trend contributed to the second problem that emerged from the corruption of and in Japan's government–business relations: public money that might have been used to reignite economic activity and lift the economy out of the doldrums in orthodox Keynesian fashion, was more often siphoned off to industries that were politically rather than economically important. The most egregious example of this possibility occurred in what Gavan McCormack (1996: ch. 1) calls the 'construction state'. Not only were most of the major public works initiatives, such as dams and roads, frequently of dubious benefit, but the bidding process was corrupt and resulted in greatly inflated costs, borne ultimately by Japanese taxpayers.

There is another, possibly even more fundamental, reason for believing that – in Japan's case, at least – the developmental state is no longer capable of playing the role it once did. The nature of contemporary technological innovation may simply not be responsive to the sorts highly interventionist, state-directed strategies employed by generations of Japanese planners (Fong 1998). Contemporary advances at the technological frontier of the most strategically important, wealth-generating industries are, it seems, more likely to occur in the sorts of diffuse networks of independent producers found in Silicon Valley (Saxenian 1994), than they are in the kinds of highly centralized projects favoured by the Japanese government (Drezner 2001). State-sponsored innovation processes seem to be effective for generating the types of incremental innovation associated with the catching-up phase of industrialization, whereas liberal market economies seem to be better at generating the kind of 'radical' innovation that occurs at the technological frontier (Hall and Soskice 2001: 41).

Japanese lessons?

Given Japan's historical importance as both a role model for other aspiring industrial economies in the region (Amsden 1995: 796), and as the principal motor of regional economic integration (Hatch and Yamamura 1996), it is worth highlighting some of the implications of the developmental state's rise and fall, before considering briefly how some of its imitators have fared elsewhere. The first point to make is that, despite the claims by some orthodox economists that the rise of Japan and the rest of East Asia is explicable simply by reference to the working of market forces (Balassa 1988), evidence about the extent, and frequently the effectiveness, of state intervention in the early phases of Japan's pre- and post-war industrialization is simply overwhelming (Dore 1986). Whatever problems Japan might have experienced during the 1990s, it is clear that for several decades after the Second World War, Japan's economic renaissance was planned and – to a significant degree – realized as a consequence of the efforts of a bureaucratic elite working in tandem with the indigenous capitalist class.

However, there are aspects of Japan's developmental trajectory that are unique and make its replication difficult – even if there is a desire to do so. Japan's specific historical experience, especially the pattern of state intervention dating from the Meiji period, coupled with the existence of established large- and small-scale industry even before the Second World War, may make this style of intervention hard to emulate. Because the Japanese economy is dominated by a handful of corporations, or *keiretsu* (Gerlach 1992), close, co-operative relations with government were relatively easy to organize – something that was facilitated by the practice, mentioned earlier, of appointing ex-bureaucrats to corporate director-ships. It is also important to recognize that alongside the massive corporate conglomerates such as Mitsui and Mitsubishi was an array of small-scale producers that provided much of the dynamism, flexibility and competitiveness of the manufacturing sector more generally (Friedman 1988).

One of the most distinctive features of the Japanese model during the high-growth era was the relative insulation of the Japanese economy. Indeed, in the first few decades after the Second World War it still made sense to speak of discrete national economies in a way that it might not now. And yet even Japan, which scrupulously avoided dependence on inward FDI, and contentiously maintained a range of highly effective formal and informal trade barriers, has been affected increasingly by external economic forces. The most important change in this regard has been the integration of the country's capital and equity markets with the wider international economy. This gradual integration has made Japanese corporations more independent of government and less reliant on their own 'main banks' for capital, and changed the ownership structures of Japanese corporations in the process.

At one level, then, the policy tools that the Japanese state employed, especially through the control of capital, have largely become unimportant and ineffective – at least as far as Japan's most competitive, internationally oriented firms are concerned. While Japan's industrial policies were clearly central to the country's overall economic renaissance, a principal shortcoming, especially in more recent times, has been a failure to discriminate between competitive and uncompetitive industries (Porter *et al.* 2000: 44). Companies and industries often received assistance or preferential treatment on the basis of their political connections or importance, rather than their economic efficiency or contribution to overall national development. As a consequence, government policy exacerbated what Pempel (1998: 212) calls 'the most central economic cleavage confronting Japan ... between its internationally competitive and non-competitive sectors, firms, and groups'. The extent of this tension and the transformation that has occurred in business–government relations in Japan can be gleaned from the fact that the *Keidanren* – Japan's most influential and important business federation – has actively lobbied the Japanese government both to open up the economy through free trade agreements (Yoshimatsu 2005) and to undertake greater deregulation of the economy and administrative reform.

The reform process has been partial and incomplete in Japan, with the consequence that the country is in some ways experiencing the worst of both worlds. The developmental state may no longer be as credible, effective or even necessary as it once was, but this does not mean that some of the relationships, institutions and patterns of behaviour associate with it have disappeared. On the contrary, as Steven Vogel (2006: 34) points out, 'Japan's error may not have been sticking with a model that was outmoded but abandoning a model that worked without converting to a new one.' Even in the financial sector, arguably the part of the economy that is most affected by global forces, the networks that constitute the sector demonstrate 'extraordinary stability'; the key obstacle to much-needed reform, according to Jennifer Amyx (2004: 34) is 'the incapacity of Japan's party system to produce bold and decisive leaders who can effectively coordinate among relevant policymaking actors'. This is what makes the emergence of so-called 'Abenomics' so potentially significant, as Shinzo Abe attempts to use the central bank and aggressive monetary policy to overcome Japan's persistent deflation (Tasker 2013). It will be a major test of both the effectiveness of Abe's leadership and the ability of a hitherto conservative institution to embrace radical policy change.

Whatever the current policy initiatives produce, there is no gainsaying Japan's former success, some of which is clearly attributable to being in the right place at the right time. On the one hand, this meant that Japan was able to take advantage of the remarkable recovery in economic activity that occurred in the aftermath of the Second World War, while on the other, it not only benefited from both American aid and demand, but also from a more indulgent American attitude towards Japanese mercantilism and interventionism. The Americans may not have liked the Japanese approach very much – it was, after all, diametrically opposed to everything the Americans stood for both normatively and practically – but they were prepared to tolerate it in the context of the wider geopolitical and strategic confrontation with the Soviet Union and its East Asian allies (Beeson 2004b). No other country has enjoyed quite such favourable conditions.

The rise of the NICs

The reason it became common to refer to the 'East Asian' miracle, rather than simply Japan's, was because Japanese-style rapid development became more widespread across the region (World Bank 1993). It is possible to identify two broad waves of development in this process. First, the newly industrializing countries (NICs) of South Korea, Taiwan, Singapore and Hong Kong followed Japan's lead during the 1960s. Latterly, the countries of Southeast Asia, and eventually China, have all attempted, with varying degrees of success, to follow in their wake. While there are significant differences between and within the various waves of developmental, it is possible to detect some important commonalities and continuities, not the least of which is the role played by the state. While none of the states considered below replicated the Japanese experience in every way, the developmental state pioneered by Japan was a model for a number of countries in the region and provides a useful comparative exemplar with which to consider developmental experiences elsewhere in East Asia.

Of the first wave of industrializing economies in the region, it is noteworthy that two of them were former Japanese colonies, and Singapore emulated a number of Japanese policy initiatives in its own push towards industrialization. Of the first wave of NICs that attracted such attention, only Hong Kong is generally thought to have deviated from the Japanese interventionist path. Even in Hong Kong, though, Castells (1992: 45) argues that 'a careful analysis of the process of economic development of Hong Kong since the mid-1950s reveals a decisive role by the state in creating the conditions for economic growth', albeit more 'subtly' and 'indirectly'. At one level this should not surprise us: as I suggested earlier, it is simply inconceivable that any form of capitalism could operate without the sort of regulatory framework that for the last several hundred years has been provided primarily by states (Heilbroner 1985). Even in Hong Kong's case, and despite the British influence, the colonial administration played an important part in creating the preconditions for the development of small-scale manufacturing through the creation of a supportive regulatory framework and the direct subsidization of labour costs (Castells 1992). Whether it is possible to draw major conclusions from atypical examples such as Hong Kong is a moot point. No such doubts apply to the other NICs.

In Korea and Taiwan the state's role and the influence of the Japanese model was more direct and unambiguous (Kohli 2004). Both countries were colonized by Japan, and despite the trauma this caused and the damage it has done to subsequent relations with Korea, both countries underwent important changes that paved the way for subsequent rapid economic development. In Korea's case in particular, the impact of Japanese colonialism in creating the preconditions for a Korean developmental state cannot be over-emphasized (Amsden 2001: 101). The Japanese created a large, centralized bureaucracy with the infrastructural capacity to reach the peripheral areas of Korea, the power of which was reinforced by a colonial police force. The net effect was a state with a 'highly centralised apex with near absolute powers of legislation and execution – and thus of setting and implementing "national" goals – and pervasive, disciplined civil service and police bureaucracies [that] constituted the core of the new state' (Kohli 1999: 105). A similar tale can be told of Taiwan, where the Japanese colonizers replaced traditional patterns of rule and authority with a centralized state. Again, despite the brutality that frequently accompanied Japanese occupation, the net effect was to transform radically Taiwan's existing social, economic and political structures and 'demonstrate to the Taiwanese the potential of capitalist industrialization' (Gold 1986: 45).

Despite this common heritage, thereafter the histories of capitalist development in Korea and Taiwan display some noteworthy differences, as well as some important continuities. The major continuity, of course, was the prevalence of authoritarian rule – something that also distinguished Singapore, as we shall see shortly. However, one of the most important differences between Korea and Taiwan is in the nature of the business organizations that came to dominate the industrial landscape in each country. The *chaebol*, the major corporate entity in Korea, is very similar to Japan's *keiretsu* networks. There is one major difference between Japan's *keiretsu* and Korea's *chaebol* that must be emphasized, however: in Japan there is a clearer separation of ownership and control, and a good deal of management autonomy as a consequence. In Korea, by contrast, the *chaebols* are dominated by the handful of families that control them (Hundt 2008). As a result, decision-making processes are highly centralized, despite the breadth of activities undertaken by the *chaebols* being generally much greater than those of their Japanese counterparts (Whitley 1990). The reason for the distinctive character of Korea's corporations is not 'Asian values' or Confucian traditions, but something rather more ubiquitous and mundane: political power.

The Korean state that Japan helped to establish subsequently became the architect of Korea's corporate development and actively encouraged the growth of the *chaebols*. As Woo (1991: 66) puts it, 'politics, and not innovative drive, has always been considered the umbilical cord nurturing big business in Korea'. While the relationship between the state and the *chaebols* has evolved, industry policy is still a more prominent part of the Korean political economy than it is in comparable Western economies (Chu 2009; Thurborn and Weiss 2006). Much the same can be said about Taiwan.

Taiwan also has a distinctive form of corporate organization and is perhaps the most important concentrated exemplar of the 'Chinese capitalism' phenomenon (Redding 2002). The key points that emerge from stylized depictions of the corporate form associated with the 'overseas Chinese'[6] are its generally small scale (especially when compared with Japan and Korea), its flexibility, and the importance of personal relationships (*gaunxi*). Significantly, in Taiwan, as in Korea, the state was involved in the systematic *creation* of an indigenous capitalist class where none had previously existed, a situation which Gold (1986: 64) considers 'offers a text-book case of elite-led revolutionary social transformation'. The impact of these efforts is not in doubt: from a position where agriculture accounted for over 90 per cent of economic activity in 1951, by 1987 it was down to barely 6 per cent; manufacturing was a mirror image, having gone from less than 10 per cent to over 90 per cent (Prybyla 1991: 53). One of Taiwan's key policy innovations – as it had also been in Korea – was to shift from a strategy of import substitution and protectionism in the 1950s, to one of export-oriented production from the 1960s onwards. Taiwan's economic take-off was also given a major economic boost by the 'massive' American aid that poured in during the Korean War – something Singapore, Malaysia, Thailand and even Korea itself would also eventually benefit from (Stubbs 2005: ch. 3).

Paradoxical as it may seem, the Korean War consolidated the position, and underpinned the success of the developmental state in Korea, though it is important to note that a truly developmental regime was not consolidated until Park came to power in 1961 (Hundt 2005). Prior to this, aid was the 'key' to Korea's initial import substitution strategies of the 1950s. Significantly, the war itself reduced American reformist pressure on authoritarian leader Syngman Rhee (Haggard 1990: 55–6). The limitations of the import substitution model, especially in terms of market size and competitiveness, became clearer in the 1950s, partly as a consequence of the comparatively poor performance of Latin America (see Gereffi and Wyman 1990). The crucial factors that allowed Korea to make a successful transition to export-oriented development were 'the concentration of power in the executive, the rationalization of the economic policy-making machinery, and the development of new instruments for steering industrialization' (Haggard 1990: 62). In other words, Korean elites developed precisely the same sort institutional innovations that had allowed Japanese policy-makers to guide development.

One of the most widely noted innovations Korean policy-makers undertook to promote development was what Alice Amsden refers to as 'getting prices wrong'. Rather than relying on market signals to allocate resources and determine economic activity, Korean officials deliberately intervened to 'distort' prices and thus encourage business to move into specific activities. Subsidies were available to those who could meet specific performance standards in a business–government relationship defined by reciprocity (Amsden 1989: 139–47). As in Japan, the state used the financial system as a mechanism for allocating credit and encouraging business co-operation through patterns of reciprocal obligation (Amsden 2001: 147–8). Consequently, 'the effectiveness of government policy in dealing with large enterprises depended crucially on the effectiveness of this instrument' (Lee 1992: 188). This is why the gradual liberalization of the financial sector in Korea was not simply an important element in the unfolding of the Asian crisis, as we shall see in the next chapter, but it also marked what Woo-Cumings (1997: 58) described as the 'historical eclipse of a developmental political economic regime'. The liberalization of the financial sector represented more than just a diminution in the effectiveness of an important policy lever as far as the state was concerned – it marked the unravelling of the state–business accommodation more generally. In sum, liberalization meant that:

> Korea's financial market would be *internationalized* and not protected ... To compete at the world level, Korean firms had to behave like capitalists and not bureaucrats, think profit and not control; and this meant the *privatization* of banks. But since banks cannot thrive in situations of financial repression, finance would have to be *deregulated*. (Woo-Cumings 1997: 80)

Despite the dramatic impact these changes would ultimately have on Korea, there are a number of comparative points that can usefully be made about the Taiwanese and Korean experiences when their respective developmental states were at their most powerful. First, the Korean developmental state was a good deal more centralized and bureaucratic than Taiwan's. In Taiwan, responsibility for industrial policy was dispersed through more agencies, and public officials had less decision-making authority in their relations with private firms. Taiwan has also used public investment to encourage particular activities, rather than the more directive approach towards domestic capital favoured in Korea, which was facilitated by the limited numbers of actors in big business noted above (Wade 1990: 324). In Korea's case, this strategy had long-term implications and dangers as far as the state was concerned, though: the very success of a state strategy designed to create large corporations inevitably changed the relationship between government and business as the *chaebols* gained more 'structural power' within the Korean political economy. By the 1990s it was becoming apparent that the *chaebols* had the capacity to resist government attempts to introduce neoliberal reforms or restructure key industries such as automotive manufacturing (Hundt 2005: 141–2). In Taiwan, in contrast, where the extent of political change has, until recently at least, been more extensive, the state was also compelled to respond to pressure from business. But while successive Taiwanese governments wound back their 'statist' approach, they found new ways to assist business through low-interest loans, R&D offsets, and improved policy co-ordination with the private sector (Noble 1999: 153) – despite the apparently ubiquitous practical and ideological constraints implied by globalization. While the state in both Taiwan and South Korea may not be as directly interventionist as it once was, it is important to recognize that in both countries it continues to play an active role in facilitating the development of strategic industries (Tzeng *et al.* 2012; Wang *et al.* 2012).

The capacity of governments to respond to changing circumstances is at the centre of contemporary debates about the role of states generally, and developmental states in particular, as we shall see below. The final member of the original NICs – Singapore – provides a useful reminder of both the variety of state strategies and situations that confronted developmental states even before the 'global' era, and of the ability of states to take advantage of changing circumstances. Indeed, like Japan, Singapore might be said to have been in the right place at the right time, particularly as far as the emerging 'new international division of labour' was concerned. In Singapore's case, its geographical location at the crossroads of Asian trade and historical role as a crucial entrepôt of the British empire, meant that it was well placed to take advantage of the expanding world economy. The key to its success, Garry Rodan (1989) argues, was an interventionist state that was able to take advantage of the opportunities offered by the international restructuring of productive capital. Singapore's limited internal market meant that the import substitution route to development was not an option, especially after the collapse of the Malay Federation. The absence of a strong domestic capitalist class meant that the Singaporean government had little choice other than to rely on FDI and multinational corporations if it wanted to integrate itself successfully into the expanding international economy.

The essence of the strategy the Singaporean government adopted was to make itself an attractive investment location for mobile international capital.[7] At one level, this resulted in the development the sort of authoritarian regime described in the last chapter. A crucially important aspect of this process was a crackdown on the labour force, plus the establishment of the Economic Development Board, in 1961, which was charged with attracting multinational capital in accordance with a preferred model of industrial development and deepening (Haggard 1990: 112–13). Through a range of incentives such as tax breaks and infrastructure provision, the government attempted to 'shape Singapore's comparative advantage in the production of labour-intensive manufactures', an export-oriented industrialization strategy that proved to be 'a spectacular success' (Rodan 1997: 153). The Singaporean government recognized the limits of this strategy in the 1980s as neighbouring economies with lower-cost labour forces jumped on the industrialization bandwagon, and converted itself successfully into a regional finance and business hub. Singapore has become an important node in regional 'growth triangles', and in the activities of the so-called 'overseas Chinese'. Part of the success of these strategies and the state's capacity to respond to changing economic circumstances is attributable to the role played by government-linked companies, such as the Government of

Singapore Investment Corporation (GIC), one of the earliest 'sovereign wealth funds' (SWFs) in the region (Clark and Monk 2010). These notoriously non-transparent entities continue to play a large part in the expansion of the Singaporean state's economic activities (Rodan 2006), in a pattern that has more in common with some of its neighbours in Southeast Asia.

Singapore's somewhat fortuitous circumstances and small scale mean that – like Hong Kong – it is difficult to draw too many conclusions from its experience. What we can say about Singapore, as of Korea and Taiwan, however, is that it is not so much the incorruptibility of the state, or even its complete autonomy from particularistic interests that seems to matter, so much as the recognition that 'even imperfect governmental machinery, operating with normally venal human beings, can still be moulded into an instrument capable of facilitating high rates of economic growth' (Evans 1998: 73). In other words, state capacity is a necessary but not sufficient cause of successful developmental outcomes. The critical variable underpinning the rise of the first generation of NICs would seem to be the willingness of states to 'intervene' to direct the course of economic development in ways that frequently defied the conventional, predominantly neoliberal, economic wisdom. In Robert Wade's view, what distinguished East Asia's developmental states was

> a consistent and coordinated attentiveness to the problems and opportunities of particular industries, in the context of a long-term perspective on the economy's evolution, and a state which is hard enough not only to produce sizable effects on the economy but also to control the direction of the effects, which is a more demanding achievement. (Wade 1990: 343)

A major question that therefore emerges from these different, but related, experiences is whether such a role is any longer possible or appropriate, and whether states are capable of 'controlling the direction of effects'. Even if the state–business relationship remains relatively uncorrupted and capable of serving some sort of 'national interest', the impact of the Asian financial crisis on the Korean economy in particular suggested that integration into the international financial sector might fundamentally undermine state-led development strategies (Wade and Veneroso 1998). Before we consider this question in any detail, it is instructive to examine the experience of Southeast Asia, an area with a patchier history of economic development.

Southeast Asia: the maligned miracles?

Once again, the diversity of the developmental experience in Southeast Asia defies easy generalization, but it still makes sense to consider the most important states in Southeast Asia – Malaysia, Thailand, Indonesia, the Philippines and Vietnam – at the same time. Not only are they the largest economies and most strategically significant countries in the region, but they all attempted to accelerate the industrialization process, and with the noteworthy and instructive exception of the Philippines, they have done so rather effectively (Amsden 1995; Beeson and Pham 2012; Jomo 2001). Thus they constitute a distinct second (or even third, in Vietnam's belated case) wave or tier of industrial development after Japan and the first generation NICs. The other reason for considering these countries together is because, despite some significant and enduring differences in developmental outcomes, their collective performance has not been as good as the NICs, and in the case of the Philippines, has been strikingly poor. Indeed, the Philippines is the quintessential exemplar of what Yoshihara famously described as Southeast Asia's 'ersatz capitalism', by which he meant its technological dependence and (in particular) the poor quality of government intervention in the development process (Yoshihara 1988). Because the Philippines is something of an outlier even in a Southeast Asian context it is instructive for comparative purposes, and thus useful to consider it first.

The primary point to make about the Philippines is that things ought to have been different. After all, as an English-speaking former American colony with relative political stability and comparatively good growth rates following independence, it looked set to be the star performer in an entire East Asian region associated with chronic economic under-development. One factor working against the Philippines and any rapid economic transformation was the legacy of the colonial period and a trade structure that revolved around a limited number of products, especially sugar. But given that, with the exception of Thailand, both generations of aspiring industrializing economies that followed in Japan's wake had to cope with some sort of colonial handicap, why was the Philippines' response so inadequate? One reason was the negative impact of the Japanese occupation. Whereas Taiwan and Korea benefited from vital bureaucratic reform and a transformation of existing class structures, the principal impact of Japanese contact as far as the Philippines was concerned was the destruction of its economy. And yet, during the 1950s, the Philippines actually experienced some of the highest growth rates in the region (Hutchison 2006: 43). So what went wrong?

One of the most distinctive characteristics of the Philippines' political economy is the enfeebled nature of the state and its vulnerability to capture by particularistic interests. The failure to institute effective land reform meant that a repressive, parasitic land-owning class remained in place and inhibited necessary structural change. Indeed, in contrast to the developmental capacities of the 'strong' states of Northeast Asia, 'the Philippines presents an insightful study of precisely what kinds of economic problems can result from insufficient development of the state apparatus' (Hutchcroft 1994: 219). Because the state was so weak, its resources were plundered systematically. Crucially, and unlike elsewhere in Southeast Asia, it was effectively looted by actors external to the state itself. The state has only been able to survive at all with the assistance of international aid from the USA and the IFIs. As a consequence, its primary function has been to act as a conduit with which to redirect external assistance to privileged insiders, rent-seekers and cronies within the wider Philippines political economy. Tragically, the developmental process in the Philippines has been made more difficult because so much government expenditure is directed towards servicing the resultant foreign debt obligations (Bello 2000: 241).

Part of the problem in the Philippines was the nature of the bureaucracy itself: whereas, in much of the region, state bureaucracies were staffed by competent, relatively incorrupt officials, in the Philippines the bureaucracy was riddled with corruption and appointment to office depended more on patronage and contacts than on competence (Kang 2002: 76). While economic activity in the Philippines is dominated, as in Korea, by a relatively small number of families, in the Philippines there are more of them, across more economic sectors. Consequently, while competition exists, it is generally not the sort advocated by orthodox economists, but rather a struggle over 'the spoils of the state, with power shifting rapidly between groups' (Kang 2002: 145). In short, the Philippines represents the nadir of bureaucratic competence and effectiveness in Southeast Asia.

However, even though the Philippines is something of an extreme case, both in terms of the ineffectiveness of the state and its consequent negative impact on development, there are parallels with some of Southeast Asia's other economies. Indonesia, for example, has until relatively recently been dominated by Suharto, another archetypal 'strong-man' leader, whose grip on power was consolidated by networks of patronage and personal links to cronies and family members. And yet, for all the undoubted corruption, nepotism and lack of transparency that distinguished the Indonesian political economy under Suharto, for the three decades before the Asian crisis hit, Indonesia experienced significant, sustained economic growth and development. Indeed, it is remarkable that, despite Suharto's military background, economic development became his ideological mantra and the key to a broader notion of security. What is less surprising, perhaps, is that the army should have been 'permitted, even encouraged, to establish or extend businesses to provide new sources of funds for their operations and, indeed, for the private gain of the officers concerned' (Elson 2001: 191). As we saw in Chapter 4, the distinctive idea of security that prevailed in Indonesia, the army's position as one of the few institutions with national reach, and Suharto's own extensive connections and control within it, help to explain the military's prominent involvement in the economy. What is more remarkable is the way that key elements of the Indonesian economy, such as the oil industry, for example, were placed under military control and became the principal source of funding for the army.

This is even more surprising when we remember that, from the outset, the Suharto regime has been closely associated with both the IFIs and the so-called 'Berkeley mafia' of Western-trained economists who played a major role in the first Suharto cabinet following the overthrow of Sukarno. In 1966, the World Bank and the IMF took a prominent role in setting the economic policy agenda and approach of the first Suharto government as it attempted to establish its economic credentials and reassure potential international investors. But despite this initial willingness to adopt the rhetoric of reform, one of the defining features of the Suharto period has been a continuing tension between technocrats and nationalists. The relative power of each faction was directly related to the price of Indonesia's most valuable resource: oil. When the price of oil was low and the Indonesian government more dependent on international aid and investment flows, the Western-oriented technocrats were in the ascendancy; but once the price rose, the nationalists held sway. As Jeffrey Winters (1996: 96) put it, 'not only the onset but also the depth and intensity of the country's policy changes can be linked to changes in the Suharto regime's access to windfall oil profits'. The general point to make is that, in contrast to some of the more effective Northeast Asian states, policy implementation of any sort in Indonesia was compromised by a lack of bureaucratic competence and capacity on the one hand, and by the patrimonial nature of ties between government and business on the other (MacIntyre 1994: 262–3). Critically, Indonesia – like the other Southeast Asian economies – failed to discipline domestic business in the way their Northeast Asian counterparts had done, consequently inhibiting the development of internationally competitive export-oriented industries (Studwell 2013).

In some ways, Indonesia seems to confirm the paradox of the 'resource curse', or the counterintuitive idea that the possession of immense resource wealth can have detrimental impacts on development and governance (Ross 1999). At one level this is plainly true: oil wealth greased the wheels of patronage politics and the distinctive, corrupt, personalized networks of power that grew up around them. And yet the Indonesian economy grew by more than 7 per cent a year between 1968 and 1981, and industrial output expanded from 13 per cent to 42 per cent of national economic activity between 1965 and 1995 (Booth 1999: 112–13). Importantly, not all of the oil wealth disappeared in conspicuous consumption or foreign bank accounts. On the contrary, in fact – for all its faults, the Suharto government's distinctive form of what Richard Robison (1997: 111) calls 'authoritarian state capitalism' was a major investor in steel, aluminium, fertilizers, petroleum refining, cement and paper; in other words, some of the basic building blocks of an industrial economy. In short, the Suharto regime was highly 'interventionist' and despite the fact that investment decisions and policies might invariably have profited particular cronies and state-sponsored business conglomerates, significant development did occur, not all of which was swept away by the Asian crisis.

One thing that *was* overthrown by the crisis was the Suharto regime itself. Given that the bases of the New Order regime's successful interventions in the economy were the authoritarian nature of the government and the state's manifold involvement in economic activity, it might be supposed that even the possibility, let alone the desire for extensive state intervention, might be a thing of the past. The reality seems to be more complex and ambiguous: on the one hand, many of the old economic and political interests associated with the former Suharto regime have reconstituted themselves within the new, democratic order, severely limiting the capacity of the state to impose systemic reform as a consequence. The difficulty of winding back protection in politically sensitive industries is testimony to this continuing reality (Bland 2012). On the other hand, decentralization initiatives, coupled with the growth of democracy and political pluralism mean that 'authority over the allocation of resources, contracts and monopolies ha[s] been shifted from a highly centralized system of state power to a more diffuse and chaotic environment of political parties, parliaments and provincial governments' (Robison and Hadiz 2004: 215). Paradoxically enough, therefore, while the downfall of the Suharto regime might have been welcomed politically, it might – in the short term, at least – have further undermined the already limited capacity of the Indonesian state to drive the developmental process (Hadiz 2011). Despite the current optimism about Indonesia's natural advantages and bright future, internal political problems, corruption and reform fatigue may yet undermine its potential (Brooks 2011).

Of all the Southeast Asian countries, Malaysia tried most actively to emulate the Japanese exemplar. This is both predictable and surprising. It is predictable because Mahathir had adopted a 'look East' policy, which set out self-consciously to emulate the Japanese model, with all the nationalist, mercantilist and interventionist underpinnings this implied (Wain 2009). Mahathir saw state-led economic development as the key to breaking the shackles of Western colonialism and contemporary economic domination that were to become such prominent parts of his anti-Western rhetoric (Khoo 1995: 65–74). Japan too has played a more direct and tangible role in Malaysian development, as Japanese multinational corporations and investment have been central to the industrialization and structural transformation of the Malay economy (Machado 1992). But while this might explain the Japanese influence on Malaysian public policy, it is also important to note that Mahathir has been disdainful about the capacity of the Malaysian state bureaucracy and has systematically wound back its influence and independence.

To understand the trajectory of Malaysia's very distinctive economic development strategies we need to remember two things. First, the 'New Economic Policy' (NEP) that was the centrepiece of Malaysia's development plan was as much driven by ethnic factors as it was by economic ones, and necessitated major state involvement in the economy to enable it to achieve its aims (Rasiah and Shari 2001). The intention was to create an indigenous capitalist class that might compete with the dominant Chinese business groups (Jesudason 1989). This complex amalgam of racial and economic goals, and the way it has been mediated by Malaysia's ethnically divided political system, explains much about the growth of 'crony capitalism' and the sorts of defensive economic policies the Malaysian government has subsequently pursued (Beeson 2000). The NEP's goal was to place 30 per cent of share capital in *Bumiputera*, or native Malay hands, by 1990. To achieve this, trust agencies were established by the government to accumulate shares on behalf of the Malay community, with the intention of redistributing them at some future date.

In consequence, the public sector and state-owned enterprises expanded dramatically during the 1970s and early 1980s, establishing the basis for the fusion of government and business interests that is so characteristic of the Malaysian political economy. The second point to emphasize about economic development in Malaysia, then, is that not only are politics and economics in the country deeply enmeshed in ways that are at odds with, and anathema to, much Western thinking, but that 'involvement in politics increasingly came to be viewed by Bumiputeras as a quick means to obtain profitable business opportunities' (Gomez and Jomo 1997: 26). The prominent role played by Mahathir in trying to push the industrialization process meant that it was always vulnerable to the possibility that he 'failed to understand the most basic prerequisites of infant industry policy: export discipline and sanctions for failure' (Studwell 2013: 86).

Like Indonesia, Malaysia was the beneficiary of windfall oil revenues, which allowed the government to accelerate the development process. Also like Indonesia – despite pervasive corruption, political interference in economic processes and a 'massive expansion of the state sector' (Searle 1999: 77) – Malaysia experienced consistently high growth rates from the 1970s onwards, as the economy switched to an export-oriented development strategy. However, while this growth and development is impressive and – at least in part – testimony to the effectiveness of government policy, it remains constrained by history and hostage to the imperatives of ethnic accommodation. At one level this is manifest in the emergence of a 'rentier class'[8] and the growth of money politics. At another level, it has raised fundamental questions about the quality of the industrialization process that has emerged from Malaysia's compromised industry policies. As Jomo (1997: 106–7) points out, the Malaysian economy has a number of structural vulnerabilities: it remains dominated by a limited number of manufactured products (primarily electronics); MNCs dominate exports; local content and value-adding is low; and the degree of industrial deepening and complex linkages within the domestic economy remains limited. As we shall see in the next chapter, the depth of the industrialization process and the nature of integration into the global economy remains an issue for all of Southeast Asia's 'late-late' industrializing economies. However, there is now a significant domestic constituency lobbying enthusiastically for greater economic liberalization (Stubbs 2000). Consequently, there is doubt about the government's capacity to direct the course of development or – more fundamentally in a Malaysian context, perhaps – willingness to underwrite the ethnic basis of the wider social compact and distribution of economic resources upon which it was predicated.

Thailand has also enjoyed a remarkable economic transformation and, like Malaysia, the Thai economy has been dominated by ethnic Chinese. But unlike Malaysia, this has not led to such racially motivated policies. On the contrary, Chinese ethnicity in not an obstacle to political or economic success in Thailand, as the remarkable rise of former prime minister Thaksin Shinawatara and his 'unprecedented fusion of political and economic power' reminds us (Wingfield 2002: 284). What Thailand does have in common with Malaysia is both the familiar transition from an import-substitution to an export-oriented development strategy and, since the 1980s, an increasing reliance on Japanese investment to underpin it. But while Japanese foreign direct investment (FDI) has been important, it is also essential to recognize that the majority of investment capital has come from domestic sources (Hewison 2001: 86–7). However, despite the fact that much capital formation was local, as in the

Malaysian case, there is lingering concern about the quality and depth of the industrialization process that has occurred, and the dependence on foreign capital generally, and Japanese multinationals in particular, that has accompanied it (Bello and Poh 1998).

Thailand also has similarities with Indonesia, in that public policy has been affected by an underlying and enduring struggle between nationalists and technocrats about the course of development. Unlike Indonesia and Malaysia, however, energy-poor Thailand has been particularly vulnerable to fluctuations in global oil prices. Significantly, this encouraged a more interventionist policy stance on the part of successive governments in the 1970s and 1980s (Bowie and Unger 1997: ch. 6). Deciding how to cope with external pressures over which domestic policy-makers have no control remains one of the defining issues in Thailand and the rest of the region. While there are currently doubts re-emerging about the stability of the Thai economy, which make generalization difficult, a few comparative points can be made.

First, as in much of the rest of the region, the state has played a 'pivotal' role in the development of the economy and an indigenous capitalist class (Hewison 1989). Second, as in Indonesia (and Korea in Northeast Asia), the emergence of major business conglomerates in Thailand owes much to government policy and the political connections of the handful of families that dominate them. Third, and following directly from the previous point, 'the power and authority of the bureaucracy – both civilian and military – has been eclipsed by the wealth and power of business interests' (Wingfield 2002: 263). The balance of power between government and business – indeed, the very distinction between the state and capital – is an underlying dynamic and contradiction common to the region as a whole, but which has become especially acute in Thailand (Hewison 2010). All of which leads to a final point: for all the talk about the levelling effects of globalization, the irresistible nature of competitive forces, and the other neoliberal shibboleths that have become so commonplace, in Thailand, at least, there has been a decisive shift back to the politics of economic nationalism. In short, 'Thaksinomics' was predicated upon the '"developmentalist" view that in catching-up economies, government has to play a positive role in protecting and promoting firms and sectors to overcome the disadvantages of competing against more advanced economies' (Phongpaichit and Baker 2004: 100).

The final Southeast Asian state to mention briefly here may ultimately prove to be the most important: Vietnam. Since finally being freed from being under one or other of the major powers, Vietnam has moved rapidly to integrate itself into the global capitalist economy. In doing so, it has had to deal with one major contradiction that has not affected the others of its peers considered above: like China, Vietnam remains notionally 'communist'. In Vietnam's case, the Communist Party of Vietnam (CPV) continues to enjoy a higher profile than its Chinese counterpart. This has involved Vietnam's leaders in some complex doctrinal shifts as it has moved to embrace and give ideological legitimacy to market forces (Beresford 2008). The key point to emphasize about Vietnam's experience for the purposes of the current discussion is that it remains highly interventionist – as we might expect from a state that until recently practised a very orthodox form of Marxist central planning.

The principal manifestation of this continuing interventionism and state control can be seen in the state-owned enterprises (SOEs). While there has supposedly been a process of privatization in Vietnam, the reality is rather different. What the Vietnamese leadership refer to as 'equitization' does little to undermine state control of what used to be referred to as the commanding heights of the domestic economy. In fact, as Martin Gainsborough (2009: 269) points out:

> equitisation should be seen not as the retreat of the state but rather as a new form of state interventionism … because the people who are ostensibly letting go (that is, authorising the sale of state assets) are doing so in such a way that they continue to exert a hold over the recipients … living in such conditions of uncertainty, equitised firms have no choice but to continue to report to the state.

The provision of scarce capital remains an important source of state influence (Fforde 2009), as it was in the Japanese prototype. Not only does state support remain critical for notionally private business in Vietnam (Hansen *et al.* 2009), but the state has also attempted to guide the course and content of indigenous economic development by the strategic use of tax revenues and state incentives (Beeson and Pham 2012). Equally significantly, the Vietnamese government has proved adept at accepting developmental assistance from international donor agencies without rigorous institution of the hoped-for reforms (Painter 2005). This sort of 'mock compliance' has been a feature of the reform process in much of Southeast Asia (Walter 2008), and serves as a reminder of the obstacles to external pressures, even where potential political leverage exists. Despite there being many problems in Vietnam, and many potential obstacles to future development – not the least of which are serious corruption and a legitimacy deficit – it is important to recognize that there has also been remarkable progress. Importantly, this has not come about by embracing the market so much as by managing its impact.

Conclusion

The remarkable economic development that occurred in East Asia in the post-war period was unprecedented and largely unexpected. While there are some important differences in the extent of the economic development that occurred and the precise strategies that were employed to encourage it, there is widespread agreement that activist state policies played an important part in most of the countries considered above. Indeed, the comparatively poor development record of the Philippines provides an illuminating example of the consequences that can flow from the absence of at least a minimally effective state. It is also clear that much can go wrong with the government–business relationship, especially where it endures beyond the 'catching-up' phase and becomes self-serving, or where it becomes the centre of a corrupt, politically unrepresentative or even a repressive regime.

But it is also clear that the existence of either authoritarianism or corruption are not of themselves necessarily an obstacle to the development process. This is not to advocate either of them, of course, but simply to point out that arguments which claim that events such as the East Asian crisis were a consequence of 'crony capitalism' need to explain why such relationships, and non-transparent, undemocratic and even authoritarian regimes more generally, were not an obstacle to development before the crisis and have endured during the recovery phase. It has also become evident that corruption is not a uniquely East Asian phenomenon. The point to emphasize is that, even where corruption threatens to impede renewed developmental efforts, as in Indonesia, reform will prove difficult where it is opposed by entrenched networks of power and interest, and where alternative institutions of 'good governance' are inadequately developed (Dick 2012).

However, even if it is accepted that states in East Asia frequently played a crucial role in mobilizing domestic savings, directing credit to strategically important industries, and generally attempting to guide the course of the developmental process, it is not clear that states can or should play such a role in the contemporary, increasingly integrated international economic and regulatory order. But, as we have seen, states are still inescapably key components of even the transnational, market-enhancing regimes. In other words, there is no such thing as a truly deregulated economy; the important issue is the *type* of regulation and the outcome it is intended to produce. It is perhaps the degree of intentionality in public policy, and the belief that the course of development could be significantly and positively influenced that really distinguishes much of East Asia. The question that the East

Asian governments must now confront is whether the types of market-friendly, 'hands-off' regulatory frameworks they have been adopting are appropriate (Stiglitz 2002). It is a question that is especially relevant in the context of East Asia's integration with the global political economy.

Chapter 8

The China Model?[1]

It is hard to overstate the significance of the 'rise of China' for the world, let alone for East Asia. Even if this is more of a *re*-emergence than an entrance on to the world stage, it is a development of long-term global significance, the consequences of which will reverberate throughout the twenty-first century. For East Asia in particular, China's re-emergence as a world power presents enormous opportunities and challenges – and even threats, perhaps. In short, whatever the leaders of China decide to do over the coming decades will have a profound influence on its neighbours and help to shape the East Asian region. As we shall see in more detail in Chapter 11, China will have a large say in deciding whether there actually is an 'East Asian region' as such, or whether the dominant rubric will be something more expansive and/or inclusive. It is therefore important to look at China's developmental experience in some detail as it is already the most significant actor in the region and is likely to become increasingly so. Indeed, for some observers, it is only a question of time before China comes to 'rule the world' (Jacques 2009).

While it is too soon to know how valid these sorts of predictions will prove to be, there is already a growing debate about the extent and impact of China's influence. For some observers, China represents an important and attractive alternative to the developmental orthodoxy that has been promoted by the USA in conjunction with powerful international financial institutions (IFIs) such as the World Bank and the International Monetary Fund (IMF) (Halper 2010). It is important, therefore, to understand how China achieved its unprecedented and monumental economic transformation, before we can see whether there is model that might be emulated by other states in much the same way that the Japanese model was adopted. While there is a good deal of scepticism about whether such a model exists and whether it is transferable even if it does (Breslin 2011a), it is worth remembering that while no other country actually replicated the Japanese experience in its entirety, it has clearly had an important demonstration effect in much of the region (Kwon 2009; Terry 2002). As with the Japanese case, it is important to unpack some of the constituent parts of the Chinese model, not least because they may have geopolitical consequences that Japan's did not. At the outset, therefore, it is worth reminding ourselves of the context from within which China re-emerged. As with all the other East Asian states we have considered so far, politics and economics are deeply interconnected and provide the context within which the economic transformation has taken place. It is important to provide a brief snapshot of political development in China, therefore, because this is a very distinctive element of the China model and one that raises immediate questions about it transferability – and its attractiveness.

Politics in China

The fact that China is a 'communist' country means that ideology plays – or ought to play – a far more important part in the political life of the nation than it does elsewhere. And yet, while Lawrence (1998: 1) may be right to suggest that, under Mao, China was 'the largest, and arguably the most devout, Marxist regime', this does not tell the whole story. As we saw in Chapter 2, part of the genius and originality of the early Chinese Communist Party (CCP) leadership was to mobilize the peasantry (in ways that would have astounded Marx) by appealing to their innate nationalism (Johnson 1962). Chinese history is punctuated by massive, traumatic upheavals, to which the communist period has not been immune. What is distinctive about the era of communist rule is that while ideology played an important part in its early phases, nationalism has become more prominent in the contemporary period (Gries 2004; Yahuda 2000). Indeed, as we saw in Chapter 4, nationalism is beginning to constrain China's foreign policy options as a consequence of non-negotiable questions of national identity and pride (Gries *et al.* 2011).

Though the comparatively recent Cultural Revolution (1966–76) demonstrated that social convulsions are still possible within the PRC, and that ideology could play a major part in their legitimation, recent leaders such as Jiang Zemin have recognized the importance of nationalism and attempted systematically to draw on nationalist sentiment and a mythologized reading of China's past to shore up support for the CCP. This was a strategy of particular importance at a time when the ideological legitimacy and practical purpose of the CCP were being undermined by rapid economic and social transformation (Terrill 2003: 147–50). William Callahan (2010) argues that China's increasingly strident nationalist sentiment is a reflection of ambivalent feelings about the country's past and present status. Callahan (2010: 27) suggests that the most important aspect of what he calls 'China's pessoptimism' is that 'it is fundamentally unstable, producing shifting feelings, which at any time can spill over into mass movements that target domestic critics, foreigners, and even the party-state itself'. In many ways nationalism has replaced Marxist ideology as the basis of Chinese identity.

Despite Marxist ideas no longer having the sort of practical importance or ideational purchase they once did, the central social fact about China is that it remains a 'communist' country. This is important, not just for China's intra- and inter-regional relations, but because it is predicated on a distinctive mode of governance and a particular role for the state. Indeed, it is important to remember that the CCP emerged from the ashes of a long, destructive civil war; the construction of a 'strong' state with which to ensure domestic control and ward off possible Cold War external predations, was consequently a key goal of the revolutionary leadership. This was (and is) no easy task, of course: the sheer extent of China and the rapidity with which the communist victory was achieved, meant that centralizing power was in itself a major undertaking. While the administration of China's vast regions was initially given over to Military Administrative Committees, the CCP set about systematically creating an entire state apparatus. Indeed, as Richard McGregor (2010: 26) points out, 'the Party's genius has been its leaders' ability in the last three decades to maintain the political institutions and authoritarian powers of old-style communism, while dumping the ideological straitjacket that inspired them.'

The upshot of political and institutional innovation in China was the development of two parallel hierarchies, the Party and the government, which shared interlocking memberships. The Party's job was primarily to provide the ideological rationale for policies, and the government's job was to implement them. Though not formally part of the decision-making process, the military, especially in this early period, was also a key political actor, whose primary job then as now was 'to keep the Party in power' (McGregor 2010: 105). The original role model for China's political system was its key ally, the Soviet Union. Consequently, its supreme political body – in theory, at least – was the National People's Congress, which was empowered to enact laws, ratify treaties and select the president and vice-president. In reality, it has been the National Party Congress and the central committee it notionally elects that has been at the centre of power in China. The central committee elects a politburo, which in turn selects a Standing Committee, whose chairman is the most powerful man in China. Importantly, however:

> While the chair normally exercises enormous authority, he is not, and never has been, a totalitarian dictator. It would be more accurate to describe him as first among almost equals. Decision-making appears to take place through coalition formation among Standing Committee members; the voice of the chair is generally, but not always, decisive. (Deyer 2000: 88)

It is worth dwelling on these rather arcane and opaque structures because they are so different from those of the West – and much of East Asia, too, for that matter – and as a consequence attract such criticism on the grounds of their non-democratic nature. But it is also worth remembering that the party had revolutionary origins, and was initially seen as the only mechanism with which to transform China's pernicious, feudal class structures and the social forces that had oppressed and exploited Chinese workers for so long. It was this historical role as the vanguard of the people that gave legitimacy to the overarching political apparatus and justified the 'dictatorship of the masses' and the paradoxical, concomitant lack of popular sovereignty. However, the net effect of the party's attempts to institutionalize this ideology has been to entrench power and leadership struggles among a handful of senior officials and the distinctive form of 'fragmented authoritarianism' that prevails to this day (Lieberthal 1992).

The nature of the Chinese political system under communist rule, and the concentration of power that occurred under dominant leaders such as Mao and Deng, meant that both leaders dominated their respective eras in ways that have few real parallels with Western democracies (Salisbury 1992). The transition between Mao and Deng, and the vicissitudes of Deng's career that preceded it, also illustrate the potential volatility of Chinese politics, the importance of personalities and personal loyalties, the informal nature of the political process, and the fluctuating fortunes of rival leadership factions in determining political outcomes (Dittmer 2002). The main achievement of Mao's chosen successor – Hua Guofeng – was to undermine the centrality and importance of revolutionary ideology. This was a pivotal moment in China's post-war history as it marked a decisive turn toward 'pragmatism'. The Eleventh Party Congress in 1977 marked Deng's re-ascent to the summit of Chinese power and a recognition that Hua lacked the authority and capacity to modernize the Chinese economy. Crucially, however, Deng's economic reforms were feasible because they did not threaten the CCP itself, and 'communist' bureaucratic institutions proved to be surprisingly flexible mechanisms with which to implement them (Shirk 1993: 17).

In addition to the economic reforms instituted by Deng, one of the most important tactics employed by him and his supporters was to dismantle the personality cult surrounding Mao (Saich 2004). From that time forward, the legitimacy of the CCP would be tied less to an inherited ideological dogma and more to the Party's ability to deliver economic development. This was to be the era of 'socialism with Chinese characteristics'. Significantly, the preoccupation with economic reform that has distinguished Chinese politics since Deng became leader, was not mirrored by similar political reforms. On the contrary, the tide of democratic reform that was sweeping through Eastern Europe and igniting hopes of similar initiatives among Chinese students in particular, was seen by the Party as something that needed to be actively suppressed. The tensions between student activists, reformists such as Hu Yaobang and Zhao Ziyang, and the PRC establishment came to a head in the demonstrations in Tiananmen Square in 1989.

That year was also significant because Jiang Zemin became General Secretary and largely continued the reformist agenda pioneered by Deng. The importance attached to economic development and the downgrading of Marxist orthodoxy was evident in Deng's rather surreal, but highly revealing, claim that 'leftists' were inhibiting the reform process and slowing China's development (Saich 2004: 76–7). Significantly, the thrust of the Dengist approach and the development of a 'socialist market economy' were endorsed by the Fourteenth Party Congress in 1992. What was significant about Jiang's role in this period was that he attempted to reimpose greater CCP control of the civil society that was developing as a consequence of economic liberalization and social transformation. And yet it is important to note that 'many of the controls have proved impossible to implement for any length of time, testifying to the decline in state capacity and threatening to result in continuing friction between the state and elements of society' (Saich 2004: 79). In short, China's elites have been forced to confront a more widespread dilemma that is one of the hallmarks of a 'global' era: greater international economic integration of the sort promoted by Deng potentially compromises the autonomy of the state. China's accession to the WTO and the domestic reforms this has necessitated are a dramatic example of this possibility (Feng 2006). In China's case, the dilemma created by diminished autonomy is especially acute, as the state has had a crucial, ideologically legitimated role as the defender of the proletariat and vanguard of progressive social development.

The degree of political and ideological change that has occurred in China can be gauged from the fact that the so-called fourth and fifth generations of leaders are generally technocrats like Hu Jintao and his successor Xi Jinping, with engineering backgrounds and seemingly little interest in ideology (Nathan and Gilley 2002). The key point to emphasize is that it is connections or *guanxi* that are crucial: patron–client networks and factional loyalty remain critical determinants of who rises to the top (Li 2012b). Indeed, it is noteworthy that capitalists are now not only seen as important elements in the development of China's productive forces, but they have actually been invited to join the CCP. There are, however, limits to which the regime is willing to go to accommodate the reformist pressures being placed on it, especially as this affects the role of the CCP itself. In a major statement on the prospects for, and view of, democratic development in China, the PRC government argues that democracy must reflect particular national circumstances. In China's case, this means that rule by the CCP is a continuing 'objective requirement' for the country's future development, stability and unity (PRC 2005).

Given the expectations about the prospects for democratic reform and transition held – if not always realized – about much of East Asia, China's political trajectory is a reminder that nothing is inevitable about the course of institutional development. Significantly, despite the rapid emergence of a middle class in China, this has not translated into direct pressure on the state for political liberalism. On the contrary, China's growing capitalist class in particular has been very happy to work closely with its authoritarian 'communist' government as long as it creates the conditions for future development and doesn't intrude too much on private prerogatives. In short, 'business owners generally rely on informal, nondemocratic means to pursue their economic interests' (Tsai 2007: 11). Indeed, Chen goes further and suggests that 'the bourgeois have prospered from the commercial privileges deriving from political lineage. They are essentially a parasitic appendage of corrupt and unrestricted political power and have a taken-for-granted personal stake in preventing regime change' (Chen 2002: 412). Far from acting as agents of political change, then, in China at least, the expanding capitalist class is actually helping to prop up and legitimate continuing 'communist' rule. As Minxin Pei (2006: 207) has pointed out, the great paradox at the centre of China's development is that 'rapid short-term economic growth may have a perversely negative impact on democratization because it provides all the incentives for the ruling elites not to seek political liberalization'.

We should not assume, therefore, that China's political future is any more likely to resemble that of the West's than its past has done (Wright 2010). This is not to suggest that the current model of political organization in China is without problems or challenges. On the contrary, there is an increasingly vocal civil society in China and it has assumed a more prominent role in criticizing the state and highlighting its failures, especially corruption, waste and environmental crises. For some observers, the situation has become so serious that it threatens the survival of the CCP itself and its distinctive form of 'resilient authoritarianism'. As Li (2012b: 606), puts it:

If middle-class Chinese begin to feel that their voices are being suppressed, that their access to information is unjustly being blocked or that their space for social action is being unduly confined, increased political dissent may begin to take shape.

However, even if Li is correct to suggest that the legitimacy of the Party is being undermined because of questions about its competence, and because new and powerful interest groups are challenging its authority, it is not obvious what direction change might take should it finally come. Much will depend on the CCP's ability to maintain the remarkable economic development that has been central to China's rise, its possible attractiveness to others, and – to this point, at least – the continuing and surprisingly high levels of support of the Chinese people themselves (Gilley 2008; Shi 2008; Wright 2010). It is important, therefore, to look more closely at the nature of and circumstances within which the economic transformation occurred.

An economy like no other?

Although China's overall rise may have occurred as a consequence of a propitious set of historical circumstances, this was not simply an inevitable function of the determinative impact of 'structural' precondi-tions. On the contrary, agency was pivotal. One man epitomized this more than any other: Deng Xiaoping (see Vogel 2011). When Deng began the process of opening up the Chinese economy as recently as the late 1970s, China was still a poor, peripheral economy known primarily for its export of revolutionary ideology rather than sophisticated manu-factured goods. It is hard to overstate the scale or significance of the subsequent transformation: double-digit economic growth rates for decades led to hundreds of millions of Chinese being lifted out of poverty at an unprecedented rate. This may have become the stuff of cliché, but it bears repeating, nevertheless: it would have been remarkable anywhere, but it is simply astounding when we remember China's marginal, impov-erished, largely agrarian status when Deng decided to encourage a process of economic opening.

While China's material transformation is the most immediate and tangible aspect of its transformation, one of the other reasons that China's rise is so significant is that it represents an alternative to the neoliberal 'Washington consensus' of market-driven development in which the state 'gets out of the way' of the private sector (Zhao 2010). Despite the fact that the Chinese economy and the regulatory framework within which it is embedded is a long way from neoliberalism, Deng's initial moves were seen as risky and controversial within China itself. Indeed, economic reform was also an important *political* achievement: when Deng oversaw the first tentative steps toward economic liberaliza-tion and integration with an international economy that remained domi-nated by capitalist powers, there were many in China who doubted its wisdom. What for some was admirable 'pragmatism' on Deng's part was seen by others as a betrayal of the socialist values that had defined the country since its reunification under Mao (Vogel 2011).

The circumstances confronting China's Party leaders in the late 1970s were very different, however, and the imperative to address declining economic productivity, especially in the countryside, was overwhelming. Once again, land reform was a crucial part of successful development (Studwell 2013): the de-collectivization and marketization of the agricultural sector brought dramatic improvements in output, making China self-sufficient by the early 1980s – no small achievement for a country whose history had been punctuated periodically by apocalyptic famines. Simultaneously, as capital accumulated and labour was freed, township and village enterprises began to spring up (Naughton 2007). Emboldened by the success of the rural reform programme, key policy-makers such as premier Zhao Ziyang began to turn their attention to reforming, liberalizing and eventually privatizing parts of the economy and the command-era institutions within which they were embedded.

The trick for China's policy-makers was to facilitate economic reforms that would galvanize the economy without undermining the role of the CCP or its place in planning China's overall development. Given the stakes involved in the economic changes, and nervousness about their impact and success, it is hardly surprising that initial efforts to liberalize and integrate with the wider international economy were confined to the sorts of special economic zones (SEZs) that had been developed successfully elsewhere in Asia, which remained relatively unconnected to the rest of the country. Despite the success of SEZs such as Shenzen, which was transformed from a sleepy fishing village in the space of forty years to become the fastest-growing city in China and a major manufacturing centre with a population of some 14 million, the impact of wrenching economic change was not welcomed by all in China. Conservative opposition to the reform and liberalization process was not defeated decisively until 1992 and Deng's celebrated tour of Southern China when he pushed for the development of a 'socialist market economy' (Breslin 2007). Ultimately, and despite paying lip service to Marxist ideology, the model China adopted was more like the developmental state pioneered by Japan than it was anything like the Soviet Union.

When the 15th Party Congress in 1997 endorsed a policy of 'grasping the large and letting go of the small' it captured the underlying attitude of the Party towards the market (Lau 1999). Strategically important elements of the state-owned enterprises (SOEs) would continue to be controlled by the state, while less significant enterprises would be hived off to the private sector. It was not simply the possible economic or even geopolitical importance of some economic sectors that influenced government thinking about policy towards the SOEs, however: the CCP ruling elite was also supposed to be acting as the vanguard of the proletariat. Many of China's workers were employed in (SOEs) that were often bywords for inefficiency and incapable of competing in the global market to which they were increasingly exposed (Yusuf *et al.* 2006). Even as late as the mid-1990s, something like 70 per cent of China's workers were employed by SOEs (Naughton 2007: 106). Privatization was bound to have far more than symbolic importance, as millions faced the prospect of losing hitherto secure employment. Nevertheless, the SOE share of national output declined from 77 per cent in 1978 at the time of initial opening, to less that 50 per cent by 1998 (Li *et al.* 2008). But despite this decline – and recent figures suggest that the state's share of industrial output had fallen further to 27 per cent by 2009 – this disguises a more important reality that in some ways defines the contemporary Chinese state and the distinctive form of capitalism it has overseen. As in Vietnam, the state in China has been careful to maintain, and even to tighten, its hold over industries it regards as strategic (Miles 2011).

The Chinese developmental state?

Like Japan, the PRC's developmental project has been influenced profoundly by the wider geopolitical context in which it was embedded. In China's case, of course, this has – until relatively recently, at least – been a major disadvantage: China found itself marginalized both politically and economically in an increasingly integrated international political economy dominated by the USA. In such circumstances, it is hardly surprising that China's leaders initially 'leaned towards' the Soviet Union, its notional ideological ally. The second point that flows from this is that, while China's political and economic regime is very different from Japan's, the PRC government has from its inception also been a developmental state, albeit one that was initially socialist and Maoist (White 1993). Indeed, it could hardly have been otherwise: states cannot be much more 'interventionist' and directive than they are under central planning.

But the limits of self-reliance and the disadvantages of isolation from global economic forces became increasingly apparent during the 1950s and 1960s. This is not to say that significant development did not occur during the Mao era – it did (Selden 1993) – but it was dwarfed by the rapid economic growth that was occurring elsewhere in the region; most gallingly in Taiwan. Even when Deng Xiaoping made the pragmatic decision to begin to open up the Chinese economy, it was not obvious whether the capitalist road and the journey from plan to market would be a success. Despite the seemingly unambiguous evidence of the success of China's economic policies, there is still a debate about some of its consequences and the character of the transformation that has occurred.

Some China specialists caution that '[r]eifying the PRC as a developmental state would reflect only the center's official aspirations, not the empirical reality within the party-state's own institutions' (Tsai and Cook 2005: 61). The key question is about how much credit the PRC government deserves for directing or managing the overall process of economic development. In other words, was it at least partly a question of being in the right place at the right time, as was plainly the case with some of Southeast Asia's economies? Japan, we need to remember, had formidable state capacity in the heyday of the developmental state. China, by comparison, has had nothing like the same bureaucratic resources, especially in the early phases of the reform process. The lack of a similar state capacity, and doubts about the state's ability to direct the course of development, have consequently led to more equivocal interpretations of the developmental process in China. Indeed, it has been argued that it is a lack of state capacity and the concomitant inability of government to direct or compel compliance with its initiatives that has actually made market-led development more attractive (Moore 2002: 279).

A number of factors seem to have stopped the state in China from playing the extensive and effective role it did in Japan. Most obviously, the fact that China is geographically and demographically massive, 'socialist', impoverished and lacking in the sort of developmental track record that led Japan to colonize China rather than vice versa, were clearly long-term handicaps. But the nature of the political relationships and economic structures that developed in the PRC meant that the course of development was shaped by contingent forces which continue to constrain policy options even in the post-Mao reform era. The sort of 'fragmented authoritarianism' noted above caused decision-making to be contested and far less coherent than in Japan, where the country's bureaucrats were less constrained by rival centres of political, ideological or even military power. This leads to some rather contradictory outcomes. On the one hand, the state in China has the same sort of control that Japanese state officials formerly enjoyed. In China, however, the policy-making process is much more factionalized and as a consequence generates sub-optimal economic outcomes. As Shi (2008: 191) points out, 'banking policies were made to bolster the short-term strength of both generalist and technocratic factions with little regard to long-term consequences'. The potentially dangerous consequences of decision-making processes that are overwhelmingly political are becoming more evident, according to some observers:

China's growing dependence on debt to drive GDP growth implies that there will be no meaningful reform of interest rates, exchange rates or material foreign involvement in the domestic financial markets for the foreseeable future. (Walter and Howie 2011: 210)

It is important not to overstate the authority and responsibility of the central government in this area, however. Another factor that limits the coherence of the 'China model' has been the contradictory impact of the process of decentralization that has been undertaken recently. What has been described as 'federalism Chinese style', is seen as having 'placed considerable limits on the discretion of the central government' (Montinola *et al.* 1995: 50). Institutions have been reconfigured in a continuing interaction between the centre and the provinces, a process in which 'local actors have exercised agency in manipulating formal institutions to their advantage' (Tsai 2006: 129).

Such changes have also had the effect of changing the distribution and nature of corruption in China as it becomes more associated with outright bribery and less with administrative abuse (Ko and Weng 2012). The expansion and transformation of the economy and its associated incentive structures has reconfigured fundamentally the position of individual cadres. The 'informal privatization' processes that have seen former Party officials become capitalist entrepreneurs has not only blurred ontological and class boundaries (Ding 2000), it has also had an impact on the state and its role. Two aspects of this process are especially noteworthy. First, the state has deviated from the sort of 'autonomous' leadership role played in Japan, partly as a consequence of some Party members' enduring 'suspicion' of the private sector (Howell 2006: 288), and partly because of the entrepreneurial, profit-seeking role of elements of the state bureaucracy (Lu 2000). Put differently, where elements of the state are engaged with the new private sector they are frequently corrupt and self-serving; where they are not, they lack the channels of communication and authority to implement policy effectively. These potential problems are exacerbated by a second distinctive feature of the embrace of capitalism: the contradictory position of capitalists themselves.

It is not only China's ideologically ambiguous relationship to capitalism that sets it apart from other developmentally oriented states such as Japan, however. What is perhaps most noteworthy about China, is that – unlike Japan – its ruling elites have been able to use foreign direct investment (FDI) to reinforce their political authority and control. As Mary Gallagher (2002: 368) has pointed out:

While foreign investment may indirectly improve the environment for future democratization, through the promotion of the rule of law, transparency, and the freer flow of information, in the short term its presence has afforded the regime more time and more political space to pursue economic reform without political liberalization.

The point to emphasize is that, even though China has been much more economically 'open' and reliant on FDI than was Japan, its political elites have managed to exert a degree of control over its possible political impact, at least – its inferior state capacity notwithstanding. The question is what impact such practices have had on the quality of the developmental process, and whether they will remain effective in the future.

The attractions of state capitalism

As Ha-joon Chang (2002) has pointed out, *all* successful industrializing and developing countries – including bastions of free market orthodoxy such as the United States and Britain – have done so with state assistance. What distinguishes China is that, first, China is still a developing economy in many ways, for all its remarkable progress. Second, the state's role in shaping this process remains an unambiguous empirical reality that China's political elites have done little to disguise. Significantly, it is not only China that is embracing forms of economic management and political organization that are sharply at odds with the neoliberal/liberal-democratic orthodoxy. On the contrary, the rise of the so-called BRIC (Brazil, Russia, India and China) economies highlights an important shift in the material distribution of power in the international system, and the emergence of very different ideas about the best ways of running an economy (Armijo 2007; Florini 2011).

The emergence of 'state capitalism' has become synonymous with the emergence of a very different style of political and economic organization from that associated with the free market orthodoxy linked to the so-called Washington consensus, which under the auspices of American hegemony has been the dominant developmental template in the post-war period – at least at the level of rhetoric and IFI-generated policy advice. State capitalism, by contrast, is associated with a very different set of principles. As Ian Bremmer (2010: 5, 23) points out, in contemporary forms of state capitalism:

the ultimate motive is not economic (maximising growth) but *political* (maximising the state's power and the leadership's chances of survival). This is a form of capitalism but one in which the state acts as the dominant economic player and uses markets primarily for political gain ... State capitalism is not the reemergence of socialist central planning in a twenty-first century package. It is a form of bureaucratically engineered capitalism particular to each government that practices it. It's a system in which the state dominates markets primarily for political gain.

Such a formulation not only helps to explain the durability, and perhaps the success, of capitalist development in China, but it also explains why it is such a challenge to the extant order that has been dominated by the West generally, and in particular for the last 150 years or so, by the USA. This form of state capitalism is entirely in keeping with the tradition of state-led development that has distinguished East Asia in the post-war period. Not only is the role of the state in China much closer to the model developed by Japan than it is to anything in the Anglo-American economies, but China's leaders' sense of 'comprehensive' security is also demonstrated in their economic policy. As we have seen, state influence over the banking sector in China remains a key tool in shaping developmental outcomes. But the retention of influence over the SOEs also remains a key part of China's overall approach to security, especially in the all-important resource sector, as we shall see in more detail in subsequent chapters. The point to note here is that:

> SOE investments and actions also reflect the long-term vision of their controlling shareholder (the Chinese government), and thus short-term profits are not necessarily their highest priority ... The top Chinese leadership has stated that SOEs will continue to be the main actors in China's going out policy, and that China will use its massive foreign exchange reserves to fuel this overseas expansion, especially targeting energy and natural resources. (Szamosszegi and Kyle 2011: 89)

The question at this stage, therefore, is what impact are such strategies having, and how attractive are they as far as other countries are concerned? If there is a China model, is it an attractive one? In the case of some of China's 'going out' policies, or the government-backed outward investment and engagement strategies, these questions are interconnected. China's burgeoning demand for resources has meant that its energy companies are not only becoming more important economic and political actors, but they are also having an impact on bilateral partners, as part of China's evolving resource diplomacy (Beeson *et al.* 2011).

As we might expect from such a complex and multifaceted process that occurs across many countries and involves multiple state and non-state actors, opinion is mixed about the impact of China's growing international presence. For some scholars, China's involvement in Africa is not only good for that continent's overall development, but also 'for those who have faith in "socialism with Chinese characteristics", China's reform experiences in the past three decades can serve as a model for developing countries in Africa on how to eliminate poverty and make strides in industrialization' (Jiang 2009: 592). Some African observers, by contrast, point to the neocolonial aspects of the relationship that is seen as primarily benefiting China rather than Africa (Sanusi 2013).

There is something of a paradox here, because the principal reason to think China may be capable of exerting an influence over the behaviour of other states is its economic success. Many outside observers, especially in countries keen to replicate China's developmental successes, want to understand how China transformed itself. Discussion about the possible existence of a distinctive Chinese model of development has centred on the so-called 'Beijing consensus' (Ramo 2004). The Beijing consensus is especially significant as it potentially provides an alternative development paradigm to the more widely known Washington consensus, which was synonymous with American hegemony, and which advocated a broadly neoliberal, free-market-oriented, small government agenda (Williamson 1994). The Beijing consensus, by contrast, is associated primarily with pragmatism and taking a non-doctrinaire approach to whatever seems to work. While some observers doubt that the Beijing consensus actually exists as a coherent framework, and question its influence or applicability (Huang 2011), it remains symbolically important if nothing else, as it highlights a decline in American influence and a recognition that there are different ways of approaching economic development. Significantly, however, the Chinese government makes a point of not talking about, much less advocating, the Beijing consensus, so its status is rather different from that of its American counterpart, variants of which have been supported enthusiastically by the USA and powerful institutions such as the World Bank and the IMF (Foot *et al.* 2003).

This point merits emphasis when thinking about the possible attractions of the China model and/or state capitalism. We have, after all, become accustomed to thinking of the USA as having 'soft power', or a non-material basis of influence over other countries, because of the apparent attractiveness of its culture, political ideas and institutions (Nye 2004). Other countries, the argument goes, are more likely to be influenced by the USA and go along with its policy preferences because they are attracted to – or at least not threatened by – what it seems to stand for. This is a possibility, it should be noted, that has not been lost on Marxist-inspired scholarship, though they are much less sanguine about its implications (Cox 1987). Be that as it may, it is remarkable that we have now begun to think of 'communist China' as having the potential to exert an ideational influence or attractiveness over other countries (Ding 2010).

There is now a substantial literature that assesses China's ability to project soft power (see Suzuki 2009). For many informed observers, especially in the West, China's soft-power appeal remains very limited. David Shambaugh (2013: 267), for example, argues that 'other countries do not want to be like China ... China's attributes may be unique, but they do not hold universal appeal'. Nevertheless, the Chinese government is expending significant resources in attempting to develop soft power resources, an effort that is manifest in the 'charm offensive' generally, and initiatives such as the increasingly ubiquitous Confucius Institutes in particular. Such efforts are unlikely to have much impact, however, while China is also engaged in a process of vigorously asserting its territorial claims with its regional neighbours. Such efforts are unlikely to cease, though, not least because of what Edney (2012: 909) claims is soft power's important domestic component: 'For the party-state, enhancing soft power is not simply a matter of more effectively using existing soft power resources at an international level through better public diplomacy, but also about building and strengthening these resources at home.' In other words, the external projection of China's collective identity is a reflection of complex, continuing debates about national identity and China's place in the international system (Callahan 2010).

Unless such debates can be resolved, China's sense of itself as a coherent entity and its ability to project soft power are likely to be constrained. In some ways, indeed, the very enterprise of seeking to construct or use soft power seems rather misconceived and redolent of a former Cold War era. It is noteworthy that America's soft power really came to the fore after the Cold War when the USA was no longer in the business of ideological struggle and active proselytizing. On the contrary, American soft power has been projected by something other than the efforts of a self-conscious state bent on winning-over converts. On the contrary – whatever we take American soft power to be, it is a product of a much wider set of cultural values, practices and products than any state authority could produce. Indeed, part of the attraction of 'American values' no doubt is precisely that they are not products of the state.

While the language and the concepts associated with soft power may be too unspecific and reified at times to be persuasive, they do point to a potentially important source of competition in the international system. It is evident that the 'American model', otherwise known as the 'Washington consensus', is no longer held in high esteem. Of course, many would argue that it never was, but was foisted upon often reluctant states as part of their acquiescence to the wishes of the wealthy and powerful IFIs (Cammack 2003). There is plainly something in this, but for better or worse, something like the Washington consensus with its commitment to free trade, financial sector liberalization and a limited role for government became the default policy setting during the heyday of American hegemony. If this period is drawing to a close, especially if this process is seen to be driven in part by the failures of the neoliberal policy paradigm, it is to be expected that there would be increased interest in other 'models'. In this context it as much the crisis of Anglo-American capitalism as it is the inherent attractions of the alternative Beijing consensus that have given the Chinese model increased salience.

Conclusion

As we might expect about something as new and ill-defined as the 'China model', there is a range of opinion about its significance, and even its existence. As Shaun Breslin (2011: 1328) points out, 'part of the problem in identifying the components of any such model is the huge diversity of developmental trajectories within China itself. To talk of a single Chinese model misses the huge variety – the different models – of economic structures within China.' Nevertheless, the *idea* of a China model stands as an important alternative to the hitherto dominant Western orthodoxy, and the possibility of an alternative model of development assumes a symbolic and discursive significance beyond any underlying coherent reality. For admirers of China's policy approach, the advantage and potential attraction of the China model is that the interventionist economic management style with which this is associated is thought to have made China less vulnerable to shocks and crises (Zhao 2010: 423). Indeed, it is the comparatively strong performance of the Chinese economy in the aftermath of recent North American and European crises that has convinced some observers that China's policy approach is both effective and attractive (Ji 2010). The validity of some of these claims is taken up in the following chapters.

Whether China does prove to be as immune to shocks as some of its admirers believe will become apparent over the next few years. However, even without knowing the answer to this profoundly important question, we can make a few observations about the Chinese developmental experience. First, while China's developmental trajectory not surprisingly reflects its own specific history and the ideas and interests that have shaped it, China's pattern of development is much closer to the broader East Asian experience described in earlier chapters than it is to the model championed by the USA or depicted in most economic textbooks. Second, given China's undoubted economic success, it is hardly surprising that its leaders may be interested in explaining it in terms that actually reflect China's particular circumstances and sensibilities. A more distinctive school of Chinese international relations theory has already begun to emerge – one that attempts to account for China's rise and role by drawing on indigenous concepts and ideas (Lynch 2009; Qin 2009; Shambaugh 2011). It would be surprising if a similar process did not happen when Chinese scholars tried to explain the country's economic performance. After all, it is no coincidence that American scholarship has dominated both economic and international relations theory, while the USA has dominated the international system more generally (Smith 2002). At a time when economic orthodoxy has suffered sustained attacks (Colander *et al.* 2009), and when the USA itself seems to be in a period of steady comparative decline, there is clearly space to develop a new conventional wisdom.

Chapter 9

East Asia and the Global Economy

It has now become something of a cliché to observe that the world's centre of economic gravity is shifting to Asia, the Asia-Pacific, or more specifically, to East Asia. It is not hard to see why: East Asia contains two of the world's three largest economies, and if we extrapolate from current growth trends, China is on track to overtake the USA as the largest economy on the planet by 2016, according to the OECD (Moulds 2012). Even if we add the customary caveat that China has a much bigger but generally less wealthy population, this is still a quite astounding transformation in the international economic order from the one that that prevailed during most of the twentieth century. It is important to remember that, for the first two-thirds of the twentieth century, much academic analysis was preoccupied with explaining the failure – indeed, the impossibility – of development occurring in what was described as the Third World.

The 'dependent' nature of development in the 'periphery' and the structural dominance of the 'core' economies (see Chase-Dunn 1998) meant that there were simply too many obstacles for would-be developing nations to overcome: existing patterns of exploitation meant that such countries were condemned to permanent under-development. The great theoretical and comparative significance of the historical transformation that has occurred in much of the East Asian region in this regard has been to overturn many of the prevailing views about the nature of development, and about relationships between core and periphery, or developed and underdeveloped parts of what was becoming an increasingly integrated and global economy. In one sense, then, the significance of the East Asian experience is as much ideational as it is material, though it is the latter that is the primary focus of this chapter, which explains the historical evolution of an increasingly regional economy. Chapter 10 looks at the contemporary picture in more detail and considers the impact of regional and global crises on East Asia.

From a historical perspective, however, it is clear that what we now think of as the East Asian region has been incorporated steadily into an expanding capitalist economy for several hundred years. Expanding

167

trade relations have been at the centre of East Asia's integration into the international economic system since the first European contact. Indeed, as we saw in Chapter 2, trade was one of the principal reasons that Europeans came to Asia in the first place. What is noteworthy more recently, however, is the rapid expansion in the flows of capital into and out of the region. This latter development has been something of a mixed blessing: while inflows of foreign direct investment (FDI) may have been welcome and central to the take-off of much of Southeast Asia and latterly China, some of the more mobile flows of capital have had much more debatable consequences, as we shall see in the next chapter. The intention of this chapter is to describe some of the most important aspects of East Asia's internal and external economic relations.

Not surprisingly, three countries loom large in the discussion that follows. The USA has, of course, played a particularly important role as the hegemonic power of the area, effectively establishing the rules and regulations within which global commerce occurs, but also acting as an important source of investment and an indispensable market for the region's export-oriented economies (Kim *et al.* 2011). This latter role remains critical, but has become more complex and controversial as a consequence of ballooning trade deficits, first with Japan and more recently with China. The latter two countries are regional economic giants and have acted as important sources of growth and dynamism, so they are the principal focus of attention in the following discussion. Their individual historical roles and mutual economic interaction are central parts of the story of East Asia's internal integration, but also of the region's relationship with the outside world. Japan's corporate networks and the development of 'greater China' as a centre of production have, at different periods, had a profound influence on the course of region-wide development, and merit detailed analysis in their own right. To understand why they have been so important, it is necessary, once again, to place these relationships in their specific historical contexts.

Japan and the growth of East Asian regionalization

One of the key points to reiterate at the outset is that, while Japan emerged as the principal regional engine of economic development and integration after the Second World War, it did so as a consequence of a unique, possibly unrepeatable set of historical circumstances. Without the direct aid and assistance of the USA and the latter's expanding domestic markets, it seems inconceivable that regional development would have occurred in the manner, or at the speed, at which it did. The potential importance of the intersection between economic development and geopolitics became even clearer in the aftermath of the Vietnam War, when Japan, having already engineered its own industrial renaissance, was ideally placed to expand into the region. Crucially, as Richard Stubbs points out in his definitive analysis of the historical origins of the 'Asian miracle':

> Japan's economic 'embrace' of East and Southeast Asia in the years after the Vietnam War could not have gone so successfully had it not been for the commitment by successive US governments of men, money and material, in a massive effort to contain the spread of communism and defend what were seen as America's vital interests. (Stubbs 2005: 154)

Economic development in the East Asian region in the post-war period has therefore been a consequence of a complex dialectical interaction between intra- and inter-regional forces. While the latter might initially have been crucial in providing the catalyst for both the re-emergence of the Japanese economy and for the politically permissive policy environment that underpinned it, we need to recognize that once under way, Japan's expansion into the region was something largely driven and managed by the Japanese themselves in line with domestic imperatives. It is also important to recognize that when Japanese companies, trade and investment began to expand outwards into the region, it was a case of *re*-engaging with the region, rather than starting from scratch. Painful and problematic as the Japanese imperial period proved to be for much of the region, it is clear that such pre-existing trade patterns facilitated regional integration (Cumings 1984; Petri 1992).

In retrospect, it is striking how early the triangular structure of Japan's relationship with the rest of East Asia on the one hand, and with the USA on the other, was established. In the immediate aftermath of World War 2, Japan imported industrial goods from the USA and exported simple manufactured goods to the East Asian region. But as Japan re-industrialized and labour costs rose, industries such as textiles were unable to compete and shifted off-shore to take advantage of lower labour costs (Steven 1990). In some ways this may be thought of as the 'normal' pattern of industrial restructuring as countries move up the value chain.[1] What is distinctive about Japan's approach to this process is that, as with its domestic development process, the course of Japan's external expansion has occurred with the extensive involvement and oversight of public officials. The tendency for the state to become involved in directing the course of Japan's external relations (as well as its internal ones), was given additional impetus by a decidedly unexpected catalyst for economic restructuring and adjustment: the first 'oil shock' of 1973. Not only did this lead directly to the development of the policy of 'comprehensive security' discussed earlier, but it triggered a burst of outward investment and aid as Japan sought to guarantee the supply of critical resource inputs on which its economic expansion was so dependent – a style of economic diplomacy that has been emulated by China in recent years (Goldstein 2003; Huang and Wang 2011).

Two points are worth emphasizing about these developments. First, the state and business generally worked collaboratively in pursuit of the 'commercial agendas of private sector actors and the strategic economic agendas of the economic ministries' (Arase 1994: 173). In other words, this co-operative approach was an extension of the domestic regime that underpinned Japan's developmental state, and was one from which both sides could expect to benefit. The Japanese government was able to encourage both the off-shore migration of declining industries and to facilitate the control of strategically important resources through the sophisticated deployment of overseas development assistance (ODA) packages for host nations, and by assisting Japanese business with technical assistance, advice, insurance and capital. While there is no doubt that much of this investment has been welcomed by the recipient countries and has played an important part in accelerating the course of development across the region, there are widely held reservations about its overall impact and intent. In one of the most persuasive and detailed analyses of Japan's economic integration with the region, Hatch and Yamamura (1996: 5) claim that Japan's business–government co-operation amounts to 'nothing less than a coordinated effort to lock up the productive resources of the world's most dynamic region'. Though this characterization of Japan's position in the region looks overblown as a consequence of competition from China and the development of other regional economies, there is no doubt that historically Japan has been a central element in East Asia's economic take-off, even if the impact of Japanese investment has been controversial at times.

Ambivalent attitudes towards Japanese investment have persisted despite the best efforts of Japan's political elites, who have done what they can to ensure that its role in the region is perceived positively. Historically, the preferred way of describing Japan's economic relationship with the rest of East Asia – at least as far as many of Japan's economic and political elites were concerned – was the 'flying geese' metaphor, in which Japan played the role of lead goose, pulling along the other industrializing nations of the region in its wake (Ozawa 2009). However, the flying geese metaphor has fallen out of favour, partly because of its historical association with Japanese imperialism (Terry 2002), and partly because of the uneven performance of the trailing geese that have not 'caught up' in quite the way that might have been expected.

One of the critical flaws in the flying geese model, and a major potential initial obstacle to industrial upgrading of a sort that the Japanese themselves achieved, has been the conspicuous reluctance of Japanese MNCs to transfer technology to would-be competitors (Bernard and Ravenhill 1995).

As a consequence of the advanced nature of Japan's industrialization and the ability of Japanese companies to use other parts of East Asia as export platforms, countries in the rest of the region, especially Southeast Asia and latterly China, became highly dependent on Japan for capital goods with which to produce manufactured products for markets in the USA and Western Europe. As a consequence, Japan invariably enjoyed trade surpluses with both the emerging economies of Southeast Asia, as well as with the wealthy industrialized nations of North America and Europe (Cai 2008). The migration of Japanese capital off-shore might have been a predictable consequence of a maturing economy and the rising cost of production in Japan, but it was given a further boost by a number of other factors. First, protectionist pressures from the United States in particular during the 1980s made it increasingly attractive for particular economic sectors in Japan, such as the automotive industry, to invest directly in the USA and to a lesser extent the European Union (EU), thus circumventing trade barriers. As a consequence, the USA has been by far the largest recipient of Japanese FDI, experiencing a major surge as a direct consequence of Japan's bubble economy (Alba *et al.* 2010). The second factor to boost outflows of Japanese capital was the Plaza Accord agreement introduced in Chapter 7: the dramatic appreciation of the yen made foreign investment increasingly attractive and encouraged many of Japan's most successful large and small companies to move parts of their operations off-shore (Katz 1998).

The rapid expansion of outward investment that occurred in the aftermath of the Plaza Accord transformed the relationship between the Japanese economy and the rest of the region, and accelerated some of the most important processes associated with globalization. As noted in Chapter 1, a key development in the international political economy over the last several decades has been the increasing disaggregation of the production process. Technical innovations, increased specialization, and improvements in transportation and communication have all meant that multinational corporations can 'slice up the value chain', separating and relocating parts of the production process to wherever the opportunities for increased profitability are greatest. Nowhere has the process been developed more dramatically or rapidly than in East Asia. In some ways, the flying geese pattern has been evident as first Japan, then the 'NICs' in Taiwan and Korea, and ultimately a number of the Southeast Asian economies, have been integrated into regional production networks

(Dent 2008). The net effect has been to spread production processes in key industries such as auto manufacture and electronics across national borders to exploit specific local advantages and resources.

Such processes have transformed economic relationships between national economies and raised difficult questions about the ways in which they should be understood. Indeed, some argue that the very idea of discrete national economies is less meaningful in an era when trade figures are a much less reliable guide to the relative standing of different economic spaces (Sturgeon and Gereffi 2009). Despite China rapidly becoming a massive trading nation, many of the most valuable elements of 'Chinese' exports are actually produced elsewhere (Breslin 2005). The fact that much trade in East Asia occurs within firms as they move components around before final assembly, means that trade figures no longer necessarily capture the nature of the production processes, or the realization of the value and wealth they generate.

What we can say is that we have seen a shift from the sort of 'Fordist' production processes based on horizontal integration in which mass production was localized, to forms of vertical integration between core companies and their production affiliates, suppliers and sub-contractors, creating a 'nexus of interconnected functions and operations through which goods and services are produced, distributed and consumed' (Henderson *et al.* 2002: 445). One of the most important long-term transformations of economic activity everywhere has therefore been a shift from trade between individual national economies, often specializing in different economic sectors or activities, to a situation where 'trade' frequently occurs between or even within individual companies as their activities have become increasingly transnational (Dicken 2011). The share of intermediate goods – which ultimately contribute to finished products that may be assembled in another country – has grown enormously across the region and represents a major part of regional economic activity. In Asia as a whole, the average percentage of intermediate goods as a share of exports is more than 50 per cent, with the likes of Taiwan, Indonesia, Malaysia and Singapore being well above that (WTO/IDE-JETRO 2011: 85, fig. 8).

The transformation of production processes is also forcing Japanese companies to change the way they approach the region. The very nature of some manufacturing processes, especially in the electronics sector, has meant that Japanese multinationals have been forced to emulate the strategies of US competitors and transfer greater technological know-how to subsidiaries in order to take advantage of local expertise and cost advantages (Ernst 2000; Sturgeon 2007). The evolution of regional production networks as a consequence of their 'strategic coupling' with multinational corporations following a global organizational logic has meant that it has become increasingly difficult for states – developmental or otherwise – to exercise the degree of influence over 'national champions' that they once did (Yeung 2009). As a result, the picture of regional production has become more complex, with a variety of forces such as ethnic business groups and sub-regional economic zones adding to an increasingly complex and fluid picture (Peng 2002).

The standard depiction of the complex production networks that have emerged as a consequence of changes in the nature of production is 'factory Asia'. More specifically, Richard Baldwin argues that such changes have come about as a consequence of the 'unbundling' of trade and production. Trade in the twenty-first century is a consequence of

> the intertwining of: 1) trade in goods, 2) international investment in production facilities, training, technology and long-term business relationships, and 3) the use of infrastructure services to coordinate the dispersed production, especially services such as telecoms, internet, express parcel delivery, air cargo, trade-related finance, customs clearance services, etc. This could be called the trade–investment–services nexus. (Baldwin 2011: 5)

Geography is potentially far less important than it once was – up to a point. While national borders are capable being transcended, this does not mean they have been erased or that distance is irrelevant. While new trade linkages have expanded around the region, the key word here, perhaps, *is* region. Regions continue to matter and – all other things being equal – will tend to encourage economic relations with immediate rather than distant neighbours. This has been the defining feature of 'factory Asia', after all. However, states continue to play an important part in encouraging or discouraging potentially footloose multinationals from investing in one location or another (Hale 2011), as the plethora of trade-facilitating bilateral agreements throughout the Asian 'noodle bowl' remind us (Baldwin 2007). As we shall see, such arrangements have major implications for regional economic diplomacy and the sorts of institutions that are constructed to try to facilitate it.

However, it is important to recognize that the apparent intensification of regional trade patterns can create a misleading picture. The disaggregation of the production process and the greatly increased, sometimes repeated, movement of parts and components across borders exaggerates greatly the significance of intra-regional imports and exports. The impression that the East Asian region has suddenly become more self-reliant is not accurate. As Athukorala and Kohpaiboon (2009: 8) point out:

the dependence of East Asia (and its individual countries) on extra-regional markets (in particular those in NAFTA [North American Free Trade Agreement] and the EU) for export-led growth is far greater than is revealed by the standard intra-regional trade ratios commonly used in the debate of regional economic integration ... the region is much more heavily dependent on extra-regional trade for its growth dynamism than what is suggested by the total regional trade share.

This is a crucial observation because of the critical role that export-led industrialization has played throughout the region, as first Japan, then the NICs and eventually the Southeast Asian economies looked to external markets as a way of accelerating growth in the absence of sufficient domestic demand. The point to emphasize, however, is that while many governments across the region may have recognized the importance of external markets in stimulating growth, this is *not* the same as leaving it to the market to determine how such markets may be exploited. Despite the possible limitations of trade figures in giving an entirely accurate picture of regional trade and the manner in which it is organized, at a broad-brush level they do give an indication of changes in the overall direction, and even geopolitical significance of, regional economic activity. Japan's trade with China and the USA has changed dramatically, despite its strategic alliance with the latter and its historically troubled relationship with the former. The reality has been – up to this point, at least – that the attractions of China's relatively cheap labour force and the growing importance of the country's domestic market have been sufficiently compelling to overcome possible political or strategic obstacles to deepening economic integration. Much the same has happened with economic ties between mainland China and Taiwan, as we shall see later. However, there may be limits to this rosy picture of pacifying mutual interdependence; as we saw in Chapter 5, the increasingly tense relationship between China and Japan that has developed as a result of their unresolved territorial dispute is having a major impact on bilateral economic ties (Murphy 2012), with Japanese multinationals now switching their investment plans from China to India (Crabtree 2013).

Whether this proves to be an aberration, and 'normal' trade patterns will be resumed between two neighbors who ought to benefit from propinquity and the benefits of comparative advantage remains to be seen. What is clear is that the position of the USA and China have changed profoundly (Kim *et al.* 2011). China has rapidly become a much more important trade partner for Southeast Asia than the USA, and this is clearly influencing the behaviour of the Southeast Asian states towards their more powerful and increasingly important neighbour. Yet despite the fact that China has become the most important trade partner for most of Southeast Asia (as it also has for Japan),[2] this has not translated seamlessly into political influence for China. On the contrary, as we saw in earlier chapters, neither China's diplomatic efforts nor its economic centrality in the region have been enough to stop a number of the Southeast Asian states from enhancing strategic ties with the USA. The other point worth noting, therefore, is that despite the USA's diminished economic significance in the region, this has not led to a concomitant shift in strategic loyalties. A crucial test of continuing American influence over economic relations will be its ability to conclude a Trans-Pacific Partnership agreement with key regional allies, a policy that reflects a move away from the sort of large-scale multilateralism of earlier periods (Aggarwal 2011; Terada 2012). The implications and motivations of such policies and their relationship to other forms of regional diplomacy are taken up in Chapter 11.

When we consider the position of a country such as Japan in a wider geopolitical and historical context, it becomes easier to understand why it has not been able to translate its undoubted economic significance in the region into international influence. Even at the height of Japan's economic success, it had little impact on the politics of regional economic development. In part this reflects the sort of low profile adopted as part of the Yoshida doctrine, its strategic subordination to the USA, and the constraints imposed by, and the failings of, Japan's domestic politics. One would not expect this to change now that Japan's regional economic significance has been eclipsed by China. This is what makes 'Abenomics' such an interesting and important experiment – something that will be taken up in more detail in the next chapter. For now, we need to consider where Japan has already exerted an influence: on the new waves of industrializing economies.

The first- and second-wave industrializing economies

The first (Northeast Asian) and second (Southeast Asian) waves of industrializing economies in East Asia 'took off' at different times, even though the general story of the declining importance of rural and resource activity, and the growth of manufacturing, would eventually become common. As it was, however, Northeast and Southeast Asia were incorporated into the global economy in rather different ways. Despite China's belated start, the sheer scale of its development means that, effectively, it represents another wave all of its own. All the major East Asian economies eventually embarked on a course of export-oriented industrialization, but the fact that they did so at different times and in different ways has had an impact on both the structures of their domestic economies and the ways in which they have been incorporated into the wider international economic order. Korea, for example, was able to follow a broadly similar path to Japan, developing one of the world's largest ship-building industries, becoming a major steel producer, and – following the growth of the *chaebols* – establishing global brand names and a corporate presence in the process. Significantly, Korea also followed Japan's lead in relying much less on inflows of FDI than other East Asian countries to underpin the initial phases of this process, and only opened up relatively recently to foreign capital inflows (Hundt 2008; Vu 2010).

Like Korea, Taiwan has also been highly successful in transforming the structure of domestic economic activity and turning itself into a manufacturing, and latterly service-oriented, economy; and, like Korea, the state continues to take an active role in this process (Wang *et al.* 2012). Unlike Korea, however, Taiwan has been more open to foreign investment and used this as a vehicle to transfer technology. Taiwan is considered to have been 'East Asia's greatest success story', mainly because of the remarkable transformation in the structure of its economy, and the rapid rise of capital- and technology-intensive manufacturing at the centre of its export industries (Camilleri 2000: 84). The most important factor influencing Taiwan's recent development has been its burgeoning economic relationship with mainland China. But before we consider that in any detail, it is important to note a distinctive feature of all the first-wave NICs: their heavy reliance on international trade. The NICs (including Singapore) are much more heavily integrated in, and exposed to, the international trading system than most of the Southeast Asian economies, Japan or even China. Indeed, given Japan's historical importance economically in the region, it is remarkable how self-contained the Japanese economy remains, despite the continuing significance of the export sector in that country's overall economic performance. However, one negative consequence of this as far as Japan's overall regional significance is concerned is that Japan has not absorbed intra-regional exports in the way its economic size suggests it might have done – something that has caused irritation among its trade partners, especially at times of crisis. China's much greater integration into the global trading system and the positive impact it has had on regional demand, stands as a revealing comparison (Roland-Holst and Weiss 2005), and one with long-term implications for the relative influence of the two countries (WTO/IDE-JETRO, 2011: 54, fig. 5).

It is also important to remember that the sheer scale of the Japanese and Chinese economies means that they have internal dynamics and potential strengths that are not applicable in many other cases. The most extreme example of this possibility, perhaps, is Singapore, which is highly dependent on, and deeply integrated into, the international economic system. Not only did Singapore rely heavily on inflows of FDI to jump-start its industrialization process, but also the manner of its integration has been heavily influenced by the nature of this investment, and as a consequence, the MNCs that provide it. Singapore has successfully moved up the value-adding chain, initially turning itself into an exporter of sophisticated manufacturing products, especially in the IT sector. Of late, it has transformed itself into a headquarters from which regional production can be co-ordinated. The fact that its trade/GDP ratio was 240 per cent in the late 2000s is a reminder of how meaningless and deceptive such figures can be (Athukorola and Hill 2010). Singapore is also a reminder that product specialization in comparatively well-run economies are vulnerable to the vicissitudes of the international economy generally, and American markets in particular (Mishkin 2012).

As the first wave of NICs have industrialized successfully and moved up the value chain, they have themselves become important sources of capital, for Southeast Asia in particular (Dixon 2010; Jarvis 2012). This has had the effect of not only deepening investment linkages within the region, but also trade. While the figures are skewed significantly by the Hong Kong–China relationship, the NICs' outward investment occurs overwhelmingly within the Asian region. The MNCs that have emerged from countries such as Korea, Taiwan and Singapore have adopted what Dicken and Yeung (1999: 118) describe as a 'regional solution' to the challenge of economic restructuring and expansion. Rather than follow-ing Japan's pioneering lead and investing primarily in the lucrative markets of North America and Europe, the NICs have attempted to exploit 'local' advantages rather than trying to compete with the estab-lished European and American MNCs on their home turf. One of the consequences of this process has been to reinforce a regional production hierarchy as the NICs export their low-end, less valuable, labour-inten-sive industries such as apparel, footwear and toys (Gereffi 1998: 50). These sorts of investment linkages between the first- and second-tier economies have contributed, like the links between Japan and the first tier before it, to the growth of intra-regional trade.

Having said that, however, it is important not to lose sight of the fact that the entire region remains highly dependent on external markets, especially America's (Athukorala and Hill 2010). In this regard, the Malaysian economy is even more exposed than Singapore's to downturns in the American economy, with some 80 per cent of IT exports going to the USA. While Malaysia's industrialization process has been compara-tively successful, it has been heavily reliant on imports of foreign capital and intermediate products, especially from Japan. One of the strategies employed by Malaysia to encourage inward investment has been the establishment of export processing zones (EPZs), in which potential investors are offered major inducements such as tax breaks and the provision of infrastructure. While Malaysia's EPZ policy is generally considered to have been at least partially effective, it highlights more general questions abut the historical effectiveness of such strategies in underpinning and deepening industrial development (Amirahmadi and Wu 1995; Hobday 2001). Malaysia has also adopted policies that are more in keeping with interventionist industry policies in other parts of the region, but with notably less success. No doubt the goal of upgrading the crucial electronics sector has been made more complex by the politics of ethnicity and the established positions of other economies in the region, but it is a reminder of important general differences between the first- and second-tier economies.

The manner in which the economies of Southeast Asia have been integrated into the wider international order has consequently given rise to continuing doubts about the quality and depth of the industrialization process. Despite the fact that some countries, such as Malaysia, have been able to attract inflows of FDI into more sophisticated manufacturing processes, overall industrial development remains 'constrained by the interests and strategies of the multinational corporations' (Jomo 2004: 64). This problem has been compounded by the emergence of China as a potential competitor. As Greg Felker (2003: 259) pointed out, Southeast Asia found itself caught in what he calls a 'structural squeeze', between a rising China and the first-tier NICs. However, much of the impact of China's rise has been felt even further down the value chain and production hierarchy in places such as Cambodia, which have specialized in low-value, low-skill textile and footwear products (Felker 2009). Nor has China's rise necessarily deprived the Southeast Asian economies of vital FDI (Ravenhill 2006).

Countries such as Indonesia and the Philippines, which face particularly difficult developmental challenges, and lack the kinds of state capacity that exist in the first-tier NICs, may find it increasingly difficult to move up the hierarchy of regional production. This is an especially important consideration, given that the state's legitimacy in the region has invariably been attached to its capacity to deliver rising living standards. Thailand highlights a more generalized dilemma in this regard: despite the industrialization process being comparatively successful, and the structure of the economy transformed, the nature of its integration with the market-oriented, neoliberal external order has tended to exacerbate the increasing polarization of income levels and life-chances that is such a characteristic feature of the contemporary international order more generally (Hewison 2006). This trend is also evident in Indonesia, the Philippines and Korea, where Haji and Zin (2005: 52) argue that 'the reduced role of government and the attendant increased role of the private sector have reversed the improving trend in income inequality'. When accounting for the less impressive economic performance of Southeast Asia, therefore, it is also important to remember that this can arguably be explained in large part by the sub-region's troubled colonial inheritance, which obviated against the creation of an effective developmental state (Kim 2009).

China and the region

Perhaps the most distinctive feature of China's rise is that it is not something confined to, or a consequence of, events that have occurred within exclusively national borders. On the contrary, 'greater China' takes in Hong Kong, Taiwan and possibly even other elements of the 'overseas Chinese' diaspora (Cheung 2012). There is a good deal of debate about the usefulness of this term, as it is applied rather loosely to the estimated 50 million or so ethnic Chinese resident in Asia outside China. As Callahan (2004: 51) suggests, 'greater China' is perhaps best thought of as 'not a territorial place, but a theoretical concept'.

While the term 'overseas Chinese' may not be sufficiently nuanced to capture the wide variety of specific political and economic contexts in which Chinese-style capitalism is realized, it is indicative of the distinctive form of economic organization associated with ethnic Chinese business in Southeast Asia in particular. Yet, while it is true that people who trace their ethnicity to China have come to assume a striking and disproportionate economic prominence in much of Southeast Asia in particular (Studwell 2007), as Goodman (1997–98: 144) points out, 'it is not clear ethnic Chineseness is the most important predictor of their economic behaviour, let alone other kinds of activity'. Be that as it may, as far as the mainland is concerned, connections with Hong Kong and Taiwan, which have clearly been facilitated by common linguistic, cultural and commercial practices, have been especially important in channelling FDI into China and restructuring economic activity across the region. It also gives rise to the some of the same kinds of anomalies that plague the trade figures: Hong Kong's apparent status as one of China's biggest investors reflects, in part, the 'round tripping' of mainland money being channelled through Hong Kong to take advantage of tax and investment incentives (Sung 2005).

Whatever the precise measures of these flows may be, however, two points are abundantly clear. First, China's economic take-off has been assisted by its relationship with Taiwan and Hong Kong, and the capital they have invested, directly or indirectly, on the mainland. Second, the degree of economic integration that has occurred between the three elements of 'greater China' has blurred national economic boundaries and effectively constituted a major trans-border 'growth triangle'. While we need to be careful about employing essentialist and possibly racist stereotypes when talking about 'Chinese business' and the supposed commonalities in the Chinese diaspora, it is clear that Southeast Asian Chinese have been key players, in what Yeung (2000b: 270) describes as a process of 'facilitating the rearticulation of their motherland, China, into the global economy'. Southeast Asia has not been the only source of FDI, of course. Indeed, one of the features of China's development that distinguishes it from Japan in particular, has been its openness to foreign investment generally. And yet it is also important to recognize that 'although China has received large amounts of foreign investment, these funds in recent years have financed only about 5 percent of capital formation' (Bergsten *et al.* 2006: 21). In other words, most of the investment that has fuelled China's unprecedented growth has come from internal sources which – as in Japan – were provided from high domestic savings rates.

The upshot of the massive investment that has taken place (and continues to materialize, as we shall see in more detail in the next chapter), has been to establish China as the 'workshop of the world' (Sung 2007). One of the principal reasons that 'factory Asia' has become such a commonplace idea is because of China's rapid integration into regional production networks since the 1990s. Crucially, however, this is not necessarily a zero sum game, even though China has rapidly become the biggest single manufacturing centre and exporter in the world. On the contrary, many of China's Southeast Asian neighbours have become suppliers of manufactured components that are eventually assembled in China, primarily for subsequent export to markets in Europe and North America (Athukorala and Hill 2010). The manufacture of Apple mobile phones has become, perhaps, the most widely cited example of just how little value is actually added by workers in China, and yet how much it contributes to China's apparent trade imbalance with the USA (Lamy 2011). Something like half of China's exports arise through joint ventures or foreign-owned enterprises. While this may not be a bad thing in itself, it is important to recognize, as Shaun Breslin points out, that the value-added of such exports that occurs within China has been 'extraordinarily low', because many of the more valuable components and capital-intensive aspects of production occur *outside* China in places such as Japan. Consequently, Breslin (2005: 743) argues, China acts as 'the manufacturing conduit through which the regional deficit is processed, with China running deficits with "supplier" states in East Asia, and surpluses with "demand" states in Europe and North America'.

This is a particularly important consideration, given the significance attached to the supposedly problematic nature of the trade surplus with China among American policy-makers. The reality, however, is that the bulk of Chinese exports to the United States are produced by firms owned by foreign companies, many of them American (N. Hughes 2005). Not only is much of the United States' trade with China actually controlled by American companies and arguably good for 'the American economy', but US-based producers also have an economic and *political* stake in good relations with China. Consequently – and unlike Japan, which still has far lower levels of foreign investment and participation in its domestic economy – in the PRC there are many MNCs and external investors that can act as a potential constraint on the US government and any attempts to penalize China for its supposedly 'unfair' economic practices (Xie 2010). It is also important to recognize how rapidly nearly everything about China continues to evolve, and how quickly its overall export structure has begun to change. China is rapidly becoming an exporter of capital goods and more sophisticated, high-value-added manufactured goods (Li 2007).

But for all their undoubted importance in underpinning rapid economic development, the industrialization process and global integration have contributed to the unevenness of income distribution and overall levels of economic development that have become such a distinctive feature of China's recent development and, as a consequence, such a potentially explosive source of domestic inequality and discontent. Such developments have led to the emergence of the 'New Left' in China which has highlighted the inequities of capitalist development (Spegele 2012). While it is important to keep such movements in perspective, there is a good deal of unhappiness in China about the rise of a privileged class, especially when its wealth is connected to their political positions, as the recent scandal over former Premier Wen Jiabao's family wealth reminds us (Branigan 2012).

The paradoxes of interdependence

One of the most visible and controversial manifestations of China's position as a source of exports for the world has been a massive build-up in its foreign reserves. Like Japan before it, this is partly a function of a significant trade surplus and the accumulation of foreign currency – mainly US dollars – in exchange for its products. In China's case, though, there is no doubt that part of the explanation for the increase in its foreign currency holdings has come about as a consequence of its efforts to 'manipulate' the value of its own currency in relation to others. This has become a major irritant in Sino–US relations, as the US tries in vain to bring about the kind of currency appreciation they achieved with Japan during the Plaza Accord. Despite China's leadership clearly realizing that such policies damage its international relations and reputation, domestic pressures make it very difficult for them to act. It is also important to note that not everyone in the USA is unhappy about the prevailing state of affairs. Ho-fung Hung (2009: 24–5) is worth quoting at length on this point:

> Beijing is well aware that further accumulation of foreign reserves is counterproductive, since it would increase the risk associated with the assets China already holds or else induce a shift to ever riskier ones. The government is also very aware of the need to reduce the country's export dependence and stimulate the growth of domestic demand by increasing the working classes' disposable income ... But the vested interests that have taken root over several decades of export-led development make this a daunting task. Officials and entrepreneurs from the coastal provinces, who have become a powerful group capable of shaping the formation and implementation of central government policies, are so far adamant in their resistance to any such reorientation. This dominant faction of China's elite, as exporters and creditors to the world economy, has established a symbiotic relation with the American ruling class, which has striven to maintain its domestic hegemony by securing the living standards of US citizens, as consumers and debtors to the world. Despite occasional squabbles, the two elite groups on either side of the Pacific share an interest in perpetuating their respective domestic status quos, as well as the current imbalance in the global economy.

The implications of some of these claims will be taken up in subsequent chapters, but there are a number of general points to note at this juncture. First, China is not the only country to have accumulated significant reserves of foreign currency: partly as a deliberate policy response to the economic crises discussed in the next chapter, and partly as a consequence of their successful export-led development strategies, all the countries of the region have seen a transformation in their balance sheets.

In China's case however, this massive influx of foreign money has proved difficult to absorb domestically. True, it gave China the wherewithal to launch a massive stimulus package in the aftermath of the most recent global financial crisis, as we shall see in the next chapter. However, not only are their concerns about how wise some of the stimulus was, and whether it might actually have contributed to domestic imbalances (Wolf 2011), but it has been central to the development of a remarkable, historically unprecedented symbiosis with the United States. What former US Treasury Secretary Larry Summers (1998) has famously called the 'balance of financial terror' describes a situation in which China has recycled much of the money it receives from its trade surplus with the USA (as well as its currency interventions), back to America. This has taken the form primarily of purchases of American treasury bonds or government debt. China already accounts for about a quarter of US foreign debt (Dept of Treasury 2012). In many ways, though, this is the proverbial win–win situation: China finds an easy way of dealing with and making money from its potentially destabilizing (politically and economically) surpluses, while the USA benefits from a source of cheap credit.

However, things are not quite so straightforward. On the one hand, thanks to Wikileaks, we know that this interdependence is something that weighs on the minds of America's most senior policy-makers. As Hillary Clinton observed when asked why she did not take a stronger line in relation to China's growing assertiveness, she replied 'How do you deal toughly with your banker?' (MacAskill 2010). In other words, the sort of liberal interdependence that is thought to have been such a distinctive feature of the post-war order created under American auspices has become a two-way street: on the one hand China's policy-makers undoubtedly have been socialized into the ways of the capitalist world. On the other hand, however, the consequence of this very successful economic integration has been effectively to shift the balance of economic power between the USA and China. It may be true that there are real limits to what China can do with this potential if it does not want to wreck the global economy from which it has benefited so much (Drezner 2009) – the essence of the balance of financial terror – but this does not mean that it is without 'structural' influence, as Clinton's remarks remind us.

Having said that we also need to be aware of two important continuing sources of American influence over China. First, despite all the attention that is rightly paid to China's growing international presence, it is not, as Peter Nolan (2012) puts it, 'buying the world'. On the contrary, at this stage, China's direct foreign investment remains a fraction of that of the USA in a world economy that remains dominated by Western companies generally, and American ones in particular. Moreover, Edward Steinfeld (2010: 18) argues that 'China today is growing not by writing its own rules, but instead by internalizing the rules of the advanced industrial West. It has grown not by conjuring up its own unique political-economic institutions but instead by increasingly harmonizing with our own.' In other words, the inward investment and presence of foreign multinationals that has been such a critical part of China's rapid development is also fundamentally reordering not just the corporate practices in China, but also the very values and expectations of its people.

While there is plainly substance to Steinfeld's arguments, the variety of capitalism literature serves to remind us of the surprising persistence of difference, even under conditions of apparent globalization. While capitalism may be the default economic option around the world, it is realized and driven by different ideas, institutions and interests. This possibility continues to be illustrated vividly in East Asia.

Conclusion

Like much else about the region, East Asia's integration into the global political economy has been distinctive. It could hardly have been otherwise. After all, the factor that distinguished the East Asian region from Western Europe, or even North America for that matter, has been that there was a wider, increasingly integrated and international economy with which to integrate. While Japan may have come to dominate the East Asian region from the 1960s through to the 1980s in particular, it did so in the context of an overarching global economy with which it was tightly connected and heavily reliant. The export-oriented industrialization that underpinned Japan's spectacular post-war renaissance was only made possible by the existence of expanding markets in North American and Europe. It was a model that would be followed, with variations in style and success, by other economies in, first, Northeast Asia and then Southeast Asia.

In that regard, for all its undoubted size and significance, China is in some ways more like its Southeast Asian predecessors than like Japan. Though it is still evolving and the picture may look very different another decade on, at this stage China's industrialization process looks more like the smaller Southeast Asian economies, which also occupied less dominant and decisive positions in the regional production hierarchy. True, China's sheer size sets it apart, but it is heavily reliant on foreign investment and markets, and it still occupies a place towards the low-value-added end of the spectrum; for all Japan's problems, it is undoubtedly at a very different stage of industrial development. As we have seen, however, things are changing rapidly, a possibility most immediately apparent in the growing integration of production across national borders in the region.

The variety of the East Asian experience also serves to remind us of the difficulty of making sense of such a complex region that has been integrated into the wider global economy – and with itself – at different times and under different circumstances. The problem is compounded by the persistence of what is described as 'methodological nationalism' in the social sciences; that is, the tendency to see national economies as discrete entities, or to focus primarily on the actions of individual nation-states when trying to make sense of complex international processes (Chernilo 2006; Hameiri 2009). For all the sometimes overblown and imprecise rhetoric associated with 'globalization', it does remind us that such apparently foundational certainties are a good deal less certain than they once were. In other words, parts of 'China' are undoubtedly moving up the value chain, just as parts of 'Japan' are highly uncompetitive and obstacles to much needed reform. A similar observation can also be made about economic sectors. One of the most notable features of the global economy since around the early 1980s in particular has been the different standing and performance of different sectors of notionally national economies. East Asia's spectacular economic growth has been associated primarily with the rise of manufacturing – as have nearly all the major economies throughout history – but that, too, has changed as the service sectors and finance have become more important over time. While this may seem to be a 'normal' part of economic development, it is not without its dangers or problems, as the next chapter makes clear.

Chapter 10

Crises and Their Consequences[1]

For much of the period following the Second World War, most of the East Asian region was synonymous with rapid, largely unexpected economic development. However, much of the positive commentary – and self-promotion – that occurred as the 'Asian miracle' spread from Northeast to Southeast Asia suddenly disappeared following the economic crisis that engulfed the region in the late 1990s. The crisis itself was consequently a profoundly important event in the history of the region. Ironically enough, however, its aftermath arguably did more than anything else in fact to help *create* a sense of a distinctive East Asian region – though this came at the cost of tremendous damage to the region's material circumstances and reputation. Devastating as the crisis was for much of the region, it is remarkable how quickly it re-emerged as a key centre of global economic activity. Indeed, when a second 'global financial crisis' (GFC) hit the region in the late 2000s, the region not only proved to be comparatively immune to its impact, but it was widely seen as one of the few bright spots and potential growth engines in the global economy.

This chapter compares these two crises and analyses their impact on the material and reputational standing of the region. I consider why the first crisis was so damaging for much of East Asia, and why the more recent one that had its origins primarily in the USA left the region comparatively unscathed. I suggest that part of the reason why the region got off lightly the second time around was because of the policies that many of the region's elites adopted in the aftermath of the first crisis. In retrospect, it can be seen that the first crisis represented the sort of 'critical juncture' that some scholars argue is necessary to enable actors to change course and deviate from otherwise institutionalized forms of 'path dependency' (Capoccia and Kelemen 2007). Put differently, without a shock to the extant system, things are likely to go along in much the same way. Given such a shock, however, new patterns of organization and behaviour are possible. Calder and Ye (2010) argue that such critical junctures have played a decisive role in the region's recent history and help to account for both the content of regional initiatives and the growth of interest in regional co-operation more generally. Before we explore this possibility in any detail, however, it is useful to remind ourselves of what happened during the first 'Asian crisis', which began in 1997.

The East Asian financial crisis and its aftermath

There is by now a voluminous literature dealing with the East Asian crisis, most of which rightly deals with those countries that bore the brunt of its impact: Indonesia, Thailand, Malaysia and – more surprisingly, perhaps – South Korea (see, for example, Haggard 2000; Pempel 1999; Robison *et al.* 2000). Rather than attempting to add significantly to that literature here, this section notes briefly some of the major impacts of the crisis while paying more attention to its longer-term implications for intra- and inter-regional relations. The key point that emerges from the subsequent discussion is that the crisis provided the proverbial wake-up call for many of the region's elites. It became painfully apparent that not only was the region as a whole exposed to the potential dangers of the sort of broadly conceived processes of globalization from which they had previously benefited, but that they also had little capacity to deal with the impact and aftermath of such shocks. It was this recognition of regional vulnerability to a combination of political and economic forces that had their origins outside the region that acted as a catalyst for regional institutional innovation (Beeson 2009a; Grimes 2009).

Though most attention was initially given to the dramatic material impact of the Asian crisis as stock markets swooned and currencies plummeted, one of the most significant consequences of the crisis was the impact on its overall standing and reputation. From being synonymous with miraculous development, the region was suddenly associated primarily with so-called 'crony capitalism' (Chang 2000). The damage to the reputation of some individual East Asian states was even greater and more pointed. In this regard, Japan – while not an immediate victim – arguably suffered the greatest long-term damage to its regional leadership ambitions and overall standing. Significantly, this process began well before the 'East Asian crisis' of 1997, suggesting that the region's economic problems were not confined to the four countries listed above, and that their antecedents can be found well before the events of the late 1990s. Japan had already experienced a 'crisis' of its own, albeit a slow-burning one that did not bring the country to its knees or affect employment and growth quite so dramatically (Katz 1998).

What Japan's crisis did, however, was to undermine the credibility of the 'Japanese model' on the one hand and – more importantly and tangibly – to add directly to the underlying economic problems of the region, on the other. This happened in two principal ways: first, distressed Japanese banks were forced to begin repatriating capital from Asia to shore up their deteriorating, post-bubble balance sheets. The net effect, King (2001: 440) argues, was to trigger the crisis 'inadvertently', as Japanese financial institutions reduced their exposure to Asia. The second problem Japan caused to much of the region was a consequence of the steady decline in the value of the yen. What Robert Brenner (2002) calls 'the reverse Plaza Accord' of 1995 saw the Japanese and American governments agree to allow the yen to decline in value, something that added dramatically to the competitiveness problems of neighbouring countries with pegged exchange rates. Furthermore, the possibility that Japan might play a positive role in soaking up exports from the region's distressed economies in the aftermath of the crisis was nullified by the impact of the crisis in Japan itself, where it further undermined domestic consumer confidence. Japan's subsequent efforts to play a leadership role in post-crisis management were undermined by the net impact of this period and the generally negative sentiment about its position – especially relative to a rising China that was rapidly assuming a more important economic *and* political place in the region (Hellman 2007).

Changes in sentiment were not confined to views about Japan. While the standing of some countries such as China may have actually been enhanced as a consequence of the crisis, there was a more generalized and negative transformation of attitudes towards the region. In this regard, the abrupt change from 'miracle to meltdown' was more than a journalistic cliché: it was testimony to both the depth of the crisis itself and the manner in which much of East Asia suddenly fell out of favour with the 'international investment community'. In reality, of course, much of the international movement of mobile capital is determined by a relative handful of money market traders and mutual fund mangers who take advantage of profit opportunities rapidly and globally. Likewise, the 'miracle' economies are, as we have seen, a highly diverse group of countries with a variety of strengths and weaknesses, and different capacities to take advantage of the evolving international economic order. Such subtleties did not appear to figure in the calculations of the 'international investment community', however. At the heart of the massive, increasingly speculative and indiscriminate inflows of capital into the region was a 'faith in the immortality of the Asian miracle that led to excessive investment in a handful of cyclically sensitive export industries and in commercial construction' (Kenen 2001: 27). The crisis highlighted dramatically what could happen when comparatively small – and not so small, in Korea's case – economies became integrated into global circuits of financial capital and thus were exposed to the actions and judgements of market actors beyond national control.

Thus the most important difference between East Asia in the late 1990s and in the late 1970s was that many of the economies of the region had become increasingly open to inflows of highly mobile portfolio capital and short-term bank-lending in a way that was not the case in the earlier period. Formerly, investment capital was raised primarily through high domestic savings or official government-to-government assistance. Gradually, however, governments across the region began to follow the neoliberal orthodoxy and open their capital accounts, allowing much greater, unregulated, movements of capital. Consequently, from the mid-1980s onwards, inflows of private capital grew much faster than government loans, and by the mid-1990s, 75 per cent of inflows were private, of which half was in the form of highly mobile portfolio capital (Beeson and Robison 2000; Winters 2000: 36). The other noteworthy feature of the borrowing patterns that emerged in the 1990s was how much of the debt incurred was short-term.[2] Sceptics doubted the wisdom of this policy, arguing that in a region where savings were extremely high, productive investment could be financed from domestic sources with much less risk; the value of encouraging further inflows of mobile capital was debatable at best and likely to encourage increasingly speculative forms of investment (Wade and Veneroso 1998). Before trying to assess the merits of this strategy and the longer-term implications of this period, it is worth rehearsing briefly the main features of the crisis itself.

A region in crisis

Famously, the crisis began with a minor currency crisis in a relatively small, peripheral Southeast Asian economy. That Thailand could prove to be the catalyst for what would rapidly become a major regional and eventually international economic downturn, as its ripples spread outwards to Russia and Latin America, is remarkable and tells us something important about the nature of the contemporary international economy and its capacity to transmit 'shocks' rapidly around the world (Krugman 1999). While international economic integration may have major benefits in potentially allowing capital-poor countries access to foreign investment, it is also clear that economic shocks are capable of being transmitted much more rapidly and widely than they once were (Bryant 2003). Indeed, this is especially the case when the type of capital that is flowing to smaller developing economies is financial capital rather than the longer-term, far more stable FDI.

The trigger that caused the initial panic about Thailand, and the subsequent 'contagion' in Indonesia, Malaysia and Korea, was concern about the Thai government's ability to maintain its 'peg' to the value of the American dollar. As investors became concerned about the value of the baht, and thus the dollar value of their investments, a self-fulfilling panic ensued as they scrambled to withdraw their cash. The Thai government was a victim of a problem that confronts even the most powerful governments, but is especially acute for smaller economies that are regarded more speculatively. While developing economies confront particularly challenging problems of risk and management, the difficulties of economic management and the consequences that flow from market-oriented policy settings are almost universal.[3] Policy-makers must contend with a well-known policy 'trilemma', or what Benjamin Cohen (1993) called an 'unholy trinity', in which they cannot simultaneously have independent monetary policies, fixed exchange rates and an open capital account. Because the Thai government had opened its capital account while trying to maintain a fixed exchange rate, it sacrificed control over monetary policy. Consequently, it was not able to use interest rates to control the domestic impact of massive capital inflows, which were simultaneously pushing up asset values and wages, fuelling a speculative construction boom, encouraging imports through increased liquidity and credit, and making Thai exports less competitive in the process.

What is striking and noteworthy in retrospect is that the structural imbalances in the Thai economy generally, and its exposure to short-term debt in particular, did not become causes for concern for outside investors sooner than they did. This is especially so, given that the other problem pegged exchange rates had created was to encourage borrowing in American dollars. Confidence – misplaced as we now know – in the durability of the exchange rate against the dollar meant that many borrowers failed to 'hedge' their positions or to insure against adverse currency movements (Jomo 1998: 6). When the baht and other regional currencies did collapse, many of the loans proved to be unserviceable. It is testimony to the positive view of potential investors before the crisis hit that they ignored warning signs that should have urged caution. In other words, the herd-like behaviour that some observers take to be a positive force in encouraging 'good' policy-making (Friedman 2000) did not have a salutary influence before the crisis. On the contrary, it appears to have contributed actively to the very problems of cronyism and non-transparency that received so much retrospective attention. Indeed, the existence of 'strong' states and close government–business relations may have encouraged a 'moral hazard' problem on the part of international investors, who were not only carried away by the general euphoria surrounding the Asian miracle, but who may have believed that states could and would indemnify them against any possible losses.

Any such lingering expectations were, however, extinguished by the rapidity and extent of the panic that took hold. Across the five most badly affected economies – Thailand, Malaysia, Indonesia, the

Philippines and Korea – a positive inflow of portfolio capital of more than US$12 billion in 1996, turned into a negative outflow of more than US$11.5 in 1997 (Beeson and Robison 2000). On top of this, the currencies of Indonesia, Thailand, Malaysia, the Philippines, Korea, and even Singapore and Taiwan, experienced major declines in value. In the case of Singapore and Taiwan, which were in comparatively good shape, and even in the Philippines, which was not as badly affected by the crisis,[4] this seemed like a case of guilt-by-association, rather than any specific failings on the part of these economies. The only East Asian countries not to experience the 'contagion effect' were Hong Kong and China. Significantly, neither of these countries had a tradable currency, and were thus insulated from the panic-stricken, herd-like behaviour that affected the rest of the region. This episode – especially its decision not to devalue the yuan in response to currency collapses elsewhere – did much to improve China's standing in the region and helps to explain their continuing nervousness about 'floating' their currency despite immense external pressure to do so (Eichengreen 2005).

Of the countries that did experience major currency movements, Indonesia was by far the most badly affected, with the rupiah losing about 80 per cent of its value in the first few months after the crisis. The upheaval this induced was not confined to the economic sphere, either. Not surprisingly, perhaps, for a regime whose legitimacy was highly dependent on the delivery of rising living standards and economic stability, the crisis was catastrophic. At the urging of the IMF, and in an effort to restore confidence and stability, interest rates were pushed up to 65 per cent, and government spending – including politically sensitive subsidies on staples such as cooking oil – were slashed in line with the IMF's standard austerity package (Stiglitz 2002). The net effect was to compound an economic crisis with a political one. While many may celebrate the downfall of the autocratic Suharto regime, which the crisis clearly brought about, it is important to recognize just how traumatic the impact of structural forces in the global economy and the direct intervention of external agencies such as the IMF were in the life of a nominally sovereign nation. Thailand and Korea experienced similar changes of government as a direct consequence of the crisis. Again, while many might welcome the ascendancy of a political liberal such as Kim Dae Jung, the impact of extraneous factors cannot be underestimated. In Korea's case, the key point to emphasize is that government liberalization of the financial sector, and a failure to exercise adequate supervision of the private sector, had established the preconditions for the subsequent economic and political crisis (Chang 1998).

Views about the merits of IMF crisis-management policies are emblematic of a fundamental division between those observers who attribute most weight to the sort of external systemic factors associated with 'globalization' when explaining the crisis (Stiglitz 2002; Wade and Venoroso 1998; Winters 2000), and those who consider that the crisis was primarily a consequence of failures of domestic governance and/or crony capitalism (Corsetti *et al.* 1999; Haggard 2000). Clearly, the sorts of reformist agendas and policy strategies that are proposed in the aftermath of the crisis will depend on the causal weight given to these factors. Even for those who take a multidimensional approach, such as that developed here, which sees the unfolding of the crisis as involving a complex interaction between structure and agency at a number of intersecting national, regional and global levels, some factors will be given more weight than others.

However, the IMF's privileging of internal factors meant it took the rather predictable view that the crisis was primarily a consequence of poor policy decisions and 'structural' problems within the affected economies. Consequently, in return for crisis management and a financial bailout, the IMF insisted on far-reaching reform packages intended to break up the distinctive patterns of business–government relations that had developed across much of East Asia (Stiglitz 2002; Wade and Veneroso 1998). This was bad enough for many of the dominant political elites of the region, whose relationships were necessarily threatened by the proposed reforms. However, when it became increasingly clear that the IMF reform strategy was not only inappropriate and actually *contributing* to the crisis by dampening demand and undermining confidence in national financial systems (Stiglitz 2002), but that it was also being actively encouraged by an American government keen to exploit a possibly unique opportunity to force liberalization on a recalcitrant region (Bello 1998), then the depth of resentment intensified (Higgott 1998). It was in this atmosphere of generalized crisis, and unhappiness about the intrusive, insensitive role played by the IMF and the USA, which 'de facto largely dictates the IMF's policies' (Krugman 1999: 114), that Malaysia broke with the ruling orthodoxy and experimented with capital controls.

A couple of points are worth making briefly about this interesting and illuminating episode. First, Malaysia's approach was something that the IMF – which had been an active proponent of precisely the sort of capital account liberalization that appeared to have drawn the crisis economies into disaster – simply could not have contemplated or sanctioned. As Stephen Grenville (2004: 82) observed, 'It was a difficult time to acknowledge the danger of excessive flows, and to contemplate restriction of inflows as part of crisis prevention would have been tantamount to heresy.' In other words, ideational influences show a remarkable degree of continuity and resilience, even in the face of powerful evidence as to their inappropriateness. Second, at the very least, it is possible to argue that whatever the motivation for Malaysia's apostasy – and a desire to shield extant networks of political and economic power from external scrutiny and reform was plainly a large part of it (Beeson 2000) – capital controls did no harm, and may in fact have saved Malaysia from experiencing the sort of economic trauma experienced by Indonesia. Given that the crisis sparked a major debate about the nature and role of the 'international financial architecture', its role in the crisis, and the possible need for reform (Armijo 2002), Malaysia's experiment also had important comparative importance, especially as far as other emerging economies were concerned (Cohen 2000). The final point to make about the Malaysian experience is that it exacerbated tensions between East Asia and the USA, giving renewed life to Mahathir's aborted proposal for an East Asian Economic Caucus – which would ultimately re-emerge as ASEAN+3 – and sparking interest in the possibility of developing regional monetary mechanisms with which to ward off future crises – issues that are considered in more detail in the next chapter.

Given that Joseph Stiglitz (2002: 99), the World Bank's former chief economist, considers that 'capital account liberalization was *the single most important factor leading to the crisis*', it is striking that the debate about the need to reform the international financial system lost much of its momentum before the second crisis. Indeed, if the lessons of the first crisis had been taken more seriously, it is possible that the second might not have happened at all – or at least not in quite the way and on the scale that it did. As we now know, of course, regulatory reform in the international financial sector was – and is – piecemeal and inadequate. The dominance of Wall Street and the continuation of relatively 'light touch' regulation in the City of London, despite their roles in the subsequent crises, is tangible evidence of this.

But before we consider the dynamics of the most recent crisis and its impact on East Asia, it is worth highlighting two things about the 'Asian crisis'. First, financial-sector interests based in the USA have lobbied the American government to promote further liberalization because, as Jagdish Bhagwati points out, 'Wall Street's financial firms have obvious self-interest in a world of free capital mobility since it only enlarges the arena in which to make money' (Bhagwati 1998: 11). But the US government has its own reasons for continuing to press for the continuing liberalization of global financial markets despite growing doubts about the wisdom of such policies for small, emerging economies with inadequate regulatory capacity and poorly developed capital markets. The second reason that the US government is an unequivocal supporter of the present highly liberal international financial order is simply that it must: the

USA's expanding current account deficits leave it highly dependent on continuing inflows of capital – primarily from East Asia – to finance its trade and budget deficits. Without such inflows, not only will domestic interest rates be higher and consumption patterns at risk, but some of the more ambitious aspects of American foreign and strategic policy would be unsupportable (Ferguson and Kotlikoff 2003; Wade 2000).

The 'global financial crisis'

The first question to ask about the 'global financial crisis' is whether it is in fact global at all. The primary impact of the crisis has been felt in North America and the European Union – East Asia has been much less badly affected, leading some to question whether it is a global crisis at all (Breslin 2011b). Indeed, one of the most interesting debates that emerged in the aftermath of the GFC was whether the entire East Asian region was becoming increasingly 'decoupled' from the problems of Europe, and the USA in particular (Athukorala and Kohpaiboon 2009; Park 2011). While some of the claims about the independence of the East Asian economies may be overstated, given their continuing reliance on North American markets, the fact that this crisis had its origins in the liberal Anglo-American economies generally and in the USA in particular was very significant (Crotty 2012). The dynamics and consequences of this crisis proved to be entirely different as a result. During the 'Asian' crisis, the United States, as the world's dominant political and economic power, was able to encourage the adoption of specific reforms within those countries judged to have failed. During the GFC, the origins of global instability were to be found in the USA itself, potentially undermining the attractiveness and authority of American-style capitalism (Posner 2010; Wu 2010).

In the first crisis, the Asian economies were subjected to withering critiques about their supposed failings as the IFIs sought systematically to undermine their credibility as an alternative, indigenous development paradigm (Hall 2003). During the GFC, even mainstream commentators expressed doubts about the ability of successive US governments to recognize the depth of the crisis, much less to address it adequately (Wolf 2009). The financial sector in the USA proved to be a powerful obstacle to reform, and this had implications for the authority of the Obama administration. As the former chief economist of the IMF has pointed out:

> elite business interests – financiers, in the case of the U.S. – played a central role in creating the crisis, making ever-larger gambles, with the

implicit backing of the government, until the inevitable collapse. More alarming, they are now using their influence to prevent precisely the sorts of reforms that are needed, and fast, to pull the economy out of its nosedive. The government seems helpless, or unwilling, to act against them. (Johnson 2009)

When the notional anchor of the international financial system has become a source of instability within an increasingly dysfunctional, polarized political system that struggles to institute much needed reform (Jacobs and King 2009; Mann and Ornstein 2012), other countries and regions are presented with an unprecedented challenge as they seek to recalibrate their domestic and foreign policies. It is important to remember that the historical record demonstrates that, when confronted with potentially conflicting domestic pressures and notional international obligations as a systemic stabilizer, the USA has put its own national interests first. There may be nothing surprising or particularly reprehensible about this – it is, after all, what all states do – but it is strikingly at odds with the sort of historical role that many American academics, policy-makers and even the general public have seen the USA playing. And yet the reality is, as the unilateral abandonment of the Bretton Woods system of managed exchange rates reminds us, that national priorities trump international obligations at times of crisis (Beeson and Broome 2010).

Anglo-American decline?

The GFC has been subjected to extensive analysis (Elliott and Atkinson 2008; Morris 2008), but it is worth recapitulating briefly its central dynamics as they continue to influence policy outcomes in the USA and elsewhere. They also shed a revealing light on the differences between the two crises, and the comparative strengths and weaknesses of capitalism in East Asia and North America in particular.

The principal features of the crisis are widely recognized and relatively uncontested: regulatory failures in the USA and Britain meant that financial-sector interests were given increasingly free rein to develop mechanisms, derivatives and innovations that generated enormous profits, but which did so by increasing, rather than diffusing, systemic risk, as their advocates had claimed previously (Crotty 2009; Tett 2009). We now know that structured investment vehicles, collateralized debt obligations and the like were little more than exercises in paper-shuffling and self-delusion, but for a number of years they generated enormous profits for the banking sectors in Wall Street and the City of London. As a consequence, neither individual financial institutions nor the regulatory authorities in the USA or Britain were motivated to question, much less to monitor effectively, such activities. On the contrary, such financial-sector innovations were actively encouraged and seen by such as former UK Chancellor of the Exchequer and later Prime Minister, Gordon Brown, as being critical to the long-term success of New York and London.

The predatory nature of Wall Street's relationship with the USA's domestic economy was revealed by the nature of the 'sub-prime crisis', in which the most vulnerable and impoverished of Americans were exploited directly by some of the most affluent and powerful of their fellow citizens (Blackburn 2008).

The dynamics of this second crisis of globalization consequently have both ideational and material effects that will shape political responses at multiple levels. At an ideational level, the diminished credibility and attractiveness of neoliberalism potentially opens up a political space for alternative models to replace the discredited Anglo-American orthodoxy. Predictably enough, given the nature of the crisis and the worrying similarities between this crisis and the Great Depression, the ideas of John Maynard Keynes have enjoyed renewed popularity and salience (Skidelsky 2009). However, it is far from clear that the USA will be able to play the same sort of role as it did in Keynes's time, when it established the Bretton Woods institutions and provided the kind of 'hegemonic' leadership that some observers consider crucial for the maintenance of international economic stability (Kindleberger 1973). Not only has the USA's own moral authority and influence been profoundly undermined by a crisis it is widely seen as having created, but there is a basic lack of agreement on what the best policies might be to revive the West's generally distressed economies – a possibility manifested in the debate about the merits of austerity versus stimulus (Posen 2013).

While it may never be possible to make a definitive judgement about universally optimal policy prescriptions at moments of crisis, a few points are clear. First, the authority and attractiveness of Anglo-American forms of capitalism has taken a severe battering on the grounds of efficacy and equity. Second, the comparative attractions of other forms of economic policy and organization can only have been enhanced by such processes. This is not to say that other countries either would want to, or even could, adopt Beijing-consensus-style policy ideas – even if it was entirely clear what such policies would actually look like. However, it is possible that the international space within which policy co-operation occurs, and in which ideas are debated, is arguably a good a deal more fluid than it has been at any time since the collapse of the Bretton Woods regime in the early 1970s.

Comparative crisis management

The USA and Britain are not the only parts of the world to have been afflicted by long-running economic problems that resist easy solutions; indeed, no part of the world has been affected more badly by recent economic problems than the European Union, where an economic crisis has become a political one that threatens the very survival of the EU itself (Barber 2012). In the context of a discussion of the impact of financial crises on different parts of the world, there are a number of comparative points to be made. The most general point is that Europe's response to the crisis has been very different from Asia's earlier efforts and is likely to have very different implications for both Europe itself, and perhaps as a consequence the wider international economy. Whatever the merits of the dramatic cuts in government spending that are being undertaken across Europe, they are bound to have a significant impact on overall global economic activity and may even trigger – according to the likes of Paul Krugman (2010) and IMF managing director Christine Lagarde (Carnegy 2011) – another Depression. Ironically, governments are hostage to precisely the same sorts of market forces that wreaked such havoc in Asia a decade earlier. Even though the 'efficient markets hypothesis' is now as discredited as the idea that financial innovation is the path to risk diversification,[5] government policy in the West remains especially vulnerable to abrupt shifts in market sentiment, and clearly constructed with this in mind. Paradoxically, though, 'embedded financial orthodoxy' in the form of balanced budgets and 'sound' money may actually exacerbate the problem and trigger the disaster that markets fear (see Cerny 1993).

The chances that a co-ordinated, state-led response to the crisis will occur have been diminished by two other factors. On the one hand, the much heralded co-ordinated action that had characterized the meeting of the G20 in the UK following the collapse of Lehman brothers had largely dissipated by the time the leaders met in Toronto a year later. The failure of the most promising part of the putative 'international financial architecture' to agree on a strategy to tackle the crisis was a major blow to both the credibility of the organization and the prospects for co-ordinated action (Wade 2011). Expectations were further dashed by the European response, which is most directly pertinent when considering East Asia's comparative crisis management.

As the benchmark for regional co-operation and integration, the EU's response to what is arguably its most serious challenge since its foundation had implications for regionalism in other parts of the world. The most striking feature of European action was not simply its ineffective and uncoordinated nature, but rather the resurgence of national interests and divisions that stymied them (Stephens 2010). Real differences emerged between individual states about both the most appropriate policy response, and about the degree to which individual members should accept responsibility for the unsustainable, and even deceptive, nature of their actions. This was demonstrated most famously in Germany's reluctance to bail out the Greeks: not only did this highlight the acutely sensitive domestic political consequences that flowed from the crisis, but it also revealed continuing differences between France and Germany over how to deal with a crisis that threatened to become much worse before it improved. It needs to be remembered that the Franco-German accord that underpinned the original implementation of the euro was essentially driven by political rather than economic priorities (Chang 2003); priorities that seemed to be in danger of being overturned by the economic crisis. In short, the very unity and future of the EU appeared to be in serious doubt – a prospect that had hitherto been unimaginable, but which opened a revealing comparative window on East Asia's past and possible future.

In the light of the European experience, the prospects for an Asian Currency Unit, which were never bright (Chung and Eichengreen 2007), but which had been floated occasionally by one policy entrepreneur or another, were effectively extinguished. In addition to the formidable technical and political obstacles involved in getting China and Japan to co-ordinate their policies, let alone the rest of East Asia's highly disparate economies, Europe's crisis suggested that it wasn't a good idea even if it could be achieved. Those sceptics who had always doubted whether a common currency could withstand either a major crisis or the undisciplined behaviour of weaker members appeared to be vindicated: not only had Greek policy-makers misrepresented the state of the economy, but they were deprived of the flexibility that a weak currency might have provided when attempting to deal with the crisis. The big lesson about optimum currency areas seemed to be that they were political rather than economic phenomena, and that common currencies might cause more problems than they solved (Eichengreen and Frieden 1995). Japan's and China's misgivings about becoming integrated too closely with some of their impoverished neighbours suddenly looked judicious and farsighted, rather than indecisive and lacking in vision (Pascha 2007). But there was, and is, one other crucial difference between East Asia and Europe, and between the first and second crises, and that is the role played by China. Despite being only a relative 'bit player' in the first crisis, China has now assumed a starring role, and the second crisis might not have occurred at all – or at least, not in quite the way it did – were it not for the part played by China.

China's growing significance

As we have seen, one of the most important long-term developments in the political economy of East Asia has been the rapid build-up of foreign exchange reserves in the region. In part this has been a consequence of a favourable trade balance between the region and the rest of the world, but it has also been a conscious policy decision, as countries across the region look to defend themselves against the sorts of vulnerabilities that were exposed so dramatically during the first crisis. Though this has become a widespread feature of the economic landscape of post-crisis Asia, nowhere has this process been more significant than in China, as we saw in the previous chapter. It has been this long-term structural transformation in the relationship between the region and the world that underpins the development of the potentially destabilizing and politically charged relationship between China and the USA. Ironically, the Asian crisis and its aftermath, which the USA played such a prominent role in overseeing, might actually have helped to create the preconditions for the GFC. It is worth spelling out why.

The structurally embedded relationship between the USA and China has been described by some as 'Bretton Woods II', because of the way it has apparently institutionalized a particular pattern of inter-regional economic and political relations. This symbiotic arrangement is based on what is thought to be an 'unlimited' appetite for US securities because the capacity for growth in East Asia is 'far from its limit' (Dooley *et al.* 2003). But even before the crisis struck, it was apparent that there were inherent dangers in this relationship, and that there *were* potential limits to the amount of American debt that other countries would be willing to absorb (Wade 2007). In the aftermath of this crisis, it is apparent that that limit may have been reached, as China in particular has reduced the level of its bond purchases, partly in response to domestic criticism of the losses incurred on failed investments in the USA (Anderlini and Alloway 2011; Bradsher 2011). The significance of these developments as far as East Asia generally is concerned is that it may compel China to reconsider its role in the international system and force a change in the regional and international order as a consequence (Chin and Thakur 2010). Unlike the earlier East Asian crisis when Japan flunked its first opportunity to provide regional leadership, it is plain that China has the capability and perhaps the desire to play a bigger international role as a consequence of its growing economic stature. The question is whether it is capable of seizing this opportunity at either the regional or international level.

China's foreign-policy-making elites have recognized, somewhat belatedly, the extent of their exposure to America's problems. Not only have some of the direct investments they have made in the USA lost money, but there is another potentially more dramatic and problematic aspect to the current crisis that has suddenly come into focus: the US dollar's continuing role as the world's reserve currency means that those countries such as China that hold huge reserves of dollars and dollar-denominated assets are effectively held hostage to the actions of the US government and the perceptions of international money markets. While the US economy was apparently booming and sucking in imports, China's dependence on the USA might have seemed like a sensible strategy and a way of underpinning Chinese exports. Now, however, it looks like dangerous over-exposure and something that urgently needs to be addressed, which has led rather ironically to Chinese officials demanding that the USA gets its fiscal house in order (Barboza 2011).

Two aspects of China's response to the crisis and the threat of a dollar devaluation are especially noteworthy in this regard. On the one hand, China's leadership is becoming increasingly outspoken and critical of the USA. For example, former premier Wen Jiabao directly repudiated the idea that China contributed to the crisis, claiming that it stemmed from an

> excessive expansion of financial institutions in blind pursuit of profit, lack of self-discipline among financial institutions and rating agencies [and] the failure of financial supervision and regulation to keep up with financial innovations which allowed the risks of financial derivatives to build and spread.[6]

Given this growing assertiveness and the analysis of the crisis that underpinned it, the widely noted remarks of Zhou Xiaochuan, Governor of the People's Bank of China, were especially significant. Zhou (2009) argued that the international monetary system needed to be reformed and an international reserve currency should be created that was 'disconnected from individual nations'. While Zhou did not mention the USA directly, the implication is clear: China wants to be one of the driving forces shaping any post-crisis international order.

However, China's ambitions and growing international status may make its regional relations more problematic. As far as the East Asian region is concerned, its institutional development and significance risks being undermined by the importance of China's bilateral relationship with the USA and by the demands of being a global power. China is facing similar problems to those Japan faced when it tried to exercise regional economic leadership: how to construct regional mechanisms in the context of an international financial architecture that remains dominated by the USA? In Japan's case, this difficulty was compounded by its strategic subordination. Even though this is less of a problem for China, dealing with the USA and the accusations of currency manipulation that have accompanied its rise is an *international* and not a regional problem. Indeed, it is striking that even in the area of financial sector reform where monetary regionalism has arguably made the most progress, initiatives by the APT grouping have remained broadly 'supportive of the existing global financial arrangements' (Grimes 2006: 371).

This is not to say that China has not been assiduously courting regional neighbours in Southeast Asia in particular – at least in the economic sphere; quite the contrary, in fact, it has. China's foreign minister, Yang Jiechi, has detailed more tangible support for the beleaguered Southeast Asian economies as a consequence of the crisis, an initiative that will help to cement China's place as the region's most important trade partner and an increasingly influential political force (Garnaut 2009). There are, however, other similarities in the Chinese approach that are reminiscent of the neo-mercantilist strategies that distinguished Japan's economic relationship with Southeast Asia during the 1980s and 1990s: China is using key bureaucratic departments and state-controlled sovereign wealth funds to monitor its overseas investment push.[7] China risks generating the same kind of resentment that sometimes accompanied Japanese investment. Moreover – and despite being potentially more assertive than Japan during its economic heyday – China may find it equally difficult to play a decisive leadership role in the region: not only is it not obvious what the 'regional interest' is at times of crisis, but it is also not clear that it is possible for China to play a role in insulating the region from the impact of the crisis without jeopardizing its own inter-regional interests.

Having said that, it is clear that China played a crucial role in mitigating the potential impact of the second crisis. China's massive domestic stimulus package inaugurated in the wake of the US downturn meant that its own growth was largely unaffected (Lardy 2010), despite America's continuing importance as an export market. It was precisely this sort of outcome that fuelled the decoupling debate. While China's actions may have left the region less exposed to external downturns, the region's growing reliance on the Chinese economy has left the Southeast Asian economies in particular vulnerable to fluctuations in Chinese demand and development (ADB 2011). In this regard, there is potentially much to be concerned about: many analysts worry about the utility and impact of China's domestic investment binge, and about the sustainability of credit creation by the so-called 'shadow banking' sector, which is increasingly difficult for the central government to monitor and control (Rabinovitch 2013; Walter and Howie 2011).

China's new leaders are increasingly concerned about the potentially negative impact of continuing credit creation and unproductive investment in real estate and redundant infrastructure (Davis and Orlick 2013). It remains to be seen whether they will be able to reconcile the domestic imperative of maintaining the growth that underpins state legitimacy without creating the preconditions for yet another economic crisis. Any future economic crisis in China would, of course, not only be potentially catastrophic for social stability and the authority of the CCP, but it would inevitably spill over China's borders to affect its neighbours too. East Asia has much at stake in the way that China's politics and economics evolve.

Conclusion

Contemporary East Asia has been shaped profoundly by crises of one sort or another. It is worth remembering that some of the most enduring and influential regional organizations, such as ASEAN, were products of earlier geopolitical crises that threatened to undermine the stability and even sovereignty of Southeast Asia's newly independent states. While such conventional strategic threats may have become less immediate – even if they remain more prominent than many expected – regional development continues to be influenced by economic crises in particular. The realization that East Asia was especially vulnerable to global economic forces has been a powerful catalyst for regional institutional innovation – the legacy of which is considered in more detail in the next chapter. The key question is whether the region has the capacity to co-ordinate its actions effectively in pursuit of common objectives. Whether such commonly held goals can be agreed upon, let alone realized, is quite another thing, of course.

The economic reality that confronts the states of East Asia is that, while they may have some common cultural traditions and political practices, they are a very diverse group of economies integrated with, and affected by, the wider international economy in different ways. True, the region is being linked more deeply by complex production networks, but at times of crisis, fault-lines, differences and potential divisions may become apparent as the strengths and weaknesses of individual economies are revealed. For all Japan's and China's possible problems, their respective roles in the regional and global order is of a significantly different order from the much smaller, more trade-exposed and vulnerable economies of Southeast Asia. While it is clear that very real progress has been made in economic development in both North and Southeast Asia, the latter remains potentially more exposed to the impact of possible future crises. It is the possibility that collective action and co-operative, institutionalized behaviour might minimize the impact of any future economic crisis that makes regionalism, as opposed to regionalization, an attractive prospect.

Chapter 11

The Evolution of East Asian Regionalism

For a region that is synonymous with difference and diversity, it is remarkable that *any* progress towards formal regional institutionalization should have taken place. After all, regionalism is associated with the self-conscious pursuit of political co-operation and co-ordination, something that the region's often traumatic history and the rather obsessive preoccupation with national sovereignty would seem to preclude. And yet this is the reality: not only is Southeast Asia home to one of the most enduring inter-governmental organizations outside Europe – ASEAN – but the region as a whole has displayed a much greater interest in the possibility of developing a wider, more ambitious and inclusive East Asian institutional architecture than history might lead us to expect. Indeed, until relatively recently, it looked as though East Asian regionalism was an idea whose time had finally come. Now, however, such prospects look rather less certain, and there is a renewed contest to define the very boundaries of the region.

As far as 'East Asia' is concerned, the most important of these initiatives, and the one with the capacity to give political expression to the idea of a discrete East Asian region, is ASEAN+3 (APT), and it looms large in the following discussion, not least because APT is China's preferred regional institution (Zhang 2006). While it is still too early to say how the APT process – which involves China, Japan and South Korea in addition to the ASEAN countries – will evolve, one thing has become clearer: growing tensions over unresolved maritime claims are making the APT's future and possible importance far less certain than seemed possible only a couple of years ago. Now other organizations, such as the East Asian Summit (EAS),[1] are vying for influence. The EAS's sudden prominence is almost entirely a consequence of the United States' 'pivot' toward East Asia and the desire to become more institutionally engaged in a region it had neglected regardless of its growing importance. Despite these competing processes, it is perhaps the fact that *anything* is happening in a region with East Asia's history and renowned heterogeneity that is interesting and worthy of further exploration. If East Asia can develop effective institutional forums to address collective action problems, and

204

give expression to some of the region's distinctive ideas about political, economic and security issues, this will be a development of long-term global significance. If it cannot, and such institutions are either not created or come to represent an alternative vision of what the region should be and who should be in it, then 'East Asia' may return to being primarily a geographical signifier.

To help make a judgement about the prospects for greater region-wide co-operation – however it is defined – it is important to look at the record of achievement so far. Consequently, I begin this chapter by looking at two of APT's most important institutional precursors: ASEAN itself and the Asia-Pacific Economic Cooperation (APEC) forum. As we shall see, the former does have the great merit of being more authentically of the East Asian region in a way that the all-encompassing, amorphous APEC grouping never was, or could be (Beeson 2006a). Both organizations have had their problems, and neither bodes well for APT's prospects – something that helps to account for the high levels of scepticism surrounding this project (Hund 2003). Nevertheless, APT has developed a degree of momentum that suggests there is a 'demand' for it, or something like it, on the part of many of the region's policy-making elites.[2] Whether this will prove sufficient to overcome some of the well-known tensions between rival regional leadership aspirants Japan and China remains to be seen. What we can say, however, is that the USA's renewed interest in and engagement with the region is changing intra-regional dynamics and the prospects for future institutional development.

ASEAN and Southeast Asian regionalism

ASEAN is very much a product of historical geopolitical circumstances. Its inauguration in 1967 occurred in the midst of the Cold War stand-off between the communist and capitalist powers, a confrontation that occasionally spilled over into actual conflict. The wars in Korea and Vietnam were vivid illustrations of the Cold War's potential to become 'hot' and move beyond ideological posturing, with catastrophic consequences for some of the countries of the region. Even where countries were not drawn directly into such conflicts, the possibility of domestic conflict or insurgency continued to haunt the region. The bloodbath associated with Suharto's rise to power and the crushing of the communist insurgency provided a salutary reminder to Southeast Asia's ruling elites about how precarious was their hold on power, and how traumatic regime change could be (see Cribb 1990). This combination of domestic fragility and a vulnerability to external forces that the individual countries of the region had little capacity to control or influence provided the catalyst for co-operation in Southeast Asia. In many ways, it still does (Beeson 2013b).

ASEAN's original members – Indonesia, Malaysia, Singapore, Thailand and the Philippines – represented the key countries of Southeast Asia, but from the outset their mutual relationships and the rationale for ASEAN itself were constrained by the overarching imperatives of the wider geopolitical context. The original Bangkok Declaration is a remarkably bland document, suggesting that ASEAN's purpose will be to

> accelerate economic growth, social progress and cultural development in the region through joint endeavours in the spirit of equality and partnership in order to strengthen the foundation for a prosperous and peaceful community of South-East Asian Nations. (ASEAN 1967)

While the emphasis here and throughout the original Declaration is on encouraging economic development, prosperity and technical co-operation, the sub-text is all about enhancing security in what was seen as a fundamentally unstable and threatening regional environment. At one level, the catalyst for co-operation was transnational and geostrategic: the Vietnam War was at its height and having a profound effect on the foreign policy orientations and calculations of political elites across the region. At another level, however, the domestic spillover of Cold War conflicts and ideological struggles was focusing the attention of regional elites on mechanisms for strengthening domestic and regional stability. The need to reintegrate post-Sukarno Indonesia into the region in a manner that shored up both Indonesia's and the region's stability was paramount in the minds of Southeast Asian policy-makers (Ba 2009; Narine 2002).

Given Southeast Asia's previous attempts at developing regionally based institutions, there was initially no reason to suppose that ASEAN would endure. The Association of Southeast Asia (ASA) between Thailand, the Philippines and Malaysia was derailed by the conflict between the Philippines and Malaysia over the disputed territory of Sabah. Similarly, the short-lived Maphilindo initiative between Malaysia, the Philippines and Indonesia was undermined by the perception that it was primarily a device with which to frustrate the emergence of the proposed Malaysian Federation. Despite the failure of these initiatives, they did pave the way for the development of ASEAN, and it drew on some of these earlier organizations' principles, especially ASA's 'institutional formlessness and lack of binding obligations' (Weatherbee 2005: 69). This sort of structure and institutional logic has been the hallmark of ASEAN; it has also been both a key to its longevity and a source of its ineffectiveness.

Despite all the talk about economic and technical co-operation, ASEAN's principal attraction in the eyes of its original members lay in its potential to enhance domestic and regional security, while simultaneously providing a forum within which to manage potentially fractious intra-regional relations. With the memories of *Konfrontasi* between Malaysia and Indonesia still fresh,[3] and Singapore feeling vulnerable following its expulsion from the Malaysian Federation, ASEAN members were understandably preoccupied with managing their inter-relationships and domestic security. The salience of strategic issues was given further weight following the enunciation of the Nixon Doctrine in 1969 and the possible winding back of America's strategic commitment to the region (Yahuda 2004). At the very least, the ASEAN grouping had the potential to give its members a greater collective presence and an enhanced capacity to respond to common threats. That it has rarely been able to do so tells us much about the challenges that continue to constrain regional co-operation.

Paradoxically, ASEAN's most distinctive institutional and ideational contribution has been central to its longevity, but also the principal reason for its ineffectiveness: the so-called 'ASEAN way'. Though it is not clear where the term came from and precisely what it means, the ASEAN way is, according to Acharya (2001: 63), 'a term favoured by the ASEAN leaders themselves to describe the process of intra-mural inter-action and to distinguish it from other, especially Western, multilateral settings'. As Acharya (2001: 64) further points out, it is indicative of a '*process* of regional interactions and cooperation based on discreteness, informality, consensus building and non-confrontational bargaining styles'. Not only is there very little chance of regional elites 'losing face' in such circumstances, but it is also a modus operandi that is contrasted favourably with what is seen as an adversarial and excessively legalistic Western model.

At the centre of the ASEAN way is the principle of non-interference in the domestic affairs of other member countries. However, according to some critics (Narine 1999; Smith and Jones 1997), it is precisely ASEAN's apparent inability to address contentious issues that makes it ineffective. The possible limitations of the ASEAN way have been highlighted by some of ASEAN's more liberal members such as Thailand, which have advocated the development of a more 'flexible' approach to intra-regional relations that would allow comment on the domestic affairs of other members (Haacke 1999). There also appears to be an increased willingness on the part of some members to overcome ASEAN's institutional limitations by employing more legalistic strategies and involving international institutions in the resolution of economic and territorial disputes within the Southeast Asian region (Kahler 2000), in a tacit acknowledgement of ASEAN's limitations. However, as Lee Jones (2010) points out, the norm of non-interference has never been absolute and ASEAN has, collectively and individually, attempted to influence the internal affairs of members at times. If the organization is to maintain any relevance and fulfil the expectations of more 'progressive' members it may need to do so even more in the future.

There are, then, a number of important issues that ASEAN's history highlights, which have implications for the future of East Asian regionalism more generally, and for comparisons with other organizations such as APEC. First, can indigenously developed norms and practices of socialization actually influence the behaviour of states, in East Asia or elsewhere? Here, the evidence is mixed. On the one hand, Charrier (2001) has argued persuasively that the very existence of ASEAN as an institution, and the repeated elite level interactions this has fostered, have actually gone a long way towards bringing the idea of a Southeast Asian region into being through sheer repetition and habituation. Similarly, Acharya (2004) has argued that ASEAN norms of consultation and consensus have become part of the institutional make-up of organizations such as the ASEAN Regional Forum (ARF), and have ultimately affected the behaviour of even the most powerful countries such as the USA. On the other hand, of course, even ASEAN's finest diplomatic hour – the resolution of the Cambodian conflict – was successful because its goals coincided with and furthered the preferences of the USA and China, and not necessarily because their behaviour was changed by ASEAN. A more nuanced position ought to recognize that simply constraining the behaviour of the likes of the USA and China is no small achievement: even if ASEAN only influences great power behaviour at the margins and it lacks any great vision for regional politics, it is an organization that others feel the need to acknowledge and cultivate (Beeson and Higgott 2013).

The second major issue that ASEAN highlights, therefore, is the role of less powerful nations in the evolution of wider regional processes (Jetschke 2012). While it needs to be acknowledged that there has not been a conflict between members since ASEAN's inauguration (Kivimaki 2001), it is impossible to know whether intra-regional conflict might have occurred in the absence of ASEAN. It seems reasonable to assume, however, that its existence and the institutionalization and regularization of intra-regional relations and interactions has contributed to stability in Southeast Asia. Likewise, it is difficult to know whether Burma's recent, apparently genuine, move towards democratic reform is primarily domestically driven, or whether ASEAN's efforts at socialization have finally produced results. Either way, the obstacles to a complete democratic transition remain substantial (Dukalskis 2009; Huang 2013), and it will provide an important test of the Southeast Asian region's ability to encourage and encompass progressive political change.

ASEAN's efforts to facilitate economic integration also face major challenges. Given the original priority attached to 'accelerating economic growth', it is surprising that trade and investment initiatives have not enjoyed a more prominent place in ASEAN's developmental priorities. Yet when we remember that ASEAN's 'real' motivation was originally geopolitical and strategic rather than economic, this is perhaps not surprising. Likewise, the fact that Southeast Asia's primary trade links lay outside the region, and that its economies were inherently competitive also made intra-regional co-operation more difficult. But in the aftermath of the Cold War, when economic issues increasingly displaced strategic ones on the agendas of policy-makers everywhere (Luttwak 1990), ASEAN was forced to pay much greater attention to facilitating economic development and co-operation. In this regard, the development of the ASEAN Free Trade Area (AFTA), was 'as much about building post-Cold War cohesion and increasing ASEAN's credibility as it was an attempt to boost the region's gross domestic product' (Henderson 1999: 22). As a consequence, utilization of the trade facilitation measures provided by AFTA have been 'exceptionally low by international standards' (Ravenhill 2010: 197).

Though most analyses of AFTA have focused on its (rather limited) impact on trade liberalization and the difficulties it has experienced in actually realizing its original, highly ambitious tariff reduction agenda, Helen Nesadurai points out that a regional investment strategy was also an important part of the AFTA process. Indeed, she makes it clear that the ASEAN states attempted to privilege indigenous investors over FDI, using regional strategies and agreements as a way of accommodating global forces and pressures. In this regard, what Nesadurai (2003: 99) calls 'developmental regionalism' offered a way of countering the 'hegemony of foreign MNCs', and was sharply at odds with the sort of 'open regionalism' that was being promoted by IFIs such as APEC, which were more attuned to the dominant Washington Consensus. Seen in this way, AFTA may have had a dual appeal for the political elites of Southeast Asia: on the one hand, it acted as a signalling device to foreign investors that the region was still broadly committed to the principles of trade integration and liberalization (Bowles 2000), and keen to facilitate regionally oriented FDI.[4] On the other hand, however, within this broader trade-oriented framework, the potential for creative political 'intervention' and investment guidance still existed.

The other point to emphasize is that the reform agenda was not necessarily an inevitable threat to those political and economic interests that were capable of responding proactively to the seemingly inevitable reformist and competitive pressures. Quite the contrary – while some of the pressures associated with globalization are necessarily universal, the way nationally embedded actors respond to them is not. Etel Solingen (2004) has detailed how 'internationalizing constituencies' in various Southeast Asian countries were able to take advantage of international restructuring to consolidate their position and power. Even where individual leaders might have been toppled, as in Indonesia, the underlying patterns of power and interest remained largely intact or were actually consolidated as they moved to exploit new opportunities (Jayasuiya 2003). The point to emphasize here is that, despite all the attention given to globalization, national political-economies continue to exert a powerful influence over domestic and foreign policy. Indeed, Jurgen Ruland has argued persuasively that the politics of Southeast Asia continue to be driven by earlier, pre-colonial ideas about order and representation. As a consequence, he suggests:

> ASEAN governments have transferred domestic organicism and its corporatist system of interest representation to regional governance. The latter tallies well with Southeast Asia's inter-governmentalist regionalism based on Westphalian sovereignty norms, which is less an institutional device for solving cross-border problems through collective action, than for strengthening the region's nation states through regional resilience. (Ruland forthcoming: 9)

In other words, far from coming to resemble the sovereignty-pooling strategies of the EU, in which national autonomy is traded off in pursuit of greater collective goods, the Southeast Asian states remain preoccupied with domestic security and seek to reinforce it at the regional level. Whatever we may think about such policies, they have important implications for other regional groupings that contain ASEAN states and pay lip service to the ASEAN way.

Post-Cold War and the rise and fall of APEC

When the APEC forum was inaugurated in 1989, it seemed like an idea whose time had come. With the Cold War at an end and economic issues appearing increasingly central to foreign policy agendas throughout the world, the establishment of an organization intended to facilitate trade relations between the eastern and western sides of the Pacific seemed both timely and appropriate. Initially, the prospects for APEC seemed relatively bright, and its inauguration in 1989 was accompanied by much optimism, especially in Australia and Japan, which had done more than any other countries to bring the APEC initiative to fruition. That such hopes and ambitions have generally not been realized tells us much about the difficulties of institutional consolidation in East Asia and beyond, and provides an insight into the sorts of problems that may confront similar initiatives, such as APT and the East Asia Summit (EAS).

The fact that it was Japan and Australia that provided much of the intellectual capital and political leadership for APEC is in itself revealing. Both countries were concerned about the development of trade blocs elsewhere and the possibility of being locked out of key markets, as well as with their relationship to the rapidly expanding East Asian region, upon which both were dependent in different ways (Beeson and Yoshimatsu 2007). Despite its own well-known shortcomings as a genuine free trader, Japan had promoted the idea of a Pacific free trade area assiduously for many years. While such an arrangement was clearly in its interests, as it was reliant on continuing access to protectionist North American markets to underpin its own economic model, it is significant that its diplomatic ambitions then, as now, were hamstrung by history. In such circumstances, the Japanese encouraged Australia to make the running in promoting a new economic grouping dedicated to trade promotion and liberalization (Funabashi 1995).

Australia had its own reasons for being enthusiastic about being a member of an institution that included its key trade partners. Indeed, so significant were trade relations considered to be during the 1980s by Australia's then Labor government, that former prime minister Bob Hawke's original proposal did not even include its key strategic partner, the USA. While such an omission is unthinkable at a time when the current Australian government has been shoring up its strategic credentials as a consequence of China's rise (White 2010), it is indicative of the concern Australian officials felt in the late 1980s about the possibility of being excluded from a region upon which Australia's economic future was increasingly dependent. While the principal driving force for this re-orientation may have been material and manifest in Australia's rapidly expanding resource exports to industrializing Asia, it also had a crucially important ideational dimension: not only was Australia involved in a long-term national discussion about identity, multiculturalism and relations with the region, but the nature of that 'engagement' with Asia was also the product of a highly influential, long-running public policy debate (Capling 2008). This debate was not only significant from an Australian perspective, but also helped to influence the development of regional relations and patterns of institutionalization more generally.

One of the most distinctive features of APEC's initial emergence was the role played by an array of path-breaking institutions and individuals that helped to shape economic debates in Australia and the wider region.

A number of 'track two' organizations[5] composed of various combinations of academics, business figures and government officials, played a pivotal part in developing and actively championing a set of beliefs that would eventually become part of APEC's agenda (see, for example, Drysdale and Garnaut 1993). Central in this context were arguments about the merits of economic integration, trade liberalization and a form of 'open regionalism' that did not discriminate against outsiders. These individuals and organizations effectively constituted an 'epistemic community',[6] assiduously promoting ideas that would ultimately – it was hoped – be translated into public policy across the region's mercantilist and comparatively closed economies in East Asia. And yet, despite the undoubted influence of such organizations and the enthusiasm of their participants, the actual appeal of the ideas they promoted and their capacity to be translated seamlessly into public policy across the region always seemed to be overstated (Beeson and Islam 2005).

One of the key difficulties that has confronted APEC from its inception has been differences between its Anglo-American and Asian members about the content and nature of the reform process. It is rather ironic, therefore, that one of the reasons that APEC's trade liberalization agenda has proved hard to implement is that – in line with ASEAN's modus operandi and in order to gain the support of Asian members – all agreements within APEC are consensual and voluntary. Similarly, APEC's secretariat – like ASEAN's, but unlike the EU's – is tiny, and has no capacity to enforce agreements or ensure member compliance. These underlying realities are reflected in APEC's distinctive reformist discourse, with its reliance on 'concerted unilateralism', which effectively recognized that many Asian governments were reluctant to sign up to binding agreements. As Ravenhill (2001: 142–3) points out, this is a major practical and conceptual problem for an agenda premised on the supposed merits of mutually beneficial trade liberalization: 'essentially, APEC's members are left to decide for themselves what their obligations are and when they will aspire to meet them' (Ravenhill 2001: 163). Not only is the contrast with the World Trade Organization (WTO) – replete, as it is, with enforcement mechanisms and binding obligations – stark and revealing, but it begs the question of what purpose APEC serves, given the existence of a more powerful inter-governmental body with a similar reform agenda.

Like ASEAN, therefore, APEC has attempted to reinvent itself and broaden the scope of its activities beyond the narrow, technocratic preoccupation with trade liberalization – an agenda that elicited less than universal enthusiasm in East Asia. One rather paradoxical consequence of this move is that APEC's greatest weakness could also become its greatest asset. One of the criticisms that has dogged APEC from the outset has revolved around the nature of its membership. APEC's original membership[7] included countries with little in common other than a fairly arbitrary relationship with the 'Asia-Pacific' region. This membership has been further expanded, or diluted, by the accession of a number of new entrants, including Russia – a country with only the most marginal claims to membership of a nominally 'regional' body. Russia's inclusion is a reminder that the composition of 'regional' organizations, and the nature of regional identity itself, is ultimately arbitrary. Important, though, some definitions of regions are inherently more plausible than others. As Barry Buzan (2012: 23) points out, 'a region that spans oceans and contains half of the world stretches the concept beyond breaking point'.

After APEC?

It is a measure of APEC's increasing irrelevance and its inability to pursue its original goals that multilateral trade liberalization is no longer a major part of regional diplomacy. Indeed, the most important development as far as trade relations is concerned, both within East Asia and within the more broadly conceived Asia-Pacific region, has been the rapid growth of *bilateral* trade agreements (Dent 2012). In this regard, APEC's record of non-achievement is partly to blame. Some member countries were concerned about APEC's inability to deliver trade liberalization, while others – especially Korea and Japan – were concerned that it might force them to open politically sensitive domestic sectors to external competition (Ravenhill 2003: 300). Either way, support for APEC waned. When combined with the failure of both the WTO and AFTA to promote trade liberalization, then the attractions of bilateral preferential trade deals increased – partly through example. As Christopher Dent (2003) pointed out, the growth in bilateral trade agreements rapidly gained a self-sustaining momentum from the late 1990s. Significantly, Singapore was an especially prominent exponent of bilateral trade agreements, being unhappy with the pace of trade liberalization in the region, but not threatening to other potential partners concerned about reciprocal access to their own protected agricultural sectors. While the USA was relatively slow to jump on the bilateral bandwagon, it has recently become heavily involved in such initiatives, and its efforts to link this to wider security objectives look likely to entrench this approach for the foreseeable future (Aggarwal 2011).

Thus, despite APEC's attempts to reinvent itself as a quasi-security organization, it already looks like a body whose time has passed. In part, this can be attributed to the narrowness of its initial agenda: not only did some of APEC's original supporters overestimate the intrinsic appeal of the rather technocratic discourse that surrounded its original trade liberalization blueprint, but they also seriously underestimated the political obstacles that confronted its implementation. Powerful vested interests, especially in agriculture and uncompetitive manufacturing industries, were always going to make compliance problematic. Likewise, the recurring divisions that distinguish East Asian and Anglo-American approaches to policy content and application were always likely to make consensus difficult, and the non-binding nature of commitments could only paper over such cracks.

The Emergence of East Asian Regionalism

The idea of a distinct East Asian region dominated by either China, or more recently Japan, is not a new phenomenon (Beeson 2009b). What is different about today's East Asian regional order, however, is that both of the regional giants are strong at the same time, and actively competing to assert themselves – an unprecedented development in regional history. The interaction between Japan and China, and their capacity to accommodate or adjust to the ambitions and development of each other will be one of the defining dynamics of the East Asian region in the twenty-first century. Thus far, the prospects for co-operation are not good, as we have seen. In whatever way Sino-Japanese relations evolve, though, it is a dynamic that will be overlaid by the influence of an international order that remains dominated by the USA. Just how important and influential the USA will continue to be is a matter of debate, but it clearly still has the capacity to influence the course of regional development in East Asia. To gain an impression of the nature of its influence and the way that American foreign policy toward the region is evolving, it is useful to revisit briefly an abortive effort to initiate a distinctively East Asian grouping.

One of the most important, prominent and outspoken advocates of the 'Asianisation of Asia' (Funabashi 1993) and the promotion of Asian values has been Malaysia's former prime minister, Mahathir Mohamad. Significantly, Mahathir was also a champion of so-called 'Asian values', which have also largely disappeared from regional political discourse. Nevertheless, from the early 1990s onwards, Mahathir promoted the idea of an exclusively 'Asian' trading bloc, in keeping with his vision of a distinct East Asian region. Despite the proposed East Asian Economic Caucus (EAEC) never actually being realized, it paved the way for APT and included all the countries that would eventually constitute the new grouping – that is, the ASEAN countries, plus China, Japan and South Korea. For Mahathir, the key to the development of an exclusively East

Asian bloc was Japan, an idea he developed in a co-authored volume with prominent Japanese nationalist Ishihara Shintaro (see Mahathir and Ishihara 1995).[8] Given Mahathir's admiration of Japan, his 'Look East' policy, his well-known antipathy towards the West, and the importance of the Japanese economy to Malaysia and the rest of the region, such views are unsurprising. What is more surprising, perhaps, was Japan's complete inability to fulfil the sort of leadership role that Mahathir envisioned.

Much of Japan's limited regional impact can be explained by the domestic political limitations and strategic subordination discussed in earlier chapters. Even during the Asian financial crisis, Japan's efforts to provide regional leadership were effectively thwarted by American foreign policy. Nevertheless, there are signs that Japan is once again attempting to assert itself, and it is clear that this has been driven in large part by the perception that it has been left at the diplomatic starting gate by what has been a surprisingly adroit and effective display of Chinese foreign policy (Yoshimatsu and Trinidad 2010). True, there may be grounds for questioning how effective China's diplomatic overtures will be as a consequence of its growing belligerence, but this should not blind us to the impact of such policies on Japan. Not only was Japan spurred into attempting to develop its own free-trade area with ASEAN (Corning 2009), for example, but it has also added its own suggestion to the ever-expanding roll call of regional initiatives. While the proposal for an 'East Asian Community' (EAC) is unlikely to be realized, it is an important indicator of Japanese policy thinking, because it arguably 'emphasizes universal values that China rejects' (Sohn 2010: 517).

There are a number of reasons why the EAC is unlikely to be realized. First, it is championed by Japan, which carries more than its fair share of historical baggage. The inability of the current Abe administration to put the past behind it and prioritize international co-operation over domestic nationalist sentiment does not augur well for a values-based approach (Hayashi 2013). Second, the demise of the Asian values discourse suggests that there is relatively little traction in trying to develop a 'master narrative' in a region that is a byword for diversity and where there is great sensitivity about national independence. As T.J. Pempel (2010: 211) observes, 'most regional bodies in East Asia continue to reflect the pre-eminence and driving force of individual state strategies rather than any collective predisposition toward regionalism or multilateralism per se'. Finally, it is striking that most progress has been made towards developing co-operation on a region-wide basis in areas of practical necessity, rather than being based on a grand vision. Nothing illustrates this better than the development of what has been called 'monetary regionalism'.

Monetary regionalism

The conspicuous failure of both APEC and ASEAN to provide leadership and support to the region's distressed economies in the aftermath of the crisis diminished both organizations significantly and made it increasingly clear that, if East Asians were to manage their own financial affairs, they would need to develop new mechanisms with which to do it. This perception was reinforced by two other developments, one long-term, the other short-term. First, the principal focus of policy attention for many of the region's political and economic elites has shifted from trade to finance (Dieter and Higgott 2003), in line with a general transformation of East Asia's links with the global economy generally, and as a consequence of the East Asian financial crisis in particular. The other factor making it clear that East Asia lacked the political weight to manage regional financial relations independently was the fate of Japan's Asian Monetary Fund (AMF) initiative (Pascha 2007).

Japan's original proposal for an AMF involved providing US$100 billion as the basis of an assistance package for economies suffering from speculative attacks on their currencies or balance of payments difficulties. Despite being widely welcomed in East Asia, the proposal was opposed vigorously, and effectively vetoed, by both the IMF and the USA, who were concerned that it would undermine their authority and control in the region (Stiglitz 2002: 112). This was a particularly sensitive issue given the widespread perception that the conditionality attached to AMF loans would be far less stringent and invasive than those of the IMF (Chang and Rajan 2001). It was, of course, for precisely these reasons that the IMF and the USA were so hostile to it. Despite Japan's initial attempt at regional leadership collapsing in the face of this opposition, for some observers this period marked a watershed in inter-regional relations generally, and between the USA and Japan in particular (Lee 2006). In Katada's (2002) opinion, Japanese policy-makers

> became more interested in taking a leadership role to define and strengthen regional monetary cooperation in reaction to the way the United States and the IMF handled the Asian financial crisis ... The idea behind these monetary initiatives is to reduce or balance Asian countries' current heavy reliance on the US dollar. Both of these initiatives appear as a large step towards the institutionalization of Asian economic regionalization in a pure 'Asian' form rather than an 'Asia-Pacific' one (which would include the major presence of the United States). (Katada 2002: 86)

Significant though this development is in terms of the evolution of both intra- and inter-regional relations, we need to be careful not to overstate its importance: not only was the original initiative squashed, but subsequent developments have been crafted carefully to comply with, and implicitly recognize the authority of, the overarching policy approach of the IMF. Similar constraints can be seen in the 'Chiang Mai Initiative' (CMI), the most significant proposal to emerge in the area of monetary co-operation. The CMI is essentially a revival and expansion of Japan's aborted AMF proposal. If it is realized successfully, it has the potential to both reinforce and give direct expression to regionally based co-operative processes such as APT, and to provide a degree of stability to the region's fragile financial structures. The CMI had two main components: an expanded currency swap arrangement among the ASEAN countries, and a network of bilateral swap agreements (BSAs) and a repurchase arrangement involving all 13 APT countries. While there are some significant limitations to the CMI, especially as far as available bail-out funds are concerned, William Grimes (2009: 81) argues that the principal significance of the CMI is that it 'increases ASEAN+3 states' leverage over the IMF by creating a credible threat of regional exit from the global regime, and it does so without exposing Japan to the political risks of a direct challenge to the United States'.

There remains a good deal of debate about the long-term efficacy and implications of these types of regional monetary initiatives. Given the rapid build-up in national defences against international financial turbulence, perhaps their greatest long-term significance will be that:

> the bilateral swap arrangements provide a focus for concrete negotiations, periodic reviews among officials within the region, and the basis for building serious policy dialogue. These advances are in fact pathbreaking: Officials within the region have never before had such intensive, continuous negotiations and policy dialogue on a regional basis on monetary and financial matters. (Henning 2002: 29)

As Jennifer Amyx observes, despite some formidable implementation problems, 'the simple *process* of negotiating and concluding the BSAs has had a major impact on the ability of countries in the region to fend off future speculative attacks by giving rise to dense networks of communication between central bankers and finance ministers in the region' (Amyx 2004: 8). The other point to emphasize is that, whatever the long-term benefits of socialization within regional economic elites might have been, it is striking that ideas about the future development of regional bond markets increasingly reflect an international consensus on the appropriate role and governance of bond markets, and not an exclusively East Asian one (Rethel 2010). In other words, there may be limits to the degree of distinctiveness to regional processes in the face of one of the more fluid and dynamic expressions of global interconnections. Nevertheless, it is clear that economic crises have been catalysts for greater co-operation rather than confrontation, and it is not entirely fanciful to suggest that the complex nature of regional–global interaction may actually be a spur to processes of regionalism. This certainly seems to have been the underlying dynamic driving the development of the APT process.

ASEAN Plus Three

If the number of emerging diplomatic initiatives, groupings and proposed institutions is any indication, East Asian regionalism is, in the words of the late Indonesian foreign minister Ali Alatas (2001), 'an idea whose time has come'. As yet, however, it is unclear which – if any – of the alternatives on offer is likely to prove to be the most important and durable. The inaugural meeting of the East Asia Summit (EAS) was held in Kuala Lumpur in December 2005 and was noteworthy primarily because it contained a number of 'outsiders' such as Australia, New Zealand and India, but not the United States, which was conspicuous by its absence. As a result, the EAS seemed unlikely to amount to much. However, now that the USA has 'rediscovered' Asia and joined the EAS things look rather different. While the EAS initially endorsed ASEAN+3 (APT) as the 'main vehicle' for achieving the longer-term goal of developing an East Asian Community (ASEAN 2005: 1), it has subsequently emerged as a potential rival and may yet become the region's most important institution (Camroux 2012). Before we consider its prospects in any detail, though, it is useful to concentrate on the earlier APT process, as it is the most developed and unambiguously East Asian grouping developed thus far, and provides a useful insight into the prospects for East Asian regional initiatives more generally.

As noted above, APT is essentially Mahathir's EAEC grouping by another name, and includes all the countries in the original proposal. The re-badged grouping emerged as a consequence of an inter-regional dialogue with Europe, which convened under the banner of the Asia–Europe Meeting (ASEM). While ASEM may not have achieved anything of great significance in itself, it did have the important long-term effect of consolidating the idea of East Asia as a coherent, collective actor with a distinct identity, and one with the potential to counterbalance American hegemony (Gilson 2012). As we saw in Chapter 1, this kind of identity-building process is a vital precursor of the institutionalization of regional processes. The key question from China's perspective is whether the APT as its preferred regional vehicle can maintain the continuing co-operation of states such as Japan, the Philippines and Vietnam (Terada 2010).

From 1998 onwards, APT summits have been held in conjunction with regular ASEAN summits, maintaining the appearance, if not the reality, that ASEAN remained the driving force of the emerging grouping. Following an APEC precedent, at the instigation of South Korean president, Kim Dae Jung, an East Asia Vision Group (EAVG) was established in 1998 to develop a blueprint for further co-operation under APT auspices. The EAVG, composed of independent experts, reported to an East Asia Study Group (EASG) composed of senior officials from member countries. The culmination of this welter of bureaucratic activity was the EASG's Final Report, which spelled out an agenda of 'concrete measures' that APT could, and should, undertake (EASG 2002). These recommendations revolve primarily around economic, financial, security, environmental and energy issues, as well as 'social, cultural and educational' co-operation.

Those who are optimistic about APT's prospects suggest that, as with the evolution of monetary co-operation, the *process* is crucial. In this context, Nick Thomas (2002: 17) argues that the expansion of the meetings of ASEAN officials to include their counterparts in Northeast Asia is 'the most significant development in regional politics', and one that could presage the development of European-style policy co-ordination in the longer term. Richard Stubbs (2002) makes an even bolder set of claims about the prospects for APT, arguing that the region's history and development are actually sources of common identity rather than an inevitable focus of dispute and division. In support of this thesis, he suggests that the distinctive institutions associated with Asian forms of capitalism, the historical circumstances from which they developed, and the values that distinguished them, provide the basis for an emerging sense of regional, *Asian* identity. Kai (2008) argues that institutions such as the APT hold out the possibility of providing new forms of 'institutional balancing' as the region evolves. Whether such processes will be able to manage, or even to withstand the pressure of more old-fashioned forms of balancing and contestation remains to be seen, however.

But even if APT proves not to be the vehicle to carry forward the process of East Asian regionalism, the idea that there are a number of underlying drivers of regional integration with the capacity to overcome long-standing animosities is shared by other astute observers of regional development. T.J. Pempel, for example, suggests that, in addition to the formal governmental processes and the integrative impact of Asian MNCs, regionalism is being consolidated by what he describes as 'ad hoc problem-oriented coalitions' of public- and private-sector organizations designed to tackle issues such as the severe acute respiratory syndrome

(SARS) emergency, water management, energy issues and other trans-boundary problems. Consequently, Pempel (2005b: 256) argues that an exclusive focus on formal, intergovernmental co-operation as a measure of the prospects for regional consolidation is misconceived, as 'the most overt and explicitly political institutions of East Asian regionalism are but a small part of the cumulative linkages that have developed across the region'.

This is a particularly important observation when we consider that the prospects for formal regional co-operation would seem to be especially bleak because of the deterioration in relations between Japan and China, and to a lesser extent, between Japan and South Korea. The key question confronting not just Japan and China, therefore, but also the region more generally, is whether the increasingly important and mutually beneficial effects of greater economic integration can overcome deep-seated and long-standing political and strategic rivalries. Whatever the future of East Asian regionalism proves to be, it is worth remembering that asking a similar question about the future of Franco-German relations in the late 1940s might have evinced levels of scepticism similar to those that revolve around the prospects for East Asian regionalism at the present time. Given the EU's current problems, however, this may not seem quite the compelling point it might once have been (see Ash 2012; Overbeek 2012). However, it is important to remember that some of the EU's problems have been self-inflicted, and the consequence of what now seems to be an ill-conceived currency union and an over-ambitious, poorly regulated programme of 'widening and deepening' (Feldstein 2012). While the EU was known primarily for significant economic development, its role in cementing closer ties between former foes seemed both unambiguous and permanent.

Therefore, despite the diminished attractiveness of some aspects of European regionalism, there are still important possible benefits to be derived from regional co-operation, even if it is simply the very idea of institutionalized patterns of co-operation itself. Whatever the potential merits of co-operation, however, the possible evolution of East Asian regionalism is unclear. While economic integration has advanced dramatically throughout the region, such processes remain vulnerable to wider political and even geopolitical events, as we saw in earlier chapters. The inability of the major Northeast Asian economies to negotiate any sort of trade deal is a reminder of just how poisonous intra-regional relationship can be at times, despite the seemingly overwhelming functional imperatives (Obe 2012). The momentum that has been achieved in monetary co-operation via the APT-sponsored CMI suggests that the demand for regional institutions and co-operation to resolve 'technical' problems may still grow despite intra-regional enmities. Whether the logic of liberal interdependence will actually prove sufficient to overcome long-standing hostilities is one of the key questions that will define the future of East Asia, and the wider international order of which it has rapidly become such a crucial part.

In this context, the role of the USA may well remain pivotal in every sense. Not only has the strategic reorientation of America's military forces changed the overall geopolitical context in significant ways, but this is linked directly to the future of institutional development in East Asia. On the one hand, the EAS has assumed an unexpected prominence and potential importance as a direct consequence of the USA's determination to re-engage institutionally with the region. In this regard, the United States has been actively encouraged by key allies such as Australia. Though former Australian prime minister, Kevin Rudd's, proposed Asia Pacific Community may also have fallen by the institutional wayside (He 2011), it has effectively remerged as an expanded and revamped EAS. On the other hand, the USA has swung behind other initiatives, such as the Trans-Pacific Partnership (TPP), which critics see as being more about trying to make economic life difficult for, if not to contain, China, rather than being about trade liberalization (Bhagwati 2012; Capling and Ravenhill 2013). The historical track record suggests that, despite US support, the EAS will confront the same sorts of problems of size and coherence that confronted APEC – especially if China remains unenthusiastic.

Conclusion

Whatever happens to the EAS in its competition with APT, one thing is clear: in many ways this evolving contest is an example of the continuing struggle to define the boundaries and make-up of the region. Though this is rarely mentioned as an explicit goal of such processes – other than by the likes of Mahathir, at least – it remains an important sub-text with much potential significance. If the EAS does emerge as the most influential organization in the region it will represent a significantly expanded vision of what the region actually looks like. Such a grouping will not only contain the liberal 'Anglo-American economies', such as the USA and Australia, but also the other potential Asian giant, India. In such circumstances, China's potential influence will be reduced dramatically and dissipated. It is hard to escape the conclusion that, from an American perspective, at least, this is precisely the point.

As far as the future of East Asian regionalism is concerned, if it is to have a distinct future and identity it is plain that those countries with the most established and enduring sense of themselves and their particular histories – such as Japan, and especially China – must find ways of reconciling these competing pressures while at the same time managing sometimes fractious international relations. There is substantial evidence about the 'socializing' effects of institutionalized interaction on member states, but China's recent pursuit of national interests at the expanse of regional harmony reminds us that there are limits to such processes. Indeed, we should not be surprised at this possibility: if nationalism can re-emerge within the much more institutionalized and established confines of the EU, it is clear that it can emerge anywhere. While we may continue to hope that China, Japan and the other East Asian states remember that they have much to lose and little to gain from any possible conflict, the ability of various countries across the region to stabilize the existing order may depend on more than state capacity, technocratic competence and functional intra-regional relations.

Chapter 12

East Asian Futures

The EU has often been taken as the role model for regional integration and co-operation. For many admirers of the EU, this was entirely appropriate, as the EU's very existence seemed to mark an epochal shift in the nature of the international system (Manners 2002). While there are still important points of comparison (Murray 2010), the EU's current problems mean that one might be forgiven for thinking that the attractiveness of regional co-operation has diminished markedly of late. One might be right. For some observers, it is now the West that should be learning from Asia, rather than the reverse (Mahbubani 2012). Plainly, the EU's problems have caused many observers to reconsider the benefits, much less the inevitability, of regional integration – especially the sorts of technically and politically complex agreements that underpinned the common currency. While there is now even less appetite in the East Asian region for such ambitious projects, as we saw in the previous chapter, there are still compelling reasons for putting in place at least some forms of co-operative arrangements, especially in areas where earlier inadequacies and vulnerabilities have painfully been exposed. At some level, therefore, East Asian regionalism is an idea that refuses to go away.

When seen in terms of the long-term development of a region famous for its heterogeneity, its privileging of national sovereignty, and its mutual distrust and hostility, to say nothing of several of the bloodiest confrontations of the twentieth century, the bland-sounding, sometimes eye-glazing efforts of regional officials to facilitate economic co-operation may not inspire, but neither should they be underestimated. Not only do they help to build transnational relationships between key regional political and economic elites (Evans 2005; Yoshimatsu 2009), but they are also suggestive of a broader recognition of the importance of continuing economic development for the region as a whole. Throughout East Asia, economic development has conferred a performance legitimacy on regional governments which means that political elites may have little choice other than to co-operate if they are to ensure the continuation of the development process in an era where 'global' forces and trans-border economic integration mean that international co-ordination is a necessity rather than an option (Gilley 2009). This is especially true for a non-democratic state such as China, which must ensure that economic development continues at all costs, if it wishes to retain any authority (Zhu 2011).

The key question that has emerged in recent years, which is embodied in both China's rise and its increasingly conflicted foreign policy, is whether the imperatives of economic development and integration will prove to be sufficiently compelling to overcome long-standing intra-regional animosities and the rising tide of nationalism. The answer to this question is far from clear, but much depends on how it is answered – and not just for East Asia. The possibility that China might go to war with Japan may still be remote, but it is far from unthinkable (White 2008), and could be triggered by accident or miscalculation, rather than any expectation of actual territorial advantage. Indeed, all the claims that have been made about the importance and advantages of economic inter-dependence under conditions of globalization remain true, but as the sobering historical precedent of the First World War reminds us, high levels of economic integration are no guarantee of peace.[1]

No doubt some will think that such comparisons are unduly alarmist or fanciful. One hopes that is just what they will prove to be, but the fact that we even need to take such issues increasingly seriously is revealing in itself. When we add some of the region's other pressing economic, polit-ical and strategic problems to the mix, one might be forgiven for think-ing that the future looks rather bleak. This too would be a surprising conclusion to arrive at about a region that has been seen as one of the few bright spots in an under-performing global economy. Indeed, the entire story of East Asian development in the period since the Second World War has generally been upbeat – two of the bloodiest wars of the twenti-eth century notwithstanding. Even here, though, the record until recently has been increasingly encouraging: despite all the predictions about the inevitability of conflict in the region, there has not been a major war since the 1970s.

Speculation about the future is necessarily a foolhardy enterprise, but it is made especially challenging by the complexity of the multi-dimen-sional factors that are likely to shape East Asia's possible future direc-tions. The diverse nature of the region's political and economic regimes, geopolitical circumstances and complex histories means that it is possible to see just about any pattern or prospect. Much depends on the predis-position and prejudices of the observer (see Beeson and Stubbs 2012). Nevertheless, as I have argued throughout this book, the economic devel-opments that have been the primary focus of attention in much of East Asia's recent history occurred within a specific geopolitical context. In this regard, broadly conceived security issues are a major determinant of political relations as well as intra- and inter-regional economic connec-tions. Consequently, East Asia's future development and its relations with other parts of the world will be determined by more than questions of economic and functional necessity. The political systems and even the economic structures of East Asia continue to display striking differences in their underlying organizational rationales and dynamics. The logic of path-dependency and the embedded nature of particular vested interests and existing power structures suggests that such differences will not easily be eroded or disappear rapidly. This is an especially important consideration when we remember that China, the country that is arguably doing the most to redefine the East Asian region, is still nominally a 'communist' country, and one with a limited capacity to make the transition to a fully market-oriented economy, even if its ruling elites wish to do so (Li 2012b; Rowen 2007; Wilson 2009).

If one prediction looks relatively uncontroversial it is that China, for better or worse, is likely to exert the greatest influence over the course of East Asian development in the foreseeable future. In the most optimistic reading of this process, China's 'peaceful rise' continues, generating rising living standards for its own population and an ever-expanding market for its neighbours. The process of political change already under way goes on, as an increasingly well-educated, politically savvy citizenry encourages further domestic political reform and greater participation in inter-governmental institutions – institutions over which China comes to play a part in keeping with its growing economic and demographic weight (Chin 2010). In this reading of possible future development, 'the United States will gladly offer China more prestige. In return, however, Washington will expect Beijing to shoulder greater international responsibilities and obligations' (Schweller and Pu 2011: 68).

While this might strike some as an excessively Panglossian picture, there are still grounds for optimism as far as China is concerned. After all, it has *already* completely overturned expectations and preconceptions about the possible course of development in a country that was until recently synonymous with poverty and under-development. Indeed, the recent history of China suggests that its populace generally seem to have a much better understanding of the prerequisites of the development process, and that development really is – to some extent, at least – a 'technical' challenge that requires some fairly basic but achievable interventions if it is to occur (Acemoglu and James 2012; Rodrik 2007). The question is, whether China can translate its economic achievements into political influence and play the sort of stabilizing, 'responsible' role that many hope for, and even expect. The way that China's leaders respond to the opportunities and responsibilities that its continuing economic expansion presents will be one of the principal influences on the evolution of regional *and* international governance. It is not obvious that China has the desire to play this sort of role, or even if its underlying material transformation will continue in quite the way it has to date.

All things being equal, we might expect that, at current rates of development and economic expansion, much of China's population could expect to enjoy living standards similar to those of other parts of developing Asia within a few decades. And yet China faces developmental challenges that are historically unprecedented and on such a scale that they are affecting profoundly not just the economic development of the region, but also the physical environment of which it is a part. The great tragedy as far as China – and the rest of the developing world, for that matter – is concerned is that, at the very moment when China's people appear to have made great strides towards solving the problem of economic development, there are fundamental doubts about its sustainability. Major cities such as Beijing are becoming unliveable – at least in the minds of the most talented and mobile elements of the labour force that are so crucial to future development (Wong 2013). Not only is China's high-speed development placing possibly unsupportable strains on the natural environment, but ensuring the supply of the resources and energy to supply China's gargantuan appetites also remains a formidable challenge. In other words, China's remarkable and welcome growth, which has excited such optimism, may be creating the preconditions for major domestic instability and a possible clash with external interests in a zero-sum scramble for rapidly diminishing resources.

The sheer scale of the transformation that has occurred in China means that its remarkable growth has begun to exercise a similarly significant impact on the outside world. This can be seen most easily in the country's seemingly insatiable demand for resources and energy to fuel its relentless growth. As Ross Garnaut (2011) notes:

> China accounted for over a fifth of the increase in global demand for petroleum, steel and copper and around half for aluminium and nickel in the late years of the 1990s ... For the first five years of the new century the Chinese share of consumption growth rose considerably for all energy and metals commodities, to over half for copper, nickel and aluminium. Between 2005 and 2010, China accounted for over four fifths of the increase in global demand for nearly all energy and metals products.

As a result, optimists rejoice at the seemingly endless growth opportunities the China market seems to hold – something that goes a long way towards explaining the remarkable amounts of foreign direct investment (FDI) that have poured into China since the 1990s in particular. Pessimists, by contrast, fret about the potential for conflict as the world's ever-expanding demand for energy – oil, in particular – meets a finite and possibly diminishing capacity to supply it. China is already the world's second-largest oil consumer, but its consumption per head remains far lower than in the USA, where access to cheap oil remains an important part of American consumption patterns and a central component of American foreign policy (Klare 2008). It is possible that the so-called 'fracking revolution' and the exploitation of new gas and oil supplies may yet entirely overturn many of the expectations that were held about a looming energy crisis – and the geopolitics associated with it (Maugeri 2012). At this stage, though, there are serious geopolitical and environmental doubts about the sustainability of China's rush for growth and the associated transformation in lifestyles and consumption patterns that is likely to accompany it.

In this final chapter, therefore, we need to consider whether East Asia and the world in general face an environmental crunch that makes the prospects for international co-operation and harmony an insubstantial pipe-dream, or whether institutionalized co-operative efforts offer the only feasible way of managing such challenges and are thus the key to the region's future development.

The material constraints on the future

Making sense of the environmental constraints that face both East Asia and the world more generally is complicated by the degree of uncertainty and unpredictability regarding some of the most basic issues. Disagreement is so widespread and ideologically loaded that it is difficult even for specialists to make definitive judgements about the implications of complex phenomena such as climate change. What we can say, though, is that there is an overwhelming consensus among the scientific community and major international agencies such as the UN that human activity is causing climate change, and that some of its impacts may be devastating (IPCC 2007). It is also important to acknowledge, however, that there are powerful vested interests at work that have done everything they can to undermine the credibility of the scientific evidence because they have powerful incentives to support the extant economic paradigm from which they benefit (Beeson and Stone 2013; Oresekes and Conway 2010).

In some ways, action on climate change faces the same sorts of obstacles that confront democratic transitions: institutionally embedded actors are resistant to changes that might undermine their power and position. In the case of climate change, entrenched authoritarian patterns of political rule may actually be reinforced by the potentially difficult and destabilizing policy options that severe climate change might bring (Beeson 2010). In other words, there may be fundamental material constraints to the sort of political and developmental options available to policy-makers in East Asia, or anywhere else for that matter. Indeed, for some observers, the key question in this context is whether the capitalist system that has been embraced so enthusiastically and successfully across Asia is actually compatible with a sustainable natural environment over the long term (Foster *et al.* 2010; Kovel 2007).

In this context, we ought to keep in mind one of the recurring themes of this book: history matters. Going early into the industrialization process had major advantages, not least of which was the capacity to exploit the environment ruthlessly before the implications and limits of such actions became all too apparent. Britain, the USA and the other early industrializing countries, along with the corporations that developed within them, enjoyed significant 'first mover advantages' in establishing dominant positions in an emerging global economy (Chandler 1990; Chang 2002). Crucially, they were able to ravage their own environments as they 'developed', free of the global constraints that are now becoming clearer. Anyone who has read Charles Dickens's novels knows that Britain's economic rise generated problems of social dislocation and environmental degradation similar to those afflicting China and the developing world today. In Britain's case, economic development clearly gave it the wherewithal to 'solve' some of its own environmental problems in ways that seem impossible today. It was able to do so, at least in part, by exploiting the resources of the developing world (Blaut 1993). Britain was also able to export some of its surplus population in ways that are simply not possible now. Indeed, it is important to remember that, for all the talk about globalization, labour migration is generally far more tightly controlled and much less significant than it was when the early industrializing nations were taking off (James 2001). The physical and political circumstances confronting would-be industrializing nations now are consequently very different from those confronting Britain, or even Japan, when they undertook similar processes.

Nevertheless, many in the developing world consider – with some justification, perhaps – that the developed world became what it is today by a fairly ruthless approach to the environment and its exploitation, so why shouldn't they do the same? There are two important differences now, of course, which highlight the importance of timing in the development process, and in determining the historical distribution of the world's resources. On the one hand, globalization has made it dramatically clear just how small the world is, and how limited its resources. Environmental issues are inescapably planetary in scope, and there is consequently a concomitant consciousness and a regulatory imperative that was simply not present during earlier periods of industrialization – even if it is proving frustratingly difficult to achieve co-operative agreements to act on commonly recognized problems (Christoff 2010). China's obstructionist behaviour at the inconclusive climate summit in Copenhagen in 2009 revealed both its growing international influence, but also the inflexible, domestically constrained nature of its foreign policy (Conrad 2012).

But China's behaviour is not as incomprehensible as some in the West might think. Not only are the governments of countries in what is still known rather patronizingly as 'the developing world' urged to uphold their responsibilities as custodians of irreplaceable fauna and flora – in a way that the West never did at a similar stage of the development process – but it is painfully clear that many of the superficially attractive economic practices that underpinned the West's rise are simply environmentally – and possibly economically – unsustainable in the long run (Angel and Rock 2009; Ophuls 1997). The other thing that is different now is what might be described as 'the logic of exploitation': the governments of many of the countries that are under the most pressure to exploit their natural resources frequently only have limited control over these, or are constrained by their relationships with external economic actors.

The extent and potentially destructive nature of these relationships can be seen in the impact of what Peter Dauvergne (1997) describes as 'Japan's ecological shadow', or the impact that the Japanese economy has on the natural environment outside Japan itself. Dauvergne details the way in which Japanese multinational corporations dominate the trade in tropical timber in Southeast Asia, using their overwhelming economic leverage ruthlessly to exploit the region's natural resources. As one resource is exhausted, Japan's locust-like MNCs simply move on to the next, working their way systematically through the forests of countries such Indonesia, the Philippines and Papua New Guinea, in a process that is emblematic of a number of the political and economic processes outlined in earlier chapters. Japan's own highly successful development process has created an insatiable appetite for resource inputs; the strategies and structures of its MNCs, the logic of resource security and the simple capacity to manipulate indigenous economic and political actors across the region has led to a brilliantly effective capacity to exploit the region's resources to satisfy such demand. In this regard there is, as Bryant *et al.* (1996: 9) point out, an 'essential continuity of processes and practices' between the colonial period and the present, even if some of the actors and methodologies have changed. Indeed, in Japan's case, the strategy of outsourcing environmental degradation was pioneered during the Tokugawa dynasty (Diamond 2005: 300). Many of the same criticisms are now being made about China as its ecological footprint expands as a consequence of the developmental imperative (Mol 2011).

For much of the region, then, environmental exploitation at the hands of outsiders is simply part of a continuing historical pattern (Crosby 2004). What is different now, of course, is the scale and 'efficiency' of the exploitation, something that is exacerbated dramatically by relentless population growth. Aat Vervoorn (1998) uses the example of Java to illustrate in microcosm – if that is the right way to describe an island with a population of more than 100 million – many of the problems that afflict developing East Asia more generally. Despite internal migration programmes, this fertile island can no longer support its burgeoning population; despite high rainfall it experiences water shortages and flash-flooding as a consequence of massive deforestation. Add to this massively depleted fish stocks around a coastline formerly rich in sea-life, and cities so overcrowded they are becoming dysfunctional, and you have a sense of some of the problems confronting much of the region (Elliott 2012). In such circumstances, the surprise is that there has not been more civil disturbance and social dislocation as a consequence of the deteriorating environment. The impact on the regional environment was bad enough while Japan was the only 'successful' source of resource demand, but now that it has been joined by China and India, the situation could prove catastrophic (Coxhead and Jayasuriya 2010). Before considering China's impact on its own, and the global environment in any detail, it is worth spelling out some of the more sobering facts about East Asia's general situation.

Perhaps the most implacable dynamic exacerbating all of the region's environmental problems is the rapid population growth that is continuing across most of the region. It is not simply the growth of Asia's population that is potentially such a problem, but that Asia is following a well-trodden path to development that inevitably has major environmental impacts. Millions of people are moving off the land into increasingly massive cities and attempting to pursue a Western, consumerist lifestyle. That such a life may be permanently beyond the reach of many of them does little to stop the overall trend, and adds to the demands on the natural environment. Seen in this context, the recent hand-wringing in Japan about the decline in the size of its population becomes rather puzzling: if population growth and consumerism really are at the heart of the planet's environmental problems, then a relative decrease in the impact of Japan's ecological shadow and resource usage should be welcomed rather than feared. It is testimony to the power of contemporary growth-oriented economic discourses and traditional notions of security that this alternative reading of Japanese demographics is generally not given much of an airing. Indeed, there is a remarkable silence about the entire issue of population growth, despite its obvious potential importance (Coole 2013).

When we consider the litany of sobering statistics that describe East Asia's environmental circumstances, it becomes clear that, at some stage, some of the more traditional notions of development, national security and transnational relations will have to be re-thought. It is important to remember that much of Southeast Asia's population remains poor, and dependent on agriculture. As recently as 1997, more than half of the rural populations of the Philippines, Vietnam and Laos were classed as living in poverty (ASEAN 2002: 16). In 2000, 45 per cent of ASEAN's total population lived on less than US$2 per day. Despite an overall slowing of population growth in Asia, demographic pressures make the continuing supply of even the most basic provisions challenging and uncertain. Most fundamentally, food insecurity continues to affect over 160 million people, or about 15 per cent of the overall population in the Asia-Pacific region despite an impressive overall increase in total output (FAOUN 2006). Destructive fishing practices and an all-too-predictable collapse in fish stocks threatened to deprive the region of a critical source of nutrition, even before the current food crisis really took hold (FAOFAD 2006). Other recent developments – partly a consequence of climate change and partly a consequence of the West's demand for 'sustainable' biofuels – have added to such problems and seen a dramatic spike in global commodity prices, and the concomitant spectre of civil disorder across parts of the region as a result (Farchy 2012).

The net effect of the relentless exploitation of the natural environment in the region, as Lorraine Elliott (2009: 252) points out, is that 'resources have been depleted and the environment polluted to the extent that so-called renewable resources and environmental services such as clean air and water are being exhausted in much the same way as non-renewable resources'. Given the devastating impact of such practices and their potential for fuelling social instability, it is worth considering what drives them, and what capacity the region as a whole has for ameliorating them. Again, no country will play a bigger role in determining the outcome of this profoundly important challenge than China, a reality that has consequences for the entire region.

Rising to the challenge?

If the region is to remain stable, let alone prosper, it will have to address a series of environmental, political, economic and strategic problems. Though it is often the latter that attract the most attention, many of the most fundamental challenges are environmental. In this context, an increasingly important source of tension between East Asian neighbours has been disputes over water usage (Chellaney 2012). Population pressures are a major contributor to the growing demand for supplies of fresh water as it is used to irrigate farmland. In Asia as a whole, per capita water availability has declined by between 40 per cent and 65 per cent since 1950 (Dupont 2001: 117). Emblematic of this problem is the potentially intractable conflict that has emerged over water usage around the Mekong River Basin. The Mekong is vital to Cambodia, Laos, Thailand and Vietnam, and these countries signed an agreement in 1995 to cooperate in its use and management. But the fact that China did not sign this agreement profoundly undermines its potential effectiveness, as this is the country with the largest capacity to control the river's flow. In addition, however, water conflict is also constraining China's foreign policy options. As Chellaney (2012: 150) points out:

> China rejects the notion of water sharing or institutionalised cooperation with downstream countries. Whereas riparian neighbours in Southeast and South Asia are bound by water pacts that they have negotiated between themselves, China does not have a single water treaty with any co-riparian country ... while promoting multilateralism on the world stage, China has given the cold shoulder to multilateral cooperation among river-basin states.

In other words, implacable material constraints are reducing dramatically the room for manoeuvre available to China's foreign-policy-making elites. While some Chinese policy-makers might like to continue the charm offensive, the reality is that they may be unable to influence the content of foreign policy in especially contentious areas such as water. It is estimated that 70 per cent of China's waterways and lakes are polluted, a problem exacerbated by high-profile chemical spills that further degrade supplies, and even spill over into neighbouring countries. China relies on underground water supplies to meet nearly 70 per cent of its drinking water needs, but an estimated 90 per cent of such supplies to China's cities are polluted. In addition, some 360 million Chinese rural residents lack access to safe drinking water, a problem compounded by illegal dumping into rivers that local officials appear unwilling or unable to stop. Nearly half of China's population lives in the arid north, which has less than 10 per cent of the country's water (Mufson 2010). Rather than confront the competing political and economic interests that vie for China's limited water sources, its leaders are embarking on massive infrastructural developments to divert existing supplies – with unknowable environmental consequences (Moore 2013).

It is possible to pile up sobering statistics about water shortages, pollution, CO_2 emissions and so on, until they become mind-numbing and incomprehensible in their sheer scale and possible implications. The general point to make is that, collectively, as Elizabeth Economy's (2004: 25) carefully researched study makes clear, 'China's environmental problems now have the potential to bring the country to its knees economically'. The problem is not simply demographic, Economy (2004: 9) argues, but a consequence of 'centuries of rampant, sometimes wilful, destruction of the environment', epitomized most comprehensively by what has been described as 'Mao's war against nature' (Shapiro 2001). As in the West, China's leaders have often had a frontier mentality, which has seen the environment as something to be systematically and ruthlessly exploited. The difference now, of course, is that there may be no new resources to discover and exploit, and no possibility of exporting significant numbers of people to virgin territories. This fundamental physical constraint is not only limiting the options available to Chinese leaders, it is also intensifying the competition for the finite resources that do remain available. China therefore highlights in dramatic form the challenges facing ruling elites across the region as they try to reconcile the potentially conflicting demands of development and conservation, exploitation and sustainability, to say nothing of domestic and international responsibilities.

China's capacity to manage some of the formidable challenges associated with continuing the process of economic development has implications that extend well beyond its own borders (Burgos and Ear 2012; Wilson 2012). The sheer scale of China's economic expansion and concomitant energy needs mean that inevitably it has a major impact on East Asia and the rest of the world. If China's population achieves 'First World' living standards it 'will approximately double the entire world's human resource and environmental impact' (Diamond 2005: 373). Evidence of its ecological footprint already extends right across the Pacific, and its rapidly growing demand for oil and other resources has had a major impact on global commodity prices. The most important question as far as the future of the region and the international system more generally is concerned is whether competition for crucial but diminishing resources can be managed within market-based processes, or whether it will spill over into outright conflict and 'resource wars' (Klare 2002). There are two major consequences of China's development that are significant when thinking about the possible future of the East Asian region: the impact on the environment and the geopolitical consequences of growing competition for scarce resources. Unless the 'externalities' associated with China's industrialization process can be managed successfully, the political and social stability of China itself and its bold experiment in capitalist economics will be in doubt.

There is, however, at least some good news on the energy front. The entirely unpredicted 'fracking revolution', which has allowed the exploitation of vast reserves of hitherto inaccessible shale gas may transform the global energy picture, and make earlier concerns about the apparent inevitability of 'peak oil' production less pressing, if not redundant. The potential implications of this development are enormous, and have major implications for the environment generally and for Sino-US relations in particular. Given that China is already the second-largest consumer of oil after the USA, the potential for friction, and even conflict, between heavily resource-dependent economies chasing dwindling supplies of energy is significant. Now, however, the picture looks rather more reassuring: there is a real possibility that the USA will move towards something like energy independence, and this also may have a positive impact on geopolitics. Not only will such an outcome have a potentially positive impact on Sino-US relations, but it may also make the USA less dependent on authoritarian regimes in the Middle East (Riley 2012).[2]

While this is a potentially positive development – at least, if we put to one side some concerns about the environmental impact of fracking – it may not be enough to transform China's relations with the USA or the region of which it is now such an important part. As we have seen, energy security remains a critical consideration for China's leaders, and there is little sign of a willingness to compromise when vital national interests are at stake. Though there are clearly powerful national undercurrents in the territorial disputes with China's neighbours, much of the implacable driving force behind these disputes, which threaten to fracture regional ties, revolve around the pursuit of the region's potential maritime riches.

The limits to interdependence

The history of East Asia provides a powerful demonstration of the transformative effects of increased interdependence and the benefits of economic opening. No country demonstrates this possibility more vividly than China. But the great challenge and contradiction confronting the leaders of authoritarian states such as China and a number of other Asian states is how to reap the benefits of economic integration while still maintaining political authority and control. When Japan made this transition it was able to do so within what turned out to be the paradoxically constructive embrace of the Cold War: not only was there less ideological pressure placed on Japan to reform, but the less extensive nature of global integration meant that it was able to maintain greater control over what were still essentially domestic economic processes. China's developmental experience – like much of the rest of the region – has been rather different in nature and timing. The penetration of foreign capital has been much greater and the pressure to reform has been more overt and pervasive.

However, none of this is to suggest that China has been unable to resist or mediate such pressures, or that different forms of capitalism are inevitably converging on some sort of universal end point – or not in the foreseeable future, at least. And yet a number of scholars, albeit principally ones from North America, continue to argue that, for political and economic development to continue, a transition has to be made to 'open access societies', which feature impersonal rule and the transformation of societies from ones based on elites to ones based on mass citizenry. What North *et al.* (2009) describe as a 'natural state' is very reminiscent of the East Asian model of close ties between political and economic actors. The problem, they argue, is that economic development is impeded, as 'the natural state cannot support creative destruction because the creation of new economic organisations directly threatens existing economic organisations and their patterns of rents' (North *et al.* 2009: 116). Acemoglu and James (2012: 86) make a similar claim when they suggest that 'economic growth is not just a process of more and better machines, and more and better educated people, but also a transformative and destabilising process associated with widespread creative destruction'.

If these authors are correct, the future looks bleak for Asian-style states and autocracies. We might expect to see an inevitable process of transformation compelling change in an ever-more-integrated, increasingly competitive global economy. Such assumptions have proved misguided in the past, however, and there is no reason to suppose they will not do so in the future. Not only are such depictions of 'open access societies' highly idealized and at odds with the actual historical record in places such as the USA, which is characterized by growing levels of inequality and political dysfunction (Mann and Ornstein 2012), but they downplay the East Asian region's historical record. The fact is that the region has amazed the world with its developmental outcomes; outcomes that have been achieved *because* rather than in spite of the sort of prominent role played by the 'natural state'. The rather lacklustre recent record of economic development in both North America and Western Europe suggests that there is nothing about the organization of economic and political activity in the West that guarantees superior developmental outcomes.

Some observers acknowledge that the West may not have a monopoly of wisdom when it comes to achieving optimal forms of broadly conceived governance. Berggruen and Gardels (2013: 13), for example, advocate a 'middle way' that draws on the experiences of the likes of the

USA and China 'to reconcile knowledgeable democracy with account-able meritocracy'. In other words, the idealized aspects of technically competent bureaucracies and electorally responsive governments may be combined to overcome the institutionalized disadvantages both systems have demonstrated in practice. Superficially attractive as such ideas may be, they are based on an assumption that 'the world is returning to the "normal pluralism" that has characterized most of human history' (Berggruen and Gardels 2013: 12). However, the historical record, especially in Asia, suggests that such assumptions are heroic, to say the least. Not only has political pluralism been the exception rather than the rule for most of East Asia's history, but non-democratic forms of political rule have proved to be surprisingly durable in parts of the region as well. It is not obvious that the interconnected challenges of maintaining economic development in a possibly degraded natural environment are going to make the prospects for widespread and enduring democratic transition any more likely (Beeson 2012).

As we have seen throughout this book, East Asia's inherent diversity means that it is possible to find evidence to support just about any thesis or perspective. In my judgement, however, the future of the region is likely to be shaped by a number of interconnected forces: the continuing influence of history and the ability (or inability) of the region's elites to reconcile potentially incompatible domestic and international impera-tives; the manner in which the region accommodates shifts in the relative importance of rising and declining powers; the way in which pressures for political reform are accommodated at the domestic level; the ability to maintain economic development and fulfil the expectations of the region's still-expanding population; and most fundamentally of all, perhaps, the capacity of the region's elites, at both a domestic and especially at a transnational level, to manage the material transformation of the environment generally and the potentially catastrophic impact of climate change in particular.

This is a formidable agenda. Deciding whether East Asia – or anywhere else for that matter – can rise to the challenge involves making a judgement about the prospects for co-operative behaviour in the inter-national system more generally. The relevant literature offers no defini-tive answers to such questions and reflects the opposing views of those who despair of the possibility of effective global governance (Bremmer 2012; Schweller 2010), and those who think the world is moving inex-orably towards greater degrees of interdependence and new forms of networked governance (Van Langenhove 2010; Wright 2000). While it is impossible to say which of these visions is more likely to be realized, it is clear that East Asia will play a big part in deciding the outcome, even if it is not as a unified collective actor. For, despite the fact that 'East Asia' contains two of the world's three largest economies, and is the site of some of the world's most important geopolitical fault-lines, this does not give it a collective identity or an overwhelming imperative to pursue economic, much less strategic, co-operation. On the contrary, East Asia's recent history serves as a reminder that if regions are to amount to anything more than geographical descriptors, they need political content and active institutional innovation.

While there is plenty of such innovation occurring among the Asian countries that have been the principal focus of this book, it has not always been centred on East Asia. On the contrary, some of the most important institutional initiatives of late have been designed to promote a much broader Asia-Pacific or even an Indo-Pacific region, in which a much wider group of states than those traditionally associated with East Asia would be involved. Under such circumstances, the very existence of East Asia as a political entity capable of exerting a consequential influence on the regional, much less the international, stage is far from certain. As the experiences of the EU, APEC and to a lesser extent ASEAN remind us, the larger any grouping becomes, the more difficult it is to organize, achieve agreement or maintain coherence. While some Asian states may think that an Asia-Pacific grouping offers the possibility of limiting China's ability to dominate East Asia, it may come at the cost of a loss of effectiveness, coherence and an inability to represent the sorts of perspectives and practises that have come to be synonymous with East Asia.

Whichever vision of the region's identity and borders comes to be the most widely accepted, it is important to remember why regionalism remains so potentially important. For all the criticisms to which the EU has recently been subjected, it was largely responsible for pacifying a European continent that had previously pioneered industrialized genocide. Despite the inefficiencies, excesses, infringements of national sovereignty and all the other costs of interdependence, if the ultimate pay-off of regional institutionalization is a more peaceful, more co-operative and even a more prosperous region, it will be a remarkably small price to pay. Given the scale of the challenges East Asia faces, it is an investment that ought to be made even if the short-term results are uncertain and contentious. Without such institutions, the chances of resolving key issues such as the ongoing territorial disputes and the challenge of environmental sustainability look remote. Equally important, the failure to develop effective forms of institutionalized co-operation could threaten some of the very real gains the region as a whole has made since the early 1960s.

Notes

1 Conceptualizing East Asia: From the Local to the Global

1 'The West' is an unsatisfactory but useful shorthand term for those countries and values that were initially associated with Western Europe, the Enlightenment and the development of political liberalism, and which are now championed primarily by the United States. For different views, see Huntington (1996) and Hall (1996).

2 For a contemporary review of this literature, see Rosamond (2005).

3 The 'Asian values' discourse emerged before the Asian crisis when the regional economic 'miracle' was in full swing. Authoritarian leaders such as Malaysia's Mahathir and Singapore's Lee claimed that distinctive Asian cultural traits and social practices such as hard work, respect for authority, filial piety and a rejection of what was seen as the destructive 'Western' vices of self-interest and individualism accounted for the region's superior economic performance. Critics claimed such ideas were self-serving justifications for the perpetuation of authoritarian rule. See Rodan (1996).

4 The literature on globalization is enormous. Good introductions are provided by Held *et al.* (1999) and Scholte (2000).

5 The GATT was replaced by the World Trade Organization (WTO) in 1995. Significantly, the WTO has far greater enforcement powers than the essentially voluntaristic GATT, though this does not mean that free trade has become universally entrenched or that tariff barriers have disappeared. See Das (2003).

6 Unless otherwise indicated, the 'post-war period' refers to post-1945, the consolidation of American hegemony and the acceleration of globalization processes.

7 The idea of the 'Third World' is increasingly being considered as unhelpful because it agglomerates disparate experiences and no longer reflects accurately the nature of the post-Cold War international order and the complex realities within it. See Berger (2004a).

8 The modern state is generally taken to have emerged from the Treaty of Westphalia of 1648, which ended the Thirty Years War and recognized the principle of state sovereignty and enshrined state borders secured by law. It became the dominant form of political organization as a consequence of a process of institutional competition because it offered specific organizational, political, economic and strategic advantages. See Spruyt (1994).

9   It is important to emphasize that states take a variety of forms and that many are 'failing' or lacking in domestic competence and capacity. Historically, East Asia has contained examples of some of the most able and interventionist states, such as Japan, as well as some of the least able and dependent, such as Cambodia.

2 Northeast Asia and the Weight of History

1   Modelski and Thompson (1996) argue persuasively that the foundations of 'globalization' and the sort of rapid economic development that characterizes the modern era were laid down in Sung dynasty China some 1,000 years ago.

2   The Mandate of Heaven was based on the belief that a ruler enjoyed the blessing of the deity, an idea with powerful legitimating potential for the ruling elite. The loss of heaven's mandate was thought to be manifested in an increase in natural disasters and a breakdown of social order.

3   The extent of China's naval capacity and the extent of its withdrawal from the world is symbolized in the voyages of Grand Eunuch Zheng He, who was commanded to survey China's trade routes in the early fifteenth century. His armada consisted of over 300 vessels, including some of the largest ever built at that time. Zheng travelled as far as India and Africa.

4   China's examination system provided a degree of social mobility through competitive entry to the civil service and thus the gentry, who constituted the governing elite between the autocracy and the peasantry. See Hsü (1983).

5   The Manchus originated in the Jurched tribes of Manchuria. The key historical point is that not only were a small group able to supplant the Ming dynasty, but that 'in reality they remained conquerors', and consequently suspicious of the Chinese – something that contributed to the Qing dynasty's ultimate demise. See Hsü (1983: 446–7).

6   The main differences in interpretation revolve around the importance of economic, political and strategic factors, the benefits that accrue to the imperial power, and the damage this inflicts on the development of the peripheral power. The relevant literature is vast, but for useful perspectives see Hobsbawm (1987) and Doyle (1986).

7   From Marco Polo onwards, European interest in China had been intense. Chinese intellectual ideas, especially Confucianism, made a substantial impact on Europe and can be seen in the writings of Montesquieu, and the ideas of the Physiocrats. See Fairbank *et al.* (1965: 64–6).

8   The self-strengthening movement developed in the latter half of the nineteenth century. It was led by prominent scholar officials like Zeng Guofan and Li Hongzhang, and was intended to adopt and learn from the West's technological expertise, but this inevitably led to a wider importation of Western ideas, some of which were political and contributed to undermining the old order. The contrast with Japan's much more successful borrowing from the West is revealing and instructive.

9   The tribute system was series of practices through which China managed its external affairs, in which barbarian states accepted their subordinate position and payed homage through gifts and emissaries to the Chinese imperial order. The pay-off for the subordinates was access to Chinese trade and reciprocal bribes. See Hamashita (1994).

10   Historically there has been a fundamental congruence between the modernization process, especially the development of a complex industrial society, and nationalism, which has provided an especially powerful force for organizing social and material resources. See Gellner (1983).

11   The May Fourth Movement refers specifically to a massive student demonstration in Peking in 1919 in response to Japan's 'Twenty-one Demands', which were endorsed by the Versailles Conference following the First World War. The long-term impact of the May Fourth Movement was to spark a more generalized intellectual revolution in China. See Fitzgerald (1996).

12   'China must cut farming population, says OECD', *Financial Times*, 14 November 2005.

13   Taiwan was formerly know as Formosa and is sometimes called 'Chinese Taipei', in deference to mainland China's sensitivities about its status.

14   Even before the fall of the Tokugawa, Japan had sent a number of missions abroad to study European styles of political, economic and, especially, military organization. These were subsequently expanded as the modernization push gained momentum.

15   Many Japanese were unhappy about the impact of the reform process – and not just marginalized feudal lords. Some samurai were concerned about the impact of Western-style reform on traditional Japanese values, and in particular their own loss of status.

16   As part of this comprehensive programme of occupation and exploitation, more than 300,000 Japanese emigrated to Manchuria during the 1930s.

17   For an interesting discussion of both Japan's wartime thinking about the West, and more recent usages of these sorts of discursively constructed cultural binaries, see Burma and Margalit (2004).

3 Southeast Asia's Dependent Development

1   By contrast, Christianity's introduction to the region, in concert with growing European trade links, was more systematic, but became dominant only in the Philippines, where the Spanish colonizers had significant state support and the experience of Latin-American colonization to draw on.

2   Patron–client ties, or patrimonialism, refers to the personal ties and loyalties that exist between superiors and subordinates, and which may be the basis of power and patronage when part of a wider social and political system. See Brown (1994: 114–17).

3   Broadly, formal rationality refers to the techniques by which ends are achieved; and substantive rationality to the norms and values that underpin such endeavours.

4   On the rivalries between the European powers that formed the backdrop of this period of colonial expansion, see Tarling (1966).
5   Saigon was re-named Ho Chi Minh City following the communist takeover of the South.
6   These intense, long-standing regional rivalries are also important in explaining contemporary tensions and problems in the region, as we shall see in subsequent chapters.
7   This way of conceptualizing relations between the developed economies of the imperial powers and the emerging colonial economies is drawn from analyses based in world systems theory, and captures something important about the enduring 'structural' nature of the relationship. See Chase-Dunn (1998).
8   This process was instrumental in cementing the dominant economic position of Chinese immigrants, the consequences of which are taken up in later chapters.
9   The *mestizo* are people of mixed Chinese–native parentage.

4 The Evolving Security Agenda

1   The JSDF were originally intended, as the name implies, for strictly defensive purposes, though it has never been entirely clear what this might mean in practice. In 1976, Prime Minister Miki placed a 1 per cent ceiling on Japanese defence spending, but, given the dramatic expansion of the Japanese economy, this has still made Japan one of the world's most significant potential military powers.
2   There are some illuminating exceptions, however. For one of these, see Brooks (2005).
3   ABRI (Angkatan Bersenjata Republik Indonesia) is the former name of the Indonesian armed forces, renamed in 1999 the Tentara Nasional Indonesia (TNI).
4   As Chapter 6 makes clear, though, this does not mean that these states do not have highly effective domestic security regimes.
5   Status-quo powers are, as the name suggests, content with the prevailing order and not intent on changing it. China's rise generally and its unhappiness about the status of Taiwan in particular, lead some observers to suggest that it is a non-status quo power and therefore a potential source of instability. See Johnston (2003a).

5 Regional Security

1   This chapter draws on Beeson (2009d).
2   North Korea plainly represents the greatest and most unpredictable challenge to this benign scenario. At the very least, it will present a formidable test of deterrence theory and practices. See Rachman (2013).

3   In addition to the ASEAN countries themselves, the ARF initially included seven 'dialogue partners' – the USA, Japan, South Korea, Australia, New Zealand, Canada and the European Union – and was subsequently expanded in 1993 to include China, Russia and Papua New Guinea, plus Vietnam and Laos who were not at that stage members of ASEAN itself. It was formally established in 1994.

4   Vietnam invaded Cambodia in 1978. Its installation of a sympathetic regime presented a major challenge for ASEAN and its capacity to deal with conflict in Southeast Asia. Vietnam saw this as a way of curbing Chinese expansionism and resolving a destabilizing domestic conflict. The fact that ASEAN was instrumental in engineering a peaceful withdrawal by Vietnam is seen by ASEAN as a triumph of its style of diplomacy and co-operation. See Acharya (2001).

5   The members of the Six Party talks are North and South Korea, Japan, China, the USA and Russia.

6   Nationalism and Domestic Politics

1   For a useful discussion of state strength in the international context and an explanation of the difficulty that many non-Western states have in shaping the international regulatory architecture, see Volgy and Bailin (2003).

2   Democracy is surprisingly hard to define, especially at a time when global processes are eroding the autonomy and authority of states – even if they are democratically elected. However, there is an assumption that this will involve some sort of procedural minimum involving 'rule by the people', a capacity for them to express their political preferences formally, and a regular turnover of political elites. On democratic forms, see Held (1987). On the 'structural' constraints that economic power present to 'authentic' democracy, see Bowles and Gintis (1996). On the capacity of global forces to undermine democracy, see Cerny (1999).

3   Japan's unusual voting system included single non-transferable votes and multi-member constituencies, and meant that voters had only one preference, but constituencies typically returned three, four or five members. Because individual parties might return more than one successful candidate from each electorate, candidates from the same party competed among themselves to try to maximize their share of the party's overall vote. To distinguish themselves from each other they frequently resorted to what were little more than bribes to lock in personal support. The consequence of this, of course, was to entrench the role and importance of 'money politics'. However, there have been significant attempts to overhaul this system, and it is important to acknowledge that it is widely considered that there is far less corruption now than there once was (Curtis 1999: 165).

4   This is how Robert Wade (1990) describes pre-democratic government in Taiwan.

5   The five principles were: 'Belief in the One and Only God'; 'Just and

Civilised Humanity'; 'the Unity of Indonesia'; 'Democracy Guided by the Inner Wisdom in the Unanimity Arising out of Deliberation amongst Representatives'; and 'Social Justice for the Whole People of Indonesia'.

6 This has now changed and present incumbent Yudhoyono was elected directly in a process that was widely seen as being fair and transparent.

7 Under Suharto, Golkar was the dominant political party and contained representatives of key 'functional' groups such as military officers, civil servants and trade unions in a highly effective, if politically unrepresentative, corporatist structure.

8 Since Suharto's downfall, Indonesia has had four leaders: Habbibie, Wahid, Megawati and the current President Yudhoyono.

9 When Ho Chi Minh declared independence – prematurely, as it turned out – in North Vietnam following the Second World War, he laced his speech with quotations from Thomas Jefferson. Significantly, Ho's friendly, potentially conflict-avoiding overtures to the USA were rebuffed on the grounds of anti-communism. See Rotter (1987: 100–01).

7 East Asia's Developmental States

1 This chapter draws on Beeson (2009c).

2 The high growth era lasted from 1955 to 1973, marking the period when the developmental state was at the height of its interventionist powers.

3 It is worth noting in passing that List's ideas also exerted considerable influence in the United States when it was going through a similar developmental stage. Alexander Hamilton, first Secretary of the Treasury, was an admirer of List's ideas and used them as the basis of his highly interventionist strategies for promoting American economic development. The idea that America prospered solely because of market forces is consequently a myth that has been – possibly conveniently – forgotten by subsequent generations of policy-makers. See Chang (2002b). On Hamilton, his ideas and place in American development, see Chernow (2004).

4 Foreign pressure, especially from the USA, has been decisive in shaping Japanese public policy, an outcome of the historical and strategic factors discussed in earlier chapters. The fact that the Japanese have a word for it – *gaiatsu* – is revealing in itself. See George (1997); Schoppa (1997).

5 This strategy was employed widely in the region, but it is fatally undermined by financial sector liberalization. On the role of financial repression in East Asian development, see the World Bank (1993: 237–9).

6 The impact and extent of the overseas Chinese is outlined in more detail in the next chapter.

7 Amsden (2001: 282) argues that all late-developing economies have to make a 'profound choice' between relying on foreign multinational companies (MNCs) or attempting to develop indigenous firms to compete internationally. Singapore's limited scale may have effectively precluded the latter option.

8   Rentier classes derive their wealth, as the name suggests, from rents, bonds and unearned income.

8 The China model?

1   This chapter draws on Beeson (2013a, 2013bc).

9 East Asia and the Global Economy

1   The 'value chain' refers to the way in which products become more valuable as they are transformed from basic commodities to finished manufactured products. More highly paid jobs and wealth-creating processes are generally found closer to the point of completion, making such activities a key focus of industrial policies. The existence of established companies and even national economies makes it much harder for new entrants to break into the more lucrative aspects of the value-creating process, however. See Kaplinsky (2000).
2   However, it is important to note that the USA has once again overtaken China as Japan's largest single export destination. While this may prove to be an aberration, it is also a reminder that economic ties can be affected negatively by a deteriorating security environment. See Wagstyl (2013).

10 Crises and Their Consequences

1   This chapter draws on previously published work in Beeson (2011).
2   By 1996, Indonesia's short-term debt was 56.7 per cent of overall liabilities, South Korea was 58.5 per cent, Thailand, 67.2 per cent, and Malaysia a massive 70.1 per cent. See Haggard (2000: 18).
3   Almost, but not quite: the USA continues to enjoy unique privileges that flow from being able to pay its debts in its own currency. See Cohen (1998).
4   That the Philippines was less badly affected by the crisis is not testimony to strong fundamentals of sound economic policy-making, but more to the fact that they had received far less investment than their neighbours, had generally poorer economic outcomes, and thus had less far to fall. See Bello (2000).
5   Perhaps the most significant point in this context is not that this thesis exercised such a surprising influence for so long, but the underlying role played by the economics profession in legitimizing uncritically a narrow set of abstractions that were at odds with empirical historical reality. See Colander *et al.* (2009).
6   Quoted in Tett and Edgecliffe-Johnson (2009).
7   The key agencies are departments such as the National Development and Reform Commission, China (NDRC); the State-owned Assets Supervision

and Administration Commission of the State Council (SASAC), which is directly under the State Council, as is the NDRC; the People's Bank of China; the Ministry of Land and Resources; the State Administration of Foreign Exchange (SAFE); and the Finance Ministry.

11 The Evolution of East Asian Regionalism

1   In addition to the APT countries, the EAS includes Australia, India, New Zealand, Russia and, most crucially, the United States.
2   Liberal theorists such as Robert Keohane (1982) argued that the demand for international institutions would increase as a consequence of their functional utility and a decline in US hegemony. While the extent of American decline remains hotly contested, Keohane was clearly right in suggesting that it would be an important factor in shaping the course of regional institutional development.
3   Indonesia challenged the legitimacy of the newly independent Malaysia, but its decision to renounce the confrontational approach 'served as a model for its neighbours and raised the possibility of a regional order based on the non-use of force in inter-state relations', Acharya (2001: 49) claims.
4   The elimination or reduction of internal trade barriers within the ASEAN grouping made the sort of cross-border production strategies employed by Japanese car manufacturers (discussed in the previous chapter) more feasible and attractive.
5   Among the most significant were the Pacific Basin Economic Council (PBEC), the Pacific Economic Cooperation Council (PECC), and the Pacific Trade and Development Conference (PAFTAD). See Woods (1993).
6   Ernst Haas (1990: 41) suggests an epistemic community is 'composed of professionals ... who share a commitment to a common causal model and a common set of political values. They are united by a belief in the truth of their model and a commitment to translate this truth into public policy.'
7   APEC's original membership included the members of ASEAN plus Australia, New Zealand, the USA and Canada. In 1991, China, Hong Kong and Taiwan (styled 'Chinese Taipei' in deference to PRC sensitivities) joined. In 1993, Mexico and Papua New Guinea (PNG) joined, then Chile in 1994, and Peru, Russia and Vietnam in 1997.
8   Significantly, Ishihara, who was instrumental in reviving the current territorial dispute between Japan and China, remains a prominent and divisive figure in Japan. See Fackler (2012).

12 East Asian Futures

1   Perhaps the most prominent example of how it is possible to over-estimate the pacifying impact of economic interdependence was made by Norman Angell (2010 [1909]) immediately before the First World War.

2   It is also worth noting that China faces much greater problems in exploiting its potential reserves of shale gas than the does the USA, giving the latter an important advantage in the race to exploit new sources of energy. See Mufson (2013).

References

Abbott, Kenneth W. and Snidal, Duncan (2009) 'The governance triangle: Regulatory standards institutions and the shadow of the state', in Mattli, W. and Woods, N., *The Politics of Global Regulation* (Princeton, NJ: Princeton University Press): 44–88.

Abernathy, David B. (2000) *Global Dominance: European Overseas Empires, 1415–1980* (New Haven, CT: Yale University Press).

Acharya, Amitav (2000) *The Quest for Identity: International Relations of Southeast Asia* (Singapore: Oxford University Press).

Acharya, Amitav (2001) *Constructing a Security Community in Southeast Asia: ASEAN and the Problem of Regional Order* (London: Routledge).

Acharya, Amitav (2002) 'Regionalism and the emerging world order', in Breslin, S. *et al.* (eds), *New Regionalisms in the Global Political Economy* (London: Routledge): 20–32.

Acharya, Amitav (2004) 'How ideas spread: Whose norms matter? Norm localization and institutional change in Asian regionalism', *International Organization*, 58: 239–75.

Acharya, Amitav (2005) 'The Bush Doctrine and Asian regional order', in Gurtov, M. and Van Ness, P. (eds), *Confronting the Bush Doctrine: Critical Views from the Asia-Pacific* (London: Routledge): 203–26.

Acemoglu, Daren and Robinson, James A. (2012) *Why Nations Fail: The Origins of Power, Prosperity, and Poverty* (New York: Crown).

ADB (Asia Development Bank) (2011) *Asian Development Outlook 2011, Update: Preparing for Demographic Transition* (Mandaluyong City, Manila: ADB).

Adler, Emanuel and Barnett, Michael (1998) 'A framework for the study of security communities', in Adler, E. and Barnett, M. (eds), *Security Communities* (Cambridge: Cambridge University Press): 29–65.

Aggarwal, Vinod K. (2011) 'Look west: The evolution of US trade policy toward Asia', *Globalizations*, 7(4): 455–73.

Agnew, John (1994) 'The territorial trap: The geographical assumptions of international relations theory', *Review of International Political Economy*, 1(1): 53–80.

Agnew, John (2005) *Hegemony: The New Shape of Global Power* (Philadelphia, PA: Temple University Press).

Ahmad, Sameena (2004) 'Behind the mask: A survey of business in China', *The Economist*, 20 March.

Alagappa, Muthiah (ed.) (1995) *Political Legitimacy in Southeast Asia: The Quest for Moral Authority* (Stanford, CA: Stanford University Press).

Alagappa, Muthiah (1998) 'Asian practice of security: Key features and explanations', in Alagappa, M. (ed.), *Asian Security Practice: Material and Ideational Influences* (Stanford, CA: Stanford University Press): 611–76.

Alagappa, Muthiah (2001) 'Introduction: Presidential election, democratization, and cross-Strait relations', in Alagappa, M. (ed.), *Taiwan's Presidential Politics* (Armonk, NY: M.E. Sharpe): 3–47.

Alagappa, Muthiah (2003) 'Managing Asian security: Competition, cooperation, and evolutionary change', in Alagappa, M. (ed.), *Asian Security Order: Instrumental and Normative Features* (Stanford: Stanford University Press): 571–606.

Alatas, Ali (2001) *"ASEAN Plus Three" Equals Peace Plus Prosperity* (Singapore: Institute of Southeast Asian Studies).

Alba, J., Park, D. and Wang, P. (2010) 'Determinants of different modes of Japanese foreign direct investment in the United States', Economics Working Paper No. 197, Asian Development Bank.

Amirahmadi, Hooshang and Wu, Weiping (1995) 'Export processing zones in Asia', *Asian Survey*, 35(9): 828–49.

Amsden, Alice H. (1989) *Asia's Next Giant: South Korea and Late Industrialization* (New York: Oxford University Press).

Amsden, Alice H. (1995) 'Like the rest: South-east Asia's "late" industrialization', *Journal of International Development*, 7(5): 791–9.

Amsden, Alice H. (2001) *The Rise of "The Rest": Challenges to the West from Late–Industrializing Economies* (Oxford: Oxford University Press).

Amyx, Jennifer (2004) *Japan's Financial Crisis: Institutional Rigidity and Reluctant Change* (Princeton, NJ: Princeton University Press).

Amyx, Jennifer (2005) 'What motivates regional financial cooperation in East Asia today?', *Asia Pacific Issues*, No. 76 (Honolulu, HI: East–West Centre).

Anderlini, Jamil and Alloway, Tracy (2011) 'Trades reveal China shift from dollar', *Financial Times*, 20 June.

Anderson, Benedict (1983) *Imagined Communities* (London: Verso).

Anderson, Benedict (1988) 'Cacique democracy and the Philippines: Origins and dreams, *New Left Review*, 169: 3–31.

Angel, David and Rock, Michael T. (2009) 'Environmental rationalities and the development state in East Asia: Prospects for a sustainability transition', *Technological Forecasting and Social Change*, 76(2): 229–40.

Angell, Norman (2010) *The Great Illusion* (New York: Cosimo).

Arase, David (1994) 'Public–private sector interest coordination in Japan's ODA', *Pacific Affairs*, 67(2): 171–99.

Arase, David (1995) *Buying Power: The Political Economy of Japan's Foreign Aid* (Boulder, CO: Lynne Rienner).

Ariely, Gal (2012) 'Globalisation and the decline of national identity? An exploration across sixty-three countries', *Nations and Nationalism*, 18(3): 461–82.

Armijo, Leslie Elliott (2002) 'The terms of the debate: What's democracy got to do with it?', in Armijo, L.E. (ed.), *Debating the Global Financial Architecture* (New York: New York State University): 2–62.

Armijo, Leslie Elliott (2007) 'The BRICs countries (Brazil, Russia, India, and

China) as analytical category: Mirage or insight?', *Asian Perspective*, 31(4): 7–42.

Art, Robert J. (2003) *A Grand Strategy for America* (Ithaca, NY: Cornell University Press).

Arthur, Brian (1989) 'Competing technologies, increasing returns, and lock-in by historical events', *The Economic Journal*, 99: 116–31.

ASEAN (1967) *The ASEAN Declaration* Available at: http://www.aseansec.org/1629.htm.

ASEAN (2002) *ASEAN Report to the World Summit on Sustainable Development* (Jakarta: ASEAN).

ASEAN (2005) 'Kuala Lumpur Declaration on the ASEAN Plus Three Summit', Kuala Lumpur, 12 December. Available at: http://www.aseansec.org/18036.htm.

Ash, Timothy G. (2004) *Free World: America, Europe, and the Surprising Future of the West* (New York: Random House).

Ash, Timothy G. (2012) 'The crisis of Europe: How the Union came together and why it's falling apart', *Foreign Affairs*, 91(2): 2–15.

Athukorala, P. and Hill, H. (2010) 'Asian trade: long–term patterns and key policy issues', *Asian-Pacific Economic Literature*, 24(2): 52–82.

Athukorala, P. and Kohpaiboon, A. (2009) 'Intra-regional trade in East Asia: The decoupling fallacy, crisis, and policy challenges', ADBI Working PaperNo. 177.

Ayoob, Mohammed (2005) 'The future of political Islam: The importance of external variables', *International Affairs*, 81(5): 951–61.

Ba, Alice D. (2003) 'China and ASEAN: Reinvigorating relations for a 21st-century Asia', *Asian Survey*, 43(4): 622–47.

Ba, Alice D. (2009) *(Re)Negotiating East and Southeast Asia: Regions, Regionalism, and the Association of Southeast Asian Nations* (Stanford, CA: Stanford University Press).

Baccini, Leonardo and Dur, Andreas (2011) 'The new regionalism and policy interdependence', *British Journal of Political Science*, 42(1): 57–79.

Back, H. and Hadenius, A. (2008) 'Democracy and state capacity: Exploring a J-shaped relationship', *Governance*, 21(1): 1–24.

Bagchi, Amiya Kumar (2000) 'The past and the future of the developmental state', *Journal of World Systems Research*, Summer /Fall: 398–442.

Balassa, Bela (1988) 'The lessons of East Asian development: An overview', *Economic Development and Cultural Change*, 36(3): 273–90.

Baldwin, Robert E. (2011) '21st century regionalism: Filling the gap between 21st century trade and 20th century trade rules', Staff Working Paper, ERSD-2011-08 (Geneva: WTO).

Baldwin, Robert E. (2007) 'Managing the noodle bowl: The fragility of East Asian regionalism', Working Paper Series on Regional Integration, No 7 (Manila: ADB).

Barber, Benjamin R. (2001) *Jihad vs. McWorld* (New York: Ballantine Books).

Barber, Tony (2012) 'Stretched at the seams', *Financial Times*, 8 November.

Barboza, David (2011) 'China tells U.S. it must "cure its addiction to debt"', *New York Times* 6 August.

Barnett, Michael and Finnemore, Martha (2004) *Rules for the World: International Organizations in Global Politics* (Ithaca, NY: Cornell University Press).

Beasley, W.G. (1989) 'Meiji political institutions', in Jansen, M.B. (ed.), *The Cambridge History of Japan, Vol. 5: The Nineteenth Century* (Cambridge: Cambridge University Press): 618–73.

Beasley, W.G. (1993) *The Rise of Modern Japan: Political, Economic, and Social Change since 1850* (London: Weidenfeld & Nicolson).

Beddoes, Zanny Minton (2005) 'The great thrift shift: A survey of the world economy', *The Economist*, 24 September.

Beeson, Mark (1999) 'Reshaping regional institutions: APEC and the IMF in East Asia', *The Pacific Review*, 12(1): 1–24.

Beeson, Mark (2000) 'Mahathir and the markets: Globalisation and the pursuit of economic autonomy in Malaysia', *Pacific Affairs*, 73(3): 335–51.

Beeson, Mark (2001) 'Globalisation, governance, and the political-economy of public policy reform in East Asia', *Governance: An International Journal of Policy, Administration and Institutions*, 14(4): 481–502.

Beeson, Mark (2003a) 'Sovereignty under siege: Globalisation and the state in Southeast Asia', *Third World Quarterly*, 24(2): 357–74.

Beeson, Mark (2003b) 'Japan's reluctant reformers and the legacy of the developmental state', in Cheung, A. and Scott, I. (eds), *Governance and Public Sector Reform in Post-Crisis Asia: Paradigm Shift or Business as Usual?* (London: Curzon Press): 25–43.

Beeson, Mark (2003c) 'ASEAN Plus Three and the rise of reactionary regionalism', *Contemporary Southeast Asia*, 25(2): 251–68.

Beeson, Mark (2004a) 'US hegemony and Southeast Asia: The impact of, and limits to, American power and influence', *Critical Asian Studies*, 36(3): 323–54.

Beeson, Mark (2004b) 'The rise and fall (?) of the developmental state: The vicissitudes and implications of East Asian interventionism', in Low, L. (ed.), *Developmental States: Relevant, Redundant or Reconfigured?* (New York: Nova Science Publishers): 29–40.

Beeson, Mark (2005) 'Re-thinking regionalism: Europe and East Asia in comparative historical perspective', *Journal of European Public Policy*, 12(6): 969–85.

Beeson, Mark (2006a) 'American hegemony and regionalism: The rise of East Asia and the end of the Asia-Pacific', *Geopolitics*, 11(4): 541–60.

Beeson, Mark (2006b) 'Southeast Asia and the international financial institutions', in Rodan, G., Hewison, K. and Robison, R. (eds), *The Political Economy of South-East Asia: An Introduction*, 3rd edn (Melbourne: Oxford University Press): 238–55.

Beeson, Mark (2008) 'Civil–military relations in Indonesia and the Philippines: Will the Thai coup prove contagious?', *Armed Forces & Society*, 34(3): 474–90.

Beeson, Mark (2009a) *Institutions of the Asia-Pacific: ASEAN, APEC and Beyond* (London: Routledge).

Beeson, Mark (2009b) 'Geopolitics and the making of regions: The fall and rise of East Asia', *Political Studies*, 57: 498–516.

Beeson, Mark (2009c) 'Developmental states in East Asia: A comparison of the Japanese and Chinese experiences', *Asian Perspective*, 33(2): 5–39.

Beeson, Mark (2009d) 'Hegemonic transition in East Asia? The dynamics of Chinese and American power', *Review of International Studies*, 35(1): 95–112.

Beeson, Mark (2010) 'The coming of environmental authoritarianism', *Environmental Politics*, 19(2): 276–94.

Beeson, Mark (2011) 'Crisis dynamics and regionalism: East Asia in comparative perspective', *The Pacific Review*, 24(3): 357–74.

Beeson, Mark (2012) 'Democracy, development, and authoritarianism', in Beeson, M. and Stubbs, R. (eds), *The Routledge Handbook of Asian Regionalism* (London: Routledge): 236–47.

Beeson, Mark (2013a) 'Can China lead?', *Third World Quarterly*, 34(2): 235–52.

Beeson, Mark (2013b) 'Living with giants: ASEAN and the evolution of Asian regionalism', *TRaNS: Trans-Regional and -National Studies of Southeast Asia*, 1(2): 1–20.

Beeson, Mark (2013c) 'The rise of China and the future of the international political economy', in Palan, Ronen (ed.), *Global Political Economy: Contemporary Theories*, 2nd edn (London: Routledge): 250–61.

Beeson, Mark (forthcoming) 'Security governance in Southeast Asia: The paradoxes of cooperation', in Sperling, James (ed.), *Handbook on Governance and Security* (Cheltenham: Edward Elgar).

Beeson, Mark and Bell, Stephen (2005) 'Structures, institutions and agency in the models of capitalism debate', in Phillips, Nicola (ed.), *Globalising International Political Economy* (Basingstoke: Palgrave Macmillan): 116–40.

Beeson, Mark and Bell, Stephen (2009) 'The G–20 and international economic governance: Hegemony, collectivism, or both?', *Global Governance* 15 (1): 67–86.

Beeson, Mark and Bellamy, Alex J. (2008) *Securing Southeast Asia: The Politics of Security Sector Reform* (London: Routledge).

Beeson, Mark and Broome, André (2010) 'Hegemonic instability and East Asia: Contradictions, crises and US power', *Globalizations*, 7(4): 479–95.

Beeson, Mark and Higgott, Richard (2005) 'Hegemony, institutionalism and US foreign policy: Theory and practice in comparative historical perspective', *Third World Quarterly*, 26(7): 1173–88.

Beeson, Mark and Higgott, Richard (2013) 'The changing architecture of politics in the Asia-Pacific: Another middle power moment?', Paper for The Role of Middle Power in the 21st Century International Relations, Korean Association of International Studies Conference, 19–20 April, Seoul.

Beeson, Mark and Islam, Iyanatul (2005) 'Neoliberalism and East Asia:

Resisting the Washington Consensus', *Journal of Development Studies*, 41(2): 197–219.

Beeson, Mark and Jayasuriya, Kanishka (1998) 'The political rationalities of regionalism: APEC and the EU in comparative perspective', *The Pacific Review*, 11(3): 311–36.

Beeson, Mark and Li Fujian (2012) 'Charmed or alarmed? Reading China's regional relations', *Journal of Contemporary China*, 21(73): 35–51.

Beeson, Mark and Li Fujian (2014) *China's Regional Relations: Evolving Foreign Policy Dynamics* (Boulder, CO: Lynne Rienner).

Beeson, Mark and Pham, H.H. (2012) 'Developmentalism with Vietnamese characteristics?: The persistence of state-led development in East Asia', *Journal of Contemporary Asia*, 42(4): 539–59.

Beeson, Mark with Stone, Diane (2012) 'A model to avoid? The European Union's declining influence in post-crisis East Asia', Paper delivered at the First Annual GR:EEN Conference, February 13–14, Milan.

Beeson, Mark and Stone, Diane (2013) 'The changing fortunes of a policy entrepreneur: The case of Ross Garnaut', *Australian Journal of Political Science*, 48(1): 1–14.

Beeson, Mark and Stubbs, Richard (2012) 'Conclusion: The future of Asian reginalism', in Beeson, M. and Stubbs, R. (eds), *The Routledge Handbook of Asian Regionalism* (London: Routledge): 420–6.

Beeson, Mark and Yoshimatsu, Hidetaka (2007) 'Asia's odd men out: Australia, Japan, and the politics of regionalism', *International Relations of the Asia-Pacific*, 7(2): 227–50.

Beeson, Mark, Soko, Mills and Wang Yong (2011) 'The new resource politics: Can Australia and South Africa accommodate China?', *International Affairs*, 87(6): 1365–84.

Bell, Stephen (2005) 'How tight are the policy constraints: The policy convergence thesis, institutionally situated actors and expansionary monetary policy in Australia', *New Political Economy*, 10 (1): 68–91.

Bell, Stephen and Feng, Steven (forthcoming) 'The politics of trade opening in post–WTO China', *Review of International Political Economy*.

Bell, Stephen and Hindmoor, A. (2009) *Rethinking Governance: The Centrality of the State in Modern Society* (Melbourne: Cambridge University Press).

Bellman, Eric and Barta, Patrick (2012) 'Indonesia says it's tackling concerns', *Wall Street Journal*, 2 March.

Bello, Walden (1998) 'East Asia: On the eve of the great transformation?' *Review of International Political Economy*, 5(3): 424–44.

Bello, Walden (2000) 'The Philippines: The making of a neo-classical tragedy', in Robison, R. *et al.* (eds), *Politics and Markets in the Wake of the Asian Crisis* (London: Routledge): 238–57.

Bello, Walden and Poh, Li Kheng (1998) *A Siamese Tragedy: Development and Disintegration in Modern Thailand* (London: Zed Books).

Beresford, Melanie (2008) 'Doi Moi in review: The challenges of building market socialism in Vietnam', *Journal of Contemporary Asia*, 38(2): 221–43.

Berger, Mark T. (2004a) 'After the Third World? History, destiny and the fate of Third Worldism', *Third World Quarterly*, 25(1): 9–39.

Berger, Suzanne (2005) *How We Compete: What Companies Around the World Are Doing to Make It in Today's Global Economy* (New York: Doubleday).

Berger, Suzanne and Dore, Ronald (eds) (1996) *National Diversity and Global Capitalism* (Ithaca, NY: Cornell University Press).

Berggruen, Nicolas and Gardels, Nathan (2013) *Intelligent Governance for the 21st Century: A Middle Way between West and East* (Cambridge: Polity Press).

Bergsten, C. Fred, Gill, Bates, Lardy, Nicholas R. and Mitchell, Derek (2006) *China: The Balance Sheet* (New York: Public Affairs).

Bernard, Mitchell and Ravenhill, John (1995) 'Beyond product cycles and flying geese: Regionalization, hierarchy, and the industrialization of East Asia', *World Politics*, 47: 179–210.

Bertrand, Jacques (1998) 'Growth and democracy in Southeast Asia', *Comparative Politics*, 30(3): 355–75.

Bevacqua, Ron (1998) 'Whither the Japanese model: The Asian economic crisis and the continuation of Cold War politics in the Pacific Rim', *Review of International Political Economy*, 5(3): 410–23.

Bezlova, Antoaneta (2004) 'The dragon stirs in a wary world', *Asia Times*, 25 December. Available at: http://www.atimes.com.

Bhagwati, Jagdish (1998) 'The capital myth', *Foreign Affairs*, 77(3): 7–12.

Bhagwati, Jagdish N. (2012) 'America's threat to trans-Pacific trade', *East Asia Forum*, 10 January.

Blackburn, Robin (2008) 'The subprime crisis', *New Left Review*, 50 (March/April): 63–106.

Blainey, Geoffrey (1975) *The Tyranny of Distance: How Distance Shaped Australia's History* (London: Macmillan).

Bland, Ben (2012) 'Protectionism hits Indonesia's reputation', *Financial Times*, 12 June.

Blaut, J.M. (1993) *The Colonizer's View of the World* (New York: Guilford Press).

Bleiker, Roland (2005) *Divided Korea: Toward a Culture of Reconciliation* (Minneapolis, MN: University of Minnesota Press).

Bobbitt, Philip (2002) *The Shield of Achilles: War, Peace and the Course of History* (New York: Knopf).

Boli, John and Thomas, George M. (1999) 'INGOs and the organisation of world culture', in Boli, John and Thomas, George M. (eds), *Constructing World Culture: International Nongovernmental Organizations since 1875* (Stanford, CA: Stanford University Press): 13–48.

Boot, Max (2002) *The Savage Wars of Peace: Small Wars and the Rise of American Power* (New York: Basic Books).

Booth, Anne (1999) 'Development: Achievement and weakness', in Emmerson, D. (ed.), *Indonesia Beyond Suharto* (Armonk, NY: M.E. Sharpe): 109–35.

Booth, Ken and Trood, Russell (eds) (1999) *Strategic Cultures in the Asia-Pacific Region* (London: Macmillan).

Börzel, Tania A. and Risse, Thomas (2012) 'From Europeanisation to diffusion: Introduction', *West European Politics*, 35(1): 1–19.

Boucher, Richard (2005) *Joint Statement of the US–Japan Security Consultative Committee* (Washington, DC: US Department of State).

Boudreau, Vince (2009) 'Elections, repression and authoritarian survival in post-transition Indonesia and the Philippines', *The Pacific Review*, 22(2): 233–53.

Bowie, Alasdair and Unger, Danny (1997) *The Politics of Open Economies: Indonesia, Malaysia, the Philippines and Thailand* (Cambridge: Cambridge University Press).

Bowles, Paul (2000) 'Regionalism and development after(?) the global financial crises', *New Political Economy*, 5(3): 433–55.

Bowles, Paul (2002) 'Asia's post-crisis regionalism: Bringing the state back in keeping the (United) States out', *Review of International Political Economy*, 9(2): 244–70.

Bowles, Paul and MacLean, Brian (1996) 'Understanding trade bloc formation: the case of the ASEAN Free Trade Area', *Review of International Political Economy*, 3(2): 319–48.

Bowles, Samuel and Gintis, Herbert (1996) *Democracy and Capitalism* (New York: Basic Books).

Boyer, Robert and Hollingsworth, J.R. (1997) 'From national embeddedness to spatial nestedness', in Hollingsworth, J.R. and Boyer, R. (eds), *Contemporary Capitalism: The Embeddedness of Institutions* (Cambridge: Cambridge University Press): 433–84.

Bradsher, K. (2011) 'Chinese Fault Beijing's Moves on Foreign Reserves', *New York Times*, 8 August.

Bradsher, K. (2012) 'China's missile advances could thwart U.S. defenses, analysts say', *New York Times*, 24 August.

Braithwaite, John and Drahos, Peter (2000) *Global Business Regulation* (Cambridge: Cambridge University Press).

Branigan, Tania (2012) 'New York Times blocked in China over Wen Jiabao wealth revelations', *The Guardian*, 26 October.

Bremmer, Ian (2010) *The End of the Free Market: Who Wins the War Between States and Corporations?* (New York: Penguin).

Bremmer, Ian (2012) *Every Nation for Itself: Winners and Losers in a G-Zero World* (New York: Portfolio/Penguin).

Brenner, Neil (1999) 'Beyond state-centrism? Space, territoriality, and geographical scale in globalization studies', *Theory and Society*, 28: 39–78.

Brenner, Neil, Peck, J. and Theodore, N.I.K. (2010) 'Variegated neoliberalization: Geographies, modalities, pathways', *Global Networks*, 10(2): 182–222.

Brenner, Robert (2002) *The Boom and the Bubble* (London: Verso).

Breslin, Shaun (2005) 'Power and production: Rethinking China's global economic role', *Review of International Studies*, 31: 735–53.

Breslin, Shaun (2007) *China and the Global Economy* (Basingstoke: Palgrave Macmillan).

Breslin, Shaun (2011a) 'The "China model" and the global crisis: from Friedrich List to a Chinese mode of governance?', *International Affairs*, 87(6): 1323–43.

Breslin, Shaun (2011b) 'East Asia and the global/transatlantic/Western crisis', *Contemporary Politics*, 17(2): 109–117.

Breslin, Shaun and Higgott, Richard (2000) 'Studying regions: Learning from the old, constructing the new', *New Political Economy*, 5(3): 333–52.

Brooks, Karen (2011) 'Is Indonesia bound for the BRICs? How stalling reform could hold Jakarta back', *Foreign Affairs*, 90(6): 109–18.

Brooks, Stephen G. (2005) *Producing Security: Multinational Corporations, Globalization, and the Changing Calculus of Conflict* (Princeton, NJ: Princeton University Press).

Brooks, Stephen G. and Wohlforth, William C. (2002) 'American primacy in perspective', *Foreign Affairs*, 81(4): 20–33.

Brown, Lester (1995) *Who Will Feed China? Wake-up Call for a Small Planet* (London: Earthscan).

Brownlee, J. (2007) *Authoritarianism in an Age of Democratization* (Cambridge: Cambridge University Press).

Bryant, Ralph C. (2003) *Turbulent Waters: Cross-Border Finance and International Governance* (Washington, DC: Brookings Institution).

Bryant, Raymond L. and Parnwell, Michael J.G. (1996) 'Introduction: Politics, sustainable development and environmental change in Southeast Asia', in Bryant, R.L. and Parnwell, M. (eds), *Environmental Change in South-east Asia: People, Politics, and Sustainable Development* (London: Routledge): 1–20.

Brzezinski, Zbigniew (2004) *The Choice: Global Domination or Global Leadership* (New York: Basic Books).

Brzezinski, Zbigniew (2012) 'Balancing the East, upgrading the west: US grand strategy in an age of upheaval', *Foreign Affairs*, 9(1): 97–104.

Buchanan, Paul G. and Nicholls, Kate (2003) 'Labour politics and democratic transition in South Korea and Taiwan', *Government and Opposition*, 38(2): 203–37.

Burgos Cáceres, S. and Ear, S. (2012) 'The geopolitics of China's global resources quest', *Geopolitics*, 17(1): 47–79.

Burke, Anthony and McDonald, Matt (eds) (2007) *Critical Security in the Asia Pacific* (Manchester: Manchester University Press).

Burma, Ian and Avishai, Margalit (2004) *Occidentalism: The West in the Eyes of Its Enemies* (New York: Penguin).

Bush, George W. (2005) 'President discusses freedom and democracy in Kyoto, Japan', The White House, 18 November. Available at: http://www.whitehouse.gov/news/releases/2005/11/print/20051116–6. html.

Buzan, Barry (1995) 'The level of analysis problem in international relations reconsidered', in Booth, K. and Smith, S. (eds), *International Relations Theory Today* (Cambridge: Polity Press): 198–216.

Buzan, Barry (2010) 'China in international society: Is a "peaceful rise" possible?', *The Chinese Journal of International Politics*, 3(1): 5–36.

Buzan, Barry (2012) 'How regions were made, and the legacies for world politics: An English School reconnaissance', in Paul, T.V. (ed.), *International Relations Theory and Regional Transformation* (Cambridge: Cambridge University Press): 22–46.

Buzan, Barry and Waever, Ole (2003) *Regions and Powers: The Structure of International Security* (Cambridge: Cambridge University Press).

Cai, Kevin G. (2008) *The Political Economy of East Asia: Regional and National Dimensions* (Basingstoke: Palgrave Macmillan).

Calder, Kent E. (1988a) 'Japanese foreign economic policy formation: explaining the reactive state', *World Politics*, 40(4): 25–54.

Calder, Kent E. (1988b) *Crisis and Compensation: Public Policy and Public Stability in Japan* (Princeton, NJ: Princeton University Press).

Calder, Kent E. (1996) *Asia's Deadly Triangle: How Arms, Energy and Growth Threaten to Destabilize Asia Pacific* (London: Nicholas Brealey).

Calder, Kent E. (2004) 'Securing security through prosperity: The San Francisco System in comparative perspective', *Pacific Review*, 17(1): 135–57.

Calder, Kent E. and Ye, M. (2010) *The Making of Northeast Asia,* (Singapore: NUS Press).

Callahan, William A. (2004) *Contingent States: Greater China and Transnational Relations* (Minneapolis, MN: University of Minneapolis Press).

Callahan, William A. (2010) *China: The Pessoptimist Nation* (Oxford: Oxford University Press).

Callon, Scott (1995) *Divided Sun: MITI and the Breakdown of Japanese High-Tech Policy, 1975–1993* (Stanford, CA: Stanford University Press).

Camilleri, Joseph A. (2000) *States, Markets and Civil Society in Asia Pacific* (Northampton, MA: Edward Elgar).

Cammack, Paul (2003) 'The governance of global capitalism: A new materialist perspective', *Historical Materialism*, 11(2): 37–59.

Camroux, David (2012) 'The East Asia Summit: Pan-Asian multilateralism rather than intra-Asian regionalism', in Beeson, M. and Stubbs, R. (eds), *The Routledge Handbook of Asian Regionalism* (London: Routledge): 375–83.

Camroux, David and Lechervy, C. (1996) '"Close encounter of the Third Kind?" The inaugural Asia–Europe meeting of March 1996', *Pacific Review*, 9(3): 442–53.

Capling, Ann (2008) 'Twenty years of Australia's engagement with Asia', *The Pacific Review*, 21(5): 601–22.

Capling, Ann and Ravenhill, John (2013) 'Australia, the United States and the Trans-Pacific Partnership: Diverging interests and unintended consequences', *Australian Journal of Political Science*, 48(2): 184–96.

Capoccia, Giovanni and Kelemen, R. Daniel (2007) 'The study of critical junctures: Theory, narrative, and counterfactuals in historical institutionalism', *World Politics*, 59(April): 341–69.

Caporaso, James A. (1996) 'The European Union and forms of state: Westphalian, regulatory or post-modern?', *Journal of Common Market Studies*, 34(1): 29–51.

Carnegy, Hugh (2011) 'IMF chief warns over 1930s style threats', *Financial Times*, 15 December.

Carpenter, Susan (2003) *Special Corporations and the Bureaucracy: Why Japan Can't Reform* (Basingstoke: Palgrave Macmillan).

Carpenter, Ted G. (2006) *America's Coming War with China: A Collision Course over Taiwan* (Basingstoke: Palgrave Macmillan).

Case, William (2002) *Politics in Southeast Asia: Democracy or Less* (London: Curzon Press).

Case, William (2010) 'Political legitimacy in Malaysia: Historical roots and contemporary deficits', *Politics and Policy*, 38(3): 497–522.

Castells, Manuel (1992) 'Four Asian tigers with a dragon head', in Applebaum, R.P. and Henderson, J. (eds), *States and Development in the Asian Pacific Rim* (Newbury Park, CA: Sage): 33–70.

Cerny, Philip G. (1993) 'American decline and the emergence of embedded financial orthodoxy', in Cerny, P.G. (ed.), *Finance and World Politics: Markets, Regimes and States in the Post-hegemonic Era* (Aldershot: Edward Elgar): 155–85.

Cerny, Philip G. (1995) 'Globalization and the changing logic of collective action', *International Organization*, 49(4): 595–625.

Cerny, Philip G. (1996) 'International finance and the erosion of state policy capacity', in P. Gummett (ed.), *Globalisation and Public Policy* (Cheltenham: Edward Elgar): 82–104.

Cerny, Philip G. (1999) 'Globalization and the erosion of democracy', *European Journal of Theoretical Research*, 36: 1–26.

Cerny, Philip G. (2005) 'Power, markets and accountability: The development of multi-level governance in international finance', in Baker, A., Hudson, A. and Woodward, R. (eds), *Governing Global Finance: International Political Economy and Multi-Level Governance* (London: Routledge): 24–48.

Cerny, Philip G. (2012) 'Globalisation and statehood', in Beeson, M. and Bisley, N. (eds), *Issues in 21st Century World Politics*, 2nd edn (Basingstoke: Palgrave Macmillan): 30–46.

Cerny, Philip G. (2013) 'Globalization and statehood', in Beeson, M. and Bisley, N. (eds), *Issues in 21st Century World Politics*, 2nd edn (Basingstoke: Palgrave Macmillan): 30–46.

Cha, Victor D. (2010) 'Powerplay: Origins of the U.S. alliance system in Asia', *International Security*, 34(3): 158–96.

Cha, Victor D. (2012) *The Impossible State: North Korea, Past and Future* (New York: Jonathan Cape).

Chaibong, Hahm (2005) 'The two South Koreas: A house divided', *Washington Quarterly*, 28(3): 57–72.

Chalk, Peter (2001) 'Separatism and Southeast Asia: The Islamic factor in Southern Thailand, Mindanao, and Aceh', *Studies in Conflict and Terrorism*, 24: 241–69.

Chan, Gerald, Lee, Pak K. and Chan, Lai-Ha (2012) *China Engages Global Governance: A New World Order in the Making?* (London: Routledge).

Chan, Steve (2008) *China, the US, and the Power-Transition Theory* (London: Routledge).

Chan, Steve (2009) 'Commerce between rivals: Realism, liberalism, and credible communication across the Taiwan Strait', *International Relations of the Asia Pacific*, 9(3): 435–67.

Chandler, Alfred (1990) *Scale and Scope: The Dynamics of Industrial Capitalism* (Cambridge, MA: Harvard University Press).

Chang, David Wen-Wei (1988) *China under Deng Xiaoping: Political and Economic Reform* (New York: St Martin's Press).

Chang, Gordon G. (2002) *The Coming Collapse of China* (London: Arrow).

Chang, Ha-Joon (1998) 'Korea: The misunderstood crisis', *World Development*, 26(8): 1555–61.

Chang, Ha-Joon (2000) 'The hazard of moral hazard: Untangling the Asian crisis', *World Development*, 28(4): 775–88.

Chang, Ha-Joon (2002) *Kicking Away the Ladder: Development Strategy in Historical Perspective* (London: Anthem Press).

Chang, Li Lin and Ramkishen, S. Rajan (2001) 'The economics and politics of monetary regionalism in Asia', *ASEAN Economic Bulletin*, 18(1): 103–18.

Chang, Michele (2003) 'Franco-German interests in European monetary integration', in J. Kirshner (ed.), *Monetary Orders: Ambiguous Economics, Ubiquitous Politics* (Ithaca, NY: Cornell University Press): 218–35.

Charrier, Philip (2001) 'ASEAN's inheritance: The regionalization of Southeast Asia, 1941–61', *Pacific Review*, 48(3): 313–38.

Chase-Dunn, Christopher (1998) *Global Formation: Structures of the World Economy* (Lanham, MD: Rowan & Littlefield).

Chellaney, Brahma (2012) 'Asia's worsening water crisis', *Survival*, 54(2): 143–56.

Chen, An (2002) 'Capitalist development, entrepreneurial class, and democratization in China', *Political Science Quarterly*, 117(3): 401–22.

Chernilo, Daniel (2006) 'Social theory's methodological nationalism', *European Journal of Social Theory*, 9(1): 5–22.

Chernilo, Daniel (2010) 'Methodological nationali sm and the domestic analogy: classical resources for their critique', *Cambridge Review of International Affairs*, 23(1): 87–106.

Chernow, Ron (2004) *Alexander Hamilton* (London: Penguin).

Cheung, Gordon C.K. (2012) 'The significance of the overseas Chinese in East Asia', in Beeson, M. and Stubbs, R. (eds), *The Routledge Handbook of Asian Regionalism* (London: Routledge): 77–89.

Chia, Siow Yue (1999) 'Trade, foreign direct investment and economic development of Southeast Asia', *Pacific Review*, 12(2): 249–70.

Chin, Gregory T. (2010) 'Remaking the architecture: the emerging powers, self-insuring and regional insulation', *International Affairs*, 86(3): 693–715.

Chin, Gregory and Thakur, Ramesh (2010) 'Will China change the rules of global order?', *The Washington Quarterly*, 33(4): 119–38.

Chin, Mikyung (2003) 'Civil society in South Korean democratization', in Arase, D. (ed.), *The Challenge of Change: East Asia in the New Millennium* (Berkeley, CA: Institute of East Asian Studies): 201–14.

China Internet Information Centre (2005) *Building of Political Democracy in China* Available at: http://english.people.com.cn/whitepaper/democracy/democracy.html.

Choi, Jang Jip (1995) 'Political cleavages in South Korea', in Koo, H. (ed.), *State and Society in Contemporary Korea* (Ithaca, NY: Cornell University Press): 13–50.

Christensen, Thomas J. (1999) 'China, the US–Japan alliance, and the security dilemma in East Asia', *International Security*, 23(4): 49–80.

Christie, Clive J. (1996) *A Modern History of Southeast Asia* (London: I.B. Tauris).

Christoff, P. (2010) 'Cold climate in Copenhagen: China and the United States at COP15', *Environmental Politics*, 19(4): 637–56.

Chu, Yin-Wah (2009) 'Eclipse or reconfigured? South Korea's developmental state and challenges of the global knowledge economy', *Economy and Society*, 38(2): 278–303.

Chung, Chin-Wee (1986) 'The evolution of political institutions in North Korea', in Scalapino, R.A., Sato, S. and Wanandi, J. (eds), *Asian Political Institutionalization* (Berkeley, CA: Institute of East Asian Studies): 18–41.

Chung, Dung-koo and Eichengreen, Barry (2007) 'Exchange rate arrangements for emerging East Asia', in Chung, D. and Eichengreen, B. (eds), *Toward an East Asian Exchange Rate Regime* (Washington, DC: Brookings Institution): 1–21.

Ciccantell, Paul S. and Bunker, Stephen G. (2004) 'The economic ascent of China and the potential for restructuring the capitalist world-economy', *Journal of World Systems Research*, 10(3): 565–89.

Clark, Gordon L. and Monk, Ashby (2010) 'Government of Singapore Investment Corporation (GIC): Insurer of last resort and bulwark of nation-state legitimacy', *The Pacific Review*, 23(4): 429–51.

Clinton, Hillary (2011) 'America's Pacific century', *Foreign Policy*, November.

Cochrane, Joe (2002) 'A military mafia', *Newsweek*, 26 August.

Cohen, Benjamin J. (1993) 'The Triad and the Holy Trinity: Lessons for the Pacific region', in Higgott, R., Leaver, R. and Ravenhill, J. (eds), *Pacific Economic Relations in the 1990s: Cooperation or Conflict?* (Boulder, CO: Lynne Rienner): 133–58.

Cohen, Benjamin J. (1998) *The Geography of Money* (Ithaca, NY: Cornell University Press).

Cohen, Benjamin J. (2000) 'Taming the phoenix? Monetary governance after the crisis', in Noble, G.W. and Ravenhill, J. (eds), *The Asian Financial Crisis and the Architecture of Global Finance*, (Cambridge: Cambridge University Press): 192–212.

Cohen, Stephen and Zysman, John (1987) *Manufacturing Matters: The Myth of the Post-Industrial Economy* (New York: Basic Books).

Cohen, Warren I. (2000) *East Asia at the Center* (New York: Columbia University Press).

Colander, David (2011) 'How economists got it wrong: A nuanced account', *Critical Review: A Journal of Politics and Society*, 23(1): 1–27.

Colander, David, Goldberg, M., Haas, A., Juselius, K., Kirman, A., Lux, T. and Sloth, B. (2009) 'The financial crisis and the systemic failure of the economics profession', *Critical Review: A Journal of Politics and Society*, 21(2): 249–67.

Collins, Alan (2003) *Security and Southeast Asia: Domestic, Regional, and Global Issues* (Boulder, CO: Lynne Rienner).

Collins, Gale and Erikson, Andrew S. (2011) 'Energy nationalism goes to sea in Asia', in G. Collins (ed.), *Asia's Rising Energy Nationalism: Implications for the United States, China, and the Asia-Pacific Region* (Seattle, WA: National Bureau of Asian Research): 15–28.

Commission on Growth and Development (2008) *The Growth Report: Strategies for Sustained Growth and Inclusive Development* (Washington, DC: World Bank).

Connors, Michael K. (2006) 'Thailand and the United States: Beyond hegemony?', in Beeson, M (ed.), *Bush and Asia: America's Evolving Relations with East Asia* (London: RoutledgeCurzon): 128–44.

Connors, Michael K. (2009) 'Liberalism, authoritarianism and the politics of decisionism in Thailand', *The Pacific Review*, 22(3): 355–73.

Conrad, Bjorn (2012) 'China in Copenhagen: Reconciling the "Beijing climate revolution" and the "Copenhagen climate obstinacy"', *The China Quarterly*, 210: 435–55.

Coole, Diana (2013) 'Too many bodies? The return and disavowal of the population question', *Environmental Politics*, 22(2): 195–215.

Corning, Gregory P. (2009) 'Between bilateralism and regionalism in East Asia: the ASEAN–Japan Comprehensive Economic Partnership', *The Pacific Review*, 22(5): 639–65.

Corsetti, Giancarlo, Pesenti, Paolo and Roubini, Nouriel (1999) 'What caused the Asian currency and financial crisis?', *Japan and the World Economy*, 11: 305–73.

Cotton, James (1999) 'The "haze" over Southeast Asia: Challenging the ASEAN mode of regional engagement', *Pacific Affairs*, 72(3): 331–51.

Cotton, James (2004) *East Timor, Australia and Regional Order: Intervention and Its Aftermath in Southeast Asia* (London: RoutledgeCurzon).

Cox, Gary W. and Thies, Michael F. (2000) 'How much does money matter? "Buying" votes in Japan, 1967–1990', *Comparative Political Studies*, 33(1): 37–57.

Cox, Robert W. (1987) *Production, Power, and World Order: Social Forces in the Making of History* (New York: Columbia University Press).

Coxhead, I. and Jayasuriya, S. (2010) 'China, India and the commodity boom: Economic and environmental implications for low-income countries', *World Economy*, 33(4): 525–51.

Crabtree, J. (2013) 'India benefits from Japan Inc shift', *Financial Times*, 3 April.

Crane, George T. (1990) *The Political Economy of China's Special Economic Zones* (New York: M.E. Sharpe).

Crane, Keith, Cliff, Roger, Mederios, Evan, Mulvenon, James and Overholt, William (2005) *Modernizing China's Military: Opportunities and Constraints* (Santa Monica, CA: Rand Corporation).

Cribb, Robert (ed.) (1990) *The Indonesian Killings of 1965–1966 : Studies from Java and Bali* (Clayton: Centre of SE Asian Studies, Monash University).

Crockett, Andrew (2002) 'Capital flows in East Asia since the crisis', Speech to the ASEAN Plus Three Deputies, Beijing, 11 October.

Croissant, Aurel and Kuehn, David (2009) 'Patterns of Civilian Control of the Military in East Asia's New Democracies', *Journal of East Asian Studies*, 9(2): 187–217.

Croissant, Aurel and Wurster, Stefan (2013) 'Performance and persistence of autocracies in comparison: Introducing issues and perspectives', *Contemporary Politics*, 19(1): 1–18.

Cronin, James E. (1996) *The World the Cold War Made: Order, Chaos, and the Return of History* (London: Routledge).

Crosby, Alfred W. (2004) *Ecological Imperialism: The Biological Expansion of Europe, 900–1900* (Cambridge: Cambridge University Press).

Crotty, James (2009) 'Structural causes of the global financial crisis: A critical assessment of the "new financial architecture"', *Cambridge Journal of Economics*, 33(4): 563–80.

Crotty, James (2012) 'The great austerity war: what caused the US deficit crisis and who should pay to fix it?', *Cambridge Journal of Economics*, 36(1): 79–104.

Crouch, Harold (1985) *Economic Change, Social Structure and the Political System in Southeast Asia: Philippine Development Compared with Other ASEAN Countries* (Singapore: ISEAS).

Crouch, Harold (1996) *Government and Society in Malaysia* (Ithaca, NY: Cornell University Press).

Cumings, Bruce (1984) 'The origins and development of Northeast Asian political economy: industrial sectors, product cycles, and political consequences', *International Organization*, 38(1): 1–40.

Cumings, Bruce (1990) *The Origins of the Korean War: Vol. II, The Roaring Cataract of 1947–50* (Princeton, NJ: Princeton University Press).

Cumings, Bruce (1997) 'Japan and Northeast Asia into the twenty-first century', in Katzenstein, P.J. and Shiraishi, T. (eds), *Network Power: Japan and Asia* (Ithaca, NY: Cornell University Press): 136–68.

Cumings, Bruce (2004) *North Korea: Another Country* (Melbourne: Scribe).

Cumings, Bruce (2009) *Dominion from Sea to Sea: Pacific Ascendancy and American Power* (New Haven, CT: Yale University Press).

Curtis, Gerald L. (1999) *The Logic of Japanese Politics: Leaders, Institutions, and the Limits of Change* (New York: Columbia University Press).

Daadler, Ivo H. and Lindsay, James M. (2003) *America Unbound: The Bush Revolution in Foreign Policy* (Washington, DC: Brookings Institution).

Das, Dilip (2003) *WTO: The Doha Agenda, The New Negotiations on World Trade* (London: Zed Books).

Dauvergne, Peter (1997) *Shadows in the Forest: Japan and the Politics of Timber in Southeast Asia* (Cambridge, MA: MIT Press).

Davis, Bob and Orlick, Tom (2013) 'Loan surge puts Beijing in quandary', *Wall Street Journal*, 11 April.

de Lombaerde, Philippe, Soderbaum, Fredrik, Van Langenhove, Luke and Baert, Francis (2010) 'The problem of comparison in comparative regionalism', *Review of International Studies*, 36(3): 731–53.

Deng, Yong (2001) 'Hegemon on the offensive: Chinese perspectives on US global strategy', *Political Science Quarterly*, 116(3): 343–65.

Deng, Yong (2008) *China's Struggle for Status: The Realignment of International Relations* (Cambridge: Cambridge University Press).

Deng, Yong (2013) 'China should abandon North Korea', *Financial Times*, 27 February.

Dent, Christopher M. (2003) 'Networking the region? The emergence and impact of Asia-Pacific bilateral free trade agreement projects', *The Pacific Review*, 16(1): 1–28.

Dent, Christopher M. (2008) *East Asian Regionalism* (London: Routledge).

Dent, Christopher M. (2010) 'Free trade agreements in the Asia-Pacific a decade on: evaluating the past, looking to the future', *International Relations of the Asia Pacific*, 10(2): 201–45.

Dent, Christopher M. (2012) Renewable energy and East Asia's new developmentalism: towards a low carbon future?, *The Pacific Review*, 25(5): 561–87.

Department of the Treasury (2012) *Report on Foreign Portfolio Holdings of U.S. Securities* (Washington, DC: Dept of the Treasury).

Deyer, June T. (2000) *China's Political System: Modernization and Tradition* (Basingstoke: Palgrave Macmillan).

Diamond, Jared (2005) *Collapse: How Societies Choose to Fail or Survive* (London: Allen Lane).

Diamond, Larry (2001) 'Anatomy of an electoral earthquake: How the KMT lost and the DPP won the 2000 Presidential election', in Alagappa, M. (ed.), *Taiwan's Presidential Politics* (Armonk, NY: M.E. Sharpe): 48–87.

Diamond, Larry (2008a) 'The democratic rollback', *Foreign Affairs*, 87(2): 36–48.

Diamond, Larry (2008b) *The Spirit of Democracy: The Struggle to Build Free Societies Throughout the World* (New York: Holt).

Dick, Howard (2012) 'Corruption in East Asia', in Beeson, M. and Stubbs, R. (eds), *The Routledge Handbook of Asian Regionalism* (London: Routledge): 375–83.

Dicken, Peter (2011) *Global Shift: Mapping the Changing Contours of the Global Economy*, 6th edn (New York: Guilford Press).

Dicken, Peter and Yeung, Henry Wai-chung (1999) 'Investing in the future:

East Asia firms in the global economy', in Olds, K. *et al.* (eds), *Globalisation and the Asia-Pacific* (London: Routledge): 106–28.

Dieter, Herbert and Higgott, Richard (2003) 'Exploring alternative theories of economic regionalism: from trade to finance in Asian co-operation?', *Review of International Political Economy*, 10(3): 430–54.

Ding, Sheng (2010) 'Analyzing rising power from the perspective of soft power: a new look at China's rise to the status quo power', *Journal of Contemporary China*, 19(64): 255–72.

Ding, X.L. (2000) 'Informal privatization through internationalization: The rise of nomenklatura capitalism in China's offshore businesses', *British Journal of Political Science*, 30: 121–46.

Dittmer, Lowell (2002) 'Modernizing Chinese informal politics', in Unger, J. (ed.), *The Nature of Chinese Politics: From Mao to Jiang* (New York: M.E. Sharpe): 3–37.

Dittmer, Lowell (2003) 'Leadership change and Chinese political development', *China Quarterly*, 176: 904–25.

Dixon, Chris (2010) 'The 1997 crisis, reform and Southeast Asian growth', in Rasiah, R. and Schmidt, J.D. (eds), *The New Political Economy of Southeast Asia* (Cheltenham: Edward Elgar): 103–38.

Dooley, Michael P., Folkerts-Landau, David and Garber, Peter (2003) 'An essay on the revived Bretton Woods system', Working Paper No. 9971 (Cambridge, MA: National Bureau of Economic Research).

Dore, Ronald (1986) *Flexible Rigidities: Industrial Policy and Structural Adjustment in the Japanese Economy 1970–80* (Stanford, CA: Stanford University Press).

Doremus, Paul N., Keller, William W., Pauly, Louis W. and Reich, Simon (1999) *The Myth of the Global Corporation* (Princeton, NJ: Princeton University Press).

Doronila, Amando (1985) 'The transformation of patron–client relations and its political consequences in postwar Philippines', *Journal of Southeast Asian Studies*, March: 99–116.

Dowdle, Michael (2012) 'Asian regionalism and the law: The continuing contribution of "legal pluralism"', in Beeson, M. and Stubbs, R. (eds), *The Routledge Handbook of Asian Regionalism* (London: Routledge): 226–35.

Dower, John (1995) *Japan in War and Peace* (London: HarperCollins).

Dower, John W. (1986) *War Without Mercy: Race and Power in the Pacific War* (New York: Pantheon).

Doyle, Michael W. (1986) *Empires* (Ithaca, NY: Cornell University Press).

Doyle, Michael W. (1997) *Ways of War and Peace: Realism, Liberalism, and Socialism* (New York: W.W. Norton).

Drezner, Daniel W. (2001) 'State structure, technological leadership and the maintenance of hegemony', *Review of International Studies*, 27: 3–25.

Drezner, Daniel W. (2009) 'Bad debts: Assessing China's financial influence in great power politics', *International Security*, 34(2): 7–45.

Drysdale, Peter and Garnaut, Ross (1993) 'The Pacific: An application of a general theory of economic integration', in Bergsten, C.F. and Noland, M.

(eds), *Pacific Dynamism and the International Economic System* (Washington, DC: Institute for International Economics): 183–223.

Dryzek, John S. (2012) 'Global civil society: The progress of post-Westphalian politics', *Annual Review of Political Science*, 15(1): 101–19.

Duffield, Michael (2002) *Global Governance and the New Wars* (London: Zed Books).

Dukalskis, Alexander (2009) 'Stateness problems or regime unification? Explaining obstacles to democratization in Burma/Myanmar', *Democratization*, 16(5): 945–68.

Dunning, John H. (1988) *Explaining International Production* (London: Routledge).

Dunning, John H. (2000) 'Globalization and the new geography of foreign investment', in Woods, N. (ed.), *The Political Economy of Globalization* (Basingstoke: Macmillan): 20–53.

Dupont, Alan (1996) 'Is there an "Asian way"?' *Survival*, 38(2): 13–33.

Dupont, Alan (2001) *East Asia Imperilled: Transnational Challenges to Security* (Cambridge: Cambridge University Press).

EASG (East Asia Study Group) (2002) *Final Report of the East Asia Study Group*, ASEAN+3 Summit, Phnom Penh.

Eastman, Lloyd E. (1986) 'Nationalist China during the Nanking decade, 1927–1937', in Fairbank, John K. and Feurwerker, Albert (eds), *The Cambridge History of China, Vol. 13: Republican China, 1912–1949* (Cambridge: Cambridge University Press): 116–67.

Eccleston, Bernard (1995) *State and Society in Post-War Japan* (Cambridge: Polity Press).

Economy, Elizabeth C. (2004) *The River Runs Black: The Environmental Challenge to China's Future* (Ithaca, NY: Cornell University Press).

Edney, Kingsley (2012) 'Soft power and the Chinese propaganda system', *Journal of Contemporary China*, 21(November): 899–914.

Edwardes, Michael (1961) *Asia in the European Age, 1498–1955* (London: Thames & Hudson).

Eichengreen, Barry (2005) 'China's new exchange rate regime', *Current History*, 104(683): 264–7.

Eichengreen, Barry and Frieden, Jeffrey (1995) 'The political economy of European monetary unification: an analytical introduction', in Eichengreen, B. and Frieden, J. (eds), *The Political Economy of European Monetary Unification* (The Hague, Netherlands: Kluwer Law International): 1–23.

Eichengreen, Barry and Kenen, Peter B. (1994) 'Managing the world economy under the Bretton Woods system: An overview', in Kenen, P.B. (ed.), *Managing the World Economy: Fifty Years after Bretton Woods* (Washington, DC: Institute for International Economics): 3–57.

Eldridge, Philip J. (2002) *The Politics of Human Rights in Southeast Asia* (London: Routledge).

Elliott, Larry and Atkinson, Dan (2008) *The Gods that Failed: How Blind Faith in Markets Has Cost Us Our Future* (London: The Bodley Head).

Elliott, Lorraine (2009) 'Environmental challenges, policy failure and regional dynamics in Southeast Asia', in Beeson, M. (ed.), *Contemporary Southeast Asia: Regional Dynamics, National Differences*, 2nd edn (Basingstoke: Palgrave Macmillan): 246–65.

Elliott, Lorraine (2012) 'Regionalizing environmental security in Asia', in Beeson, M. and Stubbs, R. (eds), *The Routledge Handbook of Asian Regionalism* (London: Routledge): 300–12.

Elson, Robert E. (1999) 'International commerce, the state and society: Economic and social change', in Tarling, N. (ed.), *The Cambridge History of Southeast Asia, Vol. 3, From c.1800 to the 1930s* (Cambridge: Cambridge University Press): 127–92.

Elson, Robert E. (2001) *Suharto: A Political Biography* (Cambridge: Cambridge University Press).

Elson, Robert E. (2004) 'Reinventing a region: Southeast Asia and the colonial experience', in Beeson, M. (ed.), *Contemporary Southeast Asia: Regional Dynamics, National Differences* (Basingstoke: Palgrave Macmillan): 15–29.

Elson, Robert E. (2005) 'Constructing the nation: Ethnicity, race, modernity and citizenship in early Indonesian thought', *Asian Ethnicity*, 6(3): 145–60.

Emmers, Ralf (2003) *Cooperative Security and the Balance of Power in ASEAN and the ARF* (London: RoutledgeCurzon).

Emmers, Ralf (2009) 'Comprehensive security and resilience in Southeast Asia: ASEAN's approach to terrorism', *The Pacific Review*, 22(2): 159–77.

Emmers, Ralf and Tan, S.S. (2011) 'The ASEAN Regional Forum and Preventive Diplomacy: Built to Fail?', *Asian Security*, 7(1): 44–60.

Emmerson, Donald K. (1984) 'Southeast Asia: What's in a name?', *Journal of Southeast Asian Studies*, 15(1): 1–21.

Emmerson, Donald K. (1988) 'The military and development in Indonesia', in Dwinandono, J.S. and Cheong, T.M. (eds), *Soldiers and Stability in Southeast Asia* (Singapore: ISEAS): 107–30.

Emmott, Bill (2005) 'The sun also rises: A survey of Japan', *The Economist*, 8 October.

Engdahl, F. William (2004) 'China lays down the gauntlet in energy war: The geopolitics of oil, Central Asia and the United States', *Asia Times*, 22 December. Available at: http://www.atimes.com.

Erlanger, Steven (2011) 'Euro, meant to unite Europe, seems to rend it', *New York Times*, 19 October.

Ernst, Dieter (2000) 'Evolutionary aspects: The Asian production networks of Japanese electronics firms', in Borrus, M. *et al.* (eds), *International Production Networks in Asia: Rivalry or Riches?* (London: Routledge): 80–109.

European Commission (2000) *Standard Eurobarometer: Public Opinion in the European Union, No. 52* (Brussels: European Commission).

Evans, Paul (2005) 'Between regionalism and regionalization: Policy networks and the nascent East Asian institutional identity', in Pempel, T.J. (ed.), *Remapping East Asia: The Construction of a Region* (Ithaca, NY: Cornell University Press): 195–215.

Evans, Peter (1995) *Embedded Autonomy: States and Industrial Transformation* (Princeton, NJ: Princeton University Press).

Evans, Peter (1998) 'Transferable lessons? Re-examining the institutional prerequisites for East Asian economic policies', *Journal of Development Studies*, 34(6): 66–87.

Evans, Peter B., Rueschemeyer, Dietrich and Skocpol, Theda (eds) (1985) *Bringing the State Back In* (Cambridge: Cambridge University Press).

Fabi, Randy and Mogato, Manuel (2012) 'Insight: Conflict looms in South China Sea oil rush', *Reuters*, 28 February.

Fackler, Martin (2012) 'A fringe politician moves to Japan's national stage', *New York Times*, 8 December.

Fairbank, John King (1994) *China: A New History* (Cambridge, MA: Harvard University Press).

Fairbank, John K., Reischauer, Edwin O. and Craig, Albert M. (1965) *East Asia: The Modern Transformation* (Boston, MA: Houghton Mifflin).

FAOFAD (FAOUN Fisheries and Aquaculture Department) (2006) *The State of World Fisheries, 2006* (Rome: United Nations).

FAOUN (Food and Agriculture Organization of the United Nations) (2006) *The State of Food Insecurity in the World 2006* (Rome: United Nations).

Farchy, Jack (2012) 'World braced for new food crisis' *Financial Times*, 19 July.

Fawcett, Louise (1995) 'Regionalism in historical perspective', in Fawcett, L. and Hurrell, A. (eds), *Regionalism in World Politics: Regional Organization and International Order* (Oxford: Oxford University Press): 9–36.

Feldstein, Martin (2012) 'The failure of the euro', *Foreign Affairs*, 91(1): 105–16.

Felker, Greg (2003) 'Southeast Asian industrialisation and the changing global production system', *Third World Quarterly*, 24(2): 255–82.

Felker, Greg (2009) 'Southeast Asian development in regional and historical perspective', in Beeson, M. (ed.), *Contemporary Southeast Asia: Regional Dynamics, National Differences*, 2nd edn (Basingstoke: Palgrave Macmillan).

Feng, Hui (2006) *The Politics of China's Accession to the World Trade Organization: The Dragon Goes Global* (London: Routledge)

Ferguson, Niall (2002) *Empire: The Rise and Demise of the British World Order and the Lessons for Global Power* (New York: Basic Books).

Ferguson, Niall (2004) *Colossus: The Price of America's Empire* (New York: Penguin).

Ferguson, Niall and Kotlikoff, Laurence J. (2003) 'Going critical: American power and the consequences of fiscal overstretch', *The National Interest*, 73: 22–32.

Fewsmith, Joseph (2001) 'The political and social implications of China's accession to the WTO', *China Quarterly*, 167: 573–91.

Fforde, Adam (2009) 'Economics, history, and the origins of Vietnam's post-war economic success', *Asian Survey*, 49(3): 484–504.

Fischer, Stanley (1998) 'The Asian crisis: A view from the IMF', Address to the Midwinter Conference of the Bankers' Association for Foreign Trade, Washington, DC, 22 January.

Fitzgerald, John (1996) *Awakening China: Politics, Culture, and Class in the Nationalist Revolution* (Stanford, CA: Stanford University Press).

Florini, Ann (2011) 'Rising Asian powers and changing global governance', *International Studies Review*, 13(1): 24–33.

Fong, Glen (1998) 'Follower at the frontier: International competition and Japanese industrial policy', *International Studies Quarterly*, 42: 339–66.

Foot, Rosemary, MacFarlane, S. Neil and Mastanduno, Michael (2003) 'Introduction', in Foot, R., MacFarlane, S.N. and Mastanduno, M. (eds), *US Hegemony and International Organizations* (Oxford: Oxford University Press): 265–72.

Foster, John B., Clark, Brett and York, Richard (2010) *The Ecological Rift: Capitalism's War on the Earth* (New York: Monthly Review Press).

Frank, Andre Gunder and Gills, Barry K. (1993) *The World System: Five Hundred Years or Five Thousand?* (London: Routledge).

Frank, Andre Gunder (1998) *ReOrient: Global Economy in the Asian Age* (Berkeley, CA: University of California).

Fravel, M. Taylor (2011) 'China's strategy in the South China Sea', *Contemporary Southeast Asia*, 33(3): 292–319.

Freyer, June T. (2000) *China's Political System: Modernization and Tradition* (Basingstoke: Palgrave Macmillan).

Friedberg, Aaron (1993/94) 'Ripe for rivalry: Prospects for peace in a multipolar Asia', *International Security*, 18(3): 5–33.

Friedberg, Aaren L. (2011) *A Contest for Supremacy: China, America, and the Struggle for Mastery in Asia* (New York: W.W. Norton).

Friedman, David (1988) *The Misunderstood Miracle: Industrial Development and Political Change in Japan* (Ithaca, NY: Cornell University Press).

Friedman, Edward (2000) 'Since there is no East and there is no West, how could either be the best?', in Jacobsen, M. and Bruun, O. (eds), *Human Rights and Asian Values: Contesting National Identities and Cultural Representations in Asia* (London: Curzon): 21–42.

Friedman, Thomas (2000) *The Lexus and the Olive Tree* (London: HarperCollins).

Froebel, Folker, Heinrichs, Jurgen and Kreye, Otto (1980) *The New International Division of Labor* (Cambridge: Cambridge University Press).

Fry, Gerald W. and Faming, Manyooch Nitnoi (2001) 'Laos', in Heenan, P. and Lamontagne, M. (eds), *The Southeast Asia Handbook* (Chicago: Fitzroy Dearborn): 145–56.

Fukuyama, Francis (1992) *The End of History and the Last Man* (New York: Avon Books).

Fukuyama, Francis (1995) *Trust: The Social Virtues and the Creation of Prosperity* (London: Hamish Hamilton).

Fukuyama, Francis (2004) *State-Building: Governance and Order in the 21st Century* (Ithaca, NY: Cornell University Press).

Funabashi, Yoichi (1993) 'The Asianisation of Asia', *Foreign Affairs*, 72(5): 75–85.

Funabashi, Yoichi (1995) *Asia Pacific Fusion: Japan's Role in APEC* (Washington: Institute for International Economics).

Fung, Edmund (1995) 'Chinese nationalism in the twentieth century', in Mackerras, Colin (ed.), *Eastern Asia* (Melbourne: Longman): 175–88.

Funston, John (2001) 'Malaysia: Developmental state challenged', in Funston, J. (ed.), *Government and Politics in Southeast Asia* (London: Zed Books): 160–202.

Gaddis, John L. (1972) *The United States and the Origins of the Cold War, 1941–1947* (New York: Columbia University Press).

Gaddis, John L. (1997) *We Now Know: Rethinking Cold War History* (Oxford: Oxford University Press).

Gaddis, John Lewis (1982) *Strategies of Containment: A Critical Appraisal of Postwar American Security Policy* (Oxford: Oxford University Press).

Gainsborough, Martin (2011) 'Present but not powerful: Neoliberalism, the state, and development in Vietnam', *Globalizations*, 7(4): 475–88.

Gallagher, Mary E. (2002) '"Reform and openness" – Why China's economic reforms have delayed democracy', *World Politics*, 54(3): 338–72.

Garnaut, John (2009) 'Chinese shares rise on ASEAN loan promise', *The Age*, 14 April.

Garnaut Ross (2011) *Australia's China resource boom*. Available at: http://www.rossgarnaut.com.au/Documents/AJARE%20Australias%20China%20Resources%20Boom%20Garnaut%20final.pdf.

Garrett, Banning (2001) 'China faces, debates, the contradictions of globalization', *Asian Survey*, 41(3): 409–27.

Garten, Jeffrey E. (2005) 'The global economic challenge', *Foreign Affairs*, 84(1): 37–48.

Gartzke, Eric (2007) 'The capitalist peace', *American Journal of Political Science*, 51(1): 166–91.

Gellner, Ernest (1983) *Nations and Nationalism* (Ithaca, NY: Princeton University Press).

George, Aurelia (1997) 'The role of foreign pressure (gaiatsu) in Japan's agricultural trade liberalization', *The Pacific Review*, 10(2): 165–209.

George Mulgan, Aurelia (2005) *Japan's Interventionist State: The Role of the MAFF* (London: RoutledgeCurzon).

George Mulgan, Aurelia (2006) 'Japan and the Bush Agenda: Alignment of divergence?', in Beeson, M (ed.), *Bush and Asia: America's Evolving Relations with East Asia* (London: RoutledgeCurzon): 109–27.

Gereffi, Gary (1998) 'More than the market, more than the state: Global commodity chains and industrial upgrading in East Asia', in Chan, S. and Clark, C. (eds), *Beyond the Developmental State: East Asia's Political Economies Reconsidered* (London: Macmillan): 38–59.

Gereffi, Gary and Wyman, D.L. (eds) (1990) *Manufacturing Miracles: Paths of Industrialization in Latin America and East Asia* (Princeton, NJ: Princeton University Press).

Gereffi, Gary, Humphrey, J. and Sturgeon, T.J. (2005) 'The governance of global value chains', *Review of International Political Economy*, 12(1): 78–104.

Gerlach, Michael (1992) *Alliance Capitalism: The Social Organization of Japanese Business* (Berkeley, CA: University of California Press).

Gerschenkron, Alexander (1966) *Economic Backwardness in Historical Perspective* (Cambridge, MA: The Belknap Press of Harvard University Press).

Giddens, Anthony (1985) *The Nation State and Violence* (Cambridge: Polity Press).

Giersdorf, Stephen and Croissant, Aurel (2011) 'Civil society and competitive authoritarianism in Malaysia', *Journal of Civil Society*, 7(1): 1–21.

Gill, Stephen (1995) 'Globalization, market civilization, and disciplinary neoliberalism', *Millennium*, 24(3): 399–423.

Gilley, Bruce (2008) Legitimacy and institutional change: The case of China. *Comparative Political Studies*, 41(3), 259–284.

Gilley, Bruce (2009) *The Right to Rule: How States Win and Lose Legitimacy* (New York: Columbia University Press).

Gilpin, Robert (1981) *War and Change in World Politics* (Cambridge: Cambridge University Press).

Gilson, Julie (2012) 'The Asia–Europe Meeting (ASEM)', in Beeson, M. and Stubbs, R. (eds), *The Routledge Handbook of Asian Regionalism* (London: Routledge): 394–405.

Glassman, Jim (2006) 'US foreign policy and the war on terror in Southeast Asia', in Rodan, Garry, Hewison, Kevin and Robison, Richard (eds), *The Political Economy of South-East Asia: An Introduction*, 3rd edn (Melbourne: Oxford University Press): 219–37.

Godement, François (1997) *The New Asian Renaissance: From Colonialism to the Post-Cold War* (London: Routledge).

Goh, Evelyn (2004) 'The ASEAN Regional Forum in United States East Asian strategy', *The Pacific Review*, 17(1): 47–69.

Gold, Thomas B. (1986) *State and Society in the Taiwan Miracle* (New York: M.E. Sharpe).

Goldstein, Avery (2003) 'An emerging China's grand strategy: A neo-Bismarkian turn?', in Ikenberry, G.J. and Mastanduno, M. (eds), *International Relations Theory and the Asia-Pacific* (New York: Columbia University Press): 57–106.

Gomez, Edmund T. and Jomo, K.S. (1997) *Malaysia's Political Economy: Politics, Patronage and Profits* (Cambridge: Cambridge University Press).

Gong, Gerrit W. (1984) *The Standard of 'Civilisation' in International Society* (Oxford: Clarendon Press).

Gonzalez, Joaquin L. (2001) 'Philippines: Counting people power', in Funston, J. (ed.), *Government and Politics in Southeast Asia* (London: Zed Books): 252–90.

Goodman, David S.G. (1997) 'China in reform: The view from the provinces', in Goodman, D.G.S. (ed.), *China's Provinces in Reform: Class, Community and Political Culture* (London: Routledge): 1–20.

Goodman, David S.G. (1997–98) 'Are Asia's "ethnic Chinese" a regional-security threat?', *Survival*, 39(4): 14–55.

Gordon, A. (1993) 'Contests for the Workplace', in Gordon, A. (ed.), *Postwar Japan as History* (Berkeley, CA: University of California Press): 373–94.

Gordon, David M. (1994) 'Twixt the cup and the lip: Mainstream economics and the formation of economic policy', *Social Research*, 61(1): 1–29.

Gourevitch, Peter A. (2005) *Political Power and Control: The New Global Politics of Corporate Governance* (Princeton, NJ: Princeton University Press).

Green, Michael (2001) *Japan's Reluctant Realism: Foreign Policy Challenges in an Era of Uncertain Power* (New York: Palgrave Macmillan).

Green, Stephen and Liu, Guy S. (2005) 'China's industrial reform strategy: retreat and retain', in Green, S. and Liu, G.S. (eds), *Exit the Dragon? Privatization and State Control in China* (London: Chatham House): 15–41.

Grenville, Stephen (2004) 'The IMF and the Indonesian crisis', *Bulletin of Indonesian Economic Studies*, 40(1): 77–94.

Gries, Peter Hays (2004) *China's New Nationalism: Pride, Politics, and Diplomacy*, (Berkeley, CA: University of California Press).

Gries, Peter Hays, Zhang, Qingmin, Crowson, H. Michael and Cai, Huajian (2011) 'Patriotism, nationalism and China's US Policy: Structures and consequences of Chinese national identity', *The China Quarterly*, 205: 1–17.

Grimes, William K. (2006) 'East Asian financial regionalism in support of the global financial architecture? The political economy of regional nesting', *Journal of East Asian Studies*, 6: 353–80.

Grimes, William W. (2009) *Currency and Contest in East Asia: The Great Power Politics of Financial Regionalism* (Ithaca, NY: Cornell University Press).

Guerin, Bill (2005a) 'Yudhoyono's bumpy first year', *Asia Times*, 28 October. Available at: http://www.atimes.com.

Guerin, Bill (2005b) 'Indonesia targets timber trafficking racket', *Asia Times*, 26 February. Available at: http://www.atimes.com.

Gundzik, Jephraim P. (2005) 'The ties that bind China, Russia and Iran', *Asia Times*, 6 June. Available at: http://www.atimes.com.

Haacke, Jurgen (1999) 'The concept of flexible engagement and the practice of enhanced interaction: intramural challenges to the "ASEAN way"', *Pacific Review*, 12(4): 581–611.

Haas, Ernst B. (1964) *Beyond the Nation State: Functionalism and International Organization* (Stanford, CA: Stanford University Press).

Haas, Ernst B. (1990) *When Knowledge Is Power: Three Models of International Organizations* (Berkeley, CA: University of California Press).

Hadiz, Vedi (2004a) 'Decentralization and democracy in Indonesia: A critique of neo-institutionalist perspectives', *Development and Change*, 35(4): 697–718.

Hadiz, Vedi (2004b) 'The politics of labour movements in Southeast Asia', in Beeson, M. (ed.), *Contemporary Southeast Asia: Regional Dynamics, National Differences* (Basingstoke: Palgrave Macmillan): 118–35.

Hadiz, Vedi R. (2011) *Localising Power in Post-authoritarian Indonesia: A Southeast Asia Perspective* (Stanford: Stanford University Press).

Haggard, Stephan (1990) *Pathways from the Periphery: The Politics of Growth in the Newly Industrialising Countries* (Ithaca, NY: Cornell University Press).

Haggard, Stephan (2000) *The Political Economy of the Asian Financial Crisis* (Washington, DC: Institute for International Economics).

Haggard, Stephan and Kaufman, Robert R. (1995) *The Political Economy of the Democratic Transitions* (Princeton, NJ: Princeton University Press).

Haggard, Stephan and Noland, Marcus (2009) 'A security and peace mechanism for Northeast Asia: the economic dimension', *The Pacific Review*, 22(2): 119–37.

Haji, Ragayah and Mat Zin (2005) 'Income distribution in East Asian developing countries: recent trends', *Asian-Pacific Economic Literature*, 19(2): 36–54.

Hale, David (2004) 'China's Growing Appetites', *The National Interest*, (Summer): 137–47.

Hale, Thomas (2011) 'The de facto preferential trade agreement in East Asia', *Review of International Political Economy*, 18(3): 299–327.

Hall, Peter A. (1986) *Governing the Economy: The Politics of State Intervention in Britain and France* (Oxford: Oxford University Press).

Hall, Peter A. (1999) 'The political economy of Europe in an era of interdependence', in Kitschelt, H. *et al.* (eds), *Continuity and Change in Contemporary Capitalism* (Cambridge: Cambridge University Press): 135–63.

Hall, Peter A. and Soskice, David (2001) 'An introduction to the varieties of capitalism', in Hall, P.A. and Soskice, D. (eds), *Varieties of Capitalism: The Institutional Foundations of Comparative Advantage* (Oxford: Oxford University Press): 1–68.

Hall, Rodney B. (2003) 'The discursive demolition of the Asian development model', *International Studies Quarterly*, 47: 71–99.

Halper, Stefan (2010) *The Beijing Consensus: How China's Authoritarian Model Will Dominate the Twenty-first Century* (New York: Basic Books).

Hamashita, Takeshi (1994) 'The tribute trade system and modern Asia', in Latham, A.J.H. and Kawakatsu, H. (eds), *Japanese Industrialization and the Asian Economy* (London: Routledge): 91–107.

Hameiri, Shahar (2009) 'Beyond methodological nationalism, but where to for the study of regional governance?', *Australian Journal of International Affairs*, 63(3): 430–41.

Hameiri, Shahar and Jayasuriya, Kunishka (2011) 'Regulatory regionalism and the dynamics of territorial politics: The case of the Asia-Pacific region', *Political Studies*, 59(1): 20–37.

Hamilton, Gary (1994) 'Civilizations and the organization of economies', in Smelser, N.J. and Swedberg, R. (eds), *The Handbook of Economic Sociology* (Princeton, NJ: Princeton University Press): 183–205.

Hamilton-Hart, Natasha (2004) 'Capital flows and financial markets in Asia: National, regional, or global?', in Krauss, E.S. and Pempel, T.J. (eds), *Beyond Bilateralism: US–Japan Relations in the New Asia-Pacific* (Stanford, CA: Stanford University Press): 133–53.

Hamilton-Hart, Natasha (2005) 'Terrorism and Southeast Asia: Expert analysis, myopia and fantasy', *Pacific Review*, 18: 303–25.

Hansen, H., Rand, J. and Tarp, F. (2009) 'Enterprise growth and survival in Vietnam: Does government support matter?', *Journal of Development Studies*, 45(7): 1048–69.

Hanson, Richard (2004) 'Japan, Iran sign major oil deal, US dismayed', *Asia Times*, 20 February. Available at: http://www.atimes.com.

Haque, M. Shamsul (2007) 'Theory and practice of public administration in Southeast Asia: Traditions, directions, and impacts', *International Journal of Public Administration*, 30(12): 1297–326.

Harris, Stuart and Mack, Andrew (1997) 'Security and economics in East Asia', in Harris, S, and Mack. A. (eds), *Asia-Pacific Security: The Economics– Politics Nexus* (Sydney: Allen & Unwin): 1–29.

Harrison, Lawrence E. and Huntington, Samuel P. (eds) (2000) *Culture Matters: How Values Shape Human Progress* (New York: Basic Books).

Hartcher, Peter (1997) *The Ministry* (Sydney: HarperCollins).

Hart-Landsberg, Martin and Paul Burkett (1998) 'Contradictions of capitalist industrialization in East Asia: A critique of "'flying geese" theories of development', *Economic Geography*, 74(2): 87–110.

Harvey, David (1988) *The Condition of Postmodernity: An Enquiry into the Origins of Cultural Change* (Oxford: Blackwell).

Hatch, Walter and Yamamura, Kozo (1996) *Asia in Japan's Embrace: Building a Regional Production Alliance* (Cambridge: Cambridge University Press).

Hawken, Paul (2005) *The Ecology of Commerce: A Declaration of Sustainability* (New York: Collins Business).

Hawken, Paul, Lovins, Amory and Lovins, L. Hunter (1999) *Natural Capitalism: Creating the Next Industrial Revolution* (Boston: Little, Brown).

Hayashi, Yuka (2012) 'Nationalist groups in Japan gain clout', *Wall Street Journal*, 14 August.

Hayashi, Yuka (2013) 'Shrine Visits by Japan Rile Neighbors', *Wall Street Journal*, 22 April.

He, Baogang (2011) 'The Awkwardness of Australian Engagement with Asia: The Dilemmas of Australian Idea of Regionalism', *Japanese Journal of Political Science* 12(2): 267–85.

Hedman, Eva-Lotta E. (2001) 'The Philippines: Not so military, not so civil', in Alagappa. M. (ed.), *Coercion and Governance: The Declining Political Role of the Military in Asia* (Stanford, CA: Stanford University Press): 165–86.

Heginbotham, Eric and Samuels, Richard J. (1998) 'Mercantile realism and Japanese foreign policy', *International Security*, 22(4): 171–203.

Heginbotham, Eric and Twomey, Christopher P. (2005) 'America's Bismarkian Asia policy', *Current History*, 104(683): 243–50.

Heilbroner, Robert (1985) *The Nature and Logic of Capital* (New York: W.W. Norton).

Heilbroner, Robert (1990) 'Analysis and vision in the history of modern economic thought', *Journal of Economic Literature*, 38: 1097–114.

Heilmann, Sebastian and Schulte-Kulkmann, Nicole (2011) 'The limits of policy diffusion: Introducing international norms of anti-money laundering into China's legal system', *Governance* 24(4): 639–64.

Held, David (1987) *Models of Democracy* (Oxford: Polity Press).

Held, David (1995) *Democracy and the Global Order* (Cambridge: Polity Press).

Held, David (2004) 'Democratic accountability and political effectiveness from a cosmopolitan perspective', *Government and Opposition*, 39(2): 364–91.

Held, David, McGrew, Anthony, Goldblatt, David and Perraton, Jonathan (1999) *Global Transformations* (Stanford, CA: Stanford University Press).

Helleiner, Eric (1994) *States and the Reemergence of Global Finance* (Ithaca, NY: Cornell University Press).

Hellmann, Donald C. (2007) 'A decade after the Asian financial crisis', *Asian Survey*, 47(6): 834–49.

Hemmer, Christopher and Katzenstein, Peter J. (2002) 'Why is there no NATO in Asia? Collective identity, regionalism, and the origins of multilateralism', *International Organization*, 56 (3): 575–607.

Henderson, Jeffrey, Dicken, Peter, Hess, Martin, Coe, Neil M. and Yeung, Henry Wai-chung (2002) 'Global production networks and the analysis of economic development', *Review of International Political Economy*, 9(3): 436–64.

Henderson, Jeannie (1999) 'Reassessing ASEAN', Adelphi Paper, vol. 328 (New York: Oxford University Press).

Henning, C. Randall (2002) *East Asian Financial Cooperation* (Washington, DC: Institute for International Economics).

Hernandez, Carolina G. (1986) 'Political institution building in the Philippines', in Scalapino, R.A., Sato, S. and Wanandi, J. (eds), *Asian Political Institutionalization* (Berkeley, CA: Institute of East Asian Studies): 261–87.

Hettne, Björn (1999) 'Globalization and the new regionalism: The second great transformation', in Hettne, B., Inotai, A. and Sunkel, O. (eds), *Globalism and the New Regionalism* (London: Macmillan): 1–24.

Hettne, Björn and Söderbaum, Fredrick (2002) 'Theorizing the rise of regionness', in Breslin, S. *et al.* (eds), *New Regionalisms in the Global Political Economy* (London: Routledge): 33–47.

Hewison, Kevin (1989) *Bankers and Bureaucrats: Capital and the Role of the State in Thailand* (New Haven, CT: Yale University Press).

Hewison, Kevin (1999) 'Political space in Southeast Asia: "Asian-style" and other democracies', *Democratization*, 6(1): 224–45.

Hewison, Kevin (2001) 'Thailand's capitalism: Development through boom and bust', in Rodan, G., Hewison, K. and Robison, R. (eds), *The Political Economy of South–east Asia* (Melbourne: Oxford University Press): 71–103.

Hewison, Kevin (2006) 'Thailand: Boom, bust, and recovery', in Rodan, G., Hewison, K. and Robison, R. (eds), *The Political Economy of South-East Asia: An Introduction*, 3rd edn (Melbourne: Oxford University Press): 72–106.

Hewison, Kevin (2010) 'Thaksin Shinawatra and the reshaping of Thai politics', *Contemporary Politics*, 16(2): 119–33.

Hicken, Allen and Martinez Kuhonta, Erik (2011) 'Shadows from the past: Party system institutionalization in Asia', *Comparative Political Studies*, 44(5): 572–97.

Higgott, Richard A. (1995) 'Economic cooperation in the Asia Pacific: A theoretical comparison with the European Union', *Journal of European Public Policy*, 2(3): 361–83.

Higgott, Richard A. (1998) 'The Asian economic crisis: A study in the politics of resentment', *New Political Economy*, 3(3): 333–56.

Higgott, Richard (2004) 'US Foreign Policy and the "Securitization" of Economic Globalization', *International Politics*, 41(2): 147–75.

Hilley, John (2001) *Malaysia: Mahathirism, Hegemony, and the New Opposition* (London/New York: Zed Books).

Hirst, Paul and Thompson, Grahame (1996) *Globalization in Question* (Oxford: Polity Press).

Hobday, Mike (2001) 'The electronics industries of the Asia-Pacific: Exploiting international production networks for economic development', *Asian Pacific Economic Literature*, 15(1): 13–29.

Hobsbawm, Eric (1987) *The Age of Empire* (London: Weidenfeld & Nicolson).

Hobsbawm, Eric (1994) *Age of Extremes: The Short Twentieth Century, 1914–1991* (London: Weidenfeld & Nicolson).

Hobson, John M. (2004) *The Eastern Origins of Western Civilization* (Cambridge: Cambridge University Press).

Hobson, John M. (2007) 'Reconstructing international relations through world history: Oriental globalization and the global–dialogic conception of inter-civilizational relations', *International Politics*, 44(4): 414–30.

Hobson, John M. (2012) *The Eurocentric Conception of World Politics: Western International Theory, 1760–2010* (Cambridge: Cambridge University Press).

Hodgson, Geoffrey M. (1996) 'Varieties of capitalism and varieties of economic theory', *Review of International Political Economy*, 3(3): 380–433.

Hogan, Michael J. (1998) *A Cross of Iron: Harry S. Truman and the Origins of the National Security State, 1945–1954* (Cambridge: Cambridge University Press).

Homer-Dixon, Thomas F. (1999) *Environment, Scarcity, and Violence* (Princeton, NJ: Princeton University Press).

Homolar, Alexandra (2012) 'Multilateralism in crisis? The character of US international engagement under Obama', *Global Society*, 26(1): 103–22.

Hoogvelt, Ankie (2001) *Globalization and the Postcolonial World*, 2nd edn (Baltimore, MD: Johns Hopkins University Press).

Hook, Glenn (1999) 'The East Asian Economic Caucus: A case of reactive subregionalism?', in Hook, G. and Kearns, I. (eds), *Subregionalism and World Order* (London: Macmillan): 223–45.

Howell, Jude (2006) 'Reflections on the Chinese state', *Development and Change*, 37(2): 273–97.

Hsiao, Frank S.T., Hsiao, Mei-chu W. and Yamashita, Akio (2003) 'The impact of the US economy on the Asia-Pacific region: Does it matter?', *Journal of Asian Economics*, 14: 219–41.

Hsü, Immanuel (1983) *The Rise of Modern China*, 3rd edn (Hong Kong: Oxford University Press).

Huang, Ray (1997) *China: A Macro History* (Armonk, NY: M.E. Sharpe).

Huang, Roger L. (2013) 'Re-thinking Myanmar's political regime: Military rule in Myanmar and implications for current reforms', *Contemporary Politics*, 19(3): 247–61.

Huang, Yasheng (2011) 'Rethinking the Beijing Consensus', *Asia Policy*, 111–26.

Huang, Yiping and Wang, Bijun (2011) 'Chinese outward direct investment: Is there a China model?', *China & World Economy*, 19(4): 1–21.

Hughes, Caroline (2009) *Dependent Communities: Aid Politics in Cambodia and East Timor* (Ithaca, NY: Cornell University Press).

Hughes, Christopher (2005) *Japan's Re-emergence as a 'Normal' Military Power*, Adelphi Papers (London: Routledge): 368–9.

Hughes, Christopher W. (2000) 'Japanese policy and the East Asian currency crisis: Abject defeat or quiet victory?', *Review of International Political Economy*, 7: 219–53.

Hughes, Neil C. (2005) 'A trade war with China?' *Foreign Affairs*, 84(4): 94–106.

Hund, Markus (2003) 'ASEAN Plus Three: Towards a new age of pan-East Asian regionalism? A sceptic's appraisal', *Pacific Review*, 16(3): 383–417.

Hundt, David (2005) 'A legitimate paradox: Neo-liberal reform and the return of the state in Korea', *Journal of Development Studies*, 41(2): 242–60.

Hundt, David (2008) *Korea's Developmental Alliance: State, Capital and the Politics of Rapid Development* (London: Routledge).

Hung, Ho-fung (2009) 'America's head servant?', *New Left Review*, 60 (November/December): 5–25.

Hunt, Michael H. (1987) *Ideology and US Foreign policy* (New Haven, CT: Yale University Press).

Huntington, Samuel (1991) *The Third Wave: Democratization in the Late Twentieth Century* (Norman, OK: University of Oklahoma Press).

Huntington, Samuel P. (1996) 'The West unique, not universal', *Foreign Affairs*, 75(6): 28–46.

Hurrell, Andrew (1995) 'Explaining the resurgence of regionalism in world politics', *Review of International Studies*, 21: 331–58.

Hutchcroft, Paul (1999) 'Neither dynamo nor domino: Reforms and crises in the Philippine political economy', in Pempel, T.J. (ed.), *The Politics of the Asian Economic Crisis* (Ithaca, NY: Cornell University Press): 163–83.

Hutchcroft, Paul D. (1995) 'Booty capitalism: Business–government relations in the Philippines', in MacIntyre, A. (ed.), *Business and Government in Industrializing Asia* (Ithaca, NY: Cornell University Press): 216–43.

Hutchcroft, Paul D. (1997) 'The politics of privilege: Assessing the impact of rents, corruption, and clientelism on Third World development', *Political Studies*, 45: 639–58.

Hutchcroft, Paul D. (1998) *Booty Capitalism: The Politics of Banking in the Philippines* (Ithaca, NY: Cornell University Press).

Hutchison, Jane (2006) 'Poverty of politics in the Philippines', in Rodan, G., Hewison, K. and Robison, R. (eds), *The Political Economy of South-East Asia: An Introduction*, 3rd edn (Melbourne: Oxford University Press): 39–71.

Huxley, Tim and Susan Willett (1999) *Arming East Asia*, Adelphi Papers (London: Routledge), 329.

ICG (International Crisis Group) (2012) *Stirring up the South China Sea (I)*, Asia Report No. 223, 23 April (Brussels: International Crisis Group).

Ikenberry, G. John (2001a) 'American power and the empire of capitalist democracy', *Review of International Studies*, 27: 191–212.

Ikenberry, G. John (2001b) *After Victory: Institutions, Strategic Restraint, and the Rebuilding of Order after Major Wars* (Princeton, NJ: Princeton University Press).

Ikenberry, G. John and Michael Mastanduno (2003) 'Conclusion: The United States and stability in East Asia', in Ikenberry, G.J. and Mastanduno, M. (eds), *International Relations Theory and the Asia-Pacific* (New York: Columbia University Press): 421–39.

Ingleson, John (1996) 'The "Asian ethic"', in Bell, R., McDonald, T. and Tidwell, A. (eds), *Negotiating the Pacific Century: The 'New' Asia, the United States and Australia* (St Leonards, NSW: Allen & Unwin): 251–267.

IPCC (2007) *Climate Change 2007: The Physical Science Basis* (Geneva: IPCC Secretariat).

Iriye, Akira (1967) *Across the Pacific: An Inner History of American–East Asian Relations* (New York: Harbinger).

Iriye, Akira (1981) *Power and Culture: The Japanese–American War, 1941–1945* (Cambridge, MA: Harvard University Press).

Iriye, Akira (1989) 'Japan's drive to great power status', in Jansen, M.B. (ed.), *The Cambridge History of Japan, Vol. 5: The Nineteenth Century* (Cambridge: Cambridge University Press): 721–82.

Islam, Iyanatul and Chowdhury, Anis (2000) *Asia–Pacific Economies: A Survey* (London: Routledge).

Jacobs, L. and King, D. (2009) 'America's political crisis: The unsustainable state in a time of unraveling', *PS: Political Science & Politics*, 42(2): 277–85.

Jacques, Martin (2009) *When China Rules the World: The Rise of the Middle Kingdom and the End of the Western World* (London: Allen Lane).

Jain, Purnendra (1997) 'Party politics at the crossroads', in Jain, P and Inoguchi, T. (eds), *Japanese Politics Today: Beyond Karaoke Democracy?* (Melbourne: Macmillan): 11–29.

James, Harold (2001) *The End of Globalization: Lessons from the Great Depression* (Cambridge, MA: Harvard University Press).

Jansen, Marius B. (1989) 'The Meiji Restoration', in Jansen, M.B. (ed.), *The Cambridge History of Japan, Vol. 5: The Nineteenth Century* (Cambridge: Cambridge University Press): 308–66.

Jarvis, Darryl Stuart (2012) 'Foreign direct investment and investment liberalisation in Asia: assessing ASEAN's initiatives', *Australian Journal of International Affairs*, 66(2): 223–64.

Jasparro, Christopher and Taylor, Jonathan (2008) 'Climate change and regional vulnerability to transnational security threats in Southeast Asia', 13(2): 232–56.

Jayasuriya, Kanishka (1996) 'The rule of law and capitalism in East Asia', *Pacific Review*, 9(3): 367–88.

Jayasuriya, Kanishka (2001) 'Globalization and the changing architecture of the state: the regulatory state and the politics of negative co-ordination', *Journal of European Public Policy*, 8(1): 101–23.

Jayasuriya, Kanisha (2003) 'Embedded mercantilism and open regionalism: the crisis of a regional political project', *Third World Quarterly*, 24(2): 339–55.

Jayasuriya, Kanisha (2009) 'Regulatory regionalism in the Asia-Pacific: drivers, instruments and actors', *Australian Journal of International Affairs*, 63(3): 335–47.

Jayasuriya, Kanisha and Rodan, Garry (2007) 'Beyond hybrid regimes: More participation, less contestation in Southeast Asia', *Democratization*, 14(5): 773–94.

Jessop, Bob (2003) *The Future of the Capitalist State* (Cambridge: Polity Press).

Jesudason, James V. (1989) *Ethnicity and the Economy: The State, Chinese Business, and Multinationals in Malaysia* (Singapore: Oxford University Press).

Jetschke, Anja (2012) 'ASEAN', in Beeson, M. and Stubbs, R. (eds), *The Routledge Handbook of Asian Regionalism* (London: Routledge): 327–37.

Jetschke, A. and Murray, Philomena (2012) 'Diffusing regional integration: The EU and Southeast Asia', *West European Politics*, 35(1): 174–91.

Ji, Boacheng (2010) 'China's economic recovery and the China model', *Journal of Chinese Economic and Business Studies*, 8(3): 215–26.

Jiang, Wenran (2009) 'Fuelling the dragon: China's rise and its energy and resources extraction in Africa', *The China Quarterly*, 199(1): 585–609.

Joffe, Josef (1995) '"Bismarck" or "Britain"? Toward an American grand strategy after bipolarity', *Foreign Affairs*, 14(4): 94–117.

Johnson, Chalmers (1962) *Peasant Nationalism and Communist Power: The Emergence of Revolutionary China, 1937–1945* (Stanford, CA: Stanford University Press).

Johnson, Chalmers (1982) *MITI and the Japanese Miracle: The Growth of Industry Policy, 1925–1975* (Stanford, CA: Stanford University Press).

Johnson, Chalmers (1987) 'Political institutions and economic performance: The government–business relationship in Japan, South Korea, and Taiwan', in Deyo, F. (ed.), *The Political Economy of the New Asian Industrialism* (Ithaca, NY: Cornell University Press): 136–64.

Johnson, Chalmers (1999) 'The developmental state: odyssey of a concept', in Woo-Cumings, M. (ed.), *The Developmental State* (Ithaca, NY: Cornell University Press): 32–60.

Johnson, Chalmers (2000) *Blowback: The Costs and Consequences of American Empire* (London: Little, Brown).

Johnson, Simon (2009) 'The quiet coup', *The Atlantic Monthly* (May).

Johnston, Alastair I. (1995) *Cultural Realism: Strategic Culture and Grand Strategy in Chinese History* (Princeton, NJ: Princeton University Press).

Johnston, Alastair I. (2003) 'Is China a status quo power?', *International Security*, 27(4): 5–56.

Johnston, Alastair I. (2008) *Social States: China in International Relations, 1980–2000* (Princeton, NJ: Princeton University Press).

Jomo, K.S. (1997) *Southeast Asia's Misunderstood Miracle: Industrial Policy and Economic Development in Thailand, Malaysia and Indonesia* (Boulder, CO: Westview Press).

Jomo, K.S. (1998) 'Introduction: Financial governance, liberalization and crises in East Asia', in Jomo, K.S. (ed.), *Tigers in Trouble* (London: Zed Books): 1–32.

Jomo, K.S. (2001) 'Introduction: Growth and structural change in the second-tier Southeast Asian NICs', in Jomo, K.S. (ed.), *Southeast Asia's Industrialization: Industrial Policy, Capabilities and Sustainability* (Basingstoke: Palgrave Macmillan): 1–29.

Jomo, K.S. (2004) 'Southeast Asian developmental states in comparative East Asian perspective', in Low, L. (ed.), *Developmental States: Relevant, Redundant or Reconfigured?* (New York: Nova Science Publishers): 57–77.

Jones, David Martin (1998) 'Democratization, civil society, and illiberal middle class culture in Pacific Asia', *Comparative Politics*, 30(2): 147–69.

Jones, David M. and Smith, M.L.R. (2007) 'Making process, not progress: ASEAN and the evolving East Asian regional order', *International Security*, 32(1): 148–84.

Jones, Eric (1981) *The European Miracle: Environments, Economies and Geopolitics in the History of Europe and Asia* (Cambridge: Cambridge University Press).

Jones, Lee (2010) 'ASEAN's unchanged melody? The theory and practice of "non-interference"' in Southeast Asia', *The Pacific Review*, 23(4): 479–502.

Kahler, Miles (2000) 'Legalization as a strategy: The Asia-Pacific case', *International Organization*, 54(3): 549–71.

Kai, He (2008) 'Institutional balancing and international relations theory: Economic interdependence and balance of power strategies in Southeast Asia', *European Journal of International Relations*, 14(3): 489–518.

Kakuchi, Suvendrini (2003) 'Japan strives to adapt to a strong China', *Asia Times*, 2 April. Available at: http://www.atimes.com.

Kaldor, Mary (2001) *New and Old Wars: Organized Violence in a Global Era* (Stanford, CA: Stanford University Press).

Kang, David C. (2002) *Crony Capitalism: Corruption and Development in South Korea and the Philippines* (Cambridge: Cambridge University Press).

Kang, David C. (2003a) 'Getting Asia wrong: The need for new analytical frameworks', *International Security*, 27(4): 57–85.

Kang, David C. (2003b) 'International relations theory and the second Korean war', *International Studies Quarterly*, 47: 301–24.

Kang, David C. (2003c) 'Transaction costs and crony capitalism in East Asia', *Comparative Politics*, 35(4): 439–58.

Kang, David C. (2009) 'The Security of Northeast Asia', *Pacific Focus*, 24(1): 1–21.

Kang, David C. (2010) *East Asia before the West: Five Centuries of Trade and Tribute* (New York: Columbia University Press).

Kaplan, R.D. (2012) *The Revenge of Geography: What the Map Tells Us about the Coming Conflicts and the Battle against Fate* (New York: Random House).

Kaplinsky, Raphael (2000) 'Globalisation and unequalisation: What can be learned from value chain analysis?', *Journal of Development Studies*, 37(2): 117–46.

Kastner, Scott L. (2009). *Political Conflict and Economic Interdependence across the Taiwan Strait and Beyond* (Stanford, CA: Stanford University Press).

Katada, Saori N. (2002) 'Japan and Asian monetary regionalisation: Cultivating a new regional leadership after the Asia financial crisis', *Geopolitics*, 7(1): 85–112.

Katz, Richard (1998) *Japan: The System that Soured* (Armonk, NY: M.E. Sharp).

Katzenstein, Peter J. (1996) *Cultural Norms and National Security: Police and Military in Postwar Japan* (Ithaca, NY: Cornell University Press).

Katzenstein, Peter J. (2005) *A World of Regions: Asia and Europe in the American Imperium* (Ithaca, NY: Cornell University Press).

Kelly, Gerard (2013) 'From the ASEAN People's Assembly to the ASEAN Civil Society Conference: The boundaries of civil society advocacy', *Contemporary Politics*, 19(4).

Kenen, Peter B. (2001) *The International Financial Architecture: What's*

New? What's Missing (Washington, DC: Institute for International Economics).

Kennedy, Paul (1989) *The Rise and Fall of Great Powers: Economic Change and Military Conflict from 1500 to 2000* (London: Fontana).

Keohane, Robert O. (1982) 'The demand for international regimes', *International Organization*, 36(25): 325–55.

Khoo, Boo Teik (1995) *Paradoxes of Mahathirism* (Oxford: Oxford University Press).

Khoo, Boo Teik (2003) *Beyond Mahathir: Malaysian Politics and Its Discontents* (London: Zed Books).

Khoo, Boo Teik (2006) 'Malaysia: Balancing development and power', in Rodan, G., Hewison, K. and Robison, R. (eds), *The Political Economy of South-East Asia: An Introduction*, 3rd edn (Melbourne: Oxford University Press): 168–94.

Kim, Soyoung, Lee, Jong-Wha and Park, Cyn-Young (2011) 'Ties binding Asia, Europe and the USA', *China & World Economy*, 19(1): 24–46.

Kim, Wonik (2009) 'Rethinking colonialism and the origins of the developmental state in East Asia', *Journal of Contemporary Asia*, 39(3): 382–99.

Kimball, Jeffrey (2006) 'The Nixon Doctrine: A saga of misunderstanding', *Presidential Studies Quarterly*, 36(1): 59–74.

Kindleberger, Charles P. (1973) *The World in Depression, 1929–1939* (Berkeley, CA: University of California Press).

Kindleberger, Charles P. (1996) *Manias, Panics, and Crashes: A History of Financial Crises* (New York: John Wiley).

King, Michael R. (2001) 'Who triggered the Asian financial crisis?', *Review of International Political Economy*, 8(3): 438–66.

Kivimaki, Timo (2001) 'The long peace of ASEAN', *Journal of Peace Research*, 38(1): 5–25.

Klare, Michael T. (2002) *Resource Wars: The New Landscape of Global Conflict* (New York: Metropolitan Books).

Klare, Michael T. (2004) *Blood and Oil: How America's Thirst for Petrol Is Killing Us* (London: Penguin).

Klare, Michael T. (2008) *Rising Powers, Shrinking Planet: The New Geopolitics of Energy* (New York: Metropolitan Books).

Ko, Kilkon and Weng, Cuifen (2012) 'Structural changes in Chinese corruption', *The China Quarterly*, 211: 718–40.

Kohli, Akue (1999) 'Where do high-growth political economies come from? The Japanese lineage of Korea's "developmental state"', in M. Woo-Cumings (ed.), *The Developmental State* (Ithaca, NY: Cornell University Press): 93–136.

Kohli, Atul (2004) *State-Directed Development: Political Power and Industrialization in the Global Periphery* (Cambridge: Cambridge University Press).

Kolko, Gabriel (1985) *Anatomy of a War: Vietnam, the United States, and the Modern Historical Experience* (New York: Pantheon).

Kolko, Gabriel (1997) *Vietnam: Anatomy of a Peace* (London: Routledge).

Korhonen, Pekka (1996) 'The Pacific age in world history', *Journal of World History*, 7(1): 41–70.

Korhonen, Pekka (1997) 'Monopolising Asia: the politics of metaphor', *The Pacific Review*, 10(3): 347–65.

Kovel, Joel (2007) *The Enemy of Nature: The End of Capitalism or the End of the World?*, 2nd edn (London: Zed Books).

Krauss, Ellis S. (1992) 'Political economy: Policymaking and industrial policy in Japan', *PS: Political Science & Politics*, March: 44–57.

Krauthammer, Charles (1990–91) 'The unipolar moment', *Foreign Affairs*, 70(1): 23–33.

Kristol, William and Kagan, Robert (1996) 'Toward a neo-Reaganite foreign policy', *Foreign Affairs*, 75(4): 18–32.

Krugman, Paul (1998) 'A desperate remedy', *Fortune*, 138(5): 179.

Krugman, Paul (2010) 'The third depression', *New York Times*, 27 June.

Krugman, Paul R. (1999) *The Return of Depression Economics* (London: Penguin).

Kuik, Cheng-Chiree (2008) 'China's evolving multilateralism in Asia', in Calder, K.E. and Fukuyama, F. (eds), *East Asian Multilateralism: Prospects for Regional Stability*, (Baltimore, MD: Johns Hopkins University Press): 109–42.

Kunz, Diane B. (1997) *Butter and Guns: America's Cold War Economic Diplomacy* (New York: Free Press).

Kwan, C.H. (2001) *Yen Bloc: Toward Economic Integration in Asia* (Washington, DC: Brookings Institution).

Kwon, Huck-ju (2009) 'Policy learning and transfer: the experience of the developmental state in East Asia', *Policy and Politics*, 37(3): 409–21.

LaFeber, Walter (1997) *The Clash: US–Japanese Relations throughout History* (New York: W.W. Norton).

Lake, David A. (1999) *Entangling Relations: America's Foreign Policy and Its Century* (Princeton, NJ: Princeton University Press).

Lam, Willy (2012) 'China's hawks in command', *Wall Street Journal*, 1 July.

Lampton, David M. (2001) 'China's foreign and national security policy-making process: Is it changing, and does it matter?', in Lampton, David M. (ed,), *The Making of Chinese Foreign and Security Policy in the Era of Reform* (Stanford, CA: Stanford University Press): 1–36.

Lamy, Pascal (2011) '"Made in China" tells us little about global trade', *Financial Times*, 24 January.

Lardy, Nicholas R. (1998) *China's Unfinished Economic Revolution* (Washington, DC: Brookings Institution).

Lardy, Nicholas R. (2002) *Integrating China into the Global Economy* (Washington, DC: Brookings Institution).

Lardy, Nicholas R. (2010) 'The sustainability of China's recovery from the global recession', Policy Brief No. PB10-7 (Washington, DC: Peterson Institute for International Economics).

Latham, Michael E. (2000) *Modernization as Ideology: American Social Science and 'Nation Building' in the Kennedy Era* (Chapel Hill, NC: The University of North Carolina Press).

Latham, Robert (1997) *The Liberal Moment: Modernity, Security, and the Making of Postwar International Order* (New York: Columbia University Press).

Lau, W.K. (1999) 'The 15th Congress of the Chinese Communist Party: Milestone in China's privatization', *Capital & Class*, 23(2): 51.

Lawrence, Alan (1998) *China Under Communism* (London: Routledge).

Layne, Christopher (2012) 'This time it's real: The end of unipolarity and the Pax Americana', *International Studies Quarterly*, 56(1): 203–13.

Lee, Chung H. (1992) 'The government, financial system, and large private enterprises in the economic development of South Korea', *World Development*, 20(2): 187–97.

Leffler, Melvyn P. (1992) *A Preponderance of Power: National Security, the Truman Administration, and the Cold War* (Stanford, CA: Stanford University Press).

Leftwich, Adrian (2000) *States of Development: On the Primacy of Politics in Development* (Oxford: Polity Press).

Leifer, Michael (1996) *The ASEAN Regional Forum*, Adelphi Papers, Vol. 302 (London: ISIS).

Leggett, Jeremy (2005) *The Empty Tank: Oil, Hot Air, and the Coming Global Financial Catastrophe* (New York: Random House).

Lemke, Douglas (2002) *Regions of War and Peace* (Cambridge: Cambridge University Press).

Leung, G.C.K. (2011) 'China's energy security: Perception and reality', *Energy Policy*, 39(3): 1330–7.

Levitsky, Steven and Way, Lucan A. (2010) *Competitive Authoritarianism: Hybrid Regimes after the Cold War* (New York: Cambridge University Press).

Leys, Colin (1996) *The Rise and Fall of Development Theory* (London: James Currey).

Li, Cheng (2007) 'China's growing external dependence', *Finance and Development*, 44(3).

Li, Cheng (2012a) 'The battle for China's top nine leadership posts', *Washington Quarterly*, 35(1): 131–45.

Li, Cheng (2012b) 'The end of the CCP's resilient authoritarianism? A tripartite assessment of shifting power in China', *The China Quarterly*, 211: 595–623.

Li, Weiye and Putterman, Louis (2008) 'Reforming China's SOEs: An overview, *Comparative Economic Studies*, 50(3): 353–80.

Liddle, R. William (1999) 'Regime: The New Order', in Emmerson, D.K. (ed.), *Indonesia Beyond Suharto* (New York: M.E. Sharpe): 39–70.

Lieberthal, Kenneth G. (1992) 'Introduction: The "fragmented authoritarianism" model and its limitations', in Lieberthal, K.G and Lampton, D.M. (eds), *Bureaucracy, Politics, and Decision Making in Post-Mao China* (Berkeley, CA: University of California Press): 1–30.

Lieberthal, Kenneth G. (1995) *Governing China from Revolution through Reform* (New York: W.W. Norton).

Liew, Leon (2001) 'What is to be done? WTO, globalisation and state–labour relations in China', *Australian Journal of Politics and History*, 47(1): 39–60.

Lin, Yi-min (2003) 'Economic institutional change in post-Mao China: Reflections on the triggering, orienting, and sustaining mechanisms', in So, A.Y. (ed.), *China's Developmental Miracle: Origins, Transformations, and Challenges* (Armonk, NY: M.E. Sharpe): 29–57.

Lincoln, Edward J. (2004) *East Asian Economic Regionalism* (Washington, DC: Brookings Institution).

Lind, Jennifer (2011) 'Democratization and stability in East Asia', *International Studies Quarterly*, 55: 409–36.

Liu, Alan P.L. (1996) *Mass Politics in the People's Republic: State and Society in Contemporary China* (Boulder, CO: Westview Press).

Lomborg, Bjorn (2001) *The Skeptical Environmentalist* (Cambridge: Cambridge University Press).

Low, D.A. (1991) *Eclipse of Empire* (Cambridge: Cambridge University Press).

Lu, Ning (2001) 'The central leadership, supraministry coordinating bodies, state council ministries, and party departments', in Lampton, D.M. (ed.), *The Making of Chinese Foreign and Security Policy in the Era of Reform* (Stanford, CA: Stanford University Press): 39–60.

Lu, Xiabao (2000) 'Booty socialism, bureau-preneurs, and the state in transition: Organizational corruption in China', *Comparative Politics*, 32(3), 273–94.

Lu, Ya-li (1991) 'Political developments in the Republic of China', in Robinson, T.W. (ed.), *Democracy and Development in East Asia* (Washington, DC: AEI Press): 35–48.

Luttwak, Edward (1990) 'From geopolitics to geo–economics', *The National Interest*, Summer: 17–23.

Lynch, Daniel (2009) 'Chinese thinking on the future of international relations: Realism as the Ti, rationalism as the Yong?', *The China Quarterly*, 197: 87–107.

MacAskill, Ewan (2010) 'WikiLeaks: Hillary Clinton's question: how can we stand up to Beijing?', *The Guardian*, 4 December.

Machado, Kit G. (1992) 'ASEAN state industrial policies and Japanese regional production strategies: The case of Malaysia's motor vehicle industry', in Clark, and Chan, S., *The Evolving Pacific Basin in the Global Political Economy* (Boulder, CO: Lynne Rienner): 169–202.

MacIntyre, Andrew (1994) 'Power, prosperity and patrimonialism: Business and government in Indonesia', in MacIntyre, A. (ed.), *Business and Government in Industrialising Asia* (Sydney: Allen & Unwin): 244–67.

Mahathir, Mohamad bin (1997) 'The Asian values debate', *The Perdana Papers* (Kuala Lumpur: ISIS).

Mahathir, Mohamad bin (1998 [1970]) *The Malay Dilemma* (Singapore: Times Books).

Mahathir, Mohamad bin and Ishihara, Shintaro (1995) *The Voice of Asia: Two Leaders Discuss the Coming Century* (Tokyo: Kodansha International).

Mahbubani, Kishore (2012) 'Western capitalism has much to learn from Asia', *Financial Times*, 7 February.

Maisrikrod, Surin and McCargo, Duncan (1997) 'Electoral politics: Commercialization and exclusion', in Hewison, Kevin (ed.), *Political Change in Thailand: Democracy and Participation* (London: Routledge): 132–48.

Majid, Munir (2010) 'Going through the democratic motions in Southeast Asia', *International Politics*, 47(6): 725–38.

Mann, Michael (1993) *The Sources of Social Power: The Rise of Classes and Nation States, 1760–1914* (Cambridge: Cambridge University Press).

Mann, Thomas E. and Ornstein, Norman J. (2012) *It's Even Worse Than It Looks: How the American Constitutional System Collided with the New Politics of Extremism* (New York: Basic Books).

Manners, Ian (2002) 'Normative power Europe: A contradiction in terms?', *JCMS: Journal of Common Market Studies*, 40(2): 235–58.

Mansfield, Edward D. and Milner, Helen V. (1999) 'The new wave of regionalism', *International Organization*, 53(3): 589–627.

Manupipatong, Worapot (2002) 'The ASEAN surveillance process and the East Asian Monetary Fund', *ASEAN Economic Bulletin*, 19(1): 111–22.

Marx, Karl and Engels, Friedrich (1978 [1872]) 'Manifesto of the Communist Party', in Tucker, R.C. (ed.), *The Marx–Engels Reader*, 2nd edn (New York: W.W. Norton): 469–500.

Mastanduno, Michael (2002) 'Incomplete hegemony and security order in the Asia-Pacific', in Ikenberry, G.J. (ed.), *America Unrivalled: The Future of the Balance of Power*. (Ithaca, NY: Cornell University Press): 181–210.

Mathews, Jessica (1997) 'Power shift', *Foreign Affairs*, 76(1): 50–66.

Maugeri, Leonardo (2012) *Oil: The Next Revolution*. (Cambridge, MA: Belfer Center for Science and International Affairs, Harvard Kennedy School).

May, R.J., Lawson, Stephanie and Selochan, Viberto (1998) 'Introduction: Democracy and the military in comparative perspective', in May, R.J. and Viberto, S. (eds), *The Military and Democracy in Asia and the Pacific* (Bathurst, NSW: Crawford House): 1–28.

McCargo, Duncan (2005) 'Network monarchy and legitimacy crises in Thailand', *The Pacific Review*, 18(4): 499–519.

McCloud, Donald G. (1995) *Southeast Asia: Tradition and Modernity in the Contemporary World* (Boulder, CO: Westview Press).

McCormack, Gavan (1996) *The Emptiness of Japanese Affluence* (St Leonards, NSW: Allen & Unwin).

McDougall, Walter A. (1997) *Promised Land, Crusader State: The American Encounter with the World since 1776* (Boston, MA: Mariner Books).

McGregor, Richard (2010) *The Party: The Secret World of China's Communist Rulers* (New York: HarperCollins).

McMahon, Robert J. (1999) *The Limits of Empire: The United States and Southeast Asia since World War II* (New York: Columbia University Press).

Mearsheimer, John J. (2001) *The Tragedy of Great Power Politics* (New York: W.W. Norton).

Mearsheimer, John J. (2006) 'China's unpeaceful rise', *Current History*, April: 160–2.

Menon, Anand (2008) *Europe: The State of the Union* (London: Atlantic Books).

METI (2005) *White Paper on International Economy and Trade 2005* (Tokyo: Ministry of Economy, Trade and Industry).

Migdal, Joel S. (1994) 'The state in society: An approach to struggles for domination', in Migdal, Joel S., Kohli, Atul, and Shue, Vivienne (eds), *State Power and Social Forces: Domination and Transformation in the Third World* (Cambridge: Cambridge University Press): 7–34.

Migdal, Joel S. (1988) *Strong States and Weak Societies: State–Society Relations and State Capabilities in the Third World* (Princeton, NJ: Princeton University Press).

Miles, James (2000–01) 'Chinese nationalism, US policy and Asian security', *Survival*, 42(4): 51–71.

Miles, James (2011) 'Rising power, anxious state', *The Economist*, 25 June.

Millar, T.B. (1978) *Australia in Peace and War: External Relations, 1788–1977* (Canberra: Australian National University Press).

Milliband, Ralph (1991) *Divided Societies: Class Struggle in Contemporary Capitalism* (Oxford: Oxford University Press).

Milne, R.S. and Mauzy, Diane K. (1999) *Malaysian Politics under Mahathir* (London: Routledge).

Milner, Helen V. and Mukherjee, Bumba (2009) 'Democratization and economic globalization', *Annual Review of Political Science*, 121: 63–181.

Milward, Alan S. (1984) *The Reconstruction of Western Europe, 1945–51* (Berkeley, CA: University of California Press).

Mishima, Ko (2005) 'After the victory, can Koizumi deliver?', *Far Eastern Economic Review*, 168(8): 13–17.

Mishkin, Sarah (2012) 'Singapore economy shrinks in fourth quarter', *Financial Times*, 3 January.

Mitrany, David (1965) 'The prospect of integration: federal of functional?', *Journal of Common Market Studies*, 4(2): 119–49.

Mol, Arthur P.J. (2011) 'China's ascent and Africa's environment', *Global Environmental Change*, 21(3): 785–94.

Montinola, Gabriella, Qian, Yingyi and Weingast, Barry R. (1995) 'Federalism, Chinese Style – the Political Basis for Economic Success in China', *World Politics*, 48(1): 50–81.

Moore, Barrington (1973) *Social Origins of Dictatorship and Democracy* (London: Penguin).

Moore, Scott (2013) 'China's Massive Water Problem'. *New York Times*, 28 March.

Moore, Thomas G. (2002) *China in the World Market: Chinese Industry and International Sources of Reform in the Post-Mao Era* (Cambridge: Cambridge University Press).

Morris, Charles R. (2008) *The Trillion Dollar Meltdown: Easy Money, High Rollers, and the Great Credit Crash* (London: Public Affairs).

Morris, Ian (2010) *Why the West Rules – For Now: The Patterns of History, and What They Reveal about the Future* (New York: Farrar, Strauss & Giroux).

Morriss, Peter (1997) 'Roh regrets: Leadership, culture and politics in South Korea', *Crime, Law & Social Change*, 28: 39–51.

Morris-Suzuki, Tessa (1989) *A History of Japanese Economic Thought* (London: Routledge).

Morris-Suzuki, Tessa (1994) *The Technological Transformation of Japan: From the Seventeenth to the Twenty-first Century* (Cambridge: Cambridge University Press).

Moulds, Josephine (2012) 'China's economy to overtake US in next four years, says OECD', *The Guardian*, 9 November.

Mufson, Steven (2010) 'As economy booms, China faces major water shortage', *Washington Post*, 16 March.

Murphy, Alexander B. (2004) 'Forum: Is there a politics to geopolitics?', *Progress in Human Geography*, 28 (5): 619–40.

Murphy, Calum (2012) 'Dispute With Japan Takes Toll on Chinese Workers', *Wall Street Journal*, 23 October.

Murphy, R. Taggart (1997) *The Weight of the Yen* (New York: W.W. Norton).

Murray, Philomena (2010) 'Comparative regional integration in the EU and East Asia: Moving beyond integration and snobbery', *International Politics*, 47(3–4): 308–23.

Narine, Shaun (1999) 'ASEAN into the twenty-first century: problems and prospects', *Pacific Review*, 12(3): 357–80.

Narine, Shaun (2002) *Explaining ASEAN: Regionalism in Southeast Asia* (Boulder, CO: Lynne Rienner).

Narizny, Kevin (2012) 'Anglo-American primacy and the global spread of democracy: An international genealogy', *World Politics*, 64(2): 341–73.

Nathan, Andrew J. and Gilley, Bruce (2002) 'The fourth generation', *Australian Financial Review*, 11 October.

Nathan, Andrew J. and Ross, Robert S. (1997) *The Great Wall and the Empty Fortress: China's Search for Security* (New York: W.W. Norton).

Naughton, B. (2007) *The Chinese Economy: Transitions and Growth* (Cambridge, MA: MIT Press).

Neher, Clark D. (2001) 'Burma', in Heenan, P. and Lamontagne, M. (eds), *The Southeast Asia Handbook* (Chicago, IL: Fitzroy Dearborn): 157–64.

Nesadurai, Helen (2006) 'Malaysia and the United States: Rejecting dominance, embracing engagement', in Beeson, M. (ed.), *Bush and Asia: America's Evolving Relations with East Asia* (London: RoutledgeCurzon).

Nesadurai, Helen E.S. (2003) *Globalisation, Domestic Politics and Regionalism: The ASEAN Free Trade Area* (London: Routledge).

Newman, Edward (2009). Failed states and international order: constructing a post-Westphalian world. *Contemporary security policy*, 30(3), 421–43.

Newman, E. (2010) 'Critical human security studies', *Review of International Studies*, 36(1): 77–94.

Newman, E. (2013) 'New forms of security and the challenge of human security', in Beeson, M. and Bisley, N. (eds), *Issues in 21st Century World Politics*, 2nd edn (Basingstoke: Palgrave Macmillan).

Noble, Gregory W. (1999) *Collective Action in East Asia: How Ruling Parties Shape Industrial Policy* (Ithaca, NY: Cornell University Press).

Nolan, Peter (2012) *Is China Buying the World?* (Cambridge: Polity Press).

North, Douglass C. and Thomas, Robert Paul (1973) *The Rise of the Western World: A New Economic History* (Cambridge: Cambridge University Press).

North, Douglass C., Wallis, John Joseph and Weingast, Barry R. (2009) *Violence and Social Orders: A Conceptual Framework for Interpreting Recorded Human History* (New York: Cambridge University Press).

Nye, Joseph S. (2004) *Soft Power: The Means to Success in World Politics* (New York: Public Affairs).

Obama, Barack (2011) 'Remarks by President Obama to the Australian Parliament', Parliament House, Canberra, 17 November.

Obe, Mitsuru (2012) 'Hopes fade for start of Japan–China–Korea trade talks', *Wall Street Journal*, 5 November.

Ockey, James (2001) 'Thailand: The struggle to redefine civil–military relations', in Alagappa, M. (ed.), *Coercion and Governance: The Declining Political Role of the Military in Asia* (Stanford, CA: Stanford University Press): 187–208.

Odgaard, Liselotte (2001) 'Deterrence and cooperation in the South China Sea', *Contemporary Southeast Asia*, 23(2): 292–306.

Office of the Secretary of Defence (2005) *Annual Report to Congress on the Military Power of the People's Republic of China*. Available at: http://www.defense.gov/pubs/pdfs/2012_CMPR_Final.pdf.

Ohmae, Kenichi (1990) *The Borderless World: Power and Strategy in the Interlinked Economy* (New York: Harper Business).

Ohmae, Kenichi (1996) *The End of the Nation State: The Rise of the Regional Economies* (London: HarperCollins).

Okimoto, Daniel (1989) *Between MITI and the Market: Japanese Industrial Policy for High Technology* (Stanford, CA: Stanford University Press).

Oman, Charles (1994) *Globalisation and Regionalisation: The Challenge for Developing Countries* (Paris: OECD).

Ophuls, William (1997) *Requiem for Modern Politics: The Tragedy of the Enlightenment and the Challenge of the New Millennium* (Boulder, CO: Westview Press).

Oreskes, Naomi and Conway, Erik M. (2010) *Merchants of Doubt: How a Handful of Scientists Obscured the Truth on Issues from Tobacco Smoke to Global Warming* (New York: Bloomsbury Press).

Organski, A.F.K. (1968) *World Politics* (New York: Knopf).

Orrù, Maria, Biggart, Nicole Woolsey and Hamilton, Gary G. (1991) 'Organizational isomorphism in East Asia', in Powell, W.W. and DiMaggio, P.J. (eds), *The New Institutionalism in Organizational Analysis* (Chicago, IL: University of Chicago Press): 361–89.

Ó Tuathail, Gearóid (1996) *Critical Geopolitics* (London: Routledge).

Overbeek, Henk (2012) 'Sovereign debt crisis in Euroland: Root causes and implications for European integration', *The International Spectator*, 47(1): 30–48.

Ozawa, Terutomu (2009) *The Rise of Asia: The 'Flying Geese' Theory of Tandem Growth and Regional Agglomeration* (Cheltenham: Edward Elgar).

Packer, George (2005) *The Assassin's Gate: America in Iraq* (New York: Farrar, Strauss & Giroux).

Page, Jeremy and Wei, Lingling (2012) 'Bo's ties to army alarmed Beijing', *Wall Street Journal*, 17 May.

Painter, Martin (2005) 'The politics of state sector reforms in Vietnam: Contested agendas and uncertain trajectories', *Journal of Development Studies*, 41(2): 261–83.

Pape, Robert A. (2009) 'Empire falls', *National Interest*, (99): 21–34.

Parello-Plesner, Jonas and Anti, Michael (2013) 'The weibo generation can reboot China', *Financial Times*, 21 January.

Park, Yung Chul (2011) *The Global Financial Crisis: Decoupling of East Asia – Myth or Reality?* (Manila: Asian Development Bank).

Parry, John Horace (1971) *Trade and Dominion: The European Overseas Empires in the Eighteenth Century* (London: Phoenix Press).

Pascha, Werner (2007) 'The role of regional financial arrangements and monetary integration in East Asia and Europe in relations with the United States', *The Pacific Review*, 20(3): 423–46.

Pauly, Louis W. (1997) *Who Elected the Bankers? Surveillance and Control in the World Economy* (Ithaca, NY: Cornell University Press).

Pei, Minxin (2006) *China's Trapped Transition: The Limits of Developmental Autocracy* (Cambridge, MA.: Harvard University Press).

Pempel, T.J. (1998) *Regime Shift: Comparative Dynamics of the Japanese Political Economy* (Ithaca, NY: Cornell University Press).

Pempel, T.J. (eds) (1999) *The Politics of the Asian Economic Crisis* (Ithaca, NY: Cornell University Press).

Pempel, T.J. (2004) 'Challenges to bilateralism: Changing foes, capital flows, and complex forums', in Krauss, E.S. and Pempel, T.J. (eds), *Beyond Bilateralism: US–Japan Relations in the New Asia-Pacific* (Stanford, CA: Stanford University Press): 1–33.

Pempel, T.J. (2005) 'Conclusion: Tentativeness and tensions in the construction of an Asian region', in Pempel, T.J. (ed.), *Remapping East Asia: The Construction of a Region* (Ithaca, NY: Cornell University Press): 256–75.

Pempel, T.J. (2010) 'Soft balancing, hedging, and institutional Darwinism: The economic-security nexus and East Asian Regionalism', *Journal of East Asian Studies*, 10(2): 209–38.

Peng, Dajin (2002) 'Invisible linkages: A regional perspective of East Asian political economy', *International Studies Quarterly*, 46: 423–47.

Petri, Peter A. (1992) *The East Asian Trading Bloc: An Analytical History*: (Waltham, MA: Department of Economics, Brandeis University).

Pew Research Centre (2003) *Views of a Changing World 2003*. Washington,

DC: Pew Research Center. Available at: http://people–press.org/reports/display.php3?ReportID=185.

Phillips, Kevin (2004) *American Dynasty: Aristocracy, Fortune, and the Politics of Deceit in the House of Bush* (New York: Viking).

Phongpaichit, Pasuk and Baker, Chris (2004) *Thaksin: The Business of Politics in Thailand* (Chiang Mai, Thailand: Silkworm Books).

Phongpaichit, Pasuk and Piriyarangsan, Sungsidh (1994) *Corruption and Democracy in Thailand* (Chiang Mai, Thailand: Silkworm Books).

Pieterse, Jan Nederveen (2004) *Globalization or Empire?* (London: Routledge).

Piling, David (2012) 'Asia's new leaders stir ancestral animosity', *Financial Times*, 19 December.

Pinker, Steven (2012) *The Better Angels of Our Nature: Why Violence Has Declined* (New York: Viking).

Pirie, Iain (2005) 'The new Korean state', *New Political Economy*, 10(1): 25–42.

Polanyi, Karl (1957) *The Great Transformation: The Political and Economic Origins of Our Time* (Boston, MA: Beacon Press).

Pomeranz, Kenneth (2000) *The Great Divergence* (Princeton, NJ: Princeton University Press).

Pomeranz, Kenneth and Steve Topik (1999) *The World that Trade Created: Society, Culture, and the World Economy* (Armonk, NY: M.E. Sharpe).

Poon, Jessie P. H., Thompson. Edmund R. and Kelly, Philip F. (2000) 'Myth of the triad? The geography of trade and investment "blocs"', *Transactions of the Institute of British Geographers*, 25: 427–44.

Porter, Michael E., Takeuchi, Hirotaka and Sakakibara, Mariko (2000) *Can Japan Compete?* (Basingstoke: Palgrave Macmillan).

Posen, Adam (2013) 'A dose of reality for the dismal science', *Financial Times*, 19 April.

Posner, Richard A. (2010) *The Crisis of Capitalist Democracy* (Cambridge, MA: Harvard University Press).

Potter, Pitman B. (2001) 'The legal implications of China's accession to the WTO', *China Quarterly*, 167: 592–609.

PRC (People's Republic of China) (2000) 'The one-China principle and the Taiwan issue', *Beijing Review*, 6 March: 16–24.

PRC (People's Republic of China) (2005) *Building of Political Democracy in China* (Beijing: Information Office of the State Council of the People's Republic of China).

Prestowitz, Clyde (2003) *Rogue Nation: American Unilateralism and the Failure of Good Intentions* (New York: Basic Books).

Pritchard, Charles L. (2007) *Failed Diplomacy: The Tragic Story of How North Korea Got the Bomb* (Washington, DC: Brookings Institution Press).

Prybyla, Jan S. (1991) 'Economic developments in the Republic of China', in Robinson, Thomas W. (ed.), *Democracy and Development in East Asia* (Washington, DC: AEI Press): 49–74.

Przeworski, Adam, Alvarez, Michael E., Cheibub, Jose A. and Limongi, F.

(2000) *Democracy and Development: Political Institutions and Well-Being in the World, 1950–1990* (Cambridge: Cambridge University Press).

Putnam, Robert D. (1992) *Making Democracy Work: Civic Traditions in Modern Italy* (Princeton, NJ: Princeton University Press).

Pye, Lucian (1985) *Asian Power and Politics: The Cultural Dimensions of Authority* (Cambridge, MA: Harvard University Press).

Pye, Lucian (1990) 'China: Erratic state, frustrated society', *Foreign Affairs*, 69(4): 56–74.

Pyle, Kenneth B. (1988) 'Japan, the world, and the twenty-first century', in Inoguchi, T. and Okimoto, D. (eds), *The Political Economy of Japan: Vol. 2, The Changing International Context* (Stanford, CA: Stanford University Press): 446–86.

Pyle, Kenneth B. (2007) *Japan Rising: The Resurgence of Japanese Power and Purpose* (New York: Public Affairs).

Qin, Yaqing (2009) 'Development of international relations theory in China', *International Studies*, 46(1–2): 185–201.

Rabinovitch, Simon (2013) 'Uncertain foundations', *Financial Times*, 2 December.

Rachman, Gideon (2013) 'North Korea tests the limits of a MAD world', *Financial Times*, 1 April.

Raine, Sarah (2011) 'Beijing's South China Sea debate', *Survival: Global Politics and Strategy*, 53(5): 69–88.

Ramo, Joshua Cooper (2004) *The Beijing Consensus* (London: The Foreign Policy Centre).

Rasiah, Rajah and Shari, Ishak (2001) 'Market, government and Malaysia's new economic policy', *Cambridge Journal of Economics*, 25: 57–78.

Ravenhill, John (2001) *APEC and the Construction of Pacific Rim Regionalism* (Cambridge: Cambridge University Press).

Ravenhill, John (2003) 'The new bilateralism in the Asia-Pacific', *Third World Quarterly*, 24 (2): 299–317.

Ravenhill, John (2006) 'Is China an economic threat to Southeast Asia?', *Asian Survey*, 46(5): 653–74.

Ravenhill, John (2010) 'The "new East Asian regionalism": A political domino effect', *Review of International Political Economy*, 17(2): 178–208.

RBA (Reserve Bank of Australia) (2004) *Reserve Bank of Australia Bulletin, August* (Sydney: Reserve Bank of Australia).

Redding, G. (2002) 'The capitalist business system of China and its rationale', *Asia Pacific Journal of Management*, 19: 221–49.

Reid, Anthony (1999) 'Economic and social change, c.1400–1800', in Tarling, Nicholas (ed.), *The Cambridge History of Southeast Asia, Vol. 2* (Cambridge: Cambridge University Press): 116–63.

Reid, Anthony (2000) *Charting the Shape of Early Modern Southeast Asia* (Singapore: ISEAS).

Reinicke, Wolfgang H. (1998) *Global Public Policy: Governing Without Government?* (Washington, DC: Brookings Institution).

Rethel, Lena (2010) 'The new financial development paradigm and Asian bond markets', *New Political Economy*, 15(4): 493–517.

Riggs, Fred (1966) *Thailand: The Modernization of a Bureaucratic Polity* (Honolulu, HI: East–West Center Press).

Riley, A. (2012) 'The Shale Revolution's Shifting Geopolitics', *International Herald Tribune*, 25 December.

Roberti, Mark (1996) *The Fall of Hong Kong: China's Triumph and Britain's Betrayal* (New York: Wiley).

Roberts, Brian and Kanaley, Trevor (eds) (2006) *Urbanization and Sustainability in Asia: Case Studies of Good Practice* (Manila: ADB).

Robinson, Thomas W. (1971) *The Cultural Revolution in China* (Berkeley, CA: University of California Press).

Robison, Richard (1996) 'The politics of "Asian values"', *Pacific Review*, 9(3): 309–27.

Robison, Richard (1997) 'Politics and markets in Indonesia's post-oil era', in Rodan, Garry, Hewison, Kevin and Robison, Richard (eds), *The Political Economy of South-East Asia: An Introduction*, 1st edn (Melbourne: Oxford University Press): 29–63.

Robison, Richard (2001) 'Indonesia: Crisis, oligarchy and reform', in Rodan, Garry, Hewison, Kevin and Robison, Richard (eds), *The Political Economy of South-East Asia: An Introduction*, 2nd edn (Melbourne: Oxford University Press): 104–37.

Robison, Richard and Hadiz, Vedi R. (2004) *Reorganising Power in Indonesia: The Politics of Oligarchy in an Age of Markets* (London: RoutledgeCurzon).

Robison, Richard, Beeson, Mark, Jayasuriya, Kanishka and Kim, H.-R. (eds) (2000) *Politics and Markets in the Wake of the Asian Crisis* (London: Routledge).

Rodan, Garry (1989) *The Political Economy of Singapore's Industrialization* (London: Macmillan).

Rodan, Garry (1996a) 'State–society relations and political opposition in Singapore', in Rodan, G. (ed.), *Political Oppositions in Industrializing Asia* (London: Routledge): 95–127.

Rodan, Garry (1996b) 'The internationalization of ideological conflict: Asia's new significance', *Pacific Review*, 9(3): 328–51.

Rodan, Garry (1997) 'Singapore: Economic diversification and social divisions', in Rodan, G., Hewison, K. and Robison, R. (eds), *The Political Economy of Southeast Asia*, 1st edn (Melbourne: Oxford University Press): 148–78.

Rodan, Garry (2005) *Transparency and Authoritarian Rule in Southeast Asia* (London: Routledge).

Rodan, Garry (2006) 'Singapore: Globalization, the developmental state and politics', in Rodan, G., Hewison, K. and Robison, R. (eds), *The Political Economy of South-East Asia: An Introduction*, 3rd edn (Melbourne: Oxford University Press): 136–67.

Rodan, Garry (2009) 'New modes of political participation and Singapore's nominated members of parliament', *Government and Opposition*, 44(4): 438–62.

Rodan, Garry and Hughes, Caroline (2012) 'Ideological coalitions and the international promotion of social accountability: The Philippines and Cambodia compared', *International Studies Quarterly*, 56(2): 367–80.

Rodrik, Dani (1997) 'The "paradoxes" of the successful state', *European Economic Review*, 41(3–5): 411–42.

Rodrik, Dani (2000) 'Institutions for high-quality growth: What they are and how to acquire them', *Studies in Comparative International Development*, 35(3): 3–31.

Rodrik, Dani (2007) *One Economics, Many Recipes: Globalization, Institutions, and Economic Growth* (Princeton, NJ: Princeton University Press).

Roland-Holst, David and Weiss, John (2005) 'People's Republic of China and its neighbours: evidence on regional trade and investment effects', *Asian-Pacific Economic Literature*, 19(2): 18–35.

Rosamond, Ben (2005) 'The uniting of Europe and the foundation of EU studies: Revisiting the neofunctionalism of Ernst B. Haas', *Journal of European Public Policy*, 12(2): 1–18.

Rosecrance, Richard (1986) *The Rise of the Trading State: Commerce and Conquest in the Modern World* (New York: Basic Books).

Ross, Michael L. (1999) 'The political economy of the resource curse', *World Politics*, 51: 297–322.

Ross, Robert S. (2005) 'Assessing the China threat', *The National Interest*, Fall: 81–7.

Ross, Robert S. (2006) 'Balance of power politics and the rise of China: Accommodation and balancing in East Asia', *Security Studies*, 15(3): 355–95.

Ross, Robert S. (2012) 'The problem with the pivot', *Foreign Affairs*, 91(6): 70–82.

Rothkopf, David (2012) *Power, Inc: The Epic Rivalry Between Big Business and Government – and the Reckoning That Lies Ahead* (New York: Farrar, Straus & Giroux).

Rotter, Andrew J. (1987) *The Path to Vietnam: Origins of the American Commitment to Southeast Asia* (Ithaca, NY: Cornell University Press).

Rowen, Henry S. (2007) 'When will the Chinese people be free?', *Journal of Democracy*, 18(3): 38–52.

Roy, Denny (2003) 'China's reaction to American predominance', *Survival*, 45(3): 57–78.

Rozman, Gilbert (2004) *Northeast Asia's Stunted Regionalism: Bilateral Distrust in the Shadow of Globalisation* (Cambridge: Cambridge University Press).

Rozman, Gilbert (2010) *Chinese Strategic Thought Toward Asia* (Basingstoke: Palgrave Macmillan).

Rozman, Gilbert (2012) 'East Asian regionalism', in Beeson, M. and Stubbs, R. (eds), *The Routledge Handbook of Asian Regionalism* (London: Routledge): 22–32.

Rueschemeyer, Dietrich, Stephens, Evelyne H. and Stephens, John D. (1992) *Capitalist Development and Democracy* (Cambridge: Polity Press).

Ruigrok, Winfried and van Tulder, Rob (1995) *The Logic of International Restructuring* (London: Routledge).

Ruggie, John Gerard (1993) 'Territoriality and beyond: Problematizing modernity in international relations', *International Organization*, 47(1): 139–74.

Ruland, Jürgen (2009) 'Deepening ASEAN cooperation through democratization? The Indonesian legislature and foreign policymaking', *International Relations of the Asia-Pacific*, 9: 373–402.

Ruland, Jürgen (forthcoming) 'The limits of democratizing interest representation: ASEAN's regional corporatism and normative challenges', *European Journal of International Relations*.

Rumsfeld, Donald (2005) Speech to the International Institute for Strategic Studies, 4 June, Singapore.

Sachs, Jeffrey D. (2005) *The End of Poverty: Economic Possibilities for Our Time* (New York: Penguin).

Saich, Tony (2004) *Governance and Politics of China*, 2nd edn (Basingstoke: Palgrave Macmillan).

Said, Edward (1985) *Orientalism* (London: Penguin).

Sakai, Kuniyasu (1990) 'The feudal world of Japanese manufacturing', *Harvard Business Review*, November/December.

Salisbury, Harrison E. (1992) *The New Emperors: Mao and Deng, A Dual Biography* (London: HarperCollins).

Samudavanija, Chai-Anan (1993) 'The new military and democracy in Thailand', in Diamond, L. (ed.), *Political Culture and Democracy in Developing Countries* (Boulder, CO: Lynne Rienner): 269–87.

Samuels, Richard J. (1987) *The Business of the Japanese State: Energy Markets in Comparative and Historical Perspective* (Ithaca, NY: Cornell University Press).

Samuels, Richard J. (1994) *Rich Nation Strong Army: National Security and the Technological Transformation of Japan* (Ithaca, NY: Cornell University Press).

Samuels, Richard J. (2007) *Securing Japan: Tokyo's Grand Strategy and the Future of East Asia* (Ithaca, NY: Cornell University Press).

Sanusi, Lamido (2013) 'Africa must get real about Chinese ties', *Financial Times*, 11 March.

SarDesai, Damodar Ramaji (1997) *Southeast Asia: Past and Present*, 4th edn (Boulder, CO: Westview Press).

Saxenian, Anna Lee (1994) *Regional Advantage: Culture and Competition in Silicon Valley and Route 128* (Cambridge: Cambridge University Press).

Sayer, Derek (1991) *Capitalism and Modernity: An Excursus on Marx and Weber* (London: Routledge).

Schaede, Ulrike (1995) 'The "old boy" network and government–business relationships in Japan', *Journal of Japanese Studies*, 21(2): 293–317.

Schaller, Michael (1997) *Altered States: The United States and Japan since the Occupation* (New York: Oxford University Press).

Schlesinger, Jacob M. (1999) *Shadow Shoguns: The Rise and Fall of Japan's Postwar Political Machine* (Stanford, CA: Stanford University Press).

Schmitter, Philip (1979) 'Still the Century of Corporatism?', in Schmitter, P. (ed.), *Trends Toward Corporatist Intermediation* (Beverly Hills, CA: Sage): 7–48.

Scholte, Jan Aart (2000) *Globalization: A Critical Introduction* (Basingstoke: Palgrave Macmillan).

Schoppa, Leonard J. (1997) *Bargaining with Japan: What American Pressure Can and Cannot Do* (New York: Columbia University Press).

Schweller, Randall (2011) 'Emerging powers in an age of disorder', *Global Governance*, 17: 285–97.

Schweller, Randall (2010) 'Ennui becomes us', *The National Interest*, 105: 27–39.

Schweller, Randall and Pu, Xiaoyu (2011) 'After unipolarity: China's visions of international order in an era of U.S. decline', *International Security*, 36(1): 41–72.

Seabrooke, Leonard (2001) *US Power in International Finance* (Basingstoke: Palgrave Macmillan).

Searle, Peter (1999) *The Riddle of Malaysian Capitalism* (St Leonards, NSW: Allen & Unwin).

Segal, Gerald (1995) 'What is Asian about Asian security?' in Rolfe, J. (ed.), *Unresolved Futures: Comprehensive Security in the Asia-Pacific* (University of Wellington: Centre for Security Studies): 107–20.

Segal, Gerald (1999) 'Does China matter?', *Foreign Affairs*, 78(5): 24–36.

Selden, Mark (1993) *The Political Economy of Chinese Development* (Armonk, NY: M.E. Sharpe).

Sen, Amartya (1999) 'Human rights and economic achievements', in Bauer, J.R. and Bell, D.A. (eds), *The East Asian Challenge for Human Rights* (Cambridge: Cambridge University Press): 88–99.

Shambaugh, David (1994) 'Growing strong: China's challenge to Asian security', *Survival*, 36(2): 43–59.

Shambaugh, David (1996) 'Containment or engagement of China? Calculating Beijing's responses', *International Security*, 21(2): 180–210.

Shambaugh, David (1999) 'China's military views the world', *International Security*, 24(3): 52–79.

Shambaugh, David (2005) 'Return to the Middle Kingdom? China and Asia in the early twenty-first century', in Shambaugh, D. (ed.), *Power Shift: China and Asia's New Dynamics* (Berkeley, CA: University of California Press): 23–47.

Shambaugh, David (2011) 'International relations studies in China: history, trends, and prospects', *International Relations of the Asia-Pacific*, 11(3): 339–72.

Shambaugh, David (2013) *China Goes Global: The Partial Power* (Oxford: Oxford University Press).

Shapiro, Judith (2001) *Mao's War Against Nature: Politics and the Environment in Revolutionary China* (Cambridge: Cambridge University Press).

Shi, Tianjian (2008) 'Democratic values supporting an authoritarian system', in, Chu, Y.-H., Diamond, L., Nathan, A.J. and Shin, D.C. (eds), *How East Asians View Democracy* (New York: Columbia University Press): 209–37.

Shih, Chih-yu (2005) 'Breeding a reluctant dragon: Can China rise into partnership and away from antagonism?', *Review of International Studies*, 31: 755–74.

Shih, Victor C. (2008) *Factions and Finance in China: Elite Conflict and Inflation* (Cambridge: Cambridge University Press).

Shin, Doh Chull, Park, Chong-Min, Hwang, Ah-Ran, Lee, Hyeon-Woo and Jang, Jiho (2003) 'The democratization of mass political orientations in South Korea', *International Journal of Public Opinion Research*, 15(3): 265–84.

Shirk, Susan L. (1993) *The Political Logic of Economic Reform in China* (Berkeley, CA: University of California Press).

Shorrock, Tim (2005) 'Bright side to Sino-Japanese ties', *Asia Times*, 15 December.

Shue, Henry (1980) *Basic Rights: Subsistence, Affluence, and US Foreign Policy* (Princeton, NJ: Princeton University Press).

Sidel, John T. (2008) 'Social origins of dictatorship and democracy revisited: Colonial state and Chinese immigrant in the making of modern Southeast Asia', *Comparative Politics*, 40(2): 122–47.

Simon, Sheldon (1998) 'Security prospects in Southeast Asia: Collaborative efforts and the ASEAN Regional Forum', *The Pacific Review*, 11(2): 195–212.

Sinclair, Timothy J. (2005) *The New Masters of Capital: American Bond Rating Agencies and the Politics of Creditworthiness* (Ithaca, NY: Cornell University Press).

Skidelsky, Robert (2009) *Keynes: The Return of the Master* (New York: Public Affairs).

Skocpol, Theda (1985) 'Bringing the state back in: Strategies of analysis in current research', in Evans, P.B., Rueschemeyer, D. and Skocpol, T. (eds), *Bringing the State Back In* (Cambridge: Cambridge University Press): 3–37.

Slater, Dan (2003) 'Iron cage in an iron fist: Authoritarian institutions and the personalization of power in Malaysia', *Comparative Politics,* 36(1): 81–101.

Slater, Dan (2010) *Ordering Power: Contentious Politics and Authoritarian Leviathans in Southeast Asia* (Cambridge: Cambridge University Press).

Smil, Vaclav (2003) *Energy at the Crossroads: Global Perspectives and Uncertainties* (Cambridge, MA: MIT Press).

Smith, Anthony D. (1998) *Nationalism and Modernism* (London: Routledge).

Smith, M.L. and Jones, D.M. (1997) 'ASEAN, Asian values and Southeast Asian security in the new world order', *Contemporary Security Policy*, 18(3): 126–56.

Smith, Steve (2002) 'The United States and the discipline of international relations: "Hegemonic country, hegemonic discipline"', *International Studies Review*, 4(2): 67–85.

Smith, Tony (1994) *America's Mission: The United States and the Worldwide Struggle for Democracy in the Twentieth Century* (Princeton, NJ: Princeton University Press).

So, Alvin Y. (2003) 'Introduction: Rethinking the Chinese developmental miracle', in So, A.Y. (ed.), *China's Developmental Miracle: Origins, Transformations, and Challenges* (Armonk, NY: M.E. Sharpe): 3–26.

Soble, Jonathan (2013) 'Shinzo Abe's nationalistic streak under scrutiny', *Financial Times*, 28 April.

Söderbaum, Frederik (2012) 'Theories of regionalism', in Beeson, M. and Stubbs, R. (eds), *The Routledge Handbook of Asian Regionalism* (London: Routledge): 11–21.

Sohn, Iujou (2008) 'Learning to co-operate: China's multilateral approach to Asian financial co-operation', *The China Quarterly*, 194: 309–26.

Sohn, Yue (2010) 'Japan's new regionalism: China shock, values, and the East Asian Community', *Asian Survey*, 50(3): 497–520.

Solingen, Etel (2004) 'Southeast Asia in a new era: Domestic coalitions from crisis to recovery', *Asian Survey*, 44(2): 189–212.

Spegele, Brian (2012) 'China's "New Left" grows louder', *Wall Street Journal*, 5 October.

Sperling, James (2010) 'National security cultures, technologies of public goods supply and security governance', in E.J. Kirchner and J. Sperling (eds), *National Security Cultures: Patterns of Global Governance* (London: Routledge): 1–17.

Spruyt, Hendrik (1994) *The Sovereign State and Its Competitors* (Princeton, NJ: Princeton University Press).

Stafford, D. Geoffrey (1997) 'Malaysia's New Economic Policy and the global economy: The evolution of ethnic accommodation', *Pacific Review*, 10(4): 556–80.

Steinfeld, Edward S. (2010) *Playing Our Game: Why China's Rise Doesn't Threaten the West* (New York: Oxford University Press).

Stephens, Philip (2010) 'Europe unravels in a tangle of national interests', *Financial Times*, 29 April.

Steven, Rob (1990) *Japan's New Imperialism* (London: Macmillan).

Stiglitz, Joseph E. (2001) 'From miracle to recovery: Lessons from four decades of East Asia experience', in Stiglitz, J.E. and Yusuf, S. (eds), *Rethinking the East Asia Miracle* (Oxford: Oxford University Press): 509–26.

Stiglitz, Joseph E. (2002) *Globalization and Its Discontents* (New York: W.W. Norton).

Stilwell, Frank (2002) *Political Economy: The Contest of Economic Ideas* (Melbourne: Oxford University Press).

Stockwell, A.J. (1999) 'Southeast Asia in war and peace: The end of European colonial empires', in Tarling, N. (ed.), *The Cambridge History of Southeast Asia* (Cambridge: Cambridge University Press): 1–58.

Stockwin, J.A.A. (1999) *Governing Japan: Divided Politics in a Major Economy* (Oxford: Blackwell).

Stockwin, J.A.A. (2002) 'Reshaping Japanese politics and the question of democracy', *Asia-Pacific Review*, 9(1): 45–59.

Strange, Susan (1987) 'The persistent myth of lost hegemony', *International Organization*, 41(4): 551–74.

Strange, Susan (1996) *The Retreat of the State: The Diffusion of Power in the World Economy* (Cambridge: Cambridge University Press).

Strange, Susan (1997) 'The future of global capitalism; or, will divergence persist forever?', in Crouch, C. and Streeck, W. (eds), *Political Economy of Modern Capitalism: Mapping Convergence and Diversity* (London: Sage): 183–91.

Strange, Susan (1998) *Mad Money: When Markets Outgrow Governments* (Ann Arbor, MI: University of Michigan Press).

Stubbs, Richard (2000) 'Signing on to liberalisation: AFTA and the politics of regional economic cooperation', *Pacific Review*, (13)2: 297–318.

Stubbs, Richard (2002) 'ASEAN Plus Three: Emerging East Asian Regionalism?', *Asian Survey*, 42(3): 440–55.

Stubbs, Richard (2005) *Rethinking Asia's Economic Miracle* (Basingstoke: Palgrave Macmillan).

Stubbs, Richard (2009) 'What ever happened to the East Asian Developmental State? The unfolding debate', *The Pacific Review*, 22(1): 1–22.

Stubbs, Richard (2012) 'The developmental state and Asian regionalism', in Beeson, M. and Stubbs, R. (eds) *The Routledge Handbook of Asian Regionalism* (London: Routledge): 90–9.

Studwell, Joe (2007) *Asian Godfathers: Money and Power in Hong Kong and Southeast Asia* (New York: Atlantic Monthly Press).

Studwell, Joe (2013) *How Asia Works: Success and Failure in the World's Most Dynamic Region* (London: Profile Books).

Sturgeon, Timothy J. (2007) 'How globalization drives diversity: The Japanese electronic industry's response to value chain modularity', *Journal of East Asian Studies*, 71–34.

Sturgeon, Timothy J. and Gereffi, Gary (2009) 'Measuring success in the global economy: International trade, industrial upgrading, and business function outsourcing in global value chains', *Transnational Corporations*, 18(2): 1–35.

Suh, Dae-sook (1988) *Kim Il Sung: The North Korean Leader* (New York: Columbia University Press).

Sung, Yun-Wing (2005) *The Emergence of Greater China: The Economic Integration of Mainland China, Taiwan and Hong Kong* (Basingstoke: Palgrave Macmillan).

Sung, Yun-Wing (2007) 'Made in China: From world sweatshop to a global manufacturing center?', *Asian Economic Papers*, 6(3): 43–72.

Sutcliffe, Bob and Glyn, Andrew (1999) 'Still underwhelmed: Indicators of globalization and their misinterpretation', *Review of Radical Political Economics*, 31(1): 111–32.

Suzuki, Shogo (2009) 'Chinese soft power, insecurity studies, myopia and fantasy', *Third World Quarterly*, 30(4): 779–93.

Swaine, Michael D. (2004) 'Trouble in Taiwan', *Foreign Affairs*, 83(2): 30–49.

Swaine, Michael D. (2012) 'Chinese leadership and elite responses to the US Pacific pivot', *China Leadership Monitor*, 381–26.

Szamosszegi, Andrew and Kyle, Cole (2011) *An Analysis of State-owned Enterprises and State Capitalism in China* (Washington, DC: Capital Trade).

Tabb, William K. (1995) *The Postwar Japanese System: Cultural Economy and Economic Transformation* (New York: Oxford University Press).

Tan, Andrew (2000) 'Intra-ASEAN Tensions', Adelphi Discussion Paper, Vol. 84. (London: RIIA).

Tang, Shiping (2003) 'The rise of China as a security linchpin', *Asia Times*, 21 June. Available at: http://www.atimes.com.

Tanter, Richard (1990) 'Oil, IGGI and US hegemony: the global pre-conditions for Indonesian rentier-militarization', in Budiman, A. (ed.), *State and Civil Society in Indonesia* (Melbourne: Monash Papers on Southeast Asia): 51–93.

Tanter, Richard (2005) 'With eyes wide shut: Japan, Heisei militarization, and the Bush Doctrine', in Gurtov, M. and Van Ness, P. (eds), *Confronting the Bush Doctrine: Critical Views from the Asia-Pacific* (London: RoutledgeCurzon): 153–80.

Tarling, Nicholas (1966) *A Concise History of Southeast Asia* (New York: Praeger).

Tarling, Nicholas (1998) *Nations and States in Southeast Asia* (Cambridge: Cambridge University Press).

Tarling, Nicholas (2001) *Imperialism in Southeast Asia* (London: RoutledgeCurzon).

Tasker, P. (2013) 'Japanomics strikes a revolutionary note', *Financial Times*, 11 January.

Terada, Takashi (2003) 'Constructing an "East Asia" concept and growing regional identity: From EAEC to ASEAN+3', *Pacific Review*, 16(2): 251–77.

Terada, Takashi (2010) 'The origins of ASEAN+6 and Japan's initiatives: China's rise and the agent–structure analysis', *The Pacific Review*, 23(1): 71–92.

Terada, Takashi (2012) 'Trade winds: Big power politics and Asia-Pacific economic integration', *Global Asia,* Spring.

Terrill, Ross (2003) *The New Chinese Empire: And What It Means for the United States* (New York: Basic Books).

Terry, Edith (2002) *How Asia Got Rich: Japan, China, and the Asian Miracle* (Armonk, NY: M.E. Sharpe).

Tett, Gillian (2009) *Fool's Gold: How Unrestrained Greed Corrupted a Dream, Shattered Global Markets and Unleashed a Catastrophe* (London: Little, Brown).

Tett, G. and Edgecliffe-Johnson, A. (2009) 'Wen blames crisis on policy mistakes', *Financial Times*, 28 January.

Thomas, Nick (1999) *Democracy Denied: Identity, Civil Society and Illiberal Democracy in Hong Kong* (Aldershot: Ashgate).

Thomas, Nick (2002) 'From ASEAN to an East Asian community? The role of functional cooperation', Working Paper Series, No 28, July, (Hong Kong: Southeast Asia Research Centre).

Thomson, James C., Stanley, Peter W. and Perry, John Curtis (1981) *Sentimental Imperialists: The American Experience in East Asia* (New York: Harper & Row).

Thurborn, Elizabeth and Weiss, Linda (2006) 'Investing in openness: The evolution of FDI strategy in South Korea and Taiwan', *New Political Economy*, 11(1): 1–22.

Tickell, Adam and Peck, Jamie (2003) 'Making global rules: Globalization or neoliberalization?', in Peck, J. and Wai-chung Yeung, H. (eds) *Remaking the Global Economy: Economic and Geographical Perspectives* (London: Sage): 163–81.

Tilly, Charles (1984) *Big Structures, Large Processes, Huge Comparisons* (New York: Russell Sage Foundation).

Tilly, Charles (1990) *Coercion, Capital, and European States* (Oxford: Blackwell).

Tow, William (2001) *Asia-Pacific Strategic Relations: Seeking Convergent Security* (Cambridge: Cambridge University Press).

Trocki, Carl A. (1999) 'Political structures in the nineteenth and early twentieth centuries', in Tarling, N. (ed.), *The Cambridge History of Southeast Asia, Vol. 3, From c.1800 to the 1930s* (Cambridge: Cambridge University Press): 75–126.

Tsai, Kellee S. (2006) 'Adaptive informal institutions and endogenous institutional change in China', *World Politics*, 59: 116–41.

Tsai, Kellee S. (2007) *Capitalism without Democracy: The Private Sector in Contemporary China* (Ithaca, NY: Cornell University Press).

Tsai, Kellee S. and Cook, Sarah (2005) 'Developmental dilemmas in China: Socialist transition and late liberalization', in Pekkanen, S.M. and Tsai, K.S. (eds), *Japan and China in the World Political Economy* (London: Routledge): 45–66.

Tzeng, C.H., Beamish, P.W. and Chen, S.F. (2012) 'Institutions and entrepreneurship development: high-technology indigenous firms in China and Taiwan', *Asia Pacific Journal of Management*, 28(3): 453–81.

UN (United Nations) (2000) *State of the Environment in Asia and the Pacific, 2000* (New York: The United Nations).

UNCTAD (United Nations Conference on Trade and Development) (2005) *World Investment Report 2005: Transnational Corporations and the Internationalization of R&D* (New York: The United Nations).

Underhill, Geoffrey R.D. (2001) 'State, market, and global political economy: Genealogy of an (inter-?) discipline', *International Affairs*, 76(4): 805–24.

Underhill, Geoffrey R.D. and Zhang, Xiaoke (2005) 'The changing state–market condominium in East Asia: Rethinking the political underpinnings of development', *New Political Economy*, 10(1): 1–24.

Vandergeest, Peter (1993) 'Constructing Thailand: Regulation, resistance and citizenship', *Comparative Studies in Society and History*, 35(1): 133–58.

Van Langenhove, Luk (2010) 'The transformation of multilateralism mode 1.0 to mode 2.0', *Global Policy*, 1(3): 263–70.

Van Ness, Peter (1970) *Revolution and Chinese Foreign Policy: Peking's Support for Wars of National Liberation* (Berkeley, CA: University of California Press).

van Wolferen, Karel (1989) *The Enigma of Japanese Power: People and Politics in a Stateless Nation* (London: Papermac).

Vatikiotis, Michael R.J. (1996) *Political Change in Southeast Asia* (London: Routledge).

Vatikiotis, Michael and Hiebert, Murray (2003) 'How China is building an empire', *Far Eastern Economic Review*: 30–3.

Vervoorn, Aat (1998) *Re Orient: Change in Asian Societies* (Melbourne: Oxford University Press).

Vogel, Ezra F. (2011) *Deng Xiaoping and the Transformation of China* (Cambridge, MA: Belknap Press).

Vogel, Steven K. (1996) *Freer Markets, More Rules: Regulatory Reform in Advanced Industrial Countries* (Ithaca, NY: Cornell University Press).

Vogel, Steven K. (2006) *Japan Remodeled: How Government and Industry Are Reforming Japanese Capitalism* (Ithaca, NY: Cornell University Press).

Volgy, Thomas J. and Bailin, Alison (2003) *International Politics and State Strength* (Boulder, CO: Lynne Rienner).

Vu, T. (2010) *Paths to Development in Asia: South Korea, Vietnam, China, and Indonesia* (Cambridge: Cambridge University Press).

Wade, Robert H. (1990) *Governing the Market: Economic Theory and the Role of Government in East Asian Industrialization* (Princeton, NJ: Princeton University Press).

Wade, Robert H. (1996) 'Japan, the World Bank, and the art of paradigm maintenance: The East Asian Miracle in political perspective', *New Left Review*, 217: 3–36.

Wade, Robert H. (2004) 'Bringing economics back in', *Security Dialogue*, 35(2): 243–9.

Wade, Robert H. (2007) 'A new global financial architecture?', *New Left Review*, 46: 113–29.

Wade, Robert H. (2011) 'Emerging world order? From multipolarity to multilateralism in the G20, the World Bank, and the IMF', *Politics & Society*, 39 (3): 347–78.

Wade, Robert H. and Veneroso, Frank (1998) 'The gathering world slump and the battle over capital controls', *New Left Review*, 23: 113–42.

Wain, Barry (2009) *Malaysian Maverick: Mahathir Mohamad in Turbulent Times* (Basingstoke: Palgrave Macmillan).

Walker, R.B.J. (1993) *Inside/Outside* (Cambridge: Cambridge University Press).

Wallace, William (1995) 'Regionalism in Europe: Model or exception?', in Fawcett, L. and Hurrell, A. (eds), *Regionalism in World Politics: Regional Organization and International Order* (Oxford: Oxford University Press): 201–27.

Wallace, William (1999) 'The sharing of sovereignty: the European paradox', *Political Studies*, 47: 503–21.

Walter, Andrew (2008) *Governing Finance: East Asia's Adoption of International Standards* (Ithaca, NY: Cornell University Press).

Walter, Carl E. and Howie, Fraser J.T. (2011) *Red Capitalism: The Fragile Financial Foundations of China's Extraordinary Rise* (Singapore: Wiley).

Waltz, Kenneth N. (1979) *Theory of International Politics* (New York: McGraw-Hill).

Waltz, Kenneth N. (1993) 'The emerging structure of international politics', *International Security*, 18(2): 44–79.

Wang, J.H., Chen, Tsing-Yuan and Tsai, Ching-Jung (2012) 'In search of an innovative state: The development of the biopharmaceutical industry in Taiwan, South Korea and China', *Development and Change*, 43(2): 481–503.

Wang, Zheng (2012) *Never Forget National Humiliation: Historical Memory in Chinese Politics and Foreign Relations* (New York: Columbia University Press).

Watson, Adam (1992) *The Evolution of International Society* (London: Routledge).

Watson Andaya, Barbara (1999) 'Religious developments in Southeast Asia, c.1500–1800', in Tarling, Nicholas (ed.), *The Cambridge History of Southeast Asia, Vol. 2* (Cambridge: Cambridge University Press): 164–227.

Weatherbee, Donald E. (2005) *International Relations in Southeast Asia: The Struggle for Autonomy* (Lanham, MD: Rowman & Littlefield).

Webber, Douglas (2001) 'Two funerals and a wedding? The ups and downs of regionalism in East Asia and Asia-Pacific after the Asian crisis', *The Pacific Review*, 14(3): 339–72.

Weiss, Linda (2003) 'Is the state being "transformed" by globalisation?' in Weiss, L. (ed.), *States in the Global Economy: Bringing Domestic Institutions Back In* (Cambridge: Cambridge University Press): 293–317.

Weiss, Linda and Hobson, John M. (1995) *States and Economic Development: A Comparative Historical Analysis* (Oxford: Polity Press).

Wesley, Michael (2006) 'The dog that didn't bark: The Bush administration and East Asian regionalism', in Beeson, M. (ed.), *Bush and Asia: America's Evolving Relations with East Asia* (London: RoutledgeCurzon): 64–79.

White, Gordon (1993) *Riding the Tiger: The Politics of Economic Reform in Post-Mao China* (Stanford, CA: Stanford University Press).

White, Hugh (2008) 'Why war in Asia remains thinkable', *Survival*, 50(6): 85–103.

White, Hugh (2010) 'Power shift: Australia's future between Washington and Beijing', *Quarterly Essay*, 39: 391–74.

Whitley, Richard (1999) *Divergent Capitalisms: The Social Structuring and Change of Business Systems* (Oxford: Oxford University Press).

Whitley, Richard D. (1990) 'Eastern Asian enterprise structures and the comparative analysis of forms of business organization', *Organization Studies*, 11(1): 47–74.

Whitlock, Craig (2012) 'U.S. eyes return to some Southeast Asia military bases', *The Washington Post*, 23 June.

Williamson, John (1994) 'In search of a manual for Technopols', in Williamson, J (ed.), *The Political Economy of Policy Reform* (Washington, DC: Institute for International Economics): 11–28.

Williamson, Oliver E. (1985) *The Economic Institutions of Capitalism: Firms, Markets, Relational Contracting* (New York: The Free Press).

Willmott, Hedley Paul (1982) *Empires in the Balance* (Annapolis, MD: Naval Institute Press).

Wilson, Jeffrey D. (2012) 'Chinese resource security policies and the restructuring of the Asia-Pacific iron ore market', *Resources Policy*, 37(3): 331–9.

Wilson, Jeffrey D. (2013) *Governing Global Production: Resource Networks in the Asia-Pacific Steel Industry* (Basingstoke: Palgrave Macmillan).

Wilson, Scott (2009) *Remade in China: Foreign Investors and Institutional Change in China* (New York: Oxford University Press).

Wingfield, Tom (2002) 'Democratization and economic crisis in Thailand', in Gomez, E.T. (ed.), *Political Business in East Asia* (London: Routledge): 250–300.

Winters, Jeffrey A. (1996) *Power in Motion: Capital Mobility and the Indonesian State* (Ithaca, NY: Cornell University Press).

Winters, Jeffrey A. (2000) 'The financial crisis in Southeast Asia', in Robison, R. *et al.* (eds), *Politics and Markets in the Wake of the Asian Crisis* (London: Routledge): 34–52.

Wittkopf, Eugene R. and McCormick, James M. (eds) (2004) *The Domestic Sources of American Foreign Policy*, 4th edn (Lanham, MD: Rowman & Littlefield),

Wolf, Eric R. (1969) *Peasant Wars of the Twentieth Century* (New York: Harper & Row).

Wolf, Martin (2009) 'Why Obama's plan is still inadequate and incomplete', *Financial Times*, 13 January.

Wolf, Martin (2011) 'Faltering in a stormy sea of debt', *Financial Times*, 19 April. Available at: http://www.ft.com/cms/s/0/ec330a70-6aaf-11e0-80a1-00144feab49a.html#axzz1K1Somwsr.

Wolters, O.W. (1999) *History, Culture, and Region in Southeast Asian Perspectives* (Ithaca, NY: Cornell University Press/SEAP).

Wong, Edward (2013) 'In China, breathing becomes a childhood risk', *New York Times*, 22 April.

Wong, Roy Bin (1997) *China Transformed: Historical Change and the Limits of the European Experience* (Ithaca, NY: Cornell University Press).

Woo, Jung–en (1991) *Race to the Swift: State and Finance in Korean Industrialization* (New York: Columbia University Press).

Woo-Cumings, Meredith (1997) 'Slouching toward the market: The politics of financial liberalization in South Korea', in Loriaux, M., Cumings, M., Calder, K.E., Maxfield, S. and Preez, S.A. (eds) *Capital Ungoverned: Liberalizing Finance in Interventionist States* (Ithaca, NY: Cornell University Press): 57–91.

Woo-Cumings, Meredith (1999) 'Introduction: Chalmers Johnson and the politics of nationalism and development', in Woo-Cumings. M. (ed.), *The Developmental State* (Ithaca, NY: Cornell University Press): 1–31.

Wood, Christopher (1992) *The Bubble Economy: The Japanese Economic Collapse* (London: Sidgwick & Jackson).

Wood, Ellen Meiksins (2002) *The Origin of Capitalism* (London: Verso).

Woodall, Pam (2004) 'The dragon and the eagle: A survey of the world economy', *The Economist*, 2 October.

Woods, Lawrence (1993) *Asia-Pacific Diplomacy: Nongovernmental Organizations and International Relations* (Vancouver, BC: UBC Press).

Woodside, Alexander (1993) 'The Asia-Pacific idea as a mobilisation myth', in Dirlik, A. (ed.), *What Is a Rim? Critical Perspectives on the Pacific Region Idea* (Boulder, CO: Westview Press): 13–28.

World Bank (1993) *The East Asian Miracle: Economic Growth and Public Policy* (Oxford: Oxford University Press).

World Bank (1997) *World Development Report 1997: The State in a Changing World* (New York: Oxford University Press).

Worldwatch Institute (2006) *State of the World 2006* (Washington, DC: Worldwatch Institute).

Wright, Robert (2000) *Nonzero: The Logic of Human Destiny* (New York: Pantheon Books).

Wright, Teresa (2010) *Accepting Authoritarianism: State–Society Relations in China's Reform Era* (Stanford, CA: Stanford University Press).

WTO/IDE-JETRO (2011) *Trade Patterns and Global Value Chains in East Asia: From Trade in Goods to Trade in Tasks* (Geneva: World Trade Organization).

Wu, Baiyi (2001) 'The Chinese security concept and its historical evolution', *Journal of Contemporary China*, 10(27): 275–83.

Wu, Xinbo (2010) 'Understanding the geopolitical implications of the global financial crisis', *The Washington Quarterly*, 33(4): 155–63.

Xie, Tao (2010) *US–China Relations: China Policy on Capitol Hill* (London: Routledge).

Yahuda, Michael (1997) 'How much has China learned about interdependence?', in Goodman, D. and Segal, G. (eds), *China Rising: Nationalism and Interdependence* (London: Routledge): 6–26.

Yahuda, Michael (2000) 'The changing faces of Chinese nationalism: The dimension of statehood', in Leifer, M. (ed.), *Asian Nationalism* (London: Routledge): 21–37.

Yahuda, Michael (2004) *The International Politics of the Asia-Pacific*, 2nd edn (London: RoutledgeCurzon).

Yeung, Henry Wai-chung (2000a) 'The dynamics of Asian business systems in a globalizing era', *Review of International Political Economy*, 7(3): 399–433.

Yeung, Henry Wai-chung (2000b) 'Economic globalization, crisis and the emergence of Chinese business communities in Southeast Asia', *International Sociology*, 15(2): 266–87.

Yeung, Henry Wai-chung (2009) 'Regional development and the competitive dynamics of global production networks: An East Asian perspective', *Regional Studies*, 43(3): 325–51.

Yoshihara, Kunio (1988) *The Rise of Ersatz Capitalism in Southeast Asia* (Manila: Manila University Press).

Yoshimatsu, Hidetaka (2005) 'Japan's Keidanren and free trade agreements', *Asian Survey*, 45(2): 258–78.

Yoshimatsu, Hidetaka (2009) 'The rise of China and the vision for an East Asian Community', *Journal of Contemporary China*, 18(62): 745–65.

Yoshimatsu, Hidetaka and Trinidad, D.D. (2010) 'Development assistance, strategic interests, and the China factor in Japan's role in ASEAN integration', *Japanese Journal of Political Science*, 11(2): 199–219.

Young, Louise (1998) *Japan's Total Empire: Manchuria and the Culture of Wartime Imperialism* (Berkeley, CA: University of California Press).

Young, Susan (1997) 'The private sector in China's economic reforms', in Hudson, C. (ed.), *The China Handbook* (Chicago, IL: Fitzroy Dearborn): 150–61.

Yuan, Jing-dong (2005) 'Hu goes to the Hermit Kingdom', *Asia Times*, 27 October. Available at: http://www.atimes.com.

Yusuf, S., Nabeshima, K. and Perkins, D.H. (2006) *Under New Ownership: Privatizing China's State-Owned Enterprises* (Washington, DC: World Bank).

Yuzawa, Takeshi (2012) 'The ASEAN Regional Forum: Challenges and prospects', in Beeson, M. and Stubbs, R. (eds) *The Routledge Handbook of Asian Regionalism* (London: Routledge): 338–49.

Zakaria, Fareed (1994) 'Culture is destiny: A conversation with Lee Kuan Yew', *Foreign Affairs*, 73(2): 109–26.

Zakaria, Fareed (2003) *The Future of Freedom: Illiberal Democracy at Home and Abroad* (New York: W.W. Norton).

Zhang, Feng (2012) 'Rethinking China's grand strategy: Beijing's evolving national interests and strategic ideas in the reform era', *International Politics*, 43(3): 318–46.

Zhang, Yongjin (1991) 'China's entry into international society: Beyond the standard of civilisation', *Review of International Studies*, 17: 3–16.

Zhao, Suisheng (2010) 'The China model: Can it replace the Western model of modernization?', *Journal of Contemporary China*, 19(65): 419–36.

Zheng, Bijian (2005) 'China's "peaceful rise" to great power status', *Foreign Affairs*, 85(5): 18–24.

Zheng, Yongnian and Lye, Liang Fook (2005) 'Political legitimacy in reform China: Between economic performance and democratization', in White, L. (ed.), *Legitimacy: Ambiguities of Political Success or Failure in East and Southeast Asia* (New Jersey: World Scientific): 183–214.

Zhou Xiaochuan (2009) 'Reform the international monetary system', People's Bank of China. Available at: http://www.pbc.gov.cn/english//detail.asp?col=6500&ID=178.

Zhu, Yuchau (2011) '"Performance legitimacy" and China's political adaptation strategy', *Journal of Chinese Political Science*, 16(2): 123–40.

Zoellick, Robert B. (2005) 'Whither China: From Membership to Responsibility?', Remarks to National Committee on U.S.–China Relations, New York City, 21 September. Available at: http://2001-2009.state.gov/s/d/ former/ zoellick/rem/53682.htm.

Zurn, M., Binder, M. and Ecker-Ehrhardt, M. (2010) 'International authority and its politicization', *International Theory*, 4(01): 69–106.

Zysman, John (1983) *Goverment, Markets, and Growth: Financial Systems and the Politics of Industrial Change* (Ithaca, NY: Cornell University Press).

Zysman, John (1996) 'The myth of the "global" economy: Enduring national foundations and emerging regional realities', *New Political Economy*, 1(2): 157–84.

Index